Essays in
Performance Practice

Studies in Musicology, No. 58

George Buelow, Series Editor

Professor of Musicology
Indiana University

Other Titles in This Series

Essays in
Performance Practice

by
Frederick Neumann

UMI RESEARCH PRESS
Ann Arbor, Michigan

Produced and distributed by
UMI Research Press
an imprint of
University Microfilms International
Ann Arbor, Michigan 48106

Library of Congress Cataloging in Publication Data

Neumann, Frederick.
    Essays in performance practice.

    (Studies in musicology ; no. 58)
    Previously published essays.
    Bibliography: p.
    Includes index.
    Contents: The use of baroque treatises on musical
performance—Robert Donington's A performer's guide to
baroque music, a review—The French inégales, Quantz and
Bach—[etc.]
    1. Music—Interpretation (Phrasing, dynamics, etc.)—
Addresses, essays, lectures. 2. Music—Performance—
Addresses, essays, lectures. 3. Embellishment (Music)—
Addresses, essays, lectures. I. Title. II. Series.
ML457.N44   781.6'3   82-6916
ISBN 0-8357-1351-2   AACR2

Contents

vi   *Contents*

Foreword

The notes in the score of a composition are not yet music, but only its image in another medium. This visual image must be converted into an acoustic phenomenon, which in turn must be subjected to interpretation by a performer in order to become living art. Such interpretation is not determined in every detail by the graphic notation; it depends on the prevailing state of musical thought and practice and on certain inherited traditions, following usages that may have solidified into rules. In the case of music from past centuries, however, both aesthetics and traditions must be re-created, because music is the most perishable of the arts and cannot be put under glass in a museum. It is not enough to restore the old instruments and study contemporaneous tracts and treatises on the art of playing and singing; we may succeed in conjuring up an acoustic replica while failing to convey the music's message because today our musical experiences, our way of hearing, and our aesthetic views and requirements are different from those of the original audience. The relationship between the sounding music and the listener is vital, but it is also most elusive.

Matters are considerably complicated by the fact that up to the late baroque era the performer was not absolutely bound to the graphic image of the score; he had great freedom in realizing it and was expected to collaborate with the composer by enriching the music text with improvised additions of his own. The rising independent instrumental music recognized the genius, so to speak, of the several instruments, their specific qualities, both euphonic and technical, creating certain turns and figures which became common property of all composers, finding their way also into vocal music. Their use depended on the reigning musical style and technique of composition as well as on the degree to which the performer's talent enabled him to surmount the formulas. Of this improvised "enrichment," the art of ornamentation was of particular importance, and since the advent of modern musicology its study and practice have become one of the particular concerns of the movement for historically authentic performance practice.

The art of ornamentation is present in the earliest monophonic music, though for our purposes it begins with the transcription of vocal into instrumental music; the oldest organ tablatures already show this natural desire for embellishment, which reached extravagant heights in French lute and clavecin music, when it became so luxuriant that it blanketed the compositions themselves. The practice was almost equally overdone in the da capo arias of the opera seria, cantata, and oratorio. Improvised embellishment, whether indicated in the score or not, outlived baroque and Rococo, continuing well into the nineteenth century. Even in that "late" period scores could be so overgrown with ornamentation of all sorts, accumulated as each new generation of performers and editors added their own, that only the core of the work remained intact—*vide The Barber of Seville.* Ornamentation was systematically taught, and there are many old and new textbooks on the subject; nevertheless, in actual practice the performer was largely on his own, and it is almost impossible to reach a consensus on the application of trills, *notes inégales,* double dotting, and all the other ingredients of the art. Toward the middle of the eighteenth century, some composers became tired of the virtuosos' excesses and began to write out the embellishments they preferred, but departed composers remain defenseless. We know, for instance that Hummel in his concerts added many ornaments to Mozart's sonatas and concertos, and so did Grieg; even Liszt, during his earlier career as a virtuoso, dressed up Beethoven's sonatas.

The field of ornamentation has become a special branch of historical musicology, studied and written about with scientific earnestness, yet it is an ambiguity-ridden discipline. The usual problem of the natural scientist is to find a better formulation for the phenomenon being studied, and he looks for regularities in experience. In scientific work there is first reduction then synthesis—there is no "may be" in mathematics. But the in history of the arts, our definition of scholarship must also include the spiritual, aesthetic, dramatic, and lyric qualities of a work of art, not only the empirically ascertainable ones, and these are highly individual/personal qualities that cannot be put under a microscope. Values and processes which have long been taken for granted are constantly brought into question, for the data obtained by historical research cannot be standardized in the arts; as they lose their force, human aspirations, taste, aesthetic concepts, and learning make them unstable, ephemeral, even open to challenge. Indeed, the historical study of music, notably of its special branch, ornamentation, is full of paradoxes; this history is a "science" in which the opposite of any generalization may be as true as the generalization itself. As a matter of fact, rigid doctrinal objectivism can endanger our contact with artistic realities; the subjective response must be and must remain at the heart of the humanistic and artistic enterprise.

Decoration is one of the oldest and most natural of creative urges. Ornamentation may have a merely decorative significance, the equivalent of chrome plating, but it also may be inventive, constructive, and even be the carrier of style. Its application calls for real insight, taste, and stylistic feeling because the slightest ornamental additions can change the character of a piece of music. There are performances in which not a single straight musical line is permitted to stand, the original design cannot be perceived because of the insistent ornamentation, but when a melodic line is thin, without a good profile, it is the ornaments which come to the rescue, and like a dowager's diamond choker hiding a sagging neck, they cover the paucity of invention. The discerning artist knows that structure and articulation, above all, must remain clear, and embellishments should never be predictable. Even subtle ideas can be trivialized by performers who proceed with the actuarist's devotion to minutiae, but in the hands of an imaginative artist the music becomes verdant.

The field of ornamentation has been so thoroughly mowed over that few new discoveries can be expected, but the same questions can yield varying answers depending on the approach, the emphasis, and the unique understanding of the researcher and performer. Unfortunately, the attitude of the researchers, and notably of the musicologically inclined performers, is often authoritarian, and differing arguments are rejected in terms not packed in cotton wool. "To understand something one must first be interested in it," said the philosopher Dewey. Frederick Neumann has been interested in these problems all his scholarly life, and does not speak with the wavering accents of the uncommitted. He respects the line between facts and surmise, but is not afraid to advance his own ideas. Sometimes these may be hyperbolic, though tempered with the ring of truth. It is my opinion that his interpretations, at times adventurous, are to be preferred to the pedantry that afflicts the strict historicists, because while his knowledge of the archival and modern literature is encyclopedic, he always starts from a musical and artistic basis, and he does not permit the extrinsic factors to outweigh the intrinsic. There is a great deal of original thought in this anthology, and it should be studied by friend and foe, for all of them will benefit from it.

Lakeville, Connecticut.   PAUL HENRY LANG

Preface

The suggestion to publish this collection of my articles came from George Buelow, editor of the UMI series "Studies in Musicology," and I wish to express my gratitude to him for this initiative and its implementation.

The purpose of these essays can best be explained by telling briefly how they came to be written. As a violinist and a teacher I had become acquainted with the main principles formulated by modern scholarship for the interpretation of early—mainly 18th-century—music. I tried to abide by them, but as the years passed by I became increasingly more disturbed by the observation that often these principles led to what seemed to me unmusical results. One day in a chance reading of an essay on rhythms that was hailed as revelatory by eminent scholars, I was surprised at its looseness of reasoning and cavalier treatment of the evidence. It was a pivotal experience because it set me to questioning whether the rules that had previously aroused my suspicion might not have been built on similarly shaky foundations. Motivated to search for the answers, I found myself drawn into a field of study that has kept me endlessly fascinated. First I turned of course to those questions that had intrigued me the most: the regimentation of ornaments, the so-called "French overture style," and the alleged international validity of the French *notes inégales.* Piece by piece my suspicions were confirmed, and I started publishing my findings in a series of articles, most of which will be found reprinted in this volume.

Articles dealing with ornamentation were to varying degrees incorporated in a later book, *Ornamentation in Baroque and Post-Baroque Music* (Princeton, 1978), and I chose for inclusion in the present volume only those items that contained additional material of sufficient substance. Unless otherwise indicated in the text, all the material is printed in its original form.

The subject matter of this volume is limited to only a few topics, but they are crucial ones. In fact, the adherence to the very rules that are challenged in these essays is considered by many to be the cornerstone of "authenticity" in baroque performance, and the research methods questioned in the very first article are the ones most commonly used by modern workers in this field. Therefore it is hoped that, in spite of the topical limitation the gathering of essays scattered over seventeen years in different publications will be of some use to students of performance practice who want to hear a counterpoint to the often powerful unison of "Establishment" thought. They might gain a more balanced view of the problems involved and be more alert to the danger of accepting any sweeping rules as would-be avenues to assured historical authenticity.

The following individuals, listed here alphabetically, have greatly obliged me by their kind permission to reprint materials from their publications, and I wish to express to each of them my sincerest gratitude: Dr. Dietrich Berke (Bärenreiter Verlag, Kassel), Mr. Alvin H. Johnson (American Musicological Society), Mr. Edward Olleson (Music & Letters), Ms. Joan Peyser (Musical Quarterly), Mr. A.F. Leighton Thomas (Music Review), and John M. Thomson (Early Music).

I would like also to express special thanks to Mr. Bruce Stevens for preparing the index entries, and to my wife Margaretta for organizing the index material into its final form.

Frederick Neumann
Richmond, Virginia

1

The Use of Baroque Treatises on Musical Performance

Research into historical performance is a surprisingly recent undertaking, since it goes back hardly more than half a century. Any young discipline may be expected to move at first gropingly by trial and error before it develops more rational research methods. However, today, though much valuable work has been accomplished, our discipline has not yet fully emerged from the first, experimental phase and continues to be beset by difficulties which are caused by questionable procedures. The latter fall into two main categories, one of which is the use of wrong sources, the other the wrong use of sources. The first of these occurs because we have so far failed to develop a reliable screening process that could establish the pertinence of a source with regard to a certain composer; the second, the wrong use of sources, occurs because inferences from the sources are often drawn too hastily and without due regard for the principles of sound reasoning. In discussing such faulty procedures I hope to avoid the impression that I am arrogating the role of a grand inquisitor of logical heresies. I am aware that principles of sound reasoning and procedure are more easily postulated than honoured. I know I have sinned against these principles during my recent endeavours in this field, and the prospects are excellent that I shall sin again. But innocence, past, present or future, should not be the prerequisite for a critic who wishes to point out mistakes that have been made and to express ideas on how to avoid similar mistakes in the future.

Of the various sources for baroque interpretation the following four are the most important: (1) historical treatises (including prefaces to compositions and explanations such as ornamentation table); (2) historical instruments and instrumental techiques; (3) pictorial evidence; (4) external and internal evidence extracted from the music itself. I shall limit myself in this article to the discussion of the difficulties that attend the correct use of historical treatises.

Reprinted by permission from *Music and Letters* 48 (1967), pp. 315-24.

Measured by the frequency of use, treatises have so far been the most important source, and probably for that statistical reason alone have provided the most fertile ground for mistaken procedures and their inevitable offspring, erroneous theories. In large part this is due to the strange fascination that treatises have exerted on many researchers, a fascination that led them to form a vastly exaggerated opinion of the revelatory power of these documents, and hence an unrealistic view of their value as sources. We shall make a great step forward if we stop looking at the authors of old treatises as if they were prophets who reveal infallible verities, and if we start seeing and treating them as what they are at best: very human witnesses who left us an affidavit about certain things they knew, certain things they believed in, certain things they wished their readers to believe. Since we want to use these testimonials as evidence for the establishment of certain unknown facts, it would behove us to take a leaf from the book of jurisprudence on principles and procedures that have been developed over thousands of years with regard to the evaluation of testimony. In so doing we learn that before the testimony of a witness in a court of law is accepted as fully valid evidence, his character, veracity, intelligence will be examined, as well as the circumstances that have a bearing on his knowledge or lack of it about the case involved; then his testimony is tempered and occasionally destroyed in the fire of cross-examination, and what remains intact is finally evaluated against the testimony of other witnesses and any other evidence that has been produced. Anything less would violate what in a civilized country is known as due process of law.

As far as historical treatises and other kinds of evidence are concerned we would do well to establish analogous requirements as "due process of research." Examination and cross-examination ought to be brought to bear (a) on the personality of the writer, (b) on the text of the treatise itself, (c) on the relationship of the latter to other sources, and (d) on its relationship to the composer and the type of composition to which it is meant to be applied. Questions like these should be asked: (a) What is the background of the author, how much did he know and to what areas did his knowledge extend? Was he a leader, and if so, how far did his influence reach; was he a follower and if so, whose ideas did he adopt? or was he a "loner," or an eccentric? Did he intend to report observed facts or propose new ideas? (b) Of what kinds, media, forms and styles of music does the book treat? Do parts of the book have a direct and close link with a definite aesthetic outlook or a definite musical style, and if so, what is the currency of such outlook or style in time and space? How clear, how consistent, how methodical is the text? Where, if at all, is literal interpretation justified? Where might we meet with over-statements and where with over-simplifications? What is the relationship of a particular passage to other parts of the book or to other books of the author: is it elsewhere qualified, modified or even contradicted? To whom is the book addressed: to beginners, advanced students or artists? (c) Are specific passages in complete or partial agreement or disagreement with other independently written treatises, or with other types of sources? What is the geographic and temporal distribution of such agreements or disagreements? (d) How does the treatise relate to any other evidence about the specific composer in whom we are interested?

These are the matters that need to be clarified before we can give a well-considered answer to the two fundamental questions which determine the genuine source value of a passage: what exactly did the author mean? With what degree of probability can it be applied to the music of a certain composer? I have no illusion about the practicability of such thorough investigation of passages in hundreds of treatises. But we must realize that a treatise is not safe for use that has not been thus filtered and distilled. The prevailing standard procedure, however, has been one borrowed from medieval theology rather than from modern jurisprudence; it consists in simply quoting chapter and verse of a single treatise and considering the evidence established, the case proved, and any further doubt proscribed as heresy. In the following pages I shall, with no pretence to completeness, discuss various types of such misguided methods.

1. The most widespread mistake is the application of a passage from a treatise outside its legitimate field of pertinence. This happens through unjustified generalization in two distinct ways: (a) horizontally, so to speak, by projecting it into contemporary space, (b) vertically, by projecting it forward and backward in time.

(a) The first of these, the horizontal projection, is made on the tacit assumption that existing conventions were universally valid and that their rules were embodied in the treatises; and conversely, that the rules we find in treatises represent such general conventions. It is on this assumption that treatises were regarded as codes of law that had jurisdiction over a wide geographic area and all the composers residing in it. Not only is this area extended over a whole nation; frontiers are crossed and a treatise is assumed to have international validity. What Couperin wrote has been taken to apply not only to the *clavecinistes* of his immediate following, not only to all other Frenchmen, but to Bach, Handel and their German contemporaries as well. This is no mere tribute to the creative genius of a man of great renown and influence, as far lesser men are accorded the same authority; and many a researcher who unearths any kind of written or printed matter believes he has struck gold of similar international currency, even if the knowledge and competence of the author quoted can in no way be established.

First we have to note that there was no such thing as a universal Baroque convention which regulated performance all over Europe. The differences of styles alone that co-existed on a national, regional, and personal level make such an assumption unrealistic, not to speak of the many contradictions we find in contemporary treatises. When two people like Quantz and C.P.E. Bach, who were closely related in aesthetic outlook and intimately associated for many years in daily music-making at the court of Frederick II of Prussia, disagree on many important principles in their respective treatises, we have to conclude that a unified practice did not prevail even within the same room, in spite of a proverbial climate of militaristic regimentation. Can we, with this in mind, seriously entertain the idea that identical practices were obligatory in vast areas, or even all over Europe? Can we seriously assume that J.S. Bach, Quantz, Couperin, Johann Stamitz, Hasse, and Pergolesi—to name but a few—held identical views, as if these views had been imposed by some totalitarian authority? In the absence of such complete uniformity of practice, it stands to reason that we cannot project the rules of a treatise upon the music of another composer, as a matter of routine, and that independent supporting evidence would have to be produced before a projection can be made with any degree of safety.

This means that, as a matter of principle, the burden of proof has to be reversed every time a composer is subjected to the jurisdiction of a treatise: cause must be shown why he should thus be subjected. In evaluating what constitutes such a cause the greatest care must be taken not to be misled by wishful thinking. Neither geographic proximity nor student-teacher relationship nor scarcity of other sources is sufficient cause. Even congeniality of style and aesthetics is not enough, as it can at best create a certain presumption of validity, but not more than that. However, in trying to establish the important fact of such spiritual kinship we must proceed with the greatest caution; in particular we must avoid the pitfalls of our own didactic classifications. In our textbooks we are told that the musical baroque lasted until 1750. This may have some meaning today because we consider Bach's music the most important phenomenon of that era; however, from the vantage point of the first half of the eighteenth century the dateline is quite unrealistic. In France the rococo had taken hold; in Italy and in the colonial empire of its music *opera buffa* was effectively burying the baroque; in Germany the flood-tide of the *galant* style had been rising since the early part of the century and under the Mannheimers had, long before Bach's death, become the dominant force in both composition and theoretical writing. Hence the idea derived from the suggestive date 1750 that every treatise written before that year reflected "Baroque" aesthetics and practices is a misconception. Writers like Heinichen, Scheibe, and even Mattheson, active well before 1750, were all committed to the aesthetics of the new style. Yet that implicative date of 1750 has drawn into its orbit even the famous treatises of Quantz (1752), C.P.E. Bach (1753), and Leopold Mozart (1756), which appeared shortly after Bach's death, since it was (not unjustly) argued that pedagogues in their books present the fruits of many years of thought, experience, and observation, and that these three books therefore presented crystallizations of pre-1750, hence baroque, practices. So we find that famous triumvirate called upon over and over again as experts for the performance of baroque composers, as lawgivers for Bach and Handel, without questioning the extent to which the aesthetics of all three books were rooted in the then 30 to 40-year-old stream of the "modern," the *galant* style.

This does not mean that certain points might not be legitimately projected from a *galant* treatise to a Baroque composer, as some practices contain an element of inertia that is unaffected by changes of taste and style. As a matter of fact, certain practices may be so linked up with the very essence of the musical impulse that they might approach a degree of universality. For such reasons it is impossible to determine the validity of a treatise in its entirety. A question, for example, as to the pertinence of a treatise like Quantz's essay would have to be answered that some of it is valid for Quantz alone, some for the other *galant* composers as well, some for Bach, some for Mozart, that some was probably valid a thousand years ago, and some is valid still today. Obviously, the greatest likelihood for the pertinence of the greatest part of a treatise is for the writer's immediate circle of influence, and the likelihood decreases in geometric proportion with the crossing of barriers of taste and style, such as the one that separates the musical world of Quantz from the world of Bach, despite the fact that the two men were almost contemporaries.

(b) The vertical species of unjustified generalization that assumes pertinence backward and forward over a long period of time is based on another unrealistic premise: the assumption that conventions remain static over a long period of time and that consequently treatises can be accorded retroactive jurisdiction for generations. Here again, the suggestive power of the "baroque" label makes itself felt. As an example may be cited the dotted notes and the so-called French style of overdotting. Based almost entirely on partly contradictory quotations from the famous triumvirate, the principle of overdotting was claimed to reach back at least as far as Lully and to embrace on the way Bach, Handel, and their contemporaries. In an article on this question I tried to show that this theory is a misunderstanding based on the misapplication of treatises.[1]

2. Another type of fallacy derives from the assumption that everything is forbidden, that nothing existed that is not specifically authorized by a treatise. This is the creed that produced such taboos as the rules against dynamic gradations, or against retarding before holds or before the final cadence, even though such practices were confirmed by many instances of internal evidence, even before direct mention of them was discovered in treatises. A specific case is that of the *Schneller,* the so-called inverted mordent. It has been argued that

it did not exist before 1750 because it supposedly makes its first appearance in C.P.E. Bach's treatise of 1753, and therefore, has "no place whatever" in the music of J.S. Bach.[2] The ornament in question, , is so simple and so obvious that most probably it has been used from time immemorial. It is hard indeed to assume that Bach did not use it before receiving printed permission from his son. Actually a good number of descriptions could be traced in treatises reaching back to the mid-sixteenth century.[3]

3. Incomplete quotations and quotations out of context are another source of error. Authors of treatises are not always paragons of either methodical thinking or precise formulation. They often make a definite statement that is later qualified or even contradicted. When they write more than one book such inconsistencies or outright discrepancies are usually more frequent and more pronounced, as they often reflect a change of opinion, attitude or actual practice. This makes it often difficult if not impossible to pin the author down to a definite meaning. The modern researcher who makes a law out of the first statement he finds misrepresents the author. A few examples follow of statements that underwent a subsequent metamorphosis.

Walther in the first part of his *Praecepta* (chap. 7, par. 7) explains and illustrates the *accentus* as an up-beat grace note:

In the second part under the title "Superjection" (chap. 4, par. 25) he gives two examples of down-beat accents, one of an up-beat grace:[4]

In his *Lexicon* of 1732 he implies in the article "Accento" a downbeat character, but in the article "Cercar della Nota" he equates this upbeat grace with the "accent." To quote one rule or one illustration without the others would be misleading. Quantz, speaking of *Vorschläge,*[5] tells us in chapter VIII, paragraph 2, that they are to be played on the beat by taking their value from the following note. Then in paragraphs 5 and 6, he introduces, as a first modification, anticipated *durchgehende Vorschläge* as passing notes between successive thirds (the French *tierces coulées*). Yet as a second modification his illustration in table VI, figures 5 and 6 would seem to contradict such limitation, as two out of the five graces do not fill the space between thirds:

As a third modification he describes in chapter XVII, ii, paragraph 20 anticipated *Vorschläge* independent of context, and illustrates them with two examples of which the following is particularly interesting:

as we have been conditioned—by unjustified generalization—to assume that this had to be a downbeat pattern resulting in four equal semiquavers. Examples like these can be multiplied where a single quotation, however categorical its formulation, is an incomplete representation of the author's ideas.

4. Closely related is the next point of too narrow interpretation. Often a treatise will present a rule that is not explicitly qualified though it ought to have been. Such omission may be an oversight, but more often than not it is prompted by eminently sound pedagogical considerations. Saint Lambert in 1702 gives in this respect some wise counsel. He tells us not to embarrass our student's memory by making fine points and distinctions out of season. The good instructor "teaches a general rule as if it had no exceptions and awaits the occasion when such an exception occurs to talk about it, because it will then be more easily understood; and if he had talked about it before, it would have interfered with the impression of the general rule."[6] We forget too readily that many treatises are elementary textbooks whose rules are to be understood as preliminary directives, as intentional oversimplifications in the sense of Saint Lambert. The modern commentator who takes such a rule at its face value is not guilty of carelessness in reading or of incomplete quotation, but he may well be guilty of too narrow interpretation.

As an example let us look at the brief ornament table which Bach wrote under the title "Explicatio" in the *Clavier-Büchlein* for his eleven-year-old son Friedemann. As one of the very few authentic documents of Bach's on interpretation it has been widely quoted and almost as widely misunderstood and misapplied. No doubt it is authoritative, but there is also no doubt that it is neither comprehensive nor exclusive nor precise,[7] and that it is a prime example of pedagogic oversimplification. For instance, it contains neither the symbols of the small-note *Vorschlag* nor that of the slide; and the *accent* is explained as a long downbeat appoggiatura when internal evidence proves that such rendition is in many cases musically impossible. In other words, this particular table covered some instances, and these by approximation only, but by no means all of them.

5. An ornament table like the "Explicatio" also illustrates the next point on our list, that of oversimplification. The nature of artistic performance is so exceedingly complicated, with all it involves in the way of fine shading of rhythm, tempo, nuance and expression, that it defies exact description or definition. Any attempt to do so is bound to be an oversimplification. This is nowhere truer than when we deal with ornamentation whose artistic function stands or falls with an imaginative rhythmic and dynamic manipulation of such subtlety that it can only be vaguely suggested by words and most imperfectly outlined by notation. That is why some of the best authors of treatises stress the inherent impossibility of teaching ornaments by book, and why they indicate that their necessarily inadequate attempts to do so have to be taken with many grains of salt. In particular, ornament tables which have to press the live irrational rhythm into the rigid mould of notation are greatly misleading if one does not bear in mind that they are meant to present rough outlines rather than exact designs, memory aids rather than definite models. Yet the misunderstanding about these facts and the frequent insistence on literal metrical rendition of ornaments has led to some of the less attractive cases of dogmatic rigour.

6. Mistranslation, misinterpretation, misrepresentation form another category with borderlines among the three sub-species often hard to trace. Such infractions are, of course, rarely prompted by an actual intention to deceive. They may be due to insufficient knowledge of the linguistic usages of a particular period, or to carelessness, but most frequently they result from the unconscious bias of a preconceived opinion, a desire to prove a pet theory, that makes a researcher read into his text what he hopes to find in it. This will naturally happen most readily when the passage is obscure or ambiguous; but it also happens when there is little room for misunderstanding. An example of mistranslation and misinterpretation can be found in Dolmetsch's version of a passage in C.P.E. Bach about the dotted notes,[8] where he inserts in the form of direct quotation additional words, phrases, and even two whole sentences which represent what he thought or hoped Bach wanted to say. In fact Bach never said it and may have had no intention of doing so.

So far I have treated of some instances where the application of a treatise was a direct and immediate one: a statement was taken and applied with varying degress of felicity to the music of a particular composer. The chances for error are multiplied and magnified when the application is not direct, when the text is used as a point of departure for theories and speculation that open new opportunities for questionable reasoning. In view of all these formidable difficulties we have to conclude that a treatise is on the whole an undependable source unless it receives decisive support from other quarters. If, for instance, many independent treatises completely agree on one point, and no other evidence to the contrary has come to light, then the probability is great that we have to do with a widespread convention. In such a case we can assume a certain likelihood that even a strong and independent personality may have adhered to it. By contrast, when we have to do with more or less isolated quotations, any projection outside the limited field of the writer is hazardous.

Another type of source—the external and internal evidence extracted from the music itself—can give the treatises perhaps their most valuable support by shedding light on the crucial question of individual pertinence. This musical source, which can achieve a high degree of reliability and is rich in yet untouched resources, actually offers the best hope for decisive progress in our field. However, its dangers parallel those of the treatises, and the key to its treasures lies in a meticulously careful analysis, evaluation, and application, based on a thorough understanding of the issues involved.[9] It is of particular importance to keep in mind that such musical evidence is directly valid only for the individual case and that one has to resist the temptation of jumping to sweeping conclusions. Only a sufficient number of identical and uncontradicted pieces of such evidence can justify, not yet the proclamation of a rule, but at best a tentative presumption for a certain regularity, a kind of working hypothesis which we have to reformulate or abandon at the first indication of conflict. Before proclaiming a definite rule, it would be necessary to prove that no possibility of any alternative solution exists; and such proof can probably never be successfully presented. We shall, therefore, have to be content to arrive at greater or lesser probabilities and stop aspiring at certainties. Our immediate aim should be to find for each particular problem as much internal and external evidence as possible, chart the latter as so many established guide-posts within unexplored territory, then try to secure them more firmly by correlation with well-screened treatises or other sources. The denser a network we can construct of such established points of reference, the smaller will be the risk of interpolation between these points through uncharted areas, the greater will be the probability of avoiding a navigational error and of setting the right course.

Donington's *A Performer's Guide to Baroque Music*—A Review

Robert Donington's book (*A Performer's Guide to Baroque Music*, New York: Charles Scribner's Sons; 1973; 320 pp.) overlaps to some extent his earlier and larger work *The Interpretation of Early Music*, of which a third and revised edition is due soon. However, the *Performer's Guide*, centered on a shorter period of time, considerably expands the treatment of certain subjects and contains new emphases and a few revisions of previously held ideas. As was to be expected, the book presents much valuable material and much sound advice, but, like its predecessor, it is not free from flaws.

Professor Donington has an enormous store of knowledge about the musical life of the period, the nature of its instruments, the treatment of the voice, and the character of its dances. He also demonstrates an impressive command of primary theoretical sources. At the onset he points out how the fragmentary notation charged the performer with vast executive powers regarding most aspects of interpretation. "In baroque music the performer is king." Donington logically infers vast freedoms and great flexibility of performance that make it impossible to establish "definitive" solutions. Approximations, he wisely states, are the only realistic aim.

In several important matters Donington dispels widely held but mistaken ideas. He notes the lack of a prevailing pitch, hence the pointlessness of lowering it for the sake of authenticity. Speaking of dynamics, he assigns the "terraced" type its rightful place but stresses, for all media capable of dynamic nuances, the important role of shadings and gradations. Concerning matters of tempo, he makes a good case for flexibility and the frequent need for cadential retards. He is gratifyingly broadminded about the question of old versus modern instruments, and, regarding research, displays refreshing common sense in such statements as: "When confronted with a musicological

Reprinted with permission from *The Musical Quarterly* 60 (1974), pp. 658-64.

solution which does not carry conviction as a musical solution, we should perhaps just bear in mind that not all musicology is successful musicology"; and "when we end up sounding rather too gimmicky and calculated . . . then something has gone wrong. . . . "

The chapter on accompaniment offers valuable advice, and the warning against realizations that "get in the way" should be taken to heart by overambitious editors or nimble-fingered improvisers. Donington offers a sample of one of his own realizations (ex. 98) that moves with pleasing fluency without obtruding itself. In the chapter on free ornamentation Donington echoes many old theories in counseling moderation and again gives a tasteful illustration of his own.

The discussion of accidentals is helpful in pointing out the many inconsistencies and ambiguities that prevailed before the natural, the double sharp, and the double flat became standard symbols, and before the bar line rule of cancellation was adopted. But at least one illustration (ex. 2e) is unrealistic: in it a B-double-flat—a late sophistication—within a signature of five flats is changed, three quarter-notes and a bar line later, into a single flat by being written as B-sharp.[1]

One weakness of the book stems from the very concept of "baroque music," for Donington implicitly ascribes to it a broader base of common style and performance practices than is justified. Even in its usual textbook definition as the era from the Italian monodists to Bach, "baroque music" encompasses such a vast number of internal differences that its common denominator, whatever it may be, is extremely small at best. Donington aggravates matters further by extending the "baroque" roof over even the homophonic *galant* style (along with its spokesmen Quantz, C.P.E. Bach, Leopold Mozart, et al.), presumably because it emerged in the first half of the eighteenth century and blossomed during Bach's lifetime. Yet it was poles apart from his or other polyphonic masters' music of the genuine "late baroque." Hence such terms as "baroque" musician, or sound, or realization, or attitude, or, indeed, style are somewhat tenuous unless focused on much narrower time spans, more limited regions, or fewer individuals. True, Donington occasionally refers to specific national practices, or to the "early" as contrasted to the "main" or "late" baroque style (designations he seems to use as synonyms), but throughout the book he tacitly assumes common practices that did not exist. It is on the basis of such assumptions that he ascribes to rules found in old treatises general "baroque" validity; and sometimes he goes further. Thus, for instance, he accepts C.P.E. Bach's directives on the appoggiatura as "standard eighteenth-century practice" (which would throw Bach and Mozart into the same pot), declares Quantz's treatise to be "invaluable for Bach and Handel," and in a similar vein cites in the same breath English, French, German, and Italian theorists, who are often separated by as much as a century and by considerable differences in style. When added to the all-too-human tendency of selecting and interpreting evidence in a way most favorable to a proposed thesis, such procedures can easily lead to a collision course with historical facts. Nowhere in the book are these weaknesses more in evidence than in the chapters on ornaments and rhythm. One example each taken at random from these two chapters may serve to show the pitfalls of such research methods.

The trill, says Donington, had, internationally and from the mid-seventeenth century on through the late baroque and beyond, primarily the harmonic function of adding an enriching dissonance. To do this, it *had* to start with the emphasized auxiliary on the beat and maintain throughout its length this upper-note emphasis (which transforms every trill into an ornamental long appoggiatura). Many objections oppose this rule. First, such rigid standardization is totally at odds with the "performer-king's" executive privilege in the very field in which it should have the widest possible range, since ornaments are the most volatile element of musical matter. Second, Donington overlooks massive evidence to the contrary in all the countries involved. Third, he does not always objectively interpret his own supportive evidence. Fourth, and most importantly, the application of the rule will in countless cases produce musical incongruities, e.g., when the trilled note is an integral part of the main melodic line, or is itself dissonant with the bass, or could not sensibly support an appoggiatura, or is an appoggiatura itself, or when the on-the-beat appoggiatura would result in offensive parallels.[2] In all such cases and similar ones Donington's trill design would not enrich the harmony, but at best impoverish it and at worst outright falsify melody, harmony, and counterpoint. Nor can we ignore the sense of tedium created by such unrelieved uniformity, which contradicts the very spirit and purpose of ornaments.

As to Donington's theoretical evidence, Hotteterre neither says nor shows anything regarding the on-the-beat start or upper note emphasis. Both Couperin's and Quantz's trill models show a clear metrical emphasis on the *main* note. Quantz's preparation by a *Vorschlag* can be from below as well as from above, and his *Vorschlag* can fall before as well as on the beat.[3] Tosi could not have made the vigorous emphasis on the main note any clearer when he writes that with singers it is difficult to discern a half-tone from a whole-tone trill "because the auxiliary due to its weakness has difficulty to make itself heard." Donington apparently fails to distinguish between the preparation of a trill with an appoggiatura (frequent at cadences, much less frequent elsewhere) and the continuously accented upper note. Actually a trill prepared by an appoggiatura of some length will logically tend to emphasize its main note in order to clarify the appoggiatura's resolution; otherwise the dissonance will keep hanging unresolved in the air. The continuous upper-note emphasis is verbally spelled out in only two post-baroque German sources (Marpurg and Türk); for some of the other cited works it is only questionably inferred from intrinsically imprecise (keyboard) ornament tables; and in Tartini and Leopold Mozart it is explicitly supplemented by several differing trill designs. If we add the available wealth of evidence for the main-note start, for the main-note emphasis whatever the start, for the pre-beat auxiliary start, and even the anticipation of the whole trill, the conclusion is inevitable that Donington's trill rule is surely too sweeping.

As an illustration of a rhythmic problem, let us look at "inequality." Donington tries to establish the French *notes inégales* convention as an international one, which it was not. He fails to distinguish between a French *obligation* in strictly circumscribed circumstances and a non-French *license* of rhythmic freedom totally uncircumscribed and totally nonobligatory. In France (1) certain evenly written, *specific* note-values in (2) certain *specific* meters (such as eighth-notes in 3 meter or sixteenth-notes in C meter) when (3) proceeding essentially stepwise, had to be rendered long-short (a 2:1 ratio being rarely exceeded), unless the composer expressly countermanded such implied rendition. By contrast, outside of France deviations from written note-values were undoubtedly very frequent (and, in a more limited scope, are so to the present day) simply as one of the many freedoms of the "performer-king," with *no* limitation whatever with regard to note values and their relationship to meter or their stepwise movement. Even where their freedom produces a chance resemblance with *notes inégales* the difference between French and non-French practices remains the important one between compulsion and freedom. In his attempt to prove the international validity of the *inégales* Donington downgrades Couperin's clear statement about their purely French character as "thoughtlessly exaggerated or incompletely expressed," even though the statement is confirmed by Loulié, Hotteterre, Corrette, J.J. Rousseau, and others. Except for Quantz, who did adopt the *inégales* as part of his avowed attempt to form a "mixed style," all the cited documents about non-French use are subjected to misunderstandings. Tosi (citation 154) speaks of a slow start, an acceleration, and ritardando; Corrette (155), though mentioning the Italian origin of various meters, speaks of French, not Italian practices, and in doing so clearly spells out Italian equality as contrasted to French *inégalité*. None of the non-French theorists (with the exception of Quantz, of course) ever mentions a note-value to meter relationship that was at the very heart of the French convention. Donington attempts to discount the importance of the meter by quoting Loulié as saying that "the practice of [those time-signatures]is not certain, some use them in one way, some in another." However, Loulié speaks here of archaic signatures used by foreigners, not of contemporary French ones that bear on *inégalité*. Caccini's models are varied rubato patterns. Alessandro Scarlatti's "si suona a tempo eguale" does not cancel *notes inégales* but indicates a steady tempo. Mary Burwell's "Instruction Book for the Lute" (like Mace's *Musick's Monument*) reflects a seventeenth-century English lute school totally beholden to the French. Example 110 from Bach's *Trauer Ode* does not at all imply a dotted adaptation of the voice. The even notation of the vocal parts juxtaposed with the dotted instrumental parts is prompted by the unvocal character of *extended* dotted rhythms. It is no coincidence that Bach wrote the voice parts too in dotted rhythms (but for no longer than a measure) so as to intensify two cadential climaxes and their parallel spots (measures 27, 36, 60, and 68). We are faced here not with *notes inégales* but simply with idiomatic writing meant to be performed as written.[4]

The attempt made on pages 259-63 to apply certain French principles to non-French music produces such complex directives that their bewildering intricacy alone suggests a love's labor lost. Unfortunately, the better part of the two chapters on ornaments and rhythm are marred by similarly one-sided presentations, producing rules that cannot stand up under close scrutiny. Such is notably the case with the discussion of the appoggiatura, the slide, the mordent, and the "overdotting" of the so-called "French Overture style."

In many matters, however, there is much to be admired and learned here, and the book, taken as a whole, represents another very significant contribution by this distinguished author. It commands thorough, if critical, study by all persons interested in historical performance.

3

The French *Inégales,* Quantz, and Bach

The field of Bach interpretation, which all too often invites comparison with a battlefield, has lately been the scene of increased activity and excitement. In addition to the many old controversies, which to be sure, were lively and heated, new ones have sprung up on matters which until fairly recently no one had suspected of harboring any problems at all. These new issues revolve around the question of rhythm, and the most provocative among them center on the performance of uneven notes where even notes were written. To put it more precisely, they have to do with the probable, or allegedly certain and obligatory, application to Bach of the French *Inégales* convention of the 17th and 18th centuries.

This upheaval was caused by a single passage in Quantz's famous *Versuch einer Anweisung die Flöte traversière zu spielen,* in which the author endorses the French convention. For almost 200 years the passage lay dormant and unnoticed in this much-praised but little-read book until, fairly recently, it was rediscovered, presented to the world, and some twelve years ago launched on a remarkable career. Quantz himself might have been surprised had he imagined that among the hundreds of paragraphs in his book this one would some day be singled out to burst into prominence as a *cause célèbre,* and that its slender substance would be used as a basis for the most far-reaching theories.

This is the passage:

I must in this connection make a necessary remark concerning the length of time that each note must be held. One must know how to distinguish in performance between *principal* notes, also called "initial" or in Italian usage *good* notes, on the one hand, and, on the other, "passing" notes, called by some foreigners *bad* notes. The principal notes must wherever possible be brought out more than the passing ones. In accordance with this rule, the fastest notes in every piece in *moderate tempo,* or in *Adagio,* despite the fact that they have in appearance the same value, must nevertheless be played a little unevenly. Thus the "initial"

Reprinted with permission from the *Journal of the American Musicological Society* 18 (1965), pp. 313-58.

notes of every group, namely, the first, third, fifth, and seventh, must be held somewhat longer than the "passing" ones, namely the second, fourth, sixth, and eighth. But this holding must not amount to as much as it would if there were dots after the notes. By the fastest notes I mean: quarters in 3/2; 8ths in 3/4 and 16ths in 3/8; 8ths in *Alla breve;* 16ths or 32nds in 2/4 or C; but only so long as no groups of notes twice as fast or once again as short are intermingled, in whatever meter, for then these last-named would have to be performed in the manner described above.

For example, if one were to play the eight 16th notes in each of the following groups taken from Table IX, Fig. I, (k) (m) (n) slowly and evenly:

Ex. 1.

they would not sound so pleasing as they would if the first and third were held somewhat longer, and played somewhat louder, than the second and fourth. This rule has the following exceptions: first, fast passages in a very fast tempo, in which there is not enough time for them to be performed unevenly, and in which accordingly only the first of each four notes can be emphasized in loudness and length. Also excepted are all fast passages for the singing voice, when they are not to be slurred; for every note in this type of vocal passage must be marked and made clear by a gentle expulsion of air from the chest, and thus unevenness has no place in such passages. Further exceptions occur: when notes have dashes or dots over them, or when there are several successive notes of the same pitch; also when there is a slur over more than two notes—that is, over four, six, or eight; and finally concerning 8th notes in gigues. All these notes must be played even, that is, one as long as the other.[1]

Dannreuther quotes a part of this passage in connection with Frescobaldi's instructions about rhythmical freedom in toccatas, and sees in Quantz's words a confirmation of the general Baroque practice of rubato playing "for certain preludes, toccatas, and the like."[2] Dolmetsch, who quotes the passage in its entirety, was probably the first to derive from it the far more sweeping conclusion that inequality should be applied to Bach as a matter of principle.[3] He states as his reason that Quantz belonged to Bach's school.

In 1952, Sol Babitz wrote an article in the form of a detailed exegesis of every sentence of this same Quantz passage.[4] He claims that the "Remark" confirms that a convention of playing evenly written pairs of notes unevenly— to wit, either long-short or short-long—had such sweeping currency at the time that it involves "nearly every measure of baroque music," including, of course, the music of Johann Sebastian Bach. He chides Quantz for hiding his remark in a dark corner of the book instead of "emblazoning it" at the beginning; neither is he happy that Quantz failed to mention the short-long variety of unequal notes. Ten years later, elaborating on his theories of 1952, he stated that even a Bach fugue ought to be played with uneven notes, arbitrarily alternating the long-short and short-long patterns:[5]

Ex. 2.

Preceding by a year Babitz's first article, Arthur Mendel expressed a certain cautious approval of Babitz's soon-to-be-published ideas, quoted the same passage, and gave examples of how Quantz's remarks about inequality might be applied to parts of the St. John Passion. However, he carefully avoided peremptory statements and pointed out that his examples were only tentative.[6]

In 1953 Curt Sachs again brought up the same passage and claimed incontrovertible proof for the use of unequal notes in baroque music, including Bach's.[7] In 1958, in the *Kritische Bericht* to the Magnificat in the *Neue Bach Ausgabe,* Alfred Dürr once more quoted the by-now famous passage, in which he saw the formulation of a "general" baroque practice and professed to have found a confirmation of its pertinence to Bach in one highly ambiguous and almost indecipherable measure of Bach's first version of the Magnificat.[8]

It might be added that Robert Donington in 1960, for once dispensing with the Quantz quotation, proposed that the French *Inégales* ought to be applied to Bach's harpsichord works because they were based on French models.[9]

This is an impressive array of authorities, and their claims are far-reaching indeed. If substantiated they would necessarily inaugurate an entirely new era of Bach interpretation. The question is—have they been proven? The main purpose of this article is to show that this has not been the case.

This article will present evidence that strongly supports the following hypotheses:

1. That the Quantz quotation has been vastly overrated; that it is not testimony to a general baroque practice, but is simply a suggestion that a French performance manner be adopted; in other words, that it is not a historian's report of what was being done in Germany, but a teacher's recommendation of what ought to be done;

2. that the arguments advanced to corroborate the passage as a description of practice in Germany are deceptive;

3. that, outside the islands of French musical influence, the *Inégales* had no currency in the Germany of Bach's time.

To support this thesis it will be necessary to discuss the French *Inégales* convention at some length in order to put the Quantz quotation into correct perspective. Against this background the Quantz passage itself will be examined and its inconsistencies will be exposed. This will be followed by an analysis and refutation of the major arguments which purport to prove the validity of the quotation for Germany and for Bach. Finally, to round out the argument, an explanation will be offered for the fact, bewildering at first glance, that Quantz included in his book a passage that had no reference to current German practice.

The French *Inégales*

The term *Inégales* will be, and ought to be, applied only in the specific sense of the French convention, namely the uneven (long-short or short-long) playing of *evenly written* pairs of notes that are subdivisions of a beat.[10] Documentation about uneven playing of evenly written notes turns up around the middle of the 16th century. At that time Santa Maria in Spain reports patterns of long-short and short-long;[11] and Bourgeois in France mentions long-short inequalities.[12] In 1602, Caccini in the *Nuove Musiche* demonstrates the long-short dotted pattern as one of many different ways in which rubato-style rhythmic manipulations can be applied to a vocal melody. Cerone, in 1613, describes long-short inequality for contiguous melodies[13] and Frescobaldi in 1614 suggests, in the Preface to his Toccatas, short-long patterns in some specific cases of 16th notes (when they are combined with 8th notes).[14] On the other hand, the dotted patterns to be found in Ganassi, Ortiz, Bovicelli, and other treatises dealing with diminutions cannot be counted as belonging to the same category. They do not refer to unequal interpretation of equally written notes, but to dotted patterns of improvised coloraturas that are based on far simpler tonal and rhythmic relationships.[15]

These rhythmic alterations of short-long and long-short execution were a form of simple ornamentation, simpler by far than the extravagant luxuriance of the diminutions. No new notes were added, and the purpose was simply to give more grace and elegance to a melody by changing a plain and square rhythmic pattern into a lilting and more varied one.

So early a writer as Bourgeois establishes a principle that became paramount in the later French convention: a definite relationship between the meter and the type of note subject to inequality. He gives as the reason that under the circumstances of this relationship the first of two notes is usually a consonance, the second a dissonance. As a further reason, however, he points to the *"meilleure grâce,"* the greater elegance, achieved by long-short inequality. The reference to consonance and dissonance is interesting because it might reveal one of the original motives for inequality. But when by the latter part of the 17th century the convention had crystallized into the form in which it remained virtually unchanged for over a hundred years (from about 1660 to about 1780) it had completely emancipated itself from the notion of consonance and dissonance, or of "good" and 'bad" notes, which played such an important part in the German and Italian musical literature of the age.

The convention which thus emerged was highly sophisticated and rather complex; so much so that practically every French treatise of the time felt compelled to deal with it in some detail.[16] From these treatises there emerges a clear picture of the convention, a picture remarkable for a high degree of uniformity with respect to 1) the manner of presentation; 2) the rules that determine which notes are to be even, and which are eligible for unevenness; 3) the nature of the inequality; and 4) the exceptions to the rules. There are to be sure, certain differences of opinion, but they are minor, and neither affect the basic principles nor mar the overall impression of near-complete agreement. These are the principles, first stated and then amplified:

1) Inequality applies to pairs of certain notes that move in stepwise progression and are subdivisions of the basic metrical unit. 2) Inequality is long-short, practically never short-long. 3) Notes not subject to inequality must be played very evenly. 4) The convention applies to French music only. 5) Inequality is subject to many exceptions.

1. *Notes eligible for inequality.* Subject to inequality are pairs of notes that move essentially in stepwise progression and are subdivisions of the beat, or, more precisely, of the basic metrical unit as indicated by the lower number of the meter signature. It emphatically never applies to the note-values representing the metrical unit itself, such as the quarter note in 4/4 or the 8th note in 3/8. The meter signature determines which notes are eligible for inequality and which have to be played evenly. In certain meters (generally speaking, in duple meters) the metrical unit has to be divided into four parts before inequality applies. This will be referred to as the *first category*. In other meters (generally speaking, the triple meters) inequality applies to the subdivision of the metrical unit into two parts. This latter will be referred to as the *second category*. The probable reasons for this distinction will be explained below.

The following simplified tabulation (table 1) shows the overall relationship of various meters; the value of their basic metrical unit; the value of the notes that were equal—that is, not subject to inequality; and those that were subject to inequality.

The next chart, table 2, documents the overall agreement of 30 contemporary authors (listed chronologically) concerning the relationship of meter to inequality, and at the same time it reveals unmistakably how Quantz's rules fit exactly into the framework of the French convention. With the exception of 3/4 meter, on which opinions are divided, the table shows only four other deviations from unanimity: those of Loulié and Choquel concerning the 2/4 meter, and of Cajon and Raparlier concerning 3/2 meter. Even though some of the general agreement may be due to the fact that some authors copied from others, the resulting picture of near-complete unanimity is none-the-less remarkable.

Table 1

The Two Categories of Inequality*

FIRST CATEGORY Meter			**2, ₵** (two beats)	$\frac{2}{4}$ **C, ₵** (four beats) $\frac{3}{4}$
Metrical unit	equal			
Subdivision in two	equal		L S L S	L S L S
Subdivision in four	unequal			

SECOND CATEGORY Meter			$\frac{3}{2}$	**3,** $\frac{3}{4}$	$\frac{3, 4, 6, 9, 12}{8}$
Metrical unit	equal		L S	L S	L S
Subdivision in two	unequal				

*In the French music of the time, meter signature still had a strong though not a rigid link with tempo. ₵ could stand for two fairly slow beats (slower than those of the 2 meter) or it could stand for four fairly fast ones. In either case inequality is of the first category. The 3/4 meter is placed by some authors in the first category, by others in the second, and is therefore listed under both headings. The rare instance of a 12/8 that is beaten in three:

may have unequal eighth-notes (Montéclair, *Principes*, p. 30). They represent in practice, though not on paper, a fourfold subdivision.

The prerequisite of stepwise progression is also well documented. Some authors state it expressly, among them Loulié, Montéclair, Couperin, and Vague: others indicate it clearly by their illustrations, among them L'Affilard, Bordet, Bordier, David, and Villeneuve.[17] The requirement must not be taken too literally, but rather flexibly, especially when a melody is predominantly linear and stepwise, as shown in the following examples from Muffat (*Florilegium Secundum,* Ex. QQ and RR).

Ex. 3.

On the other hand, a melody moving by skips implied not only equality of notes which according to the meter are eligible for inequality, but as a general rule also implied *detached* interpretation, unless expressly countermanded by a slur mark. A definite bond existed between inequality and legato; between equality and detached articulation. This explains why the terms *Détaché* or *Marqué,* or dots over the notes, indicate not only staccato playing, but also imply cancellation of inequality.

2. *Inequality is Long-short.* The long note of the unequal pair falls on the beat. Inequality is practically never short-long (with the short note falling on the beat). As mentioned earlier, our first witness, Bourgeois, mentioned only long-short inequality. The short-longs of Santa Maria and Frescobaldi find only a faint echo in France in Loulié's book of 1696, but the very way in which Loulié presents the subject suggests that it was of negligible importance. After having explained at some length in the second part of the book the various kinds of long-short *Inégales,* he proceeds in the third part to discuss the meaning of the various time signatures. At the end of this part, he adds the note: "In the second part I have forgotten to mention, when I spoke of the triple meters, that the first half of each beat can also be played in a fourth manner, to wit: by playing the first note shorter than the second: Thus".[18]

Ex. 4.

Table 2

Meter-Inequality Relationships as Formulated by 30 Contemporary Authors

	$\frac{3}{2}$	2	₵ in two	₵ in four	C	$\frac{2}{4}$	$\frac{3}{4}$	3	$\frac{6,\,9,\,12}{4}$	$\frac{3,\,4,\,6,\,9,\,12}{8}$
Rousseau (Jean) a) 1687	♩	♪	♪		♪			♪		
Loulié b) c) 1696	♩	♪	♪	♪	♪	♪	♪	♪		
L'Affilard 1697, 1705		♪	♪		♪	♪				
Muffat 1698	♩ d)	♪	♪	♪	♪	♪	♪ d)	♪ e)	♪ d)	♪ d)
Saint-Lambert f) 1702	♩	♪	♪	♪	♪			♪		
Montéclair g) 1709, 1736		♪	♪	♪	♪	♪ b)		♪	♪	♪ i)
Dupont c) 1718		♪	♪	♪	♪			♪		♪
Saurin 1722	♩	♪	♪	♪	♪	♪	♪	♪	♪	♪
Démotz j) k) 1728	♩	♪	♪	♪	♪	♪ b)	♪ b)	♪	♪	♪
Vague b) 1733	♩	♪	♪	♪	♪	♪	♪	♪	♪	
David b) 1737	♩	♪	♪	♪	♪	♪	♪	♪	♪	♪ i)
Dupuit l) 1741	♩ m)	♪	♪		♪	♪	♪	♪	♪	♪
Corrette l) n) 1741, 1770	♩ m)	♪	♪	♪	♪	♪	♪	♪	♪	♪
Duval j) 1741					♪	♪ b)	♪ b)	♪	♪	♪
Vion j) 1742	♩	♪	♪		♪			♪	♪	♪
Denis 1747					♪			♪ m)	♪	♪

Rollet 17—	*g)*	♪	♪	♪	♪	♪ *b)*	♪	♪ *b)*
QUANTZ 1752	*l)*	♪	♪	♪	♪		♪	♪ *i)*
St. Philbert 17—	♪ *m)*	♪	♪	♪	♪		♪	♪ *b)*
Bordet 1755	*l)*	♪	♪	♪	♪	♪	♪	♪ *b)*
Villeneuve 1756	♪	♪	♪	♪	♪	♪	♪	♪
Bordier 1760	♪ *m)*	♪	♪	♪	♪	♪	♪	♪
Choquel 1762		♪	♪	♪ *o)*	♪ *b)*	♪		
Brijon 1763		♪	♪	♪		♪	♪	
Duval (abbé) 1764	*j)*	♪	♪	♪	♪	♪	♪	♪
Lacassagne 1766	*l)*	♪	♪	♪	♪	♪	♪	♪
Dard 1769	*j)*	♪	♪	♪	♪	♪	♪	♪
Métoyen 17—	*l)*	♪	♪ *b)*	♪ *b)*	♪ *p)*	♪ *p)*	♪	♪ *b)*
Cajon 1772	*l)*	♪ *q)*	♪	♪	♪	♪	♪	♪
Raparlier 1772	♪	♪	♪	♪	♪	♪	♪	♪

a) Rousseau uses the term *marquer* which might imply a combination of dynamic and agogic accent. *b)* First category in duple meters, second category in triple meters. *c)* Equates equality with detached articulation. *d)* Derived from Muffat's examples. *e)* If "fairly fast" (*un peu gai*). *f)* St. Lambert's listings implied by: 8th unequal except in 4/4 where 16ths unequal; quarter-notes unequal in "slow triple meter". *g)* Any four-fold subdivision of the beat is unequal. *h)* Implied by: 8th equal. *i)* Specified for 3/8. *j)* Inequality is *cumulative*: when shorter notes occur than those eligible for inequality, both the shorter *and* the longer notes are unequal. *k)* Démotz spells out cumulative inequality in every single instance. *l)* Inequality *descends*: when many notes occur that are shorter than those eligible for inequality, the shorter ones become unequal and the longer ones become equal. *m)* 'Sometimes equal' implying unequal 8ths. *n)* No inequality in Sonatas or Concertos. *o)* With the unusual comment that only quarter and 8th notes occur in 2/4 meter, meaning probably: *if* only quarter and 8th notes occur. *p)* Equal if 16ths occur. *q)* If no 8ths occur, quarter notes are unequal.

This is the last we hear about the short-long inequality. In the 18th century none of the French authors listed in note 16 mentions the short-long pattern; what is more, several of them take pains to make sure that their explanations of inequality could not possibly be misinterpreted as a short-long pattern.

The documentation about the long-short nature of inequality is so unanimous and so massive that only a very few representative references will be cited. L'Affilard, speaking of the "2" meter, says that when the beat *(le temps)* is divided in four parts, the first note is long, the second short, the third long, the

fourth short. If a quarter note precedes two eighths ⌈ 2 ♩ ♫ ♩ ♫ ⌉ the

first is long, the second short. If an eighth rest precedes them ⌈ 2 𝄾 ♪ ♫ ⌉ then the first is short, the second long, the third short.[19]

Saint Lambert says that when inequality applies, the first note is long when the number of notes is even; the first is short and the second long when the number of notes is odd. He illustrates the odd numbers as follows: ♪ ♫ ♫ ♫ which, of course, confirms the long-short principle.[20] His illustration of what is meant by an even or odd number of notes in a measure is very important because many other French authors use the same terms to specify long-short inequality. Some, for instance Dard,[21] illustrate it in the same way; others who do not illustrate the terms (Hotteterre for instance) can be inferred to mean the same thing. That no other interpretation would seem possible is clarified by a passage from Bordet. He explains in the usual manner how meter signature determines inequality in pairs with the first long, the second short, the third long, and the fourth short. He adds that this applies as long as the same type of notes continues without interruption. Then he says:

In applying inequality one must be careful to observe that the note which is lengthened is the first of an even pair, one that either starts a measure or follows a note or a rest of a different value [meaning for instance:]

⌈ 𝄴 ♩♩♩♩ ‖   or: 𝄴 ♩ ♫ ‖   or: 2 𝄾 ♩♩ ♩♩ ♩♩ ⌉

Because if unequal notes were to start with an odd number one would have to play the first short and the next one long, in order not to disturb the natural rank order which the notes are supposed to have; whereby the odd number would derive from the fact that they are preceded either by a dot or a silence of the same value, either of which would take the place of the first lengthened note, the first of an even number[22] [meaning:]

⌈ 2 ♩ . ♪ ♫♫ ‖   or: 2 ♩ 𝄾 ♪ ♫♫ ⌉

This cumbersome passage is quoted verbatim as a reflection of the present author's concern over any possible misunderstanding about the fact that inequality must be long-short and not short-long.[23]

Yet in spite of all these unequivocal documents, much has been made lately of alleged short-long inequality. Babitz claims it for all of Europe during the baroque era, and Donington claims it as part of the *Inégales* convention. This latter convention, Donington asserts, also includes a *Lourer* (a slight long-short inequality), a *Piquer* (a pronounced long-short) and a *Couler*, which is supposed to stand for a short-long inequality.[24]

How did these claims originate? Babitz's claims are largely based on keyboard fingerings, and a separate section of this article will be devoted to them.[25] As to Donington, there is little doubt that his theory of the *Couler* as a short-long inequality is based on a misunderstanding of the following pattern from the ornamentation table in Couperin's first book of Clavecin pieces of 1713:

Ex. 5.

"Coulées dont les points marquent que la seconde note de chaque temps doit être plus appuyée."

Donington interprets Couperin's caption as a short-long *inégal* pattern which is called *Couler*. What the caption actually means is this: "If the second of two slurred notes has a dot on it, this second note should be emphasized." The term *Couler* refers to nothing but the slurred notes. Several observations have to be made to point up a misunderstanding which led to the mistaken theory that short-long *Inégales* were current in French music of the 18th century when the French contemporary writers insist that they were not.

The term *Couler*, "to flow," signifies two things in the French musical literature of the time. First, it is simply the term for legato playing or singing, or the slur on a stringed or woodwind instrument. Second, it is an agrément which "flowingly" connects notes.[26] The term is *not* used for the short-long playing of equally-written notes. Couperin's directive *"Notes égales et coulées"* in the Gavotte of the first *Concert Royal*, in the Forlane of the fourth *Concert*, or repeatedly in *l'Apothéose de Corelli (Corelli buvant a la Source d'Hypocrène; Corelli . . . s'endort)* would serve by itself to contradict such an assumption.

The term *appuyé* is ambiguous, and though for media capable of dynamic nuance it would more readily suggest an accent, it is possible that a short-long interpretation was intended for the harpsichord.[27] However this may be, the fact remains that this pattern does not consist of notes that are *equally written but unequally played*, which is the essence of the *Inégales* convention. Instead, the dot on the second note singles this pattern out for special treatment and therefore it cannot be taken as an indication that such short-long playing was practiced without any such notational directive.[28] As a matter of principle it is no more a case of inequality than are written-out dotted notes.

Still more important is that this pattern seems to have found few if any imitators, and most significant is the further fact that Couperin himself discarded it shortly afterwards. That four years later in his *L'Art de toucher le Clavecin* Couperin does not mention this pattern would not be proof in itself, since he does not again present a complete table of ornamentation. But what matters is that Couperin does not use this pattern in any of his compositions written after this date. It occurs neither in the Preludes of *L'Art de toucher*, nor in the third or fourth book of clavecin pieces, nor in the *Concerts Royaux*, nor in the 5th to the 20th Concertos, nor in the *Apothéose de Lully*, the *Apothéose de Corelli*, nor in the *Pièces de viole*. Couperin has, it seems, used his inalienable right to change his mind. It is very interesting to note that at least in one item the Couperin text of 1713 is no longer valid for the Couperin of 1717. It happens to be the very item which originated Donington's whole theory of short-long *Inégales*.[29]

With this misunderstanding cleared up, it can be safely stated that in the first part of the 18th century, which interests us most, the great mass of French documentation agrees that the *Inégales* were long-short and not short-long. If within the latitude of a performer's freedom the short-long inequality in triple meters (which Loulié almost forgot to mention) should have lingered on into the 18th century, its incidence must have been so negligible that it can well be ignored. Quantz did not forget to mention the short-long convention, as Babitz regretfully assumes. Like all the other contemporary writers on inequality he would seem to have ignored what either did not exist or was no longer worth mentioning.

As to the degree of inequality, the extent to which the first of a pair of notes is lengthened varies from very slightly to very distinctly; to the near equivalent of a dot but hardly, if ever, to more than that. It was a matter for the musical taste of the performer to decide, the *Goût* which in France at that period was always the supreme judge in all matters of interpretation. Of the various terms used, *Lourer* suggests only a small inequality, *Pointer* and *Piquer* a stronger one.

3. *The evenness of the Notes Égales.* Notes that were not eligible for inequality had to be played very evenly. In referring to examples of the first category, Montéclair tells us that each beat *(temps)* has to be divided into "two very equal parts."[30] Implying also instances of the first category, David pointedly declares that notes representing the beats, and those representing the first subdivision that are not subject to inequality, have to be played with the precision of the

pendulum of a well-adjusted clock.[31] Saint Lambert stresses that notes of equal values have to be played with great equality of timing *("Avec une grande égalité de mouvement")*[32] and all notes with great equality of proportion; a rule suspended only when *Inégales* are applied.

This French insistence on the evenness of the beats and—in the first category—of the first subdivision, must be kept in mind when later in this article the arguments will be examined which try to link the *Inégales* with the "good" and "bad" notes.

4. *The convention applies to French music only.* If borne out by the documents, such a limitation to France and French performance would, of course, be of decisive interest to our case. We have a direct statement to this effect from Loulié in 1698, who emphasizes in italics that inequality does not apply to any non-French music. In this latter, he says notes are never lengthened unless notation expressly demands it: *"dans toute sorte de Musique étrangere ou l'on ne pointe jamais qu'il ne soit marqué."*[33] *This* statement, missing in the first Paris edition, is seemingly the only addition inserted for the second, Amsterdam edition. This fact alone, as well as the italics, testifies to the importance that Loulié attached to this afterthought.

Corrette states that inequality does not apply to Italian music: "in any meter the eighth notes are played evenly in Italian music."[34] Moreover, speaking of 4/4 meters Corrette exempts from inequality Adagios, Allegros, and Prestos of Sonatas and Concertos. Since the latter were importations from Italy, this shows that even French music patterned after foreign models discarded by that very fact the typically French *Inégales.*[35]

Speaking of the *Inégales,* Couperin clearly implies their purely French character when he says that Frenchmen play foreign music better than foreigners play French music because foreign music is played as written whereas the French is not.[36]

Jean-Jacques Rousseau testifies to the same state of affairs. He tells us that "in Italian music all eighth notes are always of equal length unless they are expressly marked as dotted. By contrasts, in the French music eighth notes are equal only in 4/4 time."[37]

5. *Inequality is subject to many exceptions.* Some important ones have already been mentioned: inequality does not apply to foreign music nor to French music that is patterned after foreign models; and it does not apply to melodies that move by skips. Apart from these, the most important and sweeping exceptions issue from the general authority given to the *Goût* of the performer to decide whether the character of a piece does or does not warrant the use of the *Inégales.* There is good reason to assume that fairly complex polyphony (which was rare in any case in 18th-century French music) was not conducive to

the use of inequality; that the latter found its most natural habitat in a prominent melodic line supported by a texture more homophonic than polyphonic.

The very nature of the inequality as a free, rubato-like rhythmic manipulation predestines its use by soloists. The very fact that the degree of inequality was arbitrary would create confusion in an orchestral section and would make for difficulties in chamber music. Its most logical fields of application are organ works and harpsichord pieces, arias, songs, and instrumental solos.

Inequality is often expressly cancelled by the composer by the directive *Notes égales* or *Croches égales*. Also, as was mentioned above, markings calling for detached, staccato playing, such as the words, *Detaché, Marqué, Martelé,* as well as dots or dashes over the notes, were also understood to countermand inequality.

After 1700 differences of opinion among the French authors are by and large limited to two matters. As shown in table 2, 3/4 meter is placed by some in the first category, by others in the second. Another difference has to do with the question of what happens if note-values occur that are smaller than the *Inégales,* such as 32nd notes in 4/4 meter. According to some authors the inequality descends to the lower level of the fastest notes, with the 32nds becoming unequal and the 16ths equal. According to some authors inequality is cumulative: both the 16ths and the 32nds will be unequal (see table 2, writers marked *"j"* and *"l"*). In view of the authority given the judgment of the performer, these are minor points.[38]

Though the structure of the convention seems complicated, there is an inner logic to it which makes excellent sense of all its principles.

The true function of the *Inégales* seems to have been to grace passages that were essentially melismatic in character and partook of the nature of diminutions.[39] By contrast, inequality was *not* meant to tamper with the essence of the melody. For this reason the note-values which had structural meaning, and in particular those representing the main beats (such as the quarter note in C) had to be kept free of the encroachment of rhythmic alteration.

Actually, all the principles of the convention, its rules and its exceptions, can be deduced from the fact that melismas as a rule are a) predominantly stepwise; b) predominantly legato; and c) usually consist of the fastest notes in a piece. Both staccato articulation as well as disjunct progressions tend to confer structural meaning on single notes, however fast.

As to the fastest notes, the whole, seemingly artificial system of meter-note relationships has the aim of identifying those note-values which are apt to be melismatic in character. This made good sense in a metrical structure in which (as a legacy from the proportional system) there still prevailed a strong link between meter and tempo. The **C** meter, for example had a slow quarter note. Therefore 8th notes were still structurally important and had to be protected from inequality whereas the 16th notes in legato and in stepwise progression were likely to be ornamental in character. If the tempo was slow enough for many 32nd notes to appear, they in turn became the medium of ornamental figuration, whereas the 16ths could assume a more structural meaning. Therefore the matter of disagreement on whether inequality "descends" or is "cumulative" would resolve itself in accordance with the more ornamental or more structural character of the next-to-shortest notes.

The difference between the two categories of inequality can be explained by the fact that in triple meters, (also an inheritance from the past) the same note-values were generally considerably faster than in duple meters. Thus a quarter note in **C** was related to a half note in 3/2 and an 8th note in **C** was on the whole not much faster than a quarter note in 3. Therefore the first subdivision of the beat in triple meter (e.g. ♩ ♩ ♩ ♩ ♩ ♩ was in duration and musical function, by and large, the counterpart of the second subdivision of a corresponding duple meter (e.g. ♫♫♫ ♫♫♫).[40]

What mattered was not the dogmatic application of rules but an intelligent performer's judgment as to the nature and function of the notes involved, whether they were more nearly structural and ornamental; musical pillars rather than draperies. Viewed from this vantage point, the convention seems to reveal a true organic unity. In a way it was the gilding of the lily by further gracing ornamental figuration, thereby adding another sophistication to an already highly refined musical style.

How long did the convention last? It seems to have emerged gradually from origins that, as Bourgeois attests, go back at least to the mid-16th century. It reached maturity towards the end of the 17th century and was thoroughly codified by the beginning of the 18th. In the 1760's and 1770's many books are still full of prominently-featured references to it, and Engramelle's *Tono-technie* of 1776 clearly attests to its continued vigor. The third edition of Bailleux's treatise (a shameless plagiarism of Montéclair) came out at the eve of the Revolution and thus bears witness to the continued actuality of the convention (as well as to the "author's" intellectual dishonesty). However, a text by "citoyen" Durié published at the height of the Revolution in 1793 does not mention inequality though it otherwise conforms to the usual pattern of foundational treatises. Thus, it would seem that the *Inégales* convention, sharing the fate of other institutions of the *Ancien Régime,* did not outlast the storming of the Bastille. One thing, however, is clear. The *Inégales* were not a baroque convention, as some modern writers would have it. Their early beginnings preceded the baroque and their maturity considerably out-lasted it.

The survival span becomes still more striking if one realizes, that with Couperin and Rameau, more fittingly identified with the Rococo,[41] the terminal date for the baroque in France can be more appropriately linked to the death of Louis XIV (1715) than to the death of Bach, of whose life nobody in France had taken any notice at the time.

The Quantz Passage

Two non-Frenchmen were included in the tabulation of the *Inégales* (table 2): one is Muffat, the other Quantz. Muffat presented the *Inégales* convention at first briefly in his *Florilegium Primum* of 1695 and then at some length in the preface to his *Florilegium Secundum* in 1698. He had returned from six years of study with Lully in Paris, and clearly stated his intention of acquainting his compatriots with the French practices of the time which he considered worthy of emulation. His whole presentation of the convention as a manner "à la française" and as a part of the Lullian style leaves no doubt that at the time of his writing the convention was *not* being practiced in Germany. So far nobody seems to have misinterpreted Muffat's words as proof that the *Inégales* had currency outside of France and it would be hard indeed to do so.[42]

Sixty years after Muffat, Quantz does the same: he presents the outline of the French *Inégales* convention. He did so because he, too, found merit in it. However, he failed to attach explicitly the label of "made in France" and because of this omission, his statement was taken by some to represent what was practiced in Germany rather than in France.

There cannot be the slightest doubt that the Quantz passage embodies the essence of the French *Inégales* convention. This is borne out by the complete agreement concerning the principle of inequality (the long-short pattern by pairs of notes); concerning the most characteristic meter-to-note-value relationship, with duple meters belonging to the first, triple meters to the second category; concerning the list of exceptions to inequality which, too, is in accordance with the French tradition; and concerning the references to dots and dashes as symbols of cancellation. So far as all this goes it reads like a translation from a French treatise, and a look at table 2 confirms this complete agreement.

Yet it is interesting and significant that in spite of this agreement on the essentials of the convention, the passage deviates—inadvertently, so it seems—in a few points from the pattern of presentation set by the French authors, and it happens that these independent additions involve Quantz in inconsistencies. These are the points at issue:

1. The French authors discuss the *Inégales* in connection with meter and time values. With their strong tie to, and their dependence on, the meter, this is

their logical place. If the convention had been current in Germany, then chapter V of Quantz's book, which deals with measure and meter, would have been the obvious place to present it, but there no mention is made of it. Instead the remark is hidden away as a miscellaneous item in chapter XI, which deals with generalities about good performance.

2. At the beginning of the passage, Quantz relates the *Inégales* to the *anschlagende* and *durchgehende,* the "good" and "bad" notes. No French author after Bourgeois in 1550 seems to have done so, because in the form the convention had eventually taken there is no justification for it. The relationship of the *Inégales* to the good and bad notes will be discussed at some length, and only then will the importance of Quantz's inconsistency in this matter fully emerge.

3. At the end of the passage, Quantz lists the eighth notes in Gigues as one of the exceptions to the rules of inequality. This exception is meaningless since almost all Gigues are in a $\frac{x}{8}$ meter: $3/8, 6/8, 9/8, 12/8$, in all of which the eighth notes as the lower unit of the meter signature are equal by definition. Quantz contradicts his own statement that in a $3/8$ meter only the 16th notes are uneven.

4. The discrepancy between the clear statement that inequality descends and the apparent simultaneous inequality of 16ths and 32nds in $2/4$ or **C**.

5. The contradiction about the effect of a slur: though the latter is supposed to cancel inequality if it extends over more than two notes, one of the examples shows a slur over three notes.

Whatever the reasons for these inconsistencies, the latter must affect any evaluation of meaning and authority of the passage.[43]

Before we could be asked to accept the claim that the passage did represent and record a current German convention, the following points would have to be given convincing explanations:

1) The inconsistencies of the passage itself; 2) the apparent absence of any reference to the *Inégales,* as we know them from the French and from Quantz, in any of the numerous massive volumes written by contemporary German authors notorious for their methodical thoroughness;[44] 3) the French insistence that the *Inégales* were not practiced by foreigners; 4) the absence in German music—including, of course, that of Bach and including, as Babitz admits, even that of Quantz[45]—of the many telltale traces of the convention, such as the expressions *Notes égales, Marqué, Detaché,* or the use of dots or dashes that could be convincingly interpreted as symbols requiring cancellation of inequality.

I believe, on the other hand, that it is safe to state that the thesis as proposed for this study can be considered confirmed if it can be shown that: 1) no satisfactory explanations have been produced for the four points just listed; 2) the alleged corroborations of the Quantz passage by other German authors are illusory; 3) a plausible explanation can be given for the inclusion of the passage in Quantz's book, an explanation that will make all other known facts fall into place.

The Alleged Corroboration

We shall now examine the arguments that claim to corroborate the passage in connection with Germany and Bach. Corroboration has been alleged mainly with regard to the following: 1) good and bad notes; 2) agogic nuances suggested by slurs; 3) keyboard fingerings; 4) one measure in the first version of Bach's Magnificat; and 5) one measure in the B Minor Mass. These arguments will be investigated and a few other minor points will be touched on briefly.

1. *The Good and Bad Notes.* The most important argument centers on the different parts of the measure *(Taktteile and Taktglieder)* or different types of notes that are variously referred to by the Italians as *Note buone e cattive;* by the French as *Notes de repos et de passage, notes nobles et viles, principales et chétives,* or *temps bons et mauvais;* by the Germans as *gute and schlimme Noten,* (good and bad notes), *anschlagende* and *durchgehende* (primary and passing), notes that are *innerlich* (inwardly), or *valore intrinseca,* or *quantitate intrinseca,* or *virtualiter,*[46] long and short, or notes that are *akzentuiert* and *unakzentuiert.*

All these formidable terms were used interchangeably, and we have Scheibe's and other authors' confirmation that they all meant one and the same thing.[47] The following pages will show what this meaning is, and that it is fundamentally different from the *Inégales* as reported by Quantz.

Babitz feels that an article in Walther's Lexicon of 1732 about these two types of notes "corroborates Quantz on this subject more adequately than any other German contemporary,"[48] and Sachs supports this view.[49] In the article entitled *"Quantitas Notarum extrinseca & intrinseca"* Walther has this to say: "The outward and inward value of the notes: according to the former, notes of the same kind are performed in equal length, according to the latter in unequal length; the odd part of the measure being long and the even part short."[50]

The obscurity of this passage might seem to lend itself to various interpretations. Sachs thought he could elucidate its meaning by recourse to the Quantz Remark (in which Sachs believed he found an amplification of the Walther article) and by recourse to passages in C.P.E. Bach and Leopold Mozart. Only Mozart speaks of the same subject as Walther, namely good and bad notes. But the one sentence which Sachs quotes, to the effect that good notes are to be played "not only a little stronger but also a little longer" is a misunderstanding, since Mozart does not in that sentence refer to "good" notes, but to notes that are the first under a slur. This is a different matter altogether, as will be seen. Finally, the Quantz Remark was a misleading choice in Sach's quest for elucidation of the Walther sentences. This becomes apparent even without detailed analysis of the question through consideration of the following circumstances.

According to Walther, the "inner" inequality applies in a 4/4 measure to two half notes and, if we take the term *Taktteil* in its widest sense, to alternating quarter notes and eighth notes. By contrast, according to Quantz, in full accord with the French convention, inequality *never* applies in a 4/4 meter to half, quarter, or eighth notes, but only to the "fastest notes," to the 16ths and to those only if there were no 32nds present. Moreover, Quantz speaks of a plain, simple, and unqualified inequality of long-short, with no nonsense about *quantitas intrinseca* or *virtualiter*. From this alone it can be seen—as will emerge still more convincingly later—that the Quantz quotation is not an amplification of Walther's article, and the latter is not a confirmation of the former.

The true solution of Walther's riddle can be found very easily, since the German literature of the time abounds in references to "good" and "bad" notes under any or all of the above listed terms, and many of these discussions are extensive and explicit. What is more, these presentations show a unanimity that is a perfect counterpart to the unanimity with which the French authors treat the *Inégales* convention. Nothing dramatizes more sharply the contrast in the musical practice between the two nations than this confrontation along national lines on two issues that, apart from some superficial resemblance, have in essence nothing to do with each other.

What the German authors are concerned with is not, as Babitz supposes, a convention of Baroque "expressive rhythm" which is identical with the French *Inégales*. Instead they refer to the natural musical diction that is suggested by the bar line and the meter. Such musical prosody was by no means limited to the baroque, but has been valid and practiced ever since metrical rhythm made its appearance, which may go back as far as the 4th century and perhaps even to Greek music. Moreover, it is valid to the present day, where the bar line still suggests patterns of recurrent heavy and light beats, of stresses and releases, as it has for over 300 years.

What is meant by the expressions "long" and "short," *quantitate intrinseca* or *virtualiter* or *innerlich*, etc, is *not* an outright lengthening or shortening. If these terms had meant such a thing there would be no need whatever for all the cumbersome qualifying terms which invariably accompany the reference to "long" and "short" by German authors. What the terms mean is simply that the heavy beats of musical diction (in descending order: the beginning of a measure, of a half-measure, the main beats, the first, third, fifth notes, etc., that are subdivisions of beats) naturally attract the points of melodic, harmonic, and rhythmic emphasis; that in vocal music they have to accommodate the accented syllables of words; that they have a bearing on the choice of notes that need chordal realization in a thorough bass and those that do not; and that, by their prominence they may give the impression of being longer even if they are not.[51] The picture is very similar to that presented by the symbols used in poetry for long and short syllables (— ‿) when their actual meaning refers not to length but to accents. Words like *útmost, ínsight,* and *úpstart* would still be presented *quantitate intrinseca* by the long-short pattern — ‿ even though, according to the actual length of the syllables, *quantitate extrinseca,* they are short-long. A few quotations from contemporary sources will bear this out.

Printz, who may be among the first German authors to discuss this matter at some length, points out that certain notes which are of equal length *appear* to be longer, others *appear* to be shorter, according to their position in the measure[52] (and that among several *"der Zeit nach gleich langen Noten oder Klängen etliche länger, etliche kürzer zu sein scheinen"*). This, he says, the composer has to bear in mind in order to fit the music properly to words and in order to treat consonance and dissonance correctly. This seemingly different length "of certain notes that according to time or duration are of equal length is called *Quantitas Temporalis Intrinseca, die innerliche Zeitlänge.*"[53] He illustrates the meaning with a textual example (which was taken over 80 years later by Löhlein in his *Clavier Schule*):[54]

Ex. 6.

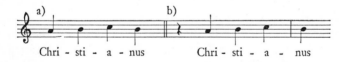

In the word "Christianus," the first and third syllables are long, and setting *a* sounds good because the long syllables are correctly placed, whereas setting *b* is "repulsive." This, he says, could not be so if there were not differences in the inward, the "innerlich" length of the notes. Another example shows how the same principle applies to subdivisions where again, 1, 3, 5, etc. are inwardly long, the even-numbered ones short: *a* is correct, *b* impossible:

Ex. 7.

From this Printz concludes that the same principle applies also to multiples of the beat, such as half notes or even whole measures, of which the first, third, etc. are inwardly long, the second, fourth, etc, inwardly short.[55] In groups of threes, when a note is divided into three parts, the first is "inwardly" long, the second and third short. In a very slow movement, Printz continues, for instance in a 6/4 meter, both parts of the measure can be considered long. The application of the terms "long" and "short" *quantitate intrinseca,* to whole measures or to two "longs" in a 6/4 meter makes it abundantly clear that what is meant cannot be an actual lengthening, but is simply a matter of emphasis. Nobody so far has advanced the claim that a long-short pattern be applied to whole measures and, of course, a long-long pattern in 6/4 would be senseless in terms of actual duration.

About the same time, Ahle presented similar examples of correct and incorrect prosody, and pointed to the need to place long syllables on the odd-numbered notes which are long *quantitate intrinseca* so that the *accentus melicus* coincides with the *accentus metricus.*[56] In 1708 Walther himself in his *Praecepta* gives a clue to his later article by identifying *quantitas extrinseca* with *quantitas tactualis,* and *quantitas intrinseca* with *quantitas accentualis.* He shows with an example that this latter has to do with prosody in the sense of Printz and Ahle, and he, too, presents a "long-long" pattern: $\frac{3}{2}$ ♩ 𝅝 that unmistakably reveals the purely accentual character of his "longs" and "shorts", *quantitate intrinseca.*[57]

The same is made very clear also in the following passage by Scheibe:

> Equal notes ... differ from each other through the natural accent, in the same way in which in the pronunciation of words one syllable differs from the other through the accent. If therefore, in 4/4 there are half notes, the first half-measure, the downbeat is long, the second, the upbeat, short, that means, the downbeat is naturally always accented, whereas the upbeat is not ...

He then says that of the quarter notes in **C**, the first and third have an accent, the second and fourth have none.

> This then, is what in music is called *Quantitas intrinseca* and the accented notes are called *anschlagende,* the unaccented *durchgehende Noten.*[58]

To leave no possible doubt that the terms "long" and "short" are not to be taken literally but, like their counterparts, the symbols of poetic meter, stand for accents, he specifies, "I call *long* what has the natural accent, as all primary notes; I call by contrast short, what has no accent, as all passing notes."[59]

Petri, in the most illuminating statement of all, tells us that one must watch out for the good and bad parts of the measure "which some musicians choose to call long and short, *although without reason.* For the duration is not changed, the difference resides only in the alternating loudness and softness, and the notes that are to be played louder are called good whereas those that are to be played softer are called bad"[60] (my italics).

Leopold Mozart too, who next to Walther is one of Babitz's chief witnesses, explains the *anschlagende* and *durchgehende Noten* (in spite of Sach's misleading quotation) strictly in terms of accents.[61] Mozart distinguishes two different kinds of good notes, the *eigentlich herrschende*, i.e. the primary good notes, and the "other good" notes, *"die andern guten Noten,"* the secondary ones. The primary good notes carry the strongest accents. These strongest accents fall on the *Taktteile*, which are explained as the halves of composite measures, such as the first and second parts of 4/4, 6/4, or 6/8. (Provided, as Mozart points out, the composer has not cancelled such accents by contrary directions.) The other good notes, the secondary ones, are the subdivisions, the first, third, fifth, etc., the quarter notes in 2/2, the eighth notes and sixteenths in 4/4 or 3/4, etc. Mozart cautions that these secondary accents for subdivisions have to be very discreet, far weaker than the primary ones on the main subdivisions of a measure.

It is important to keep in mind that the relationship of emphasized notes to meter is related by Mozart to *accents* alone and that the accents for the secondary ones are less and less distinct with every further subdivision. This shows that Babitz has misinterpreted these relationships as unequal notes in the manner of the French and of Quantz, by including them in a table entitled "Time Signatures for Unequal Notes," which purports to show the general agreement between the French writers on *Inégales* and the Germans, Quantz, Muffat, Heinichen, and L. Mozart. Here is the essence of Babitz's table: "A Problem . . . ," p. 561.

TIME SIGNATURES FOR UNEQUAL NOTES

	French Writers c. 1700	Muffat (1695)	Heinichen (1728)	Quantz (1752)	Mozart (1756)
quarter	$\frac{3}{2}$	$\frac{3}{2}$ (allegro)	$\frac{3}{2}$	$\frac{3}{2}$	$\frac{3}{2}$, ¢
8th	$2, 3, \frac{3}{4}, \frac{6}{4}, \frac{9}{4}, \frac{12}{14}$	C, ¢, $\frac{3}{4}$	C	¢, $\frac{3}{4}$	C $\frac{3}{2}, \frac{2}{4}$
16th	C, $\frac{2}{4}, \frac{3}{8}, \frac{4}{8}, \frac{6}{8}, \frac{12}{8}$	C, $\frac{12}{8}$ (adagio)	C	$\frac{2}{4}$, C, $\frac{3}{8}\,\frac{4}{8}$	C, $\frac{2}{4}\,\frac{3}{8}$ $\frac{6}{8}$

The inclusion of Mozart is a mistake for several reasons: 1) Mozart does not make any mention of inequality in connection with these meter-note relationships, but, as has been pointed out, speaks exclusively of accents; 2) Babitz lists only the *secondary* weak accents of the smaller notes, which are dealt with in paragraph 10 of chapter XII, and omits altogether any mention of the far more important primary accents dealt with in the preceding paragraph 9. He would have had to include in his table half notes and quarter notes in 4/4, dotted half notes in 6/4, and dotted quarter notes in 6/8. Even if Mozart *had* spoken of inequality rather than of accents, such inclusion would have immediately shown the utter incompatibility of Mozart with Quantz or the French, and the incongruity of Mozart's inclusion in the table.

That Muffat and Quantz agree with the French is a matter of course, since both merely report the French convention.[62] There remains Heinichen, whose contribution to the table is so meager, to begin with, that it would hardly prove anything even if his inclusion were justified, which, however, it is not. Heinichen too speaks only of "inner" length, and that alone is sufficient ground to exclude him, but beyond that he does so in connection with chordal and passing notes in thorough-bass accompaniment, which is an entirely different matter from the melodic-soloistic *Inégales*. If nothing else, his inclusion of an "inner" long-short-short pattern for ♩ ♩ ♩ in 3/2[63] would suffice to disqualify him for any association with the French writers on *Inégales*, or with Muffat and Quantz.

In other words, Babitz's table represents a misunderstanding and fails to add an element of corroboration to the Quantz Remark. Babitz's and Sach's arguments were predicated on the assumption that the *Inégales* and the "inner" length and shortness of the good and bad notes were one and the same thing, so that the German writers who discussed the good and bad notes were to be considered corroborating witnesses for Quantz. The foregoing should have shown that this assumption was incorrect.

If there are any doubts left on this matter, they are dispelled by those French authors who, in addition to the *Inégales*, also discuss the good and bad notes. These, as natural concomitants of the metrical organization, were of course present in French music and were carefully considered in its melodic-harmonic-rhythmic organization, in the prosody of vocal music,[64] and in the bowing patterns of the Lullian orchestra. However, none of the French authors listed in note 16 tried to equate the *Inégales* with the good and bad notes. So illogical a procedure would immediately boomerang, since the equality of the main beats in the *Inégales* convention is inconsistent with any true inequality that might spring from the good and bad notes. The two principles cannot be merged; they can only be treated as the separate principles they are. It was only to be expected that those French authors who do deal with them treat them accordingly.

Very characteristic is a passage from Jacob, in which he points out that even though the main beats are *even*, the requirements of musical diction imply a certain, ever-so-subtle emphasis on the heavy beats.[65] In other words, the *Notes égales* have to be given the natural dynamic inflexion that befits their place in the measure. Very interesting and revealing is that Saint Lambert, who deals with the *Inégales* in his treatise on the clavecin, discusses the good and bad notes in his treatise on thorough-bass accompaniment in the same vein as Heinichen does in his, by stating that in a faster sequence of notes only the *"Notes principales,"* those that fall on the main beats, need to be chorded, and those falling on the weak beats can be used as passing notes.[66] Similarly, Dard treats of the good and bad notes first, and then separately presents the *Inégales* as a different subject.[67] Muffat, who as a professed spokesman for the Lullian principles can be quoted among the French, makes the difference between the two principles exceptionally clear. In the *Florilegium Secundum* he discusses and illustrates inequality in section III, which deals with meter and tempo; and discusses the good and bad notes in section V, which deals mainly with agréments. He calls the good notes, *notes bonnes, nobles,* or *principales,* the bad ones *viles* or *chétives* and makes the significant statement that the principle of this polarity *applies to all notes in every composition.* This remark alone defines the contrast to inequality which applies only to specific circumstances. Muffat's further remarks and examples bring the contrast into still sharper focus.[68]

Only Quantz mixed up the two principles, and now we are at last in a position to amplify this previously noted inconsistency. He says that the good notes have to be emphasized, and therefore "the fastest notes in every piece ... must ... be played a little unevenly." There is no logic in this statement since the conclusion does not follow the premise. The logical consequence of emphasizing the good notes is not to stress the *shortest* notes, but primarily the *longest* ones, those representing the strong beats, e.g., in C the whole notes and the half notes rather than the 16ths or 32nds.

What Quantz tried to do was to present the French *Inégales* convention as a logical sequel of the principle of metrical diction, and this intermingling of two different principles not only confused the issue but misled Babitz and Sachs into believing that Walther and the other German writers could be used as corroborating witnesses.

Table 3, which follows, is a summary of the fundamental differences between the two categories.

2. *Agogic Articulation.* There is another passage in Leopold Mozart's book that Sachs and Babitz consider proof of inequality in Germany, and therefore as corroboration of the Quantz Remark. After discussing the good and bad notes, the stronger accents on the primary, the weaker accents on the secondary good notes, Mozart repeats a previous statement that of notes under a slur, the first should be somewhat accented and also slightly lengthened.[69] But by

omitting the reference to slurs, Sachs, as mentioned above, makes it appear that all good, accented notes, should also be lengthened. Mozart nowhere suggests such a principle.

Table 3
Comparison of *Inégales* and "Good" and "Bad" Notes

	INÉGALES	"GOOD AND BAD"
Name	Inégales, Lourées Pointées, Piquées	Notes de repos et de passage; Temps bons et mauvais; notes nobles et viles, principales et chétives; Note buone e cattive; gute und schlimme Noten; quantitate intrinseca or virtualiter, or innerlich, long and short; anschlagende and durchgehende; akzentuierte und unakzentuierte Noten.
Place	France	All of Europe
Period	c. 1650-1780	4th century to present
Nature	Stylized ornamentation	Musical diction suggested by meter and bar line.
Pattern	Long-short from barely noticeable to considerable (near-equivalent of a dot)	Primarily loud-soft
Application	To melody in stepwise progression; to pairs of notes, (not to groups of threes); to fourfold, sometimes twofold subdivisions of the beat; to "fastest notes" (Quantz), never to main beat.	Independent of melodic pattern; applies primarily to whole measures, then to half measures, and to main beats; to subdivisions of the beat in a secondary way and in ever diminishing strengths.

This agogic-dynamic emphasis on the first note under a slur, which could be called *agogic articulation,* is one of the many freedoms inherent in a flexible performance which can by no means be limited to any particular style-period and, like the stress on the good notes, is practiced occasionally to the present day. It is an altogether different matter from the good and bad notes. It has no reference to meter and position in the measure, and, what is more, it can apply to bad notes as well as to good ones, as Leopold Mozart expressly tells us when he points to examples like the following[70]

Ex. 8.

in which the "bad" note carries a dynamic and agogic accent because it is the first under a slur. This agogic articulation has no connection with the French *Inégales* either, since the latter were independent of slurs, worked only in pairs, and not in groups of three, four, or more notes, and had, moreover, a strict connection between note-values and meter, which is conspicuously absent in Mozart's ruling about the effect of a slur. Therefore Mozart's lengthening of the first note under a slur is an independent principle, and as such neither confirms the idea that "inner" length of notes *(quantitas intrinseca,* etc.) implies an actual lengthening, nor establishes the so-far missing link between good and bad notes on the one hand, and the *Inégales* on the other. Moreover, it cannot possibly serve to corroborate Quantz since he expressly states that inequality does *not* apply where more than two notes are slurred together.

The misunderstanding about the alleged corroboration of Quantz's Remark arose from the failure to distinguish clearly among three different issues: the *Inégales* of the remark, the good and bad notes of Walther, and the agogic articulation of Mozart. The confusion was abetted by Babitz's introduction of the dangerously vague term, "expressive rhythm," under which were lumped together all of the three principles—as well as any other kind of agogic nuance—as if they were one and the same thing.

3. *Keyboard Fingerings.* Along with the good and bad notes, and agogic articulation, another set of alleged proofs is derived from keyboard fingerings, which will now be examined.

Though the suggestion that fingerings might provide an occasional clue to interpretation has been made by several authors, among them Dannreuther, Dolmetsch, and Mellers, none went as far as Babitz, who pressed the argument to the point of extracting from baroque fingerings claims for both short-long and long-short unevenness in the performance of evenly written notes. These allegedly uneven rhythmic interpretations are intended to further confirm the currency of the Quantz quotation, or as Babitz put it, to provide "cumulative evidence." Actually Babitz aimed at far more than that; Quantz speaks only of the long-short *Inégales* of the French convention, whereas Babitz also tries to derive from fingerings evidence for a short-long performance of evenly written notes, though such a convention is mentioned neither by Quantz nor apparently by any other author of the 18th century. Babitz derived his theory from an old fingering pattern. From the 16th through the 17th and to the beginning of the 18th century, the most commonly used fingerings for the ascending scale of the right hand and the descending scale of the left hand were based on an alternation of 343434, the descending r.h. scale and ascending l.h. scale on 121212, (which had superseded a previous 232323). Babitz's main argument is that the finger-over-finger pattern of these old scale-fingerings results in an "involuntary unevenness." Therefore he argues that the use of this fingering is a clue to an intended unevenness in performance. Specifically he declares that in the 3434 sequence, 3 is always short, 4 long; just as, in the 1212 sequence 1 is short, 2 long. He explains this by the "natural tendency for a momentary delay while the stronger finger is raised over its neighbor with a compensatory acceleration, while the lower finger springs back to its normal position." One finger is too slow, and to make up for it the other finger is too fast.[71] He proceeds to call the 3434 fingering a "long-short" one if 4 is on the heavy, 3 on the light part of the beat; and vice versa, a "short-long" fingering if 3 is on the heavy beat. The long-short fingering then clearly implies to him the long-short performance, and vice versa. He uses these terms with such assurance that the reader is made to believe they represent facts that are either self-evident, generally accepted, or solidly supported by documentation. In fact they stand for a theory derived by faulty reasoning from a questionable premise.

If one asks what the meaning of "involuntary unevenness" is, would not the answer have to be: a beginner's awkwardness and lack of coordination? In other words, Babitz takes a beginner's stumbling, calls it "expressive rhythm," and proclaims it as a model for authentic interpretation. The weakness of this argument is obvious, since unevenness which is "involuntary" is by definition due not to artistic intent but to technical defect. Musically it ranks with the uneven beat of an ailing metronome. Babitz failed to realize that *every* fingering is uneven because the hand is unsymmetrical and the fingers differ in length, strength, and their degree of mobility and independence. In the modern scale fingering, for example, the action of the thumb leads instinctively to a jerk and an accent. If instinctive tendencies were a legitimate indication of a composer's wishes there would be no end to remarkable conclusions.[72] Indeed, acquisition of technical skill at all times aims at the ability to play evenly as well as accurately in any rhythmical pattern, and to overcome as much as possible the natural inequality of the fingers so that it will not interfere with phrasing, articulation, or rhythm.

There is a very interesting and pertinent passage in Quantz in which he calls as witness J.S. Bach (as identified in the index). In this passage Quantz emphasizes the importance of evenness of touch and the right kind of touch on the harpsichord, contrary to the common belief that differences of touch cannot affect the harpsichord tone. He then says "much depends on whether one hits harder with one finger than another . . . which not only causes uneven loudness *(ungleiche Stärke im Spielen)* but also prevents round, distinct, and agreeable execution of fast passages. Certain players who have to execute a scalewise run of several tones sound *as if they stumbled over the notes.*"[73] "Round" execution clearly refers to evenness and Quantz's derisive characterization of an incompetent player's stumbling would seem to describe the "involuntary unevenness" of Babitz's fingering-dictated "expressive rhythm."

Marpurg writes in a similar way when he explains how uncomfortable fingerings can endanger the round and clear performance of passages and how an effort to counteract the resulting unevenness *("das Holperichte")* will lead to forced and cramped attitudes.[74] More explicit is Rameau who, writing from the very center of the *Inégales* convention, extols the need for a complete independence of the fingers from one another, and from the hand, to achieve strength, ease, and evenness. *"De la force, de la légèreté et de l'égalité entre eux."*[75] In another treatise he urges a great regularity of the finger movements "since ease and velocity can be attained only through regularity."[76]

Quantz in his Remark actually shatters the theory of "involuntary unevenness" by telling us that two-by-two inequality disappears when the tempo is so fast that it becomes impractical. This means that inequality can neither be due to, nor associated with "involuntary unevenness," or else such stumbling will not be remedied but made worse by a faster tempo.

Babitz's theory hinges on the premise that alternation of the third and fourth fingers involves a natural tendency to lengthen the note struck by the fourth and to shorten that struck by the third. However, in a number of experiments, no such tendency could be clearly identified. On the contrary, a natural tendency to irregularity makes itself felt far more in the opposite direction, towards lengthening the third and shortening the fourth, because it is easier to flip the stronger third finger quickly over the fourth than to slide the fourth quickly from under the third toward its new key. Dolmetsch sees an "instinctive" unevenness in this fingering in this latter sense that is the opposite of Babitz's claim: the third lengthened and accented, the fourth shortened.[77] In other words, the 3434 fingering cannot, even for beginners, be considered to imply a short-long stumbling, which was the premise of the whole theory.

Babitz quotes Diruta and Santa Maria to support his thesis.[78] Diruta, writing at the end of the 16th century, established scale fingerings with good fingers on good notes and bad fingers on bad notes. He calls the second and fourth fingers good and the third and fifth bad. Though Babitz finds it "paradoxical" that Diruta names the weaker fourth finger good and the stronger third bad, Babitz speculates that Diruta intended to emphasize the good notes by lengthening them. When faced with the opposite fingerings of other authors—for instance the English virginalists, all of whom prefer the third finger on the good notes (a more natural fingering as Dolmetsch points out)—Babitz simply infers that the English emphasized the good notes by *shortening* them! Since neither Diruta nor Purcell, nor apparently anybody else mentions inequality in connection with fingerings, these inferences of Babitz are arbitrary applications of the idea that the fourth finger must be long, the third finger short. With this in mind it would be hard to explain these facts: 1) that Italians such as Penna[79] followed the English practice rather than Diruta's; 2) that French authors like Saint Lambert and Couperin, in spite of their involvement in the *Inégales* convention, present scale-fingerings with simple emphasis on the sequence of the fingers, without metrical context and hence without reference to the *Inégales*.[80] The clear inference is that these authors were in no way concerned with questions of phrasing, inequality, or other matters of interpretation, but simply with the most efficient method known to them of mastering the technical skill of a scale pattern. Saint Lambert, after presenting the usual 343434 sequence for the ascending right hand scales says, in the same vein as Santa Maria had done 150 years earlier, that apart from scales there are no rules for fingerings and that they have to be chosen to fit individual needs.[81]

That Couperin's fingerings show no bias for either the third or fourth finger on the good notes, and that he simply uses either of them according to the greater convenience of a given situation, is evident from the following examples in which scale patterns are presented in metrical context.[82]

Ex. 9.

In other examples the identical scale pattern has the third finger on the good notes in one key and on the bad notes in another key. The difference is obviously due only to the greater comfort in fitting in the black keys, and just as obviously not to an expressed intention to phrase differently in different keys. Rameau's principle, that all fingers should be trained to independence and equality, is well exemplified in his fingered model of a minuet where the same phrase is fingered differently in m. 1 and in m. 2. Again comfort and ease are the obvious criteria.[83]

Ex. 10.

Santa Maria, Babitz's other witness, does mention inequality but does not connect it at all with fingering, or fingering with inequality. Santa Maria in 1565 presents a great variety of scale fingerings.[84] Besides the 343434 and 121212 patterns he knows modern fingerings of 123123 and 12341234, as well as varieties of combinations of all these different patterns that are far ahead of his time. The decisive criteria for the choice of one or the other or the various mixtures and combinations are speed (whether quarters, 8ths, or 16ths), the number of notes in a scale-like passage, and the kind of chromatic (black) keys to be accommodated. There is never any mention of inequality. The 123123 fingering can certainly never be interpreted as either short-long or long-short, and when Babitz tried to link the 1234 fingering with rhythmical inequality he became the victim of a misinterpretation.

Santa Maria speaks of three ways of playing eighth notes "gracefully":[85] 1) long-short; 2) short-long; and 3) the first three played fast and the fourth long. However, the patterns of 3) somehow got reversed in Babitz's presentation to make the first long and the second to fourth short. Then he proceeds to find fingerings among those given by Santa Maria which are supposed to correspond to these three patterns. That he presents one that "fits" his misquoted rhythmical alteration indicates the reliability of his claims to rhythm-fingering relationships.[86]

There is no doubt that fingering can sometimes give helpful clues to interpretation, but in trying to discover such hints and read their meanings correctly, one has to avoid two distinct pitfalls. In the first place, it is one thing to state that a certain note- and rhythmic pattern, for example, a scale in long-short dotted rhythm, will be most easily performed with one particular type of fingering. It is an altogether different thing to reverse the statement and claim that therefore this fingering invariably suggests a dotted pattern only; as if one were to say that since all birds are living creatures, all living creatures are birds. Yet this is how Babitz argues his case. There is one difference: Babitz's premise, that 3434 leads to involuntary inequality with the third short and the fourth long, is not a self-evident fact, but a highly unlikely guess.

As a matter of fact, the 3434 fingering was used at the time not because it had a built-in inequality that was congenial to alleged conventions of the period, but simply because it was the best fingering for scales, regardless of their rhythm, that was known at the time.[87] It was used for scales in all kinds of rhythm patterns such as or where Babitz' long-short and short-long principle would lead *ad absurdum*. Moreover, it could be asked, if 3434 is short-long and 4343 long-short, which would have been the *even* fingering?

The second pitfall to be avoided in trying to read interpretive significance into fingerings has to do with the fact that there are two different types of fingerings that have to be kept apart in any discussion. French violinists have referred to them as *doigté du mécanisme* and *doigté de l'expression* (mechanical and expressive fingering). The first is concerned with the easiest manner in which a sequence of notes can be played with accuracy and in the required speed. The other is a fingering which will give certain more desirable musical results though it will make the execution more difficult. This is a difference which is in general far more obvious on the violin than on the keyboard,[88] but doubtless has a certain place at the keyboard too.

Of these two types of fingerings, the mechanical one can give us no interpretive information of any consequence. It can tell us something about the state of keyboard technique or something about how a beginner may have sounded in playing a passage, but not how the composer intended a passage to sound. It is futile, therefore, to search for artistic revelations in mechanical fingerings. That the fingerings for scales, arpeggios, etc. which we find in the old treatises are mechanical ones *par excellence,* is obvious, since they are presented in a musical vacuum. A fingering must be in a musical setting and be identified as an "expressive" one before it can be presumed to yield any interpretive information. We have only relatively few pieces from the Baroque era that are provided with authentic fingerings, and most of the latter are clearly mechanical ones. It is interesting that Couperin does not have a single fingering in his Clavecin Pieces, where they would belong if they were expressive ones, whereas his Treatise deals with the fingering problems of the first two books of pieces strictly in terms of their technical difficulties. He speaks of "passages in my first book of Clavecin Pieces which are hard to finger" and refers to "thorny" passages for which he gives solutions. Of the 8 didactic preludes which he included in his treatise, the first few are lavishly fingered, the last hardly at all. The purely technical-pedagogical purpose is unmistakable. The fingerings are simply designed to make the passages negotiable for students.

Exactly the same is the case with the two pieces of Bach's for which we have authenticated fingerings: the *Applicatio* and the *Präambulum* from the *Klavierbüchlein* for Wilhelm Friedemann Bach. Both were beginner's studies in which the near-complete fingerings had the obvious purpose of acquainting the child with the tools for handling simple technical problems. In view of the elementary pedagogical setting of the pieces, Babitz's attempt to read into them subtle injunctions for highly sophisticated rhythmical alterations that are of one type for the right hand, of the opposite type for the left hand, is far-fetched to a point that is hard to understand.

Example 11 is the opening of the *Applicatio* and Babitz's interpretation.[89] If apart from all the preceding arguments still more are needed to show convincingly that Babitz's interpretation of Bach's fingerings is misguided, the following can be added: 1) The lack of musical logic in having one mode of rhythmic alteration for the statement of the simple theme and the opposite one for the answer in the left hand; 2) the lack of musical logic in having the first, fifth, and ninth eighth-notes, which are weighted down by mordents, *shortened,* when if anything a lengthening would make more sense; 3) with

Quantz as Babitz's main authority for his theories of inequality, he overlooked that according to Quantz's own rules—in agreement with all French writers—inequality has no place in the *Applicatio,* since the latter is written in 4/4 where eighth notes are to be played *evenly.*

Ex. 11.

Babitz's interpretation:

The combination of all these arguments should suffice to show that Babitz's theories of unequal fingerings are untenable and must be dismissed as the "cumulative evidence" they were supposed to provide.

4. *A Measure in the Magnificat.* A further argument is presented by Alfred Dürr, the eminent Bach scholar, in his text criticism of Bach's Magnificat. This work exists in a first version in E flat and in a final version in D major. Dürr admits that the first version "shows all the earmarks of a first draft. Corrections abound everywhere and often considerably impair the legibility. In various spots there are to be found lines and spirals *(Schnörkel)* which defy interpretation."[90] On another occasion, Dürr speaks of the "sketchiness" *(Skizzenhaftigkeit)* of the first score. In contrast to this he characterizes the D major version as a "fair copy *(Reinschrift)* of exceptional clarity."

In this "sketchy" E-flat version there is one almost undecipherable measure in which Dürr sees a connection with the Quantz remark and therefore quotes the latter in full.[91] The measure in question is the first of the soprano aria, *"Quia respexit."* The following three examples show: *a)* its manuscript appearance, *b)* Dürr's transcription of the text in the new Bach edition, and *c)* the same measure in the D major version.

Ex. 12.

(a) Bach's writing:

(b) Dürr's transcription

(c) D Major version

A dotted rhythmic pattern is apparent in this first oboe entrance. As can be seen, the continuo part in the same measure has even 16th notes and from then on all the 16ths are even in all three parts. Dürr seems to think that the dotting in the first measure was an indication of unequal performance and that he can relate these dots to the "baroque performance practice" of inequality as expressed in the Quantz remark and in Père Engramelle's *Tonotechnie*.[92] Dürr's attempt to establish such a link is not convincing. As can be seen, the measure is very unclear, and even the transcription which Dürr presents in the new edition is open to many doubts. Several layers are superimposed in this measure, mirroring Bach's search for the germinal rhythmic and melodic expression of the aria. Dürr speculates that the first entry was:

he thinks that the A flat was cancelled and the second version read:

and the third version as shown above under *(b)*. But to sustain this explanation he has to assume that Bach omitted the dot after the third note and the third beam for the 32nd of the 9th note.[93]

Many things are questionable about this interpretation. That there are traces of different melodic and rhythmic ideas is clear. Their sequence is not, and their number may have exceeded three. The following idea along with others may have also been in the picture (since an 8th note flag seems to be visible for the first note):

The dots may or may not have been last and even if they were the top layer they may not represent the final idea, since they did not survive the first bar line to the second measure which was the first legible one.

Dürr ignores in his reading the A-flat which he thinks was cancelled by the second layer. However, no clear cancellation can be discerned. (The blot at the third line is occasioned by the neutral accidental.) As matters stand, not only is there a dot and a 32nd missing, but with the A-flat uncancelled and the three last notes occupying a quarter note, there is one eighth note too many in the bar. Whatever explanation one wishes to adopt, and whatever the various geological layers may have been, one thing is clear: the writing is highly ambiguous and confusing. It is most unreasonable to assume that such a defective metrical and rhythmical pattern was to serve as a model, especially if the following circumstances are considered.

First, the case is unique. There seems to be no other instance known of Bach's writing just the beginning of a theme in long-short dotted rhythm, then breaking off the pattern and continuing the rest in equal notes. Second, if it were a labor-saving device, would he not have extended the "model" for at least one legible measure? Would he not have made sure that there were neither omissions nor extra note-values, nor notes left standing which were intended to be cancelled? Third, even supposing it were a labor-saving device, directed to the copyist with the meaning of a "segue," then it had, of course, no implication about the uses of *Inégales,* just as little implication as any written-out dotted note. Fourth, Dürr admits that such inequality, as a soloist's prerogative, would not apply to Bach's orchestra and therefore seems to suggest that it was meant for the oboist alone. He does not consider that such limitation leads to musical incongruities where the oboe and the bass alternate in imitating each other. He also leaves unanswered the question of what happens to the inequality when the melody ceases to move in stepwise progression and moves by skips, in which case inequality does not usually apply. Dürr is silent about the soprano part which certainly had the soloist's prerogative, but no indication of dotting at its beginning. Should we assume that in the constant interplay of the three voices only one voice should be equal and the other two not, or two dotted and the third not? The resulting confusion would be insoluble.

The assumption of inequality thus leads to a number of unanswerable questions. On the other hand, there is a simple explanation which eliminates these difficulties. It is the supposition that during the experimentation with the first measure the dots were one of the ideas which Bach briefly considered, then discarded. Dürr thinks it unlikely that Bach wished a dotted performance in the D-major version, which would imply that sometime between the writing of the dots and the writing of the D-major version Bach rejected the idea of dottings. The likelihood is greatest that he dropped the idea almost simultaneously with its conception since this most easily explains why the pattern is incomplete: he changed his mind before he added another dot and the 32nd.

That Bach left the measure in such a state of chaos can easily be explained by the draft character of the manuscript, by the fact that the measure after a series of changes was beyond repair, and by Bach's apparent intention of either copying the oboe part himself or of giving exact instructions to a copyist. It was not the only measure of the E-flat version for which Bach was needed either as copyist or instructor.

In sum, the measure can hardly be explained by Quantz's Remark nor furnish any amount of confirmation of the Remark's validity for Bach.

6. *A Measure in the B Minor Mass.* The first measure of the *Domine Deus* has also produced speculations and claims about inequality, this time of the short-long species. In the autograph flute part *only* there appears a Lombard rhythm in the second half of the first measure:

Ex. 13.

Several scholars, among them von Dadelsen, Dürr, and with reservations, Mendel, see in the flute measure an indication that the short-long rhythm was to be used throughout the piece.[94] It is possible, however, to present on the one hand a series of counter-arguments against this view and, on the other hand, a more plausible explanation of this measure.

For reasons of space only a few of the arguments will be listed but they may suffice.

1. No genuine documentation on short-long inequality has so far been brought to light for the time and place in question.

2. With no other case on record of Bach's using such fragmentary Lombard notation as an alleged hint for inequality, it is highly improbable that he would have reserved its only use for *a)* a calligraphic[95] presentation copy to the Elector of Saxony, *b)* a performing organization unfamiliar with his ideas and methods, and *c)* a situation over which he had no control and where he could not clarify a mystifying suggestion by personal explanation.

3. The alleged hint would have been highly ambiguous since the question of who is to use the Lombard rhythm, when, and how long, has no self-evident answer. Was it to be used for the recurrent theme alone, for all 16th notes slurred by twos (which was the usual concomitant of Lombard rhythm), or for other 16ths as well? Surely not for the extended coloraturas of the singers? Yet if the latter are sung evenly we obtain incongruous rhythmical clashes in several spots like the following:

Ex. 14.

4. Had the alleged hint been in the score, a slightly better case could have been made of it, but the writing out of parts always aimed at presenting solutions not puzzles. That it is in one part *only* compounds the improbability, since it would force us to assume the existence of a convention enjoining all performers to imitate a rhythmic pattern which they hear someone else announce. With everyone having his own ideas about the what and the how of imitation, such a would-be convention would create perpetual anarchy in ensemble.

There is a far simpler explanation of this measure. The *Domine Deus*, with its stepwise 16th notes in **C** meter, was a textbook case for the use of the French

Inégales and it so happened that the chief flutist in Dresden at the time was M. Buffardin, a Frenchman. Buffardin, or, for that matter his disciple Quantz (who was still in Dresden at the time of presentation in 1733) would have been inclined to play as in example 15:

Ex. 15.

Bach's short-long at the beginning were simply an antidote against the anticipated long-shorts. They were Bach's subtle way of saying : "do not play it à la française." This would easily explain why the episode is so brief; it was enough to get the idea across and not so long as to produce actual short-longs. It also explains why it appeared in that particular flute part and not in any other part or score, and why Bach never used it anywhere else.

If this explanation is correct it will add another telling point *against* the use of inequality in Bach.

Summary and Conclusions

The corroborations claimed for the remark have failed to materialize. As compared to the torrential eloquence of the French writers on behalf of *Inégales,* Quantz stands alone with his remark in the middle of a seemingly absolute silence on the part of all contemporary German writers. No cancellation by "tell-tale" signs revealing the presence of the *Inégales* have been detected in any German music. The measures in the Magnificat and the B-minor Mass failed to establish a link. The good and bad notes were of no help; neither was the agogic articulation of Leopold Mozart. The claim of the French, that inequality was a purely national affair, remains unchallenged. The circumstantial evidence is overwhelming that inequality was not a live convention in the Germany of Bach's time. Only one question remains. If inequality was not current in Germany, why did Quantz write about it? There is a very simple and, it seems, very plausible answer.

Quantz was one of the most ardent advocates of a mixed syle in composition as well as in performance. The mixed style he advocated was one that would combine the best features of the Italian, the French, and the German practices. The idea of picking the best from various models and combining them in a higher form was not new,[96] but is had a singularly strong appeal for Quantz, who returns to it over and over again in both his treatise and his autobiography. Naturally we can expect him to select those style-elements from the various nations which pleased him the most. He had few good things to say about French composition, and nothing favorable about their style of singing. But throughout both treatise and autobiography he has nothing but high praise for French instrumental performance. Does it not stand to reason that as an ingredient of a recipe for a well-mixed style of performance he would choose an important feature of their admired performance practice?

In other words, Quantz's passage had the same meaning as Muffat's had had 60 years earlier: the suggestion of using a manner of performance which both authors considered attractive. The only difference is that Quantz failed to refer to it as a manner *"à la française."* This simple omission then became responsible for all the speculation generated by the passage and for the grossly exaggerated importance that has been ascribed to it.

This interpretation also easily explains why the passage seems to stand alone in the German literature, and why it is not where it would normally belong, in chapter V of the Quantz treatise; furthermore, it makes it quite understandable that the passage itself contained inconsistencies, since Quantz reported a convention with which he was not thoroughly conversant.

With this last question removed, the thesis of this article would seem to be vindicated: that inequality cannot be considered a general baroque practice, nor one that was current among German musicians outside islands of complete French musical domination; and that, with the possible exception of a very few marginal instances, there seems to be no reason why it should be applied to the music of J.S. Bach.

4

An Answer to Donington's Critique

[Robert Donington reacted to the preceding article (chapter 3) in a "Communication to the Editor," *JAMS* XIX (1966), pp. 112-14. His main points were answered in the following reply of mine in *JAMS* XIX (1966), pp. 435-37. "Three Further Views on *Notes inégales*" by Sol Babitz, John Byrt, and Michael Collins were published in *JAMS* XX (1967), pp. 473-85. The then-editor did not grant me space for an answer to those statements.]

In a communication in the Spring 1966 issue of this *Journal,* Prof. Robert Donington makes an eloquent plea against confinement of the *notes inégales* to France and its musical embassies abroad. In a most gentlemanly way, for which I am deeply grateful, he sees overstatement and some rigidity in my recent attempt to bar the French *inégales* from German, and in particular from Bach's, music ("The French *Inégales,* Quantz, and Bach," *JAMS* XVIII [1965], pp. 313-58). I find Prof. Donington's statement stimulating but not convincing.

Some of Donington's items of evidence had previously appeared in his *The Interpretation of Early Music;* I have taken issue with them elsewhere, and will try to avoid repetition here.

The baroque performer enjoyed vast latitude in interpretation of the score; one of the many ways in which he used this freedom was an elastic treatment of rhythmic notation. Guided by the "Affect" of a passage, he applied agogic accents, used rubato techniques of all kinds, varied the tempo, sharpened a rhythm here, softened it there. No rules governed this performance style; its only law was musical instinct and arbitrary judgment.

Prof. Donington says that some passages in Bach "cry out for inequality"—meaning *notes inégales;* had he said they cry out for rhythmic freedom, I would have completely agreed. I believe that Donington and others fail to realize the categorical difference between 1) rhythmic flexibility for the sake of a definite "Affect," and 2) the discipline of a convention that *prescribes,* independent of "Affect," a certain rhythmic alteration in certain definite

Reprinted with permission from the *Journal of the American Musicological Society,* XIX (1966), pp. 435-37.

contexts of melodic design and meter—note-value relationships. The first of these two types of "unevenness" certainly applied to Bach as to everybody else; within more modest limits it is still fully alive today. The second type, the peculiar phenomenon of a regulated irregularity, was for all practical purposes limited to France. Its origin was probably a fashion of performing improvised diminutions in quasi-dotted patterns; the fashion took hold to become a hallmark of the *"goût français"* for some 150 years.

The difference in principle between these two types is obvious enough. However, on a few rare occasions the dividing line is obscured by a chance similarity which can deceive the casual observer. An excellent example is the one sentence in C.P.E Bach's *Essay* (vol. II, chap. 29, par. 15) which Prof. Donington cites as proof that "Quantz did not stand alone," in other words as proof for *notes inégales* in Germany. Bach shows here how an agogic accent on the first of two 16th notes embedded in an 8th-note accompaniment can add life to an otherwise dull ("klinget sehr matt") phrase. Surely this is a prime example of rhythmic license for the sake of "Affect." If Bach had said that these notes ought to be played long-short because they are stepwise 16th notes in a 4/4 meter, Donington would have scored a telling point. But Bach did not even as much as list a meter signature in his example and this omission alone is proof that what might look like a reasonable facsimile of *notes inégales* had actually nothing to do with it. Moreover, one could ask how German students were to learn about the conventions for *inégales* when none of their textbooks offered them information.

Prof. Donington's quotation from Corrette is not convincing either. The passage is taken from the first in a series of more than a dozen treatises which this author wrote for a variety of media. The book in question is a flute tutor, published anonymously in 1735 and reprinted under his name some 30 years later. In this book as in most of his later ones, Corrette follows a procedure, in discussing meters, common in French treatises of that period: he takes one meter at a time, tells us how it is beaten, where it occurs, and how it affects inequality. The latter information was indispensable since every French student had to master the *inégales* rules as part of his elementary training. Arriving at 12/8, which at the time was rather new in French music, Corrette lists as an example of its occurrence in "Gigues à quatre tems" in Italian, German, French and English music, then pigeon-holes it for the *inégales* convention: the 8th notes are equal, the 16th notes unequal. He did not mean to say that the Italians, Germans and English played their Gigues with *notes inégales*. In his 'cello tutor of 1741 (partially quoted in my article) Corrette says on p. 4: "Dans chaque mesure les croches se jouent également dans la musique italienne," whereupon he lists an example from Corelli; "et dans la musique française on passe la deuxième croche de chaque tems plus vite." Immediately after this unequivocal statement he goes on to speak of the various meters, telling where they occur in French and Italian music, then listing their effect on inequality. Having just told us that the *inégales* do not apply to Italian music, he surely intended no causal link between the listing of a meter's international habitat and the listing of that meter's effect on inequality.

This is confirmed in another of his books, the tutor for the *"Par-dessus de Viole à 5 et 6 cordes..."* (Paris, n.d.), where on page 13 he has this to say: "Aux moùvemens de 2 et de 3 tems *dans la musique française,* comme Opéra ou Motets, il faut pointer les croches de deux en deux; c'est à dire la première longue en poussant et la deuxième brève en tirant: Mais *dans la musique italienne* les croches se jouent également" (my italics). For an almost literal confirmation of this statement by J.J. Rousseau see note 37 of my article. Couperin, on page 39 of his famous treatise, likens the *inégales* to the unphonetic spelling of the French language whereas "les Italiens écrivent leur musique dans les vrayes valeurs qu'ils l'ont pensée." Hotteterre in his little known *L'Art de Préluder sur la Flute traversière...* (Paris, 1719), in which he discusses meters in great detail, tells us on page 58 that in the 3 or 3/4 meter the 8th notes "sont presque toujours pointées *dans la musique française"* (my italics). Then he offers very interesting illustrations: a few French examples of inequality, then one French example (from Lully's *Armide*) where for two reasons the 8th notes are even: because they move by leaps, and because they are interspersed with 16th notes; and finally, an example from Corelli where the evenness of the 8th notes is understood.

In view of the many arguments in my articles and the new documents just presented, I believe that more convincing evidence is needed to suggest adoption of the *inégales* outside of France other than by isolated individuals like Quantz.

I am, of course, fully aware that in matters of style there are no Chinese walls around either nations or individuals. I am aware that French manners, French language, literature and sometimes even French music, held sway among the aristocracy of many a cultural center in Bach's Germany; that in various fields of endeavor many a gentleman put on French airs, affected French manners and mannerisms. Could Bach have been among the imitators? I greatly doubt it. Unquestionably he had learned a great deal from the French masters from whom he adopted the use of the Overture-Suites and many of their ornaments. But what he did and how he did it can be compared to the way in which the English language has absorbed and amalgamated more than half the French vocabulary without therefore surrendering its native genius to either French grammar, syntax or style. Had Bach written just *one* unmeasured prelude à la Chambonnières, Louis Couperin, Le Bègue, d'Anglebert, etc.; had he, à la Couperin, given just *one* suite movement a name like "Le Tic-Toc-Choc" or a sexy one like "Fureurs Bachiques" (referring to Bacchus, not to Bach), instead of a generic title like "Badinerie"; had he used *one* expression mark like *"voluptueusement sans langueur";* or had he just *once* written those revealing words *"Notes égales"* that cancel inequality, a case could have been made that Bach may on occasion have submitted to French codes of musical conduct. But in the absence of any such indication, or of any other evidence that can withstand critical scrutiny, I continue to view such a theory with utmost skepticism.

5

External Evidence and Uneven Notes

Recent publications about historical performance practice show a growing reliance on the kind of evidence that can be extracted from the old music itself. Such evidence is usually referred to as being either "internal" or "external" in nature with the borderline between the two types not always clearly drawn. The "internal" designation applies best to such clues as can be derived from the musical logic of a situation, whereby the context will either suggest, demand, or else exclude certain solutions of an interpretative problem. Evidence is "external" if it is deduced from the notation in a number of different ways.

The trend to a wider use of these sources is to be welcomed, since it holds the prospect of opening up a vast reservoir of untapped and potentially important information. However, before the hunt for such highly priced evidence could turn into the semblance of a gold rush, it might be well to recall the familiar words that all that glitters is not gold. All that looks like evidence is not real evidence, and careful analysis is needed to separate the genuine from the imitation.

Such analysis may have been missing in a few recent publications that made new claims for the use of *notes inégales* outside of France, and more specifically in Bach's music. Since an article of mine attempted to show that the *notes inégales* ought not to be applied to Bach,[1] a clarification might be in order.

A closer look into these new theories seemed to reveal that incautious use of external evidence played a leading role in their formulation and that an additional source of error sprang from a confusion of terms. Certain types of rhythmical freedom were inappropriately labelled *notes inégales* and as a consequence, this misnomer created the illusion that the French convention had a much wider currency than was actually the case. In an effort to cope with this twofold source of error I shall discuss at first what various types of external evidence can reveal to us and what they cannot; then I shall illustrate the wrong

Reprinted with permission from *The Musical Quarterly* 52 (1966), pp. 448-64.

use of such evidence with a case history that also involves confusion of terms; finally I shall attempt a classification of various types of unevenness in the hope that this might help prevent further misunderstandings.

I

External evidence can range from being direct and unquestionable to being so speculative that it practically ceases to be evidence at all. The problem is that of proper evaluation and the following discussion is meant to sound a note of caution in this respect.

1. *The testimony of the barline.* A good example of the rather rare species of direct evidence can be found in Grigny's *Premier Livre d'Orgue* (Paris, 1699), where the slide is repeatedly printed in this manner: so that the inference of an upbeat rendition is unmistakable. Both Bach and Walther copied this book, and faithfully reproduced these and other similar pre-bar notations of ornaments in their respective manuscripts; we can, therefore, be sure that they understood the upbeat implication.[2]

2. *Vertical alignment* in a manuscript can provide important information but only on the obvious condition that the writer exercised great care in this respect. Bach, for instance, did possess a remarkable sense of spatial organization and in his fair copies he carefully aligned the notes according to rhythmic relationships, though occasional lack of space led to unaligned compressions and even to overflow across barlines. What matters in a specific case is that the intentional be distinguished from the purely accidental. If we find, for example, that in the third movement of the fifth Brandenburg concerto both the calligraphic presentation score (BB. Am. B. 78) and the equally calligraphic autograph cembalo part (BB Mus. Ms. Bach St. 130) shows the triplets a few times aligned with the dotted notes in the following manner:

Ex. 1.

the intention seems unmistakable; therefore the alignment would seem to convey that in this particular instance the dotted-note pair was meant to be synchronized with the triplet. Not often is the evidence so clear; how wrong conclusions can be drawn from alignment will be shown below in part II.

3. The comparison of *simultaneous parts that move in unison* or close parallelism can also yield fairly clear-cut results in some cases, ambiguous ones in others. If for instance, as shown in example 2a, Bach writes the symbol for a

slide for one part and spells out the ornament in regular notes in a unison part, we can assume this to be a clue how the slide was to be performed in this particular instance (but by no means always).

Ex. 2.

If one voice is articulated and a unison voice is not, we may sometimes justly assume that the unmarked voice should be assimilated, especially if it belongs to the same family of instruments. If, however, both parts are articulated differently then we shall not often have a right to conclude that the discrepancy is due to oversight and that we ought to make one voice conform to the other. In Bach, such differences between the diction-implied articulation of a voice part and the specified articulation of instruments are fairly frequent and in many cases, as in example 2b, obviously intentional.

Nor should the interesting cases of different rhythm patterns in parts that are melodically in unison be prejudged as being in need of assimilation. A good illustration can be found in the *Trauer-Ode,* 1 (*Neue Bach-Ausgabe* I, 38, pp. 181-203), where Bach wrote out for the orchestra an estimated 2,500 dotted notes with unflagging consistency from beginning to end. The four voice parts, however, which move mostly but not always in melodic unison with the orchestra (see ex. 3), are written in equal notes throughout with the exception of the two (parallel) full cadences of mm. 35-36 and 67-68, and the two (parallel) half cadences of mm. 28 and 60. The exceptions make perfect sense: in these spots the vocal dotting helps to bring out the natural cadential intensification and its execution may possibly have been rendered technically more manageable by a slowing of the tempo. On the other hand a dotting throughout, in analogy to the instruments, could be vocally awkward to the point of impracticability. It is immaterial whether the rhythmical clash between voices and instruments was a free artistic choice or a grudging concession to vocal limitations. What matters is that the clash was apparently intended and inferences as to assimilation and *notes inégales* for the voice parts therefore extremely questionable. For simultaneous dotted and undotted rhythm— though not in unison—see also Cantatas 91, 5 and 207, 7.

Ex. 3.

Lass noch ei - nen_ Strahl_____ aus_ Sa - lems_ Stern - ge-wöl - ben schie-ssen

4. *The comparison of parallel spots* is still more problematical. Bach, Mozart, and many other composers often articulate a musical phrase differently when it returns a second or third time. There may be various reasons for such inconsistency, all of which we have to consider before we draw any conclusions from a comparison: 1) it may be carelessness, which the composer would have corrected had he been aware of it; 2) it may be intention to diversify; 3) it may indicate indifference to the niceties of uniformity and such indifference would in itself be an important esthetic attitude which ought to be respected.[3] Similar situations prevail with ornaments when in three parallel places they are indicated by symbol the first time, written out the second, and left out altogether the third. In such cases it is rarely possible to take identity of meaning for granted and exclude both the possibilities of intentional change and indifference to identical execution.

A change of rhythm in parallel spots may also be very difficult to evaluate. Robert Donington cites as a demonstration of *inégales* Handel's Sonata, Op. 1, No. 1, where the opening slow movement has equal notes at the beginning and dotted notes in measure 12:

Ex. 4.

"There can be no other reason than inadvertence," he says and therefore the whole movement ought to be played consistently in dotted rhythm.[4] I do not see why this conclusion should be inevitable or even likely. The simplest explanation points to intended variety. In view of the excessive freedom that Baroque performers (outside of France) arrogated to themselves in creating variety by diminutions that became more lavish with every repeat of a phrase or section, we are on shaky ground if we deny the Baroque composer the far lesser right to introduce on his own the simple ornament of a rhythmic variant. Obliteration of such diversity by arbitrary rhythmic unification is neither logically nor stylistically nor artistically convincing.[5]

5. *In comparing various versions of the same work* by the composer himself, the key to any external evidence lies in the answer to the question whether or not the two versions aim at the same musical result: whether the differences are only due to greater precision of notation or whether they embody a musical revision. The decision may at times be difficult. Bach, like many another master, increased the accuracy of his notation over the years and there are cases where a later version can illuminate the rendition of an earlier one. An example is Cantata 91, 5 where the rhythm ♪ 𝅘𝅥𝅮𝅘𝅥𝅮 𝅘𝅥𝅮 of the earlier version becomes ♪ 𝅘𝅥𝅮𝅘𝅥𝅮 𝅘𝅥𝅮 in the later one.

Especially interesting is the case of the early C minor version of Bach's French Overture, example 5a, as compared to the final engraved version in B minor, ex. 5b, which shows the kind of rhythmic sharpening that is claimed by the advocates of the so-called "French Overture style." I believe I have good reasons to assume that the sharpening of the rhythm was a second thought and not merely a more precise notation, and that the first version was by and large meant to be played as written. However, since these arguments would take up more space than is available, I shall for the time being simply submit that the possibility of a musical and not just notational revision cannot be dismissed. (The change of key certainly is a second thought.) [See pp. 181-82.]

Ex. 5.

6. If a *transcription by the composer* for another medium differs musically from the original, the need for idiomatic adaptation enhances the likelihood that the differences embody a musical revision, not just a notational improvement. In transcribing for the harpsichord the E major Violin Concerto, Bach changed in the slow movement the passages (a) into (b).

Ex. 6.

The change in m. 23 is cited by Robert Donington as a proof of short-long *inégales* in Bach.[6] However, a very plausible reason for this change can be the wish to compensate with a rhythmic inflection on the harpsichord for the unavailable tonal-dynamic nuance of the violin.[7] Moreover, the *pincé continu* of mm. 7-8 is an obvious adaptation and so are the changes in m. 35. Therefore, the conclusion that the harpsichord rhythm presents a clue to the desired violin rhythm seems quite unconvincing, and with it the claim that this case offers proof for Bach's use of *inégales* in general, their short-long variety in particular.

7. When we *compare copies, prints, or transcriptions* unsupervised by the composer, we are faced with such unending possibilities of misunderstandings, slips of the pen, misprints, arbitrary changes, etc., that external evidence can become very elusive indeed, and any inference from it extremely hazardous.

These dangers, among others, will be illustrated in the following case history, where injudicious use of external evidence, aggravated by misinterpretation of a treatise, resulted in some of the most unusual claims of rhythmic alteration yet proposed for Bach's music.

II

In a recent article[8] Ray McIntyre sets out to prove that Bach's two binary Gigues (from the first French Suite and from the sixth Partita), along apparently with all other binary Gigues, ought to be performed in a ternary rhythm by changing ♩♪ and ♫ into ♩♪, and ♫♫♫ into ♩.♫♫ or even ♫♫♫ . The agency of this transformation is supposed to be the convention of the *notes inégales*.

Like others before him, McIntyre bases his theories on the *notes inégales* on a passage in Quantz's treatise;[9] but unlike the others who have overrated the importance of the passage in question, it would appear that McIntyre misquotes it on the two crucial points that are the mainstay of his transformation theory. To call attention to these misunderstandings might perhaps be all that is necessary to disprove his theory. However, his use of external evidence calls for critical comment and so does his furtherance of a widespread confusion involving different kinds of unevenness.

In a section entitled "The Two-Note Slur,"[10] McIntyre says that "Quantz gives the two-note slur as sign for *notes inégales;* i.e. the first note in such a group should commonly be dotted in performance, thus ♪♪ = ♪.♪ with variable meaning depending upon the affect of the piece." I can find nothing in the Quantz passage that supports this statement. Neither Quantz nor any of the numerous French authors listed in my above-mentioned article[11] link the *notes inégales* with a two-note slur, or make the slur an indication or even a prerequisite of inegality. It is true that two of Quantz's three examples happen to show two-note slurs, but one does not.[12] This only shows that for Quantz two-notes slurs are compatible with, and do not prevent, inegality, but it does not at all show that the slur indicates or causes it (whereas he states that inegality does *not* apply when more than two notes are slurred).

Setting out from this misunderstanding, McIntyre presents a measure from a Gigue by Bonporti in two versions. The first, example 7a, published in Bologna (1712), shows a ternary rhythm pattern. The second, example 7b, a print by Roger in Amsterdam (1725), presents a binary one.

Ex. 7.

McIntyre concludes that "No other explanation is possible for this substitution except that the two-note slur is an orthographic variant of the trochaic rhythm pattern commonly found in gigues."[13]

Another explanation is not only possible but somewhat more plausible, namely that Roger's editor preferred the duple meter for this passage. Several reasons support this alternative explanation. 1) The idea about the transforming power of the slur is not supported by genuine evidence.[14] 2) The idea that binary rhythm is inapplicable to gigues is unfounded. 3) *Notes inégales* applied neither to Italian music, nor to eighth notes in C meter, nor to a characteristically disjointed melody. 4) It is wrong to assume that copyists or transcribers, or editors of new and mostly pirated editions[15] (Roger was a pirate king), were at all concerned with preserving the exact ideas of the composer even if they happened to know them. Respect for the composer's wishes and a reverential attitude towards tradition and authenticity of performance are modern concepts that were foreign to Bach's time.[16] Hence it is not permissible to assume that deviations in various versions of a piece aim at the same musical result and have to be "orthographic variants." The most probable explanation of a variant in this period is that it is an attempt to improve on the original. This probability would have to be convincingly discarded before any other conclusions are drawn from comparison of different versions. 5) If Roger's editor should have had an anachronistic urge for authenticity, it would be hard indeed to explain why he would have changed a perfectly clear and unambiguous notation of 2:1 rhythm into a different notation that would completely disguise such a relationship. And even if for argument's sake we were to assume that the *notes inégales* had been applicable, they would have produced a countless number of irrational rhythmic relationships rather than the exact ternary one of the original. Any way it is examined, the Bonporti-Roger evidence cannot be accepted.

To prove Bach's use of the *notes inégales*, McIntyre offers two examples. The first is from the Prelude in D major from the *Well-Tempered Clavier*, Book II, and in its analysis McIntyre makes several misjudgments. His chief evidence is the following claimed vertical lineup in measure 18 of the alleged autograph:[17]

Ex. 8.

1. First, the manuscript (see plate 1) is not an autograph but a copy assigned by the catalogue of Kast[18]—which embodies the results of the latest research—to "An[onymous] 12." It is true that until fairly recently it was taken by some to be an autograph, though Spitta knew better a hundred years ago. How it could have been taken for an autograph is hard to see, for it bears scarcely any resemblance to Bach's writing. If nothing else, the elementary mistake in m. 2 (where the second leger line of the a' is extended to become suddenly a first leger line so that the descending step a'—g' looks like an ascending one) belies any possible connection with Bach.

2. The next mistake was to read significance into the vertical alignment of a manuscript that shows great carelessness in this respect (see the very start).

3. The most serious error, however, was the actual misrendering of the original alignment: the latter is not at all of the kind claimed but as can be seen, the first eighth note is aligned not with the first but with the second sixteenth note:

Ex. 9.

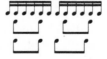

Plate 1.   The D major Prelude from Book II of the *Well-Tempered Clavier*, in the manuscript BB Bach P 416

This displacement of the first note renders invalid any inference that the second alignment might otherwise have permitted. Moreover, the manuscript shows an erasure of the third voice, which had at first been written a step too high and was, interestingly, still more wayward in its alignment: the first eighth placed under the third sixteenth! A dot after the first bass-note eighth at the beginning of this measure was claimed as further indication for the lengthening of this pulse. I would suggest that the "dot" is due to an accident of the pen, since it looks like a scratch, resembles none of the other dots on the page, and makes no notational sense, being followed by an eighth instead of a sixteenth rest.[19]

4. The fourth mistake was to see in the claimed alignment a sign for *notes inégales.* Since no autograph of this prelude is known to exist, we do not know how Bach aligned the notes in this measure. Of two important sources, one, a copy written in 1744 by Bach's pupil Altnikol (BB Bach P 430), shows clear, consistent, and unmistakable alignment of the eighth notes with the first, fourth, seventh, and tenth sixteenths, pointing to exact evenness (ex. 10a). A copy by Kirnberger (BB Bach P 209) shows the respective second eighth notes both times even earlier, between the third and fourth sixteenths. (ex. 10b).

Ex. 10a.   b.

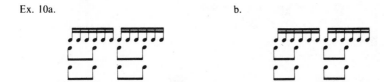

Even if we give Mr. McIntyre every benefit of the doubt and assume, against all these indications, that Bach aligned the eighth notes in the alleged two-to-one ratios, what would it prove? It would suggest that Bach intended a triplet coordination in that particular measure. If he did, which is unlikely but possible, it would simply be a case of the occasional assimilation of duple to triple rhythm, which is an entirely different matter, independent of and unrelated to the *notes inégales,* as will be explained below in some detail.[20]

The same is true of McIntyre's second example from the *Orgelbüchlein (Herr Gott, nun schleuss den Himmel auf),* where the autograph is genuine. Though the claimed line-ups: ♩   ♩ are by no means unequivocal, a double-to-triple rhythm assimilation is possibly intended, but to call it *notes inégales* is, here too, a case of mistaken identity.

Before attempting to clarify this and similar recurring misunderstandings, it is necessary to discuss briefly McIntyre's second erroneous quotation, which forms the basis of a section entitled "The Four-Note Slur."[21]

Quantz says, in the same passage, that in places where the tempo is too fast for 2 by 2 inegality, the first of four notes is to be lengthened. "For this practice," McIntyre states, "Quantz gives the four-note slur; thus ♩♫♫ = ♩. ♫♫ again with variable meaning depending upon the affect of the piece."[22] It is hard to understand how McIntyre arrived at that claim. The only link I could find between the four-note slur and *notes inégales* is Quantz's statement that inegality does *not* take place "when there is a slur over more than two notes—that is, over four, six or eight."[23] Yet even if, without the slur, Quantz's rapid-tempo one-in-four-inegality were to apply, it could not possibly bring about the transformation to ternary rhythm. Quantz tells us that the holding of the lengthened notes "must not amount to as much as it would if there were dots after the notes." That would mean that not even a lengthening by half the value would occur: ♪♫♫ Yet in McIntyre's formula the sixteenth note is lengthened to three times its value by being changed into a dotted eighth, and nothing less would do to effect the binary-ternary transformation.

Two examples are put forth to illustrate the transforming power of the four-note slur. The first is a measure from a Froberger Gigue where the "four-note slur" consists only of three notes because the first note that is to be lengthened turns out to be not a note but a rest. In the second example, from Couperin, the slur is missing for the "four-note slur." Also McIntyre has misunderstood Couperin's comment and applies the transformation formula with rather incongruous results. Here is Couperin's example and McIntyre's interpretation:

Ex. 11. Fanfare (10th Ordre)

Couperin's comment simply means that the eighth notes ⁹⁄₈ ♫♫ do not seem to relate to the sixteenth notes ³⁄₄ ♫♫♫ , which is perfectly true; they don't. But since, for the sake of a sound effect portraying a drum roll, Couperin wanted to accommodate four equal tremolo notes within a ternary beat, he had no other way of getting the idea across to the player, since the modern notation ⁹⁄₈ ♫♫♫ was not available at the time.

The other sections of McIntyre's article contain, regrettably, similar mistakes of procedure and reasoning, but a discussion of them will have to await another occasion. However, the arguments about the *notes inégales* involving the above-noted "mistaken identity" point up the need further to clear up the recurrent confusion about terms and principles in this particular field.

III

In my article on the *Inégales* I tried to set the latter apart from "good and bad" notes and from the "agogic articulation" of Leopold Mozart (mentioned above in note 14). There are, however, a number of other types of unevenness that invite misunderstandings. Since these invitations have too often been accepted, it might be useful to try to define—without claim to completeness—some of these different types of unevenness and put them into their correct relationships.

To find the common denominator of mistaken identities, the definition of unevenness has to be broadened to include any kind of deviation from the mathematical relationship of note values. Under this definition the most important genus of unevenness concerns those rhythmic manipulations for which Riemann coined the term *agogic*. The latter's species range from the "agogic accent" on a single note, over the "rubato" usually limited to a measure, to tempo variations within a phrase.[25] This kind of freedom is the manifestation of the very life-breath of music and as such is timeless and has been omnipresent ever since rhythmical notation began. The reason for it is simple. Notation, even in its modern state of sophistication, is too crude to match the infinite delicacy of rhythmic inflections, which are the sensitive performer's means of phrasing, nuance, and expressive shading. These irregularities which infuse life into the dead letter of notational mathematics have been and probably always will be an indispensable element of artistic performance. As a matter of course, Bach, like any other great interpreter, must have used agogics: tempo variations in toccatas, fantasias, and the like, rubato at least in ornamented adagios, and agogic accents probably anywhere.

It is these agogic accents, involving a slight lengthening of a single note for the sake of emphasis with a corresponding shortening of neighbor notes or note groups, that are most easily confused with the *notes inégales*. However, the agogic accent is entirely free, not regulated by any convention and dependent only on the artistic judgment and instinct of the performer. It can apply to any note without regard to its length, its relationship to the meter, to other notes, or to its place in the measure. It is, as has been said, timeless and omnipresent. When it is used in recurring patterns the chances for confusion are magnified. In a period where performers in the Italian stylistic orbit felt free, indeed obligated, to improvise on the written text, they considered certain freedoms of rhythmic manipulation as part of their prerogative. If, once in a while, such manipulation took the form of (quasi-) dotting a series of undotted notes, the result must still not be mistaken for the French type of *notes inégales*. In such cases the performer—rightly or wrongly—felt free to alter the rhythm arbitrarily, unconcerned about the composer's wishes; whereas in France there was nothing arbitrary about inegality: the performer felt bound to use it in order to conform to the composer's intentions. Herein lies the crux of the difference. The *notes inégales* were strictly regulated by a convention limited as to period, nationality, and style, and further limited for each meter to very definite note values in very definite melodic contexts. Though outwardly they might look like stylized agogic accents, the exact rules controlling their use and non-use negate such identification, and place them into a category of their own.

Another genus of unevenness is the variable rhythmic treatment of the dotted note. This practice occurred mostly in the 17th and 18th centuries and served different purposes in different contexts. Accordingly different species resulted.

1. One was the performer's franchise of lengthening or shortening the dot occasionally for reasons of the "affect," to respond to the expressive character of a passage, but *not* for purposes of assimilation to a simultaneous or prevailing rhythm of a different design (such as ternary rhythm or *notes inégales*).

2. Another species is represented by ♩. 𝅘𝅥𝅯𝅘𝅥𝅯𝅘𝅥𝅯 standing for ♩. 𝅘𝅥𝅯𝅘𝅥𝅯𝅘𝅥𝅯 .[26] This was simply the case of a notational convention clearly established by documents and countless instances of internal evidence. No element of rhythmic freedom was involved. ♩. 𝅘𝅥𝅯𝅘𝅥𝅯 𝅘𝅥𝅯𝅘𝅥𝅯𝅘𝅥𝅯 for ♩ 𝅘𝅥𝅯𝅘𝅥𝅯 𝅘𝅥𝅯𝅘𝅥𝅯𝅘𝅥𝅯 is an analogous case.

3. Categorically different from all the preceding types are those deviations from the normal value of the dotted note—and occasionally of evenly written notes—that are prompted by assimilation to concurrent or prevailing rhythm patterns of a different type. There are at least two subspecies: a) the more important of the two is the assimilation of duple to triple rhythms. It took largely the following forms:

Ex. 12.

These were simple expedients to cover a notational deficiency: the pattern of ♩ ♪ , though it turned up sporadically as early as the 17th century and was used by Bach at least twice (in the *Orgelbüchlein* and the *Canonic Variations*), did not come into general use until the middle of the 19th century. Therefore, very frequently (but by no means always) in Bach and his contemporaries, but as late as Schubert and Chopin, the dotted note was linked with triplets or sextuplets in 2:1 or 5:1 relationships. On the other hand, the triplet assimilation of evenly written notes, which was more rarely used, did not survive nearly as long. As a simple notational makeshift that, *faute de mieux,* had to be tolerated, neither of these assimilations had a connection with either the *notes inégales* or with agogic accents. b) The second subspecies of such assimilation is the limited extension of the dot in adaptation to simultaneous or prevailing *note inégales:*

Ex. 13.

where the dot takes the place of the first long eighth of a long-short pair. Such assimilation does not at all contradict the above statement that *notes inégales* are independent of another rhythm pattern: the *notes inégales* are the *independent* variable, the dotted note the dependent one.

This adaptation is probably one of the sources from which has sprung the mistaken theory of the so-called "French style" of overdotting.[27]

These are some, and probably not all, of the different types of unevenness. Only by keeping them apart and thus avoiding the risk of mistaken identities, can we dispel the fog that has beclouded these issues for too long.

6

The Dotted Note and the
So-Called French Style (FN1)

[This and the following four articles deal critically with the so-called "French overture style," one of the chief pillars of today's performance practice canon. For the sake of easier reference these articles are identified and referred to as FN1, FN2, FN3, FN4, and FN5. The first of these (FN1) was written originally in French and published in the *Revue de Musicologie* of 1965; the reprint here is in an English translation by R. Harris and E. Shay that *Early Music* published twelve years later (1977). The next four articles (1974, 1977, 1979, and 1981) were written partly in response to criticism but mainly in an attempt to support with new evidence and new reasoning my original thesis about the fictional nature of the doctrine.]

Among the many problems that beset the pursuit of historic performance, few are as complex as the uncertainties surrounding the rendition of the dotted note. The issue was controversial even among the theorists of the 17th and 18th centuries—hence it need not surprise us that the controversy has persisted to the present day. There are various facets to the issue and only one of these has to do with the "French style" of required strong overdotting—a modern doctrine widely accepted today as authentic. The article that follows, written in 1965, was to my knowledge the first published attempt to question its validity. This unorthodox attempt was bound to elicit a strong reaction. Michael Collins wrote an article "A Reconsideration of French Double-Dotting" (*Music & Letters,* Jan. 1969, pp. 111-23) in which he tried to disprove my arguments and Robert Donington lent his support to Collins *(The Interpretation of Early Music,* New Version, London, 1974, p. 451). In the meantime I have dealt with one part of Collins's arguments in a paper "The Question of Rhythm in the Two Versions of Bach's French Overture BWV 831"*(Studies in*

Reprinted with permission from *Early Music* 5 (1977), pp. 310-24, with original reprint permission from *Revue de Musicologie* 51 (1965). The research for this article was helped by a grant from the American Council of Learned Societies. Edmund Shay, concert organist, is professor of music and director of the early music consort at Columbia College, Columbia, South Carolina; Raymond Harris, formerly professor of music at Weslyan College, has performed extensively as an organist, harpischordist, and recorder player.

Renaissance and Baroque Music in Honor of Arthur Mendel, Kassel, 1974, pp. 183-94). Furthermore, in an article "Facts and Fiction about Overdotting" that appeared in the April 1977 issue of the *Musical Quarterly,* I introduced new evidence in support of my thesis; then set out to dispel the confusion surrounding the various categories of rhythmic alteration for dotted notes, and finally dealt with the remainder of Collins's arguments. After this new exchange of ideas I stand with increased confidence behind my first article. Since in my recent papers I had to refer frequently to this article, its availability in English could not have come at a more propitious time. I am very grateful to Messrs Raymond Harris and Edmund Shay for their fine translation and to *Early Music* for opening its pages to this study.

F.N.   *15 April 1977*

The authentic interpretation of early music is a topic that creates the most lively interest among musicologists and intelligent performers in our time. This interest, however, and the specific discipline that emanated from it are of a somewhat recent date, since the first historically oriented essays about interpretation only began to appear at the end of the 19th century. Consequently, one can easily understand how this young discipline might suffer from childhood diseases. The most serious disease with which it is afflicted is caused by a somewhat naive trust in the infallibility of historical treatises, and the symptoms of it are manifested in a faulty interpretation of these documents. Previously the treatises were either unknown or ignored, then towards the end of the 19th century the enthusiasm of their discovery incited musicologists to exaggerate their importance. This exaggeration persists in our own day; it is evident in the tendency to extend the application of treatises beyond their legitimate scope, to generalize certain isolated passages too freely, and to consider as law that which was simply a general rule subject to many exceptions.

The infant stage is now passed, and it is time we judged these documents with more discrimination regarding the facts that can or cannot be obtained from them. Undoubtedly the treatises are sources of important information, but we must develop better methods for deciding more circumspectly and with better judgement what their validity in each case is, according to the period, the personality of the author, the region and the country.

If a large number of treatises are found to be in complete accord concerning a problem, one has the right to infer the existence of a convention for the country and period in question. If, on the other hand, it is a question of isolated documents, it is rash, lacking any supplementary proof, to claim a validity outside the immediate circle of influence of the author; if lacking other evidence, generalizations are deduced that cross the boundaries of style, period, and nationality, it is no longer rashness, but pure and simple naiveté.

Among the questions concerning rhythm in old French music, there are two which, in point of view of the documentation, are situated at opposite poles. One, the convention of unequal notes *(notes inégales),* is established and clarified by an abundance of French documents which, by their quantity and complete accord, are impressive. The other, the dotted note and the so-called French style of overdotting, is proclaimed as a well-established principle; however, the documents are foreign, sporadic, late, and in part contradictory.

This theory of performing dotted notes is the subject of the present study. First, the facts will be stated, then the principal documents which have occasioned the formulation of the theory will be examined. Given the problematic character of the documents, an attempt will be made to find other sources of information that can shed light on the problem. In evaluating all of the evidence, the conclusion will be reached that the theory of the French style of obligatory overdotting is based, in large part, more on legend than historical fact, and that it is, in effect, one of the manifestations of "childhood diseases," an illegitimate interpretation of historical treatises.

Of what does the French style consist? It consists essentially of two elements: one is overdotting, and the other synchronization. Overdotting means that the dot after a note is to be lengthened by a second or even a third dot, or a corresponding silence, and that the short note that follows the dot is to be played as late as possible. Synchronization means that if, for example, there are dotted quarters in one voice and dotted eighths in the other, the short notes following the dot must be played simultaneously and as quickly as possible.

This manner of performance supposedly originated in France, where it permeated the overtures and dance music of the Lullian era. Thanks to the extraordinary vogue of the French overture and suite, it is then supposed to have spread across the whole of Europe, imposing something like an international convention that lasted until the end of the 18th century, embracing not only Couperin and Rameau, but Bach and Handel as well. According to Donington, it would be appropriate to employ double dotting whenever dotted rhythms are a characteristic element of a composition.[1] Although of an international currency, it is always in the entrées, sarabandes, courantes, chaconnes, passacailles, but above all in overtures in the French style, that this manner of performance would have been most appropriate, and its usage mandatory.

The principle of this application is formulated most clearly by Thurston Dart, who tells us that overtures, for example, ought to be played "jerkily" with all the notes following the dots synchronized and reduced to the shortest rhythmic denominator.[2] His description of this manner of execution is so picturesque, that we shall call it the "jerky style." This theory has succeeded in establishing itself so firmly that one generally believes it to be based on incontestable evidence. In this connection one continually finds the phrases "it is well known . . . ," "it is firmly established," etc. The question arises, what is the nature and the source of this certitude?

It seems that Arnold Dolmetsch was the first to proclaim this thesis, which he maintains is applicable in the works of Handel and Bach.[3] As an example he gives the overture from *Messiah* which, according to him, should be played in the manner illustrated in example 1. The principal documents on which he bases his theory are the texts of Quantz (1752) and of C.P.E. Bach (1753). Dolmetsch concedes that he was unable to find any earlier document, and it seems no other writer has been able to find one either. In his recent book, A. Geoffroy-Dechaume, who subscribes to the same theory, calls upon the same two authors.[4] In the Donington book these two sources, Quantz and Bach, are again the principal basis on which this theory is built. They are weakly corroborated by Leopold Mozart and by an example of doubtful worth by Couperin; these will be examined later in the paper. It will therefore be necessary to carefully examine the doctrines of these two Berlin authors.

Ex. 1.   Handel *Messiah,* Interpretation by Dolmetsch

In his famous book on the flute, Quantz deals with the question of dotted notes principally in two places.[5] The first of these passages is found in chapter V, which deals with metre and note values. Quantz tells us first, as do moreover all the treatises without exception, that the dot is worth half of the value of the note which precedes it, and he demonstrates the principle with the illustration of a dotted half-note and a dotted quarter-note (para. 20). In the next paragraph he reveals the exceptions. He explains that for dotted eighths, sixteenths and thirty-seconds, one deviates from this rule because of the "liveliness" (Lebhaftigkeit) which these notes ought to express, and indicates that all of the short notes in examples 2, 3, and 4 are of the same duration, that is to say, like a sixty-fourth-note. (He simply wanted to express that they were played as fast as possible.) In order to be more explicit he indicates in examples 5, 6 and 7, the long prolongation of the dot for the notes of the upper voice by lining up their sixteenth and thirty-second-notes with the sixty-fourth-notes of the lower voice 5 and 6. It is believed these examples indicated that it was always necessary to synchronize the short notes that follow a dot in different voices, after reducing them to the smallest value. Here is the original source of the "jerky style," a modest source which, fed by a generous flow of ink, has grown into a mighty river that threatens to inundate the music of two centuries.

Ex. 2.   Ex. 3.   Ex. 4.

Ex. 5.   Ex. 6.   Ex. 7

However, if one reads the text attentively one perceives that Quantz does not in any way speak of such a synchronization of two voices. Alone our example 7, the like of which never occurs in actual notation, shows that Quantz did not try to demonstrate the functional relationship between two independent voices but resorted to a pedagogical device that would indicate the nature and extent of rhythmic alteration for a single voice.

In some circumstances a radical shortening certainly ought to produce synchronization, and there is no doubt that synchronization was practised from time to time. But his fact does not permit one to consider synchronization, based on Quantz, as a general principle, the less so, since Quantz does not mention it in his text.

Until now Quantz has dealt with interpretation in general, without mentioning a specific national style that was connected with certain forms. Only in the chapter dealing with the duties of the accompanist (chap. XVII, sec. VII) does he specifically speak about French dance music. He tells us there that, in general, it is necessary to use heavy and detached bow strokes, to play dotted notes with emphasis, and the notes that follow them briefly in an incisive manner. Then in par. 58, he specifies that in ¢ and in the 3/4 metre of loures, sarabandes, courantes, and chaconnes, one must play the eighth-notes following dotted quarters not according to their normal value, but in a very short and sharp manner. It is important to note that, in speaking of the dotted quarter-note, he does not mention the overture. The only mention of the overture is made in a somewhat incidental way in the following sentence: "If a dot or a rest is followed by three or more thirty-second notes, these are played, especially in slow pieces . . . at the extreme end of the time allotted to them, and with the greatest possible speed, as is frequently [öfters] the case in overtures, entrées and furies."[6] Several modern authors seem to have ignored the limitation of this directive to thirty-second-notes, and in invoking the authority of Quantz, have applied the same principle without hesitation to sixteenth-notes. Geoffroy-Dechaume, for example, cites the same passage by Quantz on thirty-second notes, and as illustration follows it with the *Alceste* overture of Lully presented in the "jerky style," although it concerns itself with sixteenth and not thirty-second notes (ex. 8). He continues his illustration of Quantz's doctrine by demonstrating the necessity of subjecting the overture from J.S. Bach's Suite in B Minor for flute and strings to the jerky treatment.[7]

Ex. 8.   Lully, Overture to *Alceste*

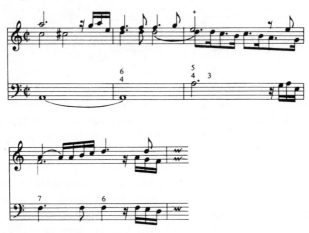

Interpretation by Geoffroy-Dechaume

Let us try in a few words to summarize the meaning of Quantz's instructions. He tells us that the notes that follow dotted eighths or sixteenths must be played as fast as possible because of the liveliness of expression. This appears to imply that if the character of the piece or of the dotted passage does not incline toward liveliness, then the principle would not be applicable. Although, in certain cases the shortening of quick notes implies a synchronization with notes of different values, Quantz does not mention it. When writing about French dance music he describes the overdotting of quarter-notes in certain characteristic pieces, [the overdotting interpretation of Quantz's directive was mistaken; see FN5], but does not mention overtures. He then speaks only of the shortening of thirty-second notes, provided there are at least three or four of them. In all, Quantz says less than one generally attributes to him. Before posing the question of the validity and scope of his opinions, let us examine the doctrines of the second witness, C.P.E. Bach.

The passages dealing with dotted notes are found in both sections of C.P.E. Bach's book, originally published nine years apart.[8] The first part deals with the art of the soloist (1753), and the second with the art of accompaniment (1762). In part one (chap. III, par. 23), Bach tells us that: "The short notes which follow dotted ones are always shorter in execution [werden . . . kürzer abgefertigt] than their notated length; hence it is superfluous to mark them with dots or dashes [mit Puncten oder Strichen]. One can see their execution in example 9." This sentence is the cause of two distinct misunderstandings. First, Dolmetsch[9] and Geoffroy-Dechaume[10] have misunderstood the *Puncte* and *Striche,* which mean that the articulation is to be detached and marked. However, both authors believed it was a question of a second dot to lengthen the first note, and an additional flag for the second.[11] For the second misunderstanding, Dolmetsch and Donington have interpreted this phrase as signifying that the value of the short note in examples 9(a), (b) and (c), is always the same, namely that of a thirty-second note. Nevertheless, one finds nothing in the text or in the three examples to support the idea of exaggerated overdotting.[12] However, even though the letter of the text does not seem to admit it, it is probable that Bach had a certain prolongation of the dot in mind. In an additional note to the third edition, inserted in the course of this paragraph, the term *kürzer abgefertigt* is used undoubtedly to suggest rhythmic contraction. In addition, example 9(e) and a passage from the second part of the book, which will be referred to later, could lead us to believe that Bach wanted to speak of prolongation in this passage. If one assumes this, then the first sentence of the text becomes incoherent. If one does not assume it, then the use of the term *kürzer abgefertigt* only leads to confusion. Example 9(e) shows, without further comment, a case of double dotting in which two parallel voices of a purely homophonic nature are synchronized (one of the voices is simply a little more ornamented than the other). In contrast, example 9(f) illustrates the case of two independent, i.e. polyphonic, voices where such an overdotting would corrupt the counterpoint. Bach's commentary is significant: "Occasionally the interplay of the voices requires one to use the notated values [Zuweilen erfordert die Eintheilung, dass mann der Schreib-Art gemäss verfährt]." This is a very important principle that Bach reiterates even more explicitly in the second part of the book.

Ex. 9.   C.P.E. Bach

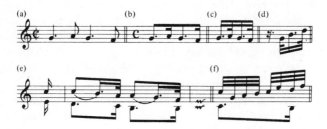

The passage continues: "Dots after long notes as well as those after short ones in a slow movement, and also isolated dots are held [Die Puncte... werden gehalten]." Here again we have an ambiguous expression. *Die Puncte halten* normally means to hold the dots for their entire value (the same thing that is indicated by the Italian term *ten(uto)* above a note). But if Bach, as is probable, wanted to indicate prolongation rather than the exact holding [of the dot], he has not expressed himself clearly, and the vagueness and indifference of the expression do not suggest a marked prolongation. Moreover, in the next sentence he uses the word *halten* clearly in the sense of holding to the exact value: "If several dotted notes succeed each other, particularly in a rapid movement, they are seldom held, *even though the notation demands it* [Kommen aber, zumal in geschwindem Tempo, viele (Puncte) hinter einander vor, so werden sie oft nicht gehalten, ohngeacht die Schreib-Art es erfordert] (italics added)." This means that in place of holding *(halten)* the dots for their exact value, corresponding to the notation, they must be shortened.[13] Bach continues: "Given this alternative, it would be best to indicate everything in an exact manner [in the notation]; if this is not done, then the content of the piece will clarify it for us." The alternative of which he speaks is probably that between prolongation and shortening. "One holds the dots of short notes which are followed by groups of shorter ones" (ex. 10). If he is speaking of double dotting, then he contradicts himself in the following sentences, which are the beginning of the original insertion for the third edition: "In figures *(Figuren)* where dotted notes are followed by four or more notes, these last are [already] sufficiently short because of their number [Bey Figuren, wo auf die Puncte vier und noch mehrere kurze Noten folgen, werden diese durch ihre Vielheit kurz genug]." Therefore, Bach is explaining that they are played according to the notation, because there is no need to shorten them more.[14] "The same applies to the figures in example 11 and, if the tempo is not too slow, to the figure in example 12." This means that in the case of examples 11 and 12 overdotting does not take place.

·Ex. 10.   Ex. 11.

Ex. 12.

This is all quite different from what Quantz said. There is also divergence with Quantz regarding the treatment of *lombard* rhythm, where a short note placed on the beat is followed by a dotted note. According to Quantz, the short note is shortened both in the allegro and in the adagio; according to Bach, it is not necessary to shorten it when the movement is slow or of an expressive character.[15]

In reviewing the entire passage of which a painfully detailed analysis has just been presented, one cannot avoid the conclusion that much of it is obscure, ambiguous, and even contradictory. This does nothing to increase its authority, since even the reader of the original text would not know how to draw the author's exact opinion from it without recourse to conjecture. And it was only by excessive abuse of conjecture in the French and English translations that several writers have succeeded in transforming this passage into a manifesto of decided overdotting. Fortunately, a paragraph in the second part of the book illuminates very many of these uncertainties, and repudiates many of these conjectures. In this passage (Part II; chap. 29, par. 15) Bach returns to the problem and summarizes his ideas about it in a clearer and more orderly manner. Here is the passage: "In writing dotted notes the needed precision is often lacking. A general rule regarding the execution of these notes has been advanced which, however, *allows for many exceptions*. According to this rule, the notes that follow dots should be played very quickly, and often this rule is correct. However, there are some cases where the rule cannot be applied, because the disposition of notes in different voices requires their exact coordination [Allein bald machet die Eintheilung gewisser Noten in verschiedenen Stimmen, vermöge welcher sie in einem Augenblicke zusammen eintreten müssen, eine Aenderung]. In other cases a tender [flatierend] expression would hardly survive the defiant effect [das Trotzige] produced by dotted notes; this is one reason to shorten the duration of the dots. *If only one type of execution is allowed, one loses the other types* (italics added)."[16] This last sentence seems to repudiate the "style" which admits of only one type.

In the light that this paragraph sheds on the former passages, it is possible to formulate the quintessence of Bach's ideas as follows: 1) In homophonic pieces and in pieces of a vivacious or energetic character, dots are often lengthened; 2) In polyphonic pieces it is necessary in general to respect the precise duration of the dot in order not to disturb the mutual rapport of the independent voices; 3) In pieces of a tender character, it is often necessary to shorten dots so as not to introduce a contradictory expression. The same shortening often takes place in a rapid tempo when there is a succession, or series of dotted notes.

The limitation of overdotting to a homophonic structure is not only dictated by musical logic, but is clearly implied when, in both passages, Bach speaks of the necessity of the agreement between different voices; a necessity which would forbid a deviation from the notated values. Example 9(f) serves as illustration.

In all of this discussion Bach speaks of music in general and, it goes without saying, principally of his own. He mentions neither French music, nor particular forms to which his principles would apply more than to others. In short, what he tells us is scarcely more than what, for a long time, was part of the interpretative freedom of the soloist, an implicit freedom seen as an authority conferred by "taste," combined with an attitude much less rigid than ours towards notation. Nothing in his writing suggests the idea that overdotting was mandatory, or a stylistic demand of certain musical forms like the French overture; nothing suggests the notion of the "jerky style." The important issue, therefore, is that Bach has not confirmed Quantz, and the mutual agreement of these authors is only a reality concerning the fact that in certain circumstances the dot is lengthened, and perhaps in others, synchronized. This is not at all sufficient evidence to support "the style," which in the end finds its only endorsement in the testimony of Quantz.

In spite of their limited accord, these two authors are, nevertheless, considered the principal source of the "French style." The question of their authority on French practice from Lully to Rameau, the peak period for French overtures and suites, is then of primary importance. One has an obligation to question the credentials of these two authors, their sphere of influence, and the period for which their jurisdiction extends.

Let us first observe that both were Germans who wrote after 1750, and that their treatises were re-edited towards the end of the century; that of Quantz after his death, without alteration in 1780 and 1789, while Bach prepared the third enlarged edition himself in 1787, from which some of the above-mentioned additions were taken. The possible conclusion would seem to be that these two authors, *in as much as they are in agreement,* could reflect certain German practices between 1750-1790, and of the galant style that both represented.

As for the agreement—or disagreement—between the two, their divergences are not limited to those which were already noticed on the subject of dotted notes. In addition, numerous cases can be found where they contradict each other completely, notably in the area of ornaments. These contradictions are even more significant if we take into account that both were employed at the same time by the King of Prussia, Frederick II, and belonged to the same musical establishment. If, in spite of their daily collaboration for the royal music each evening, there was discord between the two, one could hardly avoid the conclusion that neither can claim to reflect unquestionably the practices of the very place and epoch where they worked.[17] However, we are asked to accept their authority without further corroboration, not only for the contemporary practices of all Germany and France, but also for those of three or four previous generations: for the music of J.S. Bach, Handel, Rameau, Couperin and Lully, and all of their contemporaries. By what right? By none other than the fact that their ideas were printed in an old treatise, and treatises are venerated as sources of the last word.

But let us not reject their testimony before examining it more. It is self-evident that both authors were writing about their epoch and their performance practices; an historical interest was foreign to the century. C.P.E. Bach does not mention French music or French practices. Quantz, when he speaks of French dance music, does not say, as he specifies in other places, that it is the way the French perform it; it is therefore probable that his remarks only reflect his personal taste. But in order to strengthen the argument, let us admit the possibility that the ideas of Quantz were shared by some French interpreters of his generation. What right do we have to confer on these precepts a kind of retroactivity to include J.S. Bach and Lully? Barring other evidence—and it is always necessary to add this proviso—it would only be under the following conditions that a French-German retroactivity could even be a debatable idea: 1) that there was an international style and convention, 2) that this style and this convention would have remained static from 1660-1790. It is enough to state these conditions to realize their absurdity. How can we suppose a unified international convention existed, if, as we have seen, there was not even a unified convention at the court of Frederick II?

As to the second condition, the static state, such a thing never existed in the realm of Western art. If one merely thinks of the profound change that took place between the aesthetic of J.S. Bach and C.P.E. Bach (between father and son-student), then the thought of a static set of performance conventions crossing national boundaries and embracing five generations from Lully to Mozart becomes an untenable one. The intervening changes between J.S. Bach and the new galant style, moreover, had some important implications for our question of the dotted note.

The new style in Germany had abandoned the complexity of polyphony for a less sophisticated musical style which was based, above all, on the charm of simple melodies. In this kind of music, marked changes of rhythm were not only possible but often desirable in order to ornament and compensate a little for the lean musical substance. By contrast, in music that is essentially polyphonic, particlarly the music of J.S. Bach, a marked change from the notated rhythm would not fail, in most cases, to distort the rapport of the voices and falsify the counterpoint. We recall that C.P.E. Bach refers twice to this important fact.

Therefore, what is desirable for the music of Quantz and his contemporaries, is not appropriate for the music of J.S. Bach, nor for the overtures, chaconnes, etc., of Lully or Rameau. There are good reasons to suppose that marked overdotting was a new fashion, one of the manneristic exaggerations which often characterize the terminal phase of a development. Moreover, it is possible that the origin of Quantz's version was more Prussian than French, and that the new Frederician climate of strict regimentation in Berlin had transformed French flexibility into Prussian rigidity, the dance style into a military march style.

The objection could be made that even if the testimony of the authors were judged inapplicable, it does not prove the nonexistence of the alleged convention. However, if the convention did exist, it should be possible to find some traces of it either in treatises or in the music itself.

We are not lacking a trail of investigation regarding the treatises. Dolmetsch followed it first, but in vain. Others after him have not had much more success. We have found nothing in German treatises prior to Quantz, nor in French treatises, even from the second half of the century. As for the latter, their silence contrasts dramatically with the eloquence of about 40 others on the subject of *notes inégales*. If the convention known as the "French style" existed, then such a silence would be all the more striking, since each treatise deals with the dot and gives the exact rule for it. Is it not astonishing that none of the authors, in connection with this rule, thought to mention some obvious exceptions to it? The silence could not be more remarkable than in a publication by Lully's student G. Muffat, in which he intended to initiate his German compatriots into the style of his master.[18] Being, as he himself asserts, the first to undertake such a task, he takes great pains in a long quadralingual foreword not to omit any details. The music contained in this publication is full of dotted notes, and though he discusses in great detail the bow-strokes that are strongly affected by the "style," he does not mention the latter with a single word.

Would it not be asking too much of our trustfulness to accept such a collective silence as the result of pure chance—a generalized amnesia lasting for more than a century? Or quite simply, are we to assume that the "style" did not actually exist? This is the fundamental question. Since the treatises offer no help, other sources must be investigated in the hope of shedding light on the problem. It is said that there is no smoke without fire. Since there is plenty of smoke about the French style, perhaps it would be possible fo find the fire by other means. In order to find it, I shall attempt to explore three new lines of approach; first, the music itself, from the point of view of the notation and musical logic; second, what Pincherle calls the "rights of the interpreter," and third, the convention of *notes inégales.*

Before embarking upon this analysis, let us remember that there are two aspects of the style: one is overdotting, and the other synchronization. Any proof against one or the other must seriously compromise the theory.

First, concerning notation, an erroneous notion about the use of the double dot must be dispelled. It was not invented by Quantz or any of his contemporaries, as is generally supposed. It was known in France in the second half of the 17th century. Chambonnières and Louis Couperin used it from time to time, and André Raison used it regularly. It is true that Lully did not use it, and that after him the double dot seems to have disappeared during the first half of the 18th century. Nevertheless I have found some additional examples from this period in the music of Clérambault and Michel Corrette. Since the convention, according to Thurston Dart, dates from the beginning of the seventeenth century, it will be interesting to see what kind of information can be deduced from the notation.

André Raison is probably the better witness because he uses the double dot so systematically, notating the dotted rhythm so precisely in each case, that his intention cannot be misinterpreted. Therefore, the conclusion is justified that the absence of a second dot must be interpreted literally. The following examples are all extracts from the original edition of André Raison's *Livre d'Orgue,* published in Paris in 1688. In example 13, from the second Kyrie (p. 2), double dots such as those at (a) are replaced at the end by single dots at (b). This last measure, therefore, must be played with broadness and solemnity, and without double dotting. In example 14, from Christe (p. 4), the double dots in the third measure place the single dots of the first in relief; hence an effect full of the charm of rhythmic variety, which would be obliterated by double dotting in the first measure. Example 15 of the same piece is most interesting, because the exact value of the dot after the first note is confirmed in the rhythmic imitation of the second voice, written as a quarter-note tied to an eighth without a dot. Example 16 (first Kyrie on the sixth tone, p. 20) is in the form of an overture, and the absence of double dots here demonstrates that double dotting was not characteristic of this style. Example 17 (*Benedicimus te,* p. 54) presents another case of rhythmic variety. The next example from the same piece (ex. 18) is of very special interest: the absence of a double dot in the lower voice, and the position of the eighth-note exactly below the dot in the upper voice, proves that synchronization in the "French style" was not desired, but rather an enrichment of the structure by what might be called "rhythmic counterpoint." The book is full of many different examples such as these.

Ex. 13.   André Raison

Ex. 14.

Ex. 15.

Ex. 16.

Ex. 17.

Ex. 18.

An advocate of the "style" might say: Raison has shown us that doubly-dotted rhythms were certainly in vogue; consequently since Lully and his successors did not make use of the double dot, we can conclude that a great many of their single dots ought to be interpreted as double ones. Such an argument is not convincing. Lully and the masters who succeeded him, among them Couperin and Rameau, certainly knew how to use the tied-over note or the rest to express double dotting, and they did use them often.

If, as in the overture to *Amadis,* Lully writes a tied-over note in the third measure that is equivalent to a double dot (ex. 19), it follows that the dotted notes in the first two measures were not intended to be double dotted. Several measures later, example 20 demonstrates that synchronization in the third and fourth quarters could not have been the intention of the composer, that the "jerky" style had no place there, and finally, that the intended aim was precisely a conflict of rhythm, a "rhythmic counterpoint" which would augment the richness and interest of the structure, and allow the independent voices of the polyphonic writing to stand out. Many examples of this kind by all composers in this period, German as well as French, indicate that it was a rhythmic conflict (ex. 21a) and not a jerky synchronization (ex. 21b) that was characteristic of the style. A confirmation quite capable of proving this idea is furnished in the second measure of example 22 (*Amadis,* second act, last scene), where the notational differences of the first violins and bass on one side, and the second violins and voice part on the other, leave no doubt about the intention of rhythmic conflict. In cases where Lully wanted synchronization, he specified it, as in example 23 (ritornello, *Le Mariage forcé*) and in example 24 (overture from *Les Amants magnifiques).* Couperin, Rameau, Handel, Telemann, and Bach did the same.

Ex. 19.   Lully, *Amadis*

Ex. 20.

Ex. 21. (a)   (b)

Ex. 22.   *Amadis* Act II. last scene

[L'en] fer   a   for - mé   de ter - rib - le
                        4   6

Ex. 23.   *Le mariage forcé*

Ex. 24.   *Les Amants magnifiques*

It is interesting and revealing to examine the scores of Lully that were used for performances during the 18th century, because they contain modifications and alterations which reflect a change of taste. There is a copy of the opera *Amadis,* preserved in the library of the Paris Opera, which was used in the first half of the 18th century.[19] Among other things we find the changes shown in example 25 (referring to II.ii), where the passage shown at line (a) is changed to that of (b), and line (c) to that of (d); exactly the kind of change required by the "style." Also found there is the following interesting directive of the editor, addressed, it would appear, to the copyist: "Revise the inside voices for change of metre and note values." (The score was a condensed version containing only the outer voices.) The changes reveal first of all that the reviser felt the need in this particular scene of a bit more rhythmic seasoning. But, even more important, they reveal that *a convention did not exist that demanded such a doubly-dotted execution without exact indication in the notation.*[20] If such a convention had existed in the first half of the 18th century, the changes in the outer voices and the remark about the necessity of changing the inner voices would have been superfluous. Further, it is interesting that such a change is found only in this scene in the midst of the opera, and that similar rhythms everywhere else have remained in their original form.[21]

Ex. 25.   *Amadis* II. ii

In a Sarabande by Louis Couperin (ex. 26) the second voice, with its quarter and eighth-note, is only intelligible if the eighth after the dot enters exactly in rhythm.[22] In example 27 by Le Bègue, synchronization of the two upper voices is possible. However, the bass with its two equal eighth-notes (in C time eighth-notes are equal) provides the rhythmic conflict which, in its turn, confirms that of the middle voice.

Ex. 26.   L. Couperin *Sarabande*

Ex. 27.   Le Bègue, *Allemande*

There is an example from the 18th century by François Couperin (the passacaille *L'Amphibie* from the 24th Ordre of the *Pièces de Clavecin*) in which a theme with a rhythm of singly dotted notes (ex. 28a) is found doubly dotted in the second variation (ex. 28b). This proves that contrast was a deliberate choice; consequently, the theme should not be played according to the "French style."

Ex. 28.   F. Couperin, *L'Amphibie* (Passacaille)

Ex. 29.   Händel, Overture to *Berenice*

Some examples by foreign masters who adopted French forms will now be examined. Handel is in the first rank of composers whose works, particularly his overtures, have been claimed by the "jerky style." In the overture to *Bérénice* (ex. 29) we see how Handel introduced the same variety of dotted rhythms, alternating what could be called "dull" with "sharpened" rhythms. Notice, particularly in the upper voice, the transition from one pattern to the other in the second half of the second measure. In the overture to *Xerxes* (ex. 30) a rhythmic conflict in the first measure caused by the eighth-note E flat in the first violins (and by the eighth-note in the bass) against the sixteenth-note C in the second violins is corroborated by the two equal eighth-notes A-G in the viola. In the second bar, a clearly doubly-dotted synchronization is specified by the notation. This gives way in the third bar to a new broadening of the rhythm with a rhythmic conflict against the bass; a captivating variety whose arbitrary leveling by the "French style" would cause a deplorable impoverishment. A similar alternation of both rhythmic types occurs in an anonymous overture (ex. 31) from an important manuscript known as the *Möllersche Handschrift;* it originates from J.S. Bach's circle.[23]

Ex. 30.   Overture to *Xerxes*

Ex. 31.   *Möllersche Handschrift,* anonymous overture

These illustrations, and a great number of similar examples that could be cited, seem to confirm the supposition that the "French style" did not exist in the form stated by its advocates.

Ex. 32.   Boyvin, Trio

Concerning the evidence that the music itself can furnish, attention must again be called to an argument of Donington on the subject of an unusual notation used by Couperin. As proof of double dotting Donington cites the sixth movement of *L'Apothéose de Corelli* (ex. 33), where Couperin is supposed to have used the dot to represent a double dot.[24] It is improbable, if not impossible, for the dots in this example to be equivalent to double dots because: 1) in the rapid tempo demanded by the word "vivement," double dots would be absolutely unplayable, 2) in a context of triplets it is more natural, in a fast tempo, for short notes to be infected by the triplets; one can see this especially in the unison entrance of the second voice in the second measure—a formula often repeated in this piece—the sixty-fourth-note enters naturally with the thirty-second-note of the triplet figure; 3) the rests are written in such a way that, if the sixty-fourth-notes were true sixty-fourths, there would be another thirty-second-note rest missing before each of them.

Ex. 33.   F. Couperin, *L'Apothéose de Corelli.*

We can probably find the solution to this small mystery in Gigault, who also uses a similar notation. In advising the readers of his book of organ music he says: " . . . eighth-notes that are barred several times need not frighten one, since they ought to be considered as if they were merely sixteenth-notes."[25]

Perhaps it is from Gigault that Couperin adopted this notational caprice which he uses from time to time in many of his compositions.

It is true that this notation does give the impression of a double-dotted rhythm, but on the other hand, it is not solely with dotted notes that we find such notational deviations. In the Sarabande *L'Unique* from the 8th Ordre of his clavecin pieces, Couperin writes the following (ex. 34). One could suppose, perhaps, that it was a question of indicating *inégalité*. But, aside from the fact that such a rhythmic formula does not lend itself to inequality, this hypothesis is refuted in example 35 (*Pièces de violes,* 1st suite, Passacaille) where, for a similar formula, Couperin specifies: "Notes égales." Therefore the fourth beam has no musical meaning.

Ex. 34. Sarabande *L'Unique*

Ex. 35. *Passacaille (Pièces de violes)*

One might think this was nothing more than a caprice. Although possible, it is not a very satisfactory explanation.

Perhaps a solution of a psychological nature can be found. As every pedagogue knows, a dotted rhythm is difficult to execute, and there is always a tendency of not holding the dot long enough, which makes it sound like a triplet. The same can be said for the rhythm of a sixteenth followed by two thirty-second-notes: there is a tendency to play the sixteenth too quickly and the thirty-seconds too sluggishly. It is possible that similar experiences with his students induced Couperin to use notational exaggerations, such as an excessive number of beams, simply for their suggestive force (their shock value as one might say in America), in order to persuade performers at first sight not to yield to natural inertia, and to play the notes in a well-defined rhythm.

Whatever the explanation, it is difficult to see how this little eccentricity could confirm the "style," since it has been demonstrated that a double-dotted interpretation was impossible in certain cases, very doubtful in others, and that often there was no dot at all present in the notation.

Still remaining for consideration is an examination of two other approaches: the "rights of the performer," and the ramifications of *notes inégales*.

The rights of the performer have been incidentally mentioned earlier in the discussion, but it is necessary to return briefly to the subject. It must first be recognized that one of the greatest sources of misunderstanding and erroneous notions about historical interpretation is the fact that we are too inclined to project the principles, ideas, and demands of today's performances into the past. For example, in our day the musical education of a performer insists on technical virtuosity and mathematical exactness of rhythm—points of view which were far removed from the concerns of the 17th and 18th centuries. Our orchestras are machines of precision, and if one did not play a dotted note in the exact ratio of 3:1, or a doubly-dotted note in that of 7:1, it would be tantamount to a crime in the eyes of our dictator-conductors. This mentality gave birth to the idea that a deviation from the mathematical values of dotted rhythms in old music was only possible if it was specifically required by a convention. However, all that actually existed as a "convention" was a greater degree of adaptability in the interpretation of the musical text, and this adaptability implied a flexibility towards the relative value of the notes. Above all it was the privilege of the soloist to determine whether or not the character of the piece or passage demanded a certain "softening" or "sharpening" of the rhythm. He had to adjust the interpretation of the dot to a given situation, that was all; this includes the question of triplets combined with dotted notes, and that of synchronization. The first of these questions recently gave rise to a heated controversy in German periodicals, where each party claimed a definitive convention: one supported the solution of C.P.E. Bach, to shorten the value of the dot to that of a triplet (see note 15); in opposition, the other supported the rule of Quantz which demands a distinct prolongation. Both parties were wrong, because here also there was no definitive convention that demanded one solution more than the other. It was simply a question for the performer to choose which he judged the most musical solution, and the most natural in a particular situation. Therefore, the intelligent performer sometimes chose one, and sometimes the other.

The same thing can be said for the synchronization of various kinds of short notes that follow dotted ones. It was undoubtedly practised from time to time when the logic of the situation appeared to demand it, even before the period of the galant style. For example, Gigault tells us that: "In order to animate one's playing, some dots can also be added, more or less where one wishes. Where there is a sixteenth-note above an eighth, they are played simultaneously."[26] However, this situation, apparently, does not present itself in his book of organ music. But in a passage such as that of Boyvin's (ex. 32), which is concerned with strictly parallel voices, i.e. homophonic writing, a "rhythmic counterpoint" would not be appropriate, and for this reason synchronization was the natural solution. Therefore, some deviation from the mathematical value was practised long before Quantz, and the choice was determined by the performer as one of his "rights," but the idea of a convention that *demanded* these kinds of specific deviations is a misconception. It is important to stress that there is a profound and categorical difference between the freedom to lengthen, shorten, or synchronize *according to musical taste,* and a so-called law that would force us to do one or the other. The first partakes of freedom, the second of tyranny.

Aside from individual freedom, there are some cases where prolongation of the dot was actually based on a real and firmly established convention: that of *notes inégales*. One French quotation on this subject by Hotteterre tells us that: "Sometimes dots are placed after notes which lengthen them by half of their value. ... In movements where eighth-notes are unequal, a dot following a quarter-note is equivalent to a dotted eighth; hence the eighth-note which follows a dotted quarter is always short."[27] At first glance one might believe this to be a confirmation of Quantz and the "jerky style." However, after a second look this idea can be rejected.

The *inégalité* of eighth- and sixteenth-notes occurs only in certain metres, and then in principle only when there is a series of eighths in pairs which proceed essentially in conjunct motion. A series of dotted quarters followed by eighths, a rhythmic model for many overtures, does not lend itself in principle to *inégalité*. The situation to which Hotteterre refers (where the dot takes the place of the first long eighth, causing the eighth that follows it to be short) could happen only under two circumstances: 1) when more or less isolated dotted quarter-notes are, in a manner of speaking, linked to a series of continuous eighths (ex. 36), and 2) when there is a succession of unequal eighths in one voice and dotted-quarters in another (exx. 37 and 38). In this situation a harpsichordist would certainly, and an orchestra probably, prolong the dot in order to adapt naturally and spontaneously to the unequal subdivision of the beats.

Ex. 36.   Gavotte

Ex. 37.   Rameau, Courante

Ex. 38.   Lully, *Alceste*

Plate 2. Handel's Overture to *Orlando*, autograph. Note the double-dotting of the *quarter-notes* by explicit and consistent insertion of rests except for the last two bars with their natural cadential broadening (British Library)

Plate 3.   Handel's Overture to *Rinaldo*, autograph. Note in bars 4-6 the tell-tale inalterable lack of rhythmic sharpness. With three brief and precisely spelled-out exceptions this informs the whole introduction (to be played as written, but at a faster pace than usually taken). (British Library)

In order to obtain a perspective on the scope and importance of this principle of Hotteterre's as compared to the "French style" and the "jerky style," we must realize that, 1) the cases where it can be applied are not frequent, and 2) *inégalité* is nearly always subtle, often almost imperceptible, and very rarely attains the 3:1 ratio of an actual dotted note. Therefore, even in cases where the *inégalité* of the eighth-notes involves a prolongation of dots, the prolongation could not reach the extremes claimed by the "style" or by Quantz, and could approach them only very rarely. The difference here is not only of degree, but of principle.

In summarizing the arguments of this study, it can be said that the lack of French sources to corroborate Quantz suggests that a pronounced and obligatory style of overdotting did not exist. This supposition is verified by the evidence drawn from the music itself, and in many cases the evidence shows that the application of the alleged rules was impossible, illogical, or clearly refuted by the notation. Moreover, it has been pointed out that individual freedom permitting some flexible manipulation of the dot, balancing a little from one side to the other, was a different thing in principle from a convention which would have demanded a decisive prolongation. Likewise, it has been shown that an occasional prolongation of the dot within the framework of inequality cannot offer the missing proof for what Quantz wrote about French dance music, nor can it give his remarks a retroactive validity. As for Quantz— and the concern is almost exclusively with him—it may be that his instructions concerning French music are only an expression of his personal taste. Perhaps they reflect a new German fashion of the mid-eighteenth century, a fashion where French flexibility, emanating from *notes inégales* and the freedom of the soloist, was exaggerated by imitators and transformed into rigid mannerisms.

Indeed, for the period from Lully to Rameau, the so-called French style is essentially a legend, and its first formulation by Dolmetsch is an invention which has been wrongly taken for a discovery.

When we play the overtures, sarabandes, chaconnes, etc., of Lully, Rameau, Handel, and Bach, it is a mistake to deprive them of their majestic dignity in favor of the frantic style of jerks and jolts. In any case, for many listeners a prolonged series of such jerks and jolts can be rather irritating. Others might find such a style stimulating, perhaps because it reflects the nervous tensions of our age; they have the privilege of their taste, but they must cease the claim of historical authenticity.

Rhythm in the Two Versions of Bach's French Overture, BWV 831 (FN2)

Bach's French Overture-Suite for harpsichord exists in two versions: an earlier one in C minor, a later in B minor. The principal source of the C-minor version is a manuscript by Anna Magdalena Bach at the *Deutsche Staatsbibliothek* in Berlin (*Mus. ms. Bach, P 226,* hereafter referred to as P 226). Its title page is written by Bach himself whose hand can also be seen, according to Walter Emery, in a few editorial additions and emendations.[1] The exact date of this manuscript cannot be established, but Emery, on the basis of the watermark and the character of Anna Magdalena's handwriting considers a date prior to July 1733 as most likely. A second source is a manuscript by Johann Gottlieb Preller, written probably in the 1730s, and contained in the extensive "Mempell-Preller" collection of Bach manuscripts in the Leipzig *Musikbibliothek* (Ms 8).[2] As Emery convincingly shows, this second source is not derived from P 226, but from a third source, presumably Bach's autograph sketch. Very little is known about Preller except that he was an organist born around 1700 and that his Bach manuscripts date from the 1730s and 40s.

The second version of the Overture in B minor is the one which Bach published in 1735 together with the Italian Concerto as the second part of his *Clavier Übung.*[3]

Apart from the altered key the main differences between the two versions concern the first movement, the overture proper, in which the rhythm is strikingly changed by being sharpened throughout in the manner shown in example 1 for the opening measures.

Both change of key and change of rhythm for this overture have given rise to much speculation.

Reprinted with permission from *Studies in Renaissance and Baroque Music in Honor of Arthur Mendel,* ed. Robert L. Marshall (Kassel, 1974), pp. 183-94.

Ex. 1.

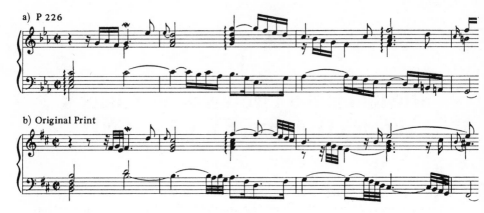

a) P 226

b) Original Print

Concerning the reason for the changed key, the first explanation that comes to mind—that the transposition may have resulted in a better adjustment to the compass of the instrument—does not answer the question. As was already pointed out by Hans Bischoff in his Steingräber edition of the 1880s and confirmed in more detail by Emery, the transposition to B minor not only offers no advantages in the upper register but in fact is a liability in the bass where two cadences had to be modified.

Bischoff (relating a private communication by Spitta), Hans David in his Schott edition of 1935 (presenting the C-minor version), Erwin Bodky, and recently Rudolf Eller, attempted explanations for the change of key that would integrate the first and the second parts of the *Clavier Übung* into a unified scheme of key relationships.[4] Each explanation is different (which in itself arouses skepticism), and none is convincing. This is not surprising, since it is unlikely that Bach would have linked into a single key scheme two publications of totally different inner organization. The first part is homogeneous with its six Partitas; the second part is heterogeneous: its very point is to contrast the two leading national styles, the Italian and the French, in the form of their most typical representatives: the concerto and the overture-suite. This purpose lends support to Hermann Keller's suggestion that Bach wanted to underline the antithesis by juxtaposing the two prototypes in the sharpest possible key contrast, the tritone relationship of F major and B minor. Christoph Wolff has recently expressed the same idea and strengthened its case.[5] This seems to be the most plausible explanation, though we cannot entirely dismiss the possibility that Bach had no profound symbolism in mind and may have chosen the B-minor key for no more mysterious reason than that he preferred its characteristic sound for this particular work.

More intriguing than the change of key is the change of rhythm. Whenever we find notational deviations in second versions of a piece, the simplest explanation is that the second version represents a second thought—and usually the simplest explanation turns out to be the best. The sharpening of a rhythm as a second thought is not foreign to Bach. We find such specimens for instance in the aria, "Süßes Kreuz," from the *St. Matthew Passion,* where certain rhythms of the autograph score *(P 25),* given in example 2a, are changed in the equally autograph gamba part *(St 110)* to those of example b; or in the lute transcription (BWV 955) of the Suite for Unaccompanied Cello in C minor (BWV 1011). The autograph of the latter (in the Bibliothèque Royale de Belgique) contains, in the Allemande, the alterations shown in examples 2c and d, respectively, as well as in all parallel spots.

Ex. 2.

The case of the rhythmic alterations in the French overture could rest with the simple explanation of a second thought were it not for the fact that a Bach scholar of Emery's eminence saw in the change not a conscious revision but rather a more precise notation for the same intended rhythm. (As will be presently shown, this opinion is shared by Michael Collins.) Emery feels that the pervasive rhythmic design of the C-minor version: ♩ ♬ was only a more convenient way of writing the sharper rhythms of the printed edition. If taken literally, the slower rhythms are "dull", he says, in response to Hans David who did believe in their literal meaning and found the early version "grander and more natural" than the "fashionable" revision. Emery, in making his claim for the sharpening of the rhythm, tacitly assumed the existence of an alleged convention. For this reason we have to take a brief look at the latter which was first formulated by Arnold Dolmetsch in 1916 and widely accepted since as authoritative.[6] Its gist is that all dotted rhythms in French overtures and suite movements must be sharpened so decisively that they move together "jerkily" (as a wellknown modern writer put it).[7] Thus ♩. ♪ or ♩. ♫ are to be rendered approximately ♩.. ⅞♪ and ♩.. ⅞♫ respectively. Because such rhythmic incisiveness or "jerkiness" became to be considered an essential element of the style, the idea was extended to other rhythmic designs that occur frequently in French overtures, where an upbeat figure of three or more notes is separated from its left neighbor by a rest such as ♩ ⅞♫♩ or ♩. ⅞♫♩ and, in analogy, as we have seen, even to the pattern ♩ ♫♫ of the C-minor version.

A few years ago I examined the whole issue of this French overture style and found that the doctrine of its obligatory sharp "overdotting" (a term coined by Bodky) was built on defective evidence.[8] I pointed out that the alleged French convention, which is supposed to apply to overtures and suite movements from Lully to Rameau and to include Bach and Handel, is not supported by any French theoretical source. Instead, the doctrine is based on two German sources of the mid-18th century, namely, passages from the treatises of J.J. Quantz (1752) and C.P.E. Bach (1753). Of these two, C.P.E. Bach has to be eliminated on two counts: 1) he makes no reference to French music—let alone to overtures and suites; 2) the confused and obscure passage which Dolmetsch used (but misquoted by adding two whole sentences which Bach did not write), does not say what it is alleged to say. This is made evident in a lucid passage in the second volume of the treatise. In the latter Bach says that the dot is often lengthened, but sometimes played precisely, and sometimes shortened, and that it would be a mistake to limit its rendition to one style only: "if one makes a rule of one type of execution, one loses the other ones."[9] Speaking of *German* music and rejecting a limiting manner of execution, C.P.E. Bach can hardly be a convincing witness for obligatory sharp overdotting in the French overture style. Quantz alone remains, and he, too, presented the overdotting first as a *general* practice which has become somewhat of a mannerism in the Germany of the *galant* era. Only in a later chapter, devoted to the duties of accompanists, does he apply the principle of overdotting to French dances.[10] I explained also why certain French musical evidence—such as the peculiarities in the notation of Gigault and Couperin who often added one or more extra flags or beams to their short notes—carried no implication for overdotting. Finally, I was able to present much musical evidence that contradicted the doctrine. (More remains to be presented on another occasion.)

As is so often the case with mistaken theories, the Dolmetsch doctrine contains kernels of truth. But it mistakes an artistic license for a strict obligation, and it has been projected far beyond its legitimate range of application.

One of the "kernels" resides in the thoroughly documented French *notes inégales* convention according to which certain evenly written notes in certain specific meters (such as eighth-notes in 2 meter) were rendered unevenly, to wit: short-long, in a lilting pulse. The degree of unevenness varied, ranging from an approximately 3:2 to a 2:1 ratio, rarely exceeding the latter. When a greater unevenness was intended, the French wrote dotted notes.[11] As a consequence of this uneven pulse, we find that in such works where the eighths are *inégales* the dotted quarter-notes will be somewhat lengthened, the companion eighths correspondingly shortened because the dot takes the place of the longer first of the uneven notes[12]:

This is what Jacques Hotteterre had in mind when he wrote in his *Méthode pour la Musette* (1738), that in movements in which the eighth-notes are *inégales,* the dot after a quarter-note is the equivalent of a dotted eighth-note (using the dotted note here as a makeshift symbol for a generally lesser inequality). As I pointed out in discussing this quotation, the usually mild lengthening of the *notes inégales* is a far cry from the extremes postulated by the doctrine.[13] Moreover, it applies to *all* French music, not only to overture-suites.

Being tied to the *Inégales* convention, such lengthening of the dot does *not* occur in C meter in which all eighth-notes are strictly equal. Hence in such overtures as Lully's *Bellérophone,* or in all of Dieupart's overture-suites for the harpsichord, the *notes inégales* would not have affected the length of the dotted quarter-notes; even assuming against all probability that Handel had honored the French *inégales* convention, not a single one of his overtures would be thus affected, since they are all written in C meter.

The second kernel of truth resides in the imprecision of the dot during most of the 17th and 18th centuries in *all* national styles. Though theoretically the dot stood for one half of the principal note's value, in practice it was flexible in both directions. Usually it did have its exact meaning, but it could simply stand for an undetermined increment. Often it signified exactly one fourth: for instance when Bach and many of his contemporaries and predecessors wrote ♩. ♫ they meant ♩ ♫ The latter is simply a more precise notation for such "underdotting". More frequently still the dot signified one third when the pair ♫ was a makeshift notation for the unavailable ♩₃♪ .[14] Similar shortenings of the dots were practiced when the "affect" of the piece called for gentler rhythms. On the other hand, the dot could be lengthened when the textbook relationship of 3:1 was, as Leopold Mozart put it, "too sleepy." The above-mentioned *galant* mannerism of such frequent lengthening, is reflected in a number of German treatises after those of Quantz and C.P.E. Bach. Some authors (Löhlein, for example) advocate it as a quasi-rule; others take note of this practice but (as C.P.E. Bach did in the above quotation) qualify it strongly as only one of several manners; some condemn it outright, for instance Marpurg and G.F. Wolf, or reject it implicitly as did Hiller.[15] Moreover, what all these Germans in the second half of the 18th century wrote about overdotting (including Quantz's *first* statement) is totally unrelated to the French overture-suite which by mid-17th century had actually gone out of fashion.

These, then, are in briefest summary the meager facts behind the legend of "jerkiness" as an essential feature of the French overture-suite style: a mild lengthening of the dot whenever *notes inégales* applied, valid for *all* French music with no specific link to the overtures and often not even applicable to the latter; secondly, the freedom of the performer to lengthen as well as shorten the dot according to the "affect," valid for *all* music of *all* nations; thirdly, a—spotty—German *galant* mannerism with no reference to any kind of French style.

Michael Collins attempted to salvage the Dolmetsch theory of obligatory intense overdotting in the French overture-suite (thereby revising his own earlier theory of obligatory *under*dotting in the "French style").[16]

Here I shall deal with Collins's arguments only as far as they concern Bach's French Overture with its central rhythm pattern: ♩ 𝄢 (hereafter referred to as the "C-minor pattern") but shall discuss on another occasion his ideas regarding the simple dotted pattern of French overtures.

Collins shows the opening measures of both versions of Bach's French Overture (see above, ex. 1) and declares that "obviously" they have to be played in the same rhythm.[17] It is not clear why the identity of rhythm should be obvious, not even if one were to take the Dolmetsch doctrine for granted: the C-minor pattern can not be "overdotted" for the simple reason that it contains no dot. The only known theoretical source that might appear to link this pattern with the alleged convention of obligatory overdotting, is a passage in Quantz (chap. 17, sec. 7, par. 58) where, speaking of the orchestra accompanying French dances, he says: "when three or more thirty-seconds follow a dot or rest they are not always played according to their proper value, especially in slow pieces, but at the extreme end of their assigned time and with the greatest of speed." Then he points to their frequent occurrence in *"Overtures, Entrées and Furies."*

If, just for argument's sake, we assume the Quantz's (dance orchestra) rule applies to Bach—which is far from self-evident—it would apply to the B-minor version where Quantz's conditions are fulfilled since we find three or more thirty-seconds after dots. These figures would then have to be played as fast as possible. The rule would *not* apply to the C-minor pattern that has neither dots, nor rests, nor thirty-seconds: all three of Quantz's conditions are missing. In claiming that the C-minor pattern has to follow Quantz's directives, Collins overlooks the absence of dots and rests[18] but is concerned about the absence of thirty-seconds. He tries to overcome this difficulty by claiming that the notation has changed. Lully, Georg Muffat, and D'Anglebert, he says, never place three or more thirty-seconds after dots or rests in their overtures. Instead they use the sixteenths figures: [musical notation] . On the other hand, Collins says, Gottlieb Muffat, Dieupart, J.K.F. Fischer, and Rameau all use thirty-seconds: [musical notation] .[19] Handel's practice he continues, is especially illuminating. With only *two* exceptions those overtures between 1705 and 1738 that have upbeat figures, have them in sixteenth-notes. After 1738 Handel "modernizes his notation" to thirty-seconds. "All this clearly shows that as the eighteenth century progressed composers turned to a somewhat more accurate representation of musical meaning. It is therefore not surprising that Quantz in 1752 speaks only of the demisemiquavers in common usage at the time he was writing." The argument which is meant to prove that Quantz's rule regarding thirty-seconds, applies to sixteenths as well, fails to convince. Even if later masters had written *only* thirty-second upbeat figures where Lully had written sixteenths, and if Handel had used exclusively sixteenths until 1738 and exclusively thirty-seconds after that date, such developments could still be more plausibly explained by a change of style than by a change of notation. However, no such simple shift from sixteenths to thirty-seconds has taken place. The later masters used the thirty-second upbeat figures not in place of, but concurrently with sixteenths, as well as with sixty-fourths and with eighth-note figures. This simply shows that after Lully's time the rhythmic scope of the overtures expanded to cover a wider range of designs from mild and stately to sharp and agitated ones.[20] Concerning the Handel evidence, there were not two, but eighteen Overtures written between 1705 and 1738 with upbeat figures of three or more thirty-second-notes after dots or rests, and three more Overtures with thirty-second-notes starting from a tie.[21] Regarding Handel's "modernized" notation after 1738, the upbeat figures in Overtures are now rare, but here, too, no new developments could be discerned. In the Overture to his last opera, *Deidamia* of 1740, Handel uses sixteenths: [musical notation] side by side with thirty-seconds: [musical notation] . *Susanna* of 1748 has the pattern: [musical notation] and the C minor pattern: [musical notation] and in *Theodora* of 1749 the latter pattern occurs in the following combination: [musical notation] no less than fourteen times. Clearly there was no change in Handel's notation of the upbeat figures. Thus the theory of notational development failed to restore *one* of Quantz's three conditions for use in Bach's C minor version. Since the two other conditions, the "dots or rests," were absent and overlooked, the only theoretical source for the compression of the upbeat figures has to be disqualified on all three counts.

The *notes inégales* are no help here either. They would only result in the pattern: ♩ 𝅘𝅥𝅯𝅘𝅥𝅯𝅘𝅥𝅯   but not in rhythmic contraction. Neither can the flexible dot be invoked, because there is no dot; on the contrary, as mentioned above, the notation   ♩ 𝅘𝅥𝅯𝅘𝅥𝅯𝅘𝅥𝅯   was a more accurate, more "modern" spelling for ♩. 𝅘𝅥𝅯𝅘𝅥𝅯   and indeed was used as an antidote against the flexible dot, as protection against the very danger of extending its meaning for more than the intended one-fourth of the principal's note value.

But let us go one step further: let us, again for argument's sake, assume that the alleged convention did exist and did apply to the C-minor pattern, then take a look at the implications.

In the second source of this early version, the Preller manuscript, the upbeat figures are throughout strewn with ornaments of which example 3 gives a characteristic illustration. The graces would be unplayable in contracted rhythm. Whether these ornaments have any connection with Bach is impossible to establish, but Preller obviously was not aware of the alleged convention.[22]

Ex. 3.

MS J. G. Preller

In measures 11 and 12 (given in ex. 4a in the P 226 reading, in b in the B-minor version) we would have to assume that whereas Bach spelled out the sharpened rhythms for the left hand he relied on the convention to achieve the same effect for the right hand. The next measure presents a special problem with sixteenth-note upbeat figures in both hands which seem to call for synchronization. Yet to match the solution of the B-minor version, the player would have to guess that the convention applied to the right hand but not to the left. Then in measures 17—20 (given for P 226 in ex. c) we find upbeat patterns for both hands written in the identical sharpened rhythm of the B-minor version. True, Bach was often inconsistent but never in a way and to a degree that would completely confuse the performer or present him with such near-insoluble puzzles as offered in measure 13.

Ex. 4.

Ex. 5.

Greater trouble still awaits the convention in the overtures to Bach's orchestral suites. The first two measures of the C-major Overture (BWV 1066), given in example 5, already lead the convention *ad absurdum.* Many similar spots in the same work repeat the message. In Overture No. 3 in D major (BWV 1068), measures 5, 13, and 14 in the continuo; measure 15 in oboes, violins and continuo; in Overture No. 4 in D major (BWV 1069), measure 3 in oboes and violins, offer similar evidence. So does the opening of Cantata 119 whose first movement is a French overture that contains many thirty-second figures; its first measure has sixteenth-note upbeat figures that are not contractable.

These examples should prove that the sixteenth-note upbeat figures starting from a tie were meant to be played as written. Yet stronger evidence is still available. Not infrequently the upbeat figures are written in eighth-notes in which case no theory of notational evolution could conceivably link them with Quantz's thirty-second patterns. Lully's Overture to *Proserpine* (1680) has such figures as shown in example 6a. D'Anglebert in his harpsichord transcription of this overture (in his *Pièces de Clavecin* of 1689) emphasizes the slowness of these figures by adding ornaments (ex. b gives a brief excerpt; the comma after the note stands for a mordent).

Ex. 6.

a) Lully, Ouverture to *Proserpine* (Skeleton Score)

b) d'Anglebert's transcription
m. 5

Dieupart uses upbeat figures in three of six overtures, (from his *Six Suittes de Clavessin . . .* of ca. 1702) and in all three of these, they are written in eighth-notes (exx. 7 a-c give their starting measures). Rameau's similar figures from his Overture to *Les Indes Galantes* are shown in example 7d.

Ex. 7.

d) Rameau, *Les Indes galantes*, Ouverture

For German illustrations examples 8a and b show the start of two Overtures by Mattheson, one from his Sonata op. 1 No. 2 for two flutes, the other from Sonata op. 1 No. 7 for three flutes. Both contain upbeat figures in eighth-notes which resist any attempt at contraction into sharper rhythms.

The sixteenth-note figures have shown, and the eighth-note figures emphatically underscored, the fact that rhythmic sharpness, let alone jerkiness was not an essential characteristic of the French overture.

Ex. 8.

Mattheson a) Sonata for two flutes op. 1 No. 2, Ouverture

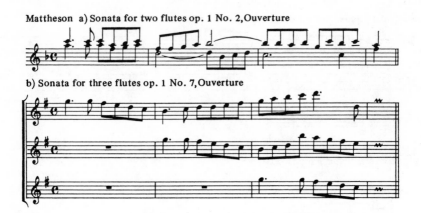

b) Sonata for three flutes op. 1 No. 7, Ouverture

Returning to Bach's two versions, it should now be clear that the first was meant as written. Whether we agree with Emery that such a rendition is "duller," or with David that it is "grander and more natural," is purely a matter of individual taste; it has no bearing on the question of historical performance.

8

Facts and Fiction About Overdotting (FN3)

Paul Henry Lang, in his review of Daniel Heartz's edition of *Idomeneo* for the *Neue Mozart-Ausgabe* (in the January 1974 issue of *The Musical Quarterly*) mentions "Aufführungspraxis-mad editors and performers, who go strictly by the book," and with a felicitous expression speaks of a "demi-science" whose exponents and disciples misuse ornamentation and apply "double dotting" or *notes inégales* in improper contexts. As an example he cites a recording of *Don Giovanni* in which the conductor doubledots the heavily striding basses at the beginning of the overture and in the great final scene. This unsettling report prompted me to return to the question of doubledotting in the seventeenth and eighteenth centuries. "Return," because I have previously published a study that challenged the prevailing doctrines on this matter.[1] These doctrines claim a so-called "French overture style" in which dotted notes are supposed to be strongly overdotted[2] by excessive lengthening of the dot or by corresponding insertion of rests.

The present vogue of this performing manner may have possibly started in nineteenth-century England, where, according to Peter Larsen, the overdotting of the overture to *Messiah* has been the leading tradition since Ebenezer Prout (1835-1909).[3] However, by far the most powerful impulse came from Arnold Dolmetsch, who, in his famous book of 1915, culled the principle of sharp overdotting from two passages in Quantz and C.P.E. Bach.[4] Though admitting he had found no earlier sources, Dolmetsch applies the procedure of vigorously sharpened rhythms to Bach and Handel. He illustrates how the Sinfonia from *Messiah* (a French overture), though written thus, $\overset{\text{Grave}}{\mathbf{¢}}$ ♩. ♪♩. ♪| ♩. ♫♩. ♪, should be played ♩. ⁊ ♪♩. ⁊♪ | ♩. ⁊♫♩. ⁊♪ . He gives analogous interpretations for the E-flat Minor Prelude and the D major Fugue from Bach's *Well-Tempered Clavier,* Book I, and lists a number of other works by

Reprinted with permission from *The Musical Quarterly* 63 (1977), pp. 155-85.

these two composers that should be comparably treated. Dolmetsch did not refer to this practice of overdotting as being of French origin, and he mentions neither French overtures nor dance forms. The connection was made by his followers, who coined the term "French overture style" to indicate the archetype of the practice.

Among Dolmetsch's followers, Thurston Dart gave us perhaps the most succinct formulation of this doctrine when he wrote: "In an overture in the French style...all the parts should move together, *jerkily* [italics mine] even when their written note-values do not suggest that this is how they should be played. *All* dotted rhythms should be adjusted so that they fit the shortest one in the piece."[5] This rule is to be applied also to the dance movements of the French ballet suite, such as, notably, the courantes, sarabandes, gigues, and chaconnes. Robert Donington likewise speaks of the "French overture style" and sees in it a convenient term for a general baroque practice of overdotting, acknowledging its spread to other nations, forms, and styles.[6] Michael Collins writes that overdotting applies at least "from the time of Lully to that of Haydn and Mozart and that the practice was introduced into Germany along with French ornamentation by Muffat and J.K.F. Fischer. That it applies at least to the works in French style—*overtures, courantes, sarabandes,* etc. of J.S. Bach, Handel, Telemann is certain, and it no doubt applies to all music except that of a languid, expressive character in the *galant* and classical style."[7] Perhaps the only Frenchman to endorse this essentially Anglo-Saxon/Germanic doctrine, A. Geoffroy-Dechaume relies, like Dolmetsch, on Quantz and C.P.E. Bach, and applies overdotting to Lully's *Alceste* Overture,[8] as had Dart before him. Daniel Heartz, in the preface to his above-mentioned edition of *Idomeneo*, suggests doubledotting for that opera's overture, giving as a rationale the strong French style elements in that opera. Even the skeptical Paul Henry Lang is willing to acquiesce in this suggestion in that one is moving within the frame of the French style, where he, too, feels that overdotting has a rightful place.

Many other musicologists accept the "French overture style" as fact so solidly established that, outside of France, very few (Hans T. David was one of these) have ever questioned its legitimacy or felt the need to take a closer look at its credentials. In my above-mentioned article I tried to do just that and came to the conclusion that the "French overture style" is essentially a myth wrapped around a small nucleus of fact. As this article of mine has since been strongly challenged, my purpose in the present study is to reaffirm and strengthen my original findings by presenting new evidence, both theoretical and musical, and by attempting to clarify widespread confusions, to answer specific criticism, and in the process to separate fact from fiction.

The confusion that envelops the question of overdotting in the seventeenth and eighteenth centuries is due to the complexity of the issue, which cannot be reduced to a single "convention" with a clearcut set of simple rules. Overdotting certainly was practiced (and so was underdotting), but it was done under various musical categories. A failure to distinguish these different and in some instances totally unrelated categories has disposed researchers to trace them all to a single chimerical source, the "French overture style." The following are some of the more important relevant categories that will be here discussed in some detail: 1) in France (and France alone)[9] the *notes inégales;* 2) inaccuracies of notation; 3) *occasional* synchronization; 4) *Nachschlag*-type ornaments that follow a dot; 5) freedom of the performer in the interpretation of the score; and 6) a (spotty) German *galant* mannerism of doubledotting. In order to place these categories in better perspective, I shall first present some documents that stress the regularity of the dot, with special emphasis on France, the alleged homeland of the style.

In France every single one of the numerous treatises of the seventeenth and eighteenth centuries that mention the dot describes it unfailingly as signifying one-half of the preceding note's value. Not one mentions in this connection— the obvious place to refer to exceptions—*any* kind of lengthening. This total reticence contrasts strikingly with a correspondingly total coverage of the *notes inégales* rules in all treatises on performance, even the briefest and simplest ones addressed to children. Georg Muffat, in his long and detailed preface to his *Florilegium secundum* of 1698, dedicated to the purpose of introducing his German compatriots to all the fine points of the "Lullian style" as embodied in the overture and dance suite, follows the same pattern. He, too, carefully explains the *notes inégales;* he, too, omits any mention of overdotting, though the main body of his volume consists only of French overtures and dances.

Inferences about the basic precision of the dot can also be gathered from mechanical instruments. Engramelle, in his *Tonotechnie* of 1776, as well as in the section written by him on the mechanical organ in Bedos de Celles's monumental work on organ-building,[10] discusses extensively the *notes inégales* and applies them in their proper contexts. By contrast, the dotted notes are mentioned only in connection with articulation. Engramelle displays through-out an encompassing concern for articulation, notably for the time a note is actually held, as opposed to the time literally implied by its notation. He speaks of a *silence d'articulation* that occupies the time difference between notated and executed length, and distinguishes *tenues,* i.e., notes that are followed by a relatively short rest, and *tactées,* composed of a very short sound and a long rest. He states the principle that of two quarter-notes or eighth-notes that move by twos the first is always a *tenue,* the second a *tactée* (thus, c ♩ ♩ would be performed approximately ♪· 𝄽 ♪ 𝄾). This principle of alternation of *tenues* and *tactées* in binary patterns allows, he says, so few exceptions that in cases where a dotted quarter-note is followed by an 8th-note, this dot which lengthens the quarter-note by one-half, takes the place of a first eighth-note, hence the eighth-note that follows the dot, being a second one, must be a *tactée*.[11] This is *not* overdotting; the *tactée* is strongly clipped at the end, but enters exactly on time.

In the music examples with corresponding cylinder notations (which are found only in Bedos de Celles's treatise) there happen to be very few dotted notes, perhaps only three. One of these is an illustration of the *cadence jettée* (plate 107), which incidentally shows the complete anticipation of the trill. In its attendant cylinder notation we can measure that the eighth-note following the dot enters mathematically on time—even though in 3 meter the eighth-notes are *inégales*—but it is, like the first eighth-note of the example, a *tactée* with a length of slightly more than a sixty-fourth-note. There are two similar cases of dotted notes in Balbastre's *Barcelonette* (plate 118). Both show the same pattern: mathematically exact entrance, with extreme shortness of articulation.

The *vielle*, a mechanical string instrument activated by the turning of a wheel, offers similar information. Michel Corrette in his method for this instrument writes: "Since the dot after a note lengthens it by one half, one must consequently extend the turn of the wheel by one-half. In ₵ or 2 meter, the dotted half-note gets one and a half turns of the wheel, the dotted quarter-note three-fourths of a turn; in this meter the eighth-notes are played *inégales*."[12] Again we find side by side a mention of the *notes inégales* and a mathematically exact dot.

This mathematical evidence is matched by C.R. Brijon's instructions about the disposition of the bow in playing dotted notes on the violin. In his treatise of the instrument Brijon discusses various dotted patterns, and in all of them the dot turns out to be of exact standard length.[13] Speaking of the dotted quarter-note, Brijon asks that the whole bow be used for either note. In so doing for the eighth-note, he specifies that it be played "with three times the speed of the dotted note." With equal expenditure of bow, the triple speed mathematically establishes the 3:1 ratio. Regarding the pattern 2 ⌐⌐⌐⌐ Brijon says: "If the first dotted eighth is taken on the upbow, one uses three-quarters of the bow beginning at the point; one slightly takes the bow off the string, and with the remaining length one takes the sixteenth-note still on the upbow. For the third note one takes the whole length of the downbow, moving the bow one-quarter faster than for the first note. The fourth note is taken in upbow, starting it in the middle of the bow and moving fast to the frog at twice the speed used for the second of the four notes." Here again the exact prescription for bow length and speed relationships confirms the mathematical exactness of the dot's standard value. This second example is even more remarkable than the first, because in 2 meter the eighth-notes are *inégales* and would therefore be susceptible to a slight lengthening of the dot. Even if we were to ignore the conclusive directives about bow speed, a division of the bow in 2:1 ratio would, at the implied lively speed (eighth-notes in 2 meter), be more conducive to a shortening of the dot, while totally precluding any overdotting. Finally, speaking of the figure 𝆕 𝆔 in 2 or 3 meter, Brijon's instructions call for alternating bows, , and the use of one-quarter bow for each sixteenth-note, which again favors shortening of the dot and effectively prevents its lengthening. To play the short notes in the "French style" would call for the extreme end of the bow.

The standard value of the single dot is also indicated when it is juxtaposed with its lengthening in exact notation either by the use of the double dot, or by a tie, 𝆕 𝅘𝅥· 𝅘𝅥, or a rest, 𝆕· 𝄾𝅘𝅥. The double dot was used by a number of French masters in the late seventeenth century. It can be found profusely in André Raison, is frequent in the famous seventeenth century Bauyn manuscript, is used by Chambonnières and later, more sporadically, by Clérambault, Corrette, and Hotteterre. Thus when Raison writes as shown in example 1a or Chambonnières as in example 1b, the presumption is strong that the single dots were meant as written.

Ex. 1a. Raison, *Benedicimus te*   Ex. 1b. Chambonnières, *Second Livre,* Allemande

Lully did not use the double dot, nor did François Couperin, Rameau, nor any Italian or German master before the mid-eighteenth century. But all masters, with hardly an exception, used the tie or the rest to indicate doubledotting. When Lully starts the prologue to *Armide* as given in example 2, the doubledotted quarter-notes of the violins in the second and third measures contrast with the single dotted notes that precede and follow; at the same time they clash rhythmically in the second measure with the eighth-notes of the violas and the bass. The very explicitness of the ties excludes the assumption of inadvertence.

Ex. 2. Lully, *Armide,* Prologue

The advocates of the "French overture style" would eliminate both types of variety, by treating every dotted note with equal sharpness and synchronizing the companion notes in all the voices after reducing them to the smallest "jerk" value. However, it makes no musical sense to deny a composer the precious musical resource of both horizontal and vertical rhythmic variety by the free use of milder and sharper dotted rhythms in melodic succession as well as in polyphonic interplay. And he would be denied this resource if his precise notation were to be automatically obliterated by the leveling procedures of the doctrine. Notated variety would be turned into monumental rhythmic monotony. The principle of nonsynchronization is particularly vital for polyphonic textures, because it helps to bring the independence of the voices into plastic relief. To expect voices to be melodically independent but rhythmically handcuffed is self-defeating, because their melodic independence would for all practical purposes become inaudible.

Similar examples are legion. Michael Collins is disturbed by the fact that Handel uses both ♩· ♪ and ♩· 𝄾♪ in the same overtures, the first of which he considers an old-fashioned, the second a modernized notation: he considers this a "vagary" and says that "there seems . . . to be a tendency to use the latter pattern when it coincides with ♩· 𝄾♪ the better to indicate the simultaneity of the last notes of each pattern." The facts do not bear this out. Like Lully, Handel uses the milder and sharper rhythms both in succession and simultaneity—even more so than Lully, since he used a wider range of rhythmic figures as shown, e.g., in example 3.[14]

Ex. 3.   Handel, *Alexander's Feast* (1736), Overture

To prove synchronization by overdotting, Collins cites the sinfonia from *Hercules* (1751), where the oboes and first violins have throughout the pattern ♩· 𝄾♪ against the simple dots ♩· ♪ of the harmony parts. "Surely the lead of the melodic part is to be followed by the rest." Why? Such rhythmic diversity might surprise the eye but pleases the ear. How are we to resolve the opposite situation, e.g., in Oriana's aria from *Amadigi* (1715) where the voice sings throughout in single dotted notes and all the instruments including the unison violins play in sharpened rhythm:

The same is the case in Handel's Funeral Anthem No. 2 of 1737.[15] Are the accompanying instruments here, too, to follow the melodic lead and give up their sharpened rhythms? And how about Don Ottavio's aria (see ex. 4), where the first violins in melodic unison with the voice have in measure 1 and 4 a sharpened rhythm and in measures 2 and 4 a sharpened articulation; or Pedrillo's "Romance" from *Die Entführung* with the unison dotted pizzicato violins in measures 8 and 12-16 and in parallel spots. Of course nobody is to follow anybody. Mozart, and Handel before him, meant what they put down, because they wrote idiomatically for the voice that calls for rounder lines, while adding a delightful touch of rhythmic spice through the sharper dotting of the instruments. It is the same rhythmic spice that enriched the flavor of the *Hercules* sinfonia.[16]

Ex. 4.   Mozart, *Don Giovanni*

Ex. 5.   Bach, Cantata 29, first mvt.

Horizontal alternation of single and double dots in a homophonic setting is shown in example 5, from Bach's Cantata 29/1. We see in the melody a double dot, written by a tie, sandwiched between two single dots. This is no "vagary" that calls for assimilating overdotting. The exact meaning of the single dots is confirmed by the notation of the third trumpet and the timpani.

With respect to polyphonic settings examples 6a and b show two specimens from calligraphic Bach autographs, where the clear vertical line-up reveals the rhythmic clash of a longer and shorter dotted note, not their overdotted synchronization.[17] In the Contrapunctus 6 "in stile francese" of the second example the clashes are imperative, because the dotted theme is repeatedly set against its own diminution. That the dotted chaconne rhythms in Bach's work for violin solo were meant as written is obvious from (among others) the passage of example 6c.

Ex. 6.   a.   BWV 654 (autograph)   b.   *Art of Fugue*, Contrapunctus 6 (autograph)

c.   Ciaccona

With all due allowance for inconsistencies on the part of many great masters—whenever it mattered little—we have to assume a modicum of rationality in their notation. Thus when they wrote ♩. ♪♩. ⅞ ♪ or the like, not once, but innumerable times, the explanation that they meant the identical doubledotting, but wrote the first half of the bar in old-fashioned, the second in modern notation, is suspect by its weird complexity, when a far simpler one is available: that they meant what they wrote. In science the superiority of simplicity is axiomatic. The same should be true of musicology.

The "French overture style" is the alleged fountainhead of all sharp overdotting in Western music from Lully to Mozart. Yet, in spite of intensive search, nobody has so far found a genuine French documentation to authenticate the doctrine. Such documentation as has been brought forward by Collins and Donington is misleading, chiefly because of a confusion with the *notes inégales*. Since the latter present, for France, a hard kernel of fact related to occasional lengthening of dots, we have to take a look at them and dwell in particular on their mildness, because this very mildness disqualifies them as the missing link to the doctrine.[18]

The *notes inégales* were part of the French musical syntax from the seventeenth century (with earlier roots) to about the Revolution. Several things about them are pertinent to our quest.

1. The application of the *notes inégales* was regulated by strict principles of meter/note-value relationships, as well as by the requirement of essentially stepwise motion. Thus eighth-notes were *inégales* in 3, 2, and ₵ meter, sixteenth-notes in C meter, etc. Whenever the *notes inégales* applied to a piece, the subdivisions of a beat moved in a lilting long-short rhythm. Hence in the pattern ♩ the dot takes the place of the first and

   longer eighth-note and is therefore extended according to the degree of *inégalité* applied on the occasion.
2. *Inégalité* applies to *all* kinds of French music, with the exception of the Italianate sonatas and concertos.
3. The *inégalité* was predominantly mild, as is attested by a wide consensus of theorists. It ranged, directed by the *goût,* from an almost imperceptible unevenness to an approximate maximum of a 2:1 ratio. Its range was much narrower than has been assumed by most modern writers. Thus, among others, Donington (who erroneously claims an international currency for the *inégalité* rules) describes its range as extending from a mild "lilting" triplet rhythm or smoother, to a "vigorous" one of "dotted rhythm or sharper."[19]

Such misconceptions about strong *inégalité* stem from two main sources, both related to the dot. One is the fact that in the absence of the unavailable notation the dotted note was the only available graphic device to represent *any* kind of long-short unevenness. Theorists who have used this notation to illustrate *inégalité* (among them Georg Muffat, Hotteterre, La Chapelle) have misled some modern researchers into taking this makeshift device on its face value. The second source of misunderstanding is the term *pointer* (used by many French theorists to indicate *inégalité* ["nous pointons les croches"]) which was again too readily taken in its literal sense of standard dotting. Actually the term denoted an increment of undetermined and often minuscule size. Thus, the author of a famous vocal treatise of 1668, Bénigne de Bacilly, in recommending *notes inégales* for improvised diminutions, speaks of "poincts alternatifs" but cautions that they be applied with such subtlety that the "dotting" is hardly noticeable [notes *pointées si finement* (italics mine) que cela ne paroisse pas].[20] Hotteterre defines *pointer* as making (in C meter) of two sixteenth-notes one long and one short [une longue et une brève], which certainly falls short of suggesting a 3:1 ratio.[21] Buterne writes that *passer* and *pointer* mean that the first of the *inégales* is "longer than the second" [la premiére... plus longue que la seconde].[22] Duval, concerned about the misleading use of the word *pointer,* says: " 'Dotting' is an improper term for *inégalité"* [Pointer se dit improprement pour faire les croches inégalles].[23] Couperin gives for his allemande *La Laborieuse* the instruction "the sixteenth-notes ever so slightly dotted" [Les double croches un tant soit peu pointées].[24]

The deceptiveness of the dotted illustrations and of the term *pointer* is confirmed by other important theorists who specify the mildness of *inégalité.* Loulié speaks of two types of unevenness. The first, contingent on stepwise motion, he calls *lourer,* whereby the first of a pair of notes is held "a little longer" [un peu plus longue]. The second type, in which the first is "much longer than the second," he calls *pointer* or *piquer* but this type "has to be marked with a dot" [doit avoir un point].[25] Clearly only the *lourer* with its mild unevenness represents *notes inégales,* since the concept of *inégalité* refers solely to evenly written pairs of notes. Loulié, in manuscript supplements to his treatise, indicates the mildness of the *lourer* by the ingenious design ♩. ♩♩. ♩.[26] Montéclair says the first note should be held "a little longer" ("un peu plus longue") than the second one and, by illustrating this explanation as follows— 2 ♪♪♪♪ like ♪♪♪♪ —offers incidentally the clearest possible proof that the dotted representation of *inégalité* can stand for a very mild ratio of unevenness.[27] He confirms this fact in a later and more detailed treatise by saying that the second eighth-note must be rendered "a little faster" than the first [cette seconde croche doit passer un peu plus vite que la première].[28] Similary, Villeneuve—"one renders the second eighth-note a little faster" [un peu plus vite];[29] Choquel—"the first of two even notes that form a beat must be held a little longer than the second"[la première des deux qui forment un temps doit estre tenue un peu plus longtemps que la seconde];[30] Mercadier de Belesta—"the first a little longer than the second" [la première un peu plus longue que la seconde];[31] and Jean Jacques Rousseau—"In Italian music, all eighth-notes are always of equal length, except when followed by a dot. In French music, however, the eighth-notes are equal only in C meter; in all others one dots them always a little [on les pointe toujours un peu] except when *Croches égales* is written."[32] And so it goes on and on with the monotonous refrain not contradicted by a single theorist, that *inégalité* was a gentle lilt ("a little longer... ") and nothing more, proving conclusively that the idea of vigorous inequality, equivalent to and occasionally exceeding a dotted note, is based on misunderstanding.

Finally let us look again at Engramelle—at both his *Tonotechnie* and his essay for Bedos de Celles's book. Though in theory he stakes out a range of *inégalité* from a 7:5 to a 3:1 ratio (the latter reserved for marches and their like), in practice, in the given examples—even in the *Marches du Roy* Nos. 1 and 2 from the *Tonotechnie*[33]—and in the cylinder notations in *L'Art du facteur d'orgue* the sharpest ratio to be found is 2:1, and this occurs only when in an assimilation to triplets in the *Romance* by Balbastre. Everywhere else the ratio is throughout milder. Interesting is Engramelle's comment that *inégalité* is stronger in lively than in slower or graceful pieces,[34] for this observation permits us to infer very mild *inégalité* only for overtures, chaconnes, sarabandes, and loures.

As an inescapable conclusion from the evidence presented we see that the *notes inégales* fail to support the "French overture style": their mildness sets them far apart from the "jerky" style of the doctrine. Dotted illustration of them was a makeshift device, the term *pointer* a misnomer. Besides, they have no special relationship to either overtures or dance movements, and often, when the meter is not right, they are not even applicable at all to this central core of the doctrine.

Further cause for the dot's changing value in *both* directions lay in certain inaccuracies or limitations of notation as practiced in those times. The pattern: ♩ ♪ was, as mentioned above, unavailable, and to fill the gap the dotted note was used as a makeshift substitute.[35] Thus, when in a binary meter, triplets in one voice are set against dotted notes in another (♩. ♩) as well as where a

dotted note is embedded in a sequence of triplets (⁹₄ ♫ ♫ ♫) the probability is strong that the dotted note is used in ternary meaning. This makeshift use of the dotted note was common throughout the seventeenth and eighteenth centuries and well into the nineteenth, Schubert and Chopin included. In Bach innumerable are the examples in which external or internal evidence point to this meaning. For him this meaning was so routine that he often used the dotted note even in a triple meter where he did not need a makeshift. A particularly telling example occurs in the autograph organ chorale BWV 626 where he writes as shown in example 7a; another in the late autograph of Cantata 110/1 (ex. 7b). In this French overture (parodied from the Fourth Orchestral Suite) the middle section of 9/8 is filled with dotted eighth-notes instead of the logical ♩ ♪ . Still more striking for the spontaneous synonymity of such notation is example 7c (which I owe to the late Walter Emery), where, for the same spot, the continuo in the autograph score has a ternary notation in a binary meter, the autograph organ part has dotted notes in an (alternative) ternary meter.

Ex. 7a. BWV 626 (autograph)

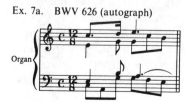

Organ

Ex. 7b. Cantata 110, first mvt. (autograph)

Ob. III

Vln. II

Ex. 7c.   Cantata 94, sixth mvt.

In spite of all this, such ternary synonymity, though with Bach probably intended in the vast majority of cases, is not a foregone conclusion. In certain works by him and by other composers[36] the short note after the dot *could*, especially in slow tempos, be meant to be played after the third note of the triplet; either in its exact value, to clarify an intended binary/ternary contrast, or in an overdotted 5:1 relationship, dividing the last note of the triplet in half, which is easier to do and can be musically satisfying.

A shortening of the dot to exactly one fourth of the value of the preceding note occurred in the frequent notation of ♩· 𝄽 taking the place of ♩ 𝄽 . Since the tie was available, this imprecision was avoidable but widely used and understood. Among theorists we find this notation explained by Sperling in 1705 and Schmelz in 1752.[37] Bach used it throughout his life side by side with the precise notation offered by the tie.[38] We also find Bach using the dot with similarly halved value in such rhythmic designs as

found in measures 2, 3 (twice), and 11 of the allemande of the A Minor Partita for harpsichord.

Notational irregularites that lengthen as well as shorten the dot are explained in the above-cited manuscript fragments by Loulié. After giving the standard rule for the dot, he writes that it sometimes "augments the note by 1/8, or 1/4, or 3/8, or 1/2, or 5/8, or 3/4, or 7/8 . . . in any given place, the time-value of the dot is regulated by the notes which follow." Meaning that the dot simply fills the space left, he gives, as illustrations for the above, the following rhythms:[39]

Though many of these patterns are very rare in French music, the fourth example is of particular interest to us because it shows that the dot in its standard notation has its exact value of 3:1. We must realize that, though these patterns illustrate the variability of the dot, they are not, properly speaking, cases of over- or underdotting. These terms are logically applicable only to dots that are written in standard fashion but performed with nonstandard values.

This is no semantic hairsplitting, because an *irregular notation* that implies an exact nonstandard length of the dot does not admit the inference of an obligatory over- or underdotting for a dot written in standard notation—and that is what the whole issue is about.

While the principle of an obligatory synchronization whatever the style or form is untenable, there are situations where a musical need for synchronization arises that has to be met by genuine overdotting. Such a need will most likely occur in a homophonic setting where simultaneous harmonic progressions are more convincing than rhythmically disparate ones. Though some cases will leave little room for doubt, there will often remain a grey area of ambiguity for which the composer has to bear the blame if he is not properly interpreted.

An early theoretical mention for such synchronization is made by Gigault, who writes in 1685: "Whenever a sixteenth-note is placed on top of an eighth-note, they have to be played simultaneously."[40] The importance of this rule could not have been great, since not a single such instance occurs in the music of this book. (However, to illustrate this rule I have, in example 32 of my article "La Note pointée," given an illustration from Boyvin which I believe is unambiguous.)

We even find spots in Bach where such synchronization through doubledotting of one voice is likely to be the authentic rendition. In the organ obbligato of Cantata 170/3 (example 8a) there is an obvious need to synchronize it with the same pitch in the left hand to a thirty-second-note. At the very start of Cantata 127 the logical synchronization in the first beat of the second measure is presumably matched by a horizontal assimilation in the first measure and throughout the movement (example 8b). In the autograph of the A Minor Partita (in Anna Magdalena's Notebook of 1725) the sixteenth-note of the middle voice shows clear and seemingly intentional vertical alignment with the thirty-second-notes in the outer voices, thus suggesting a doubledotting of the eighth-note (example 8c). In the original print of the G Major Partita (for which no autograph survived) we find in measures 9 and 23 of the sarabande the last eighth-note exactly aligned with the sixteenth-note below. Though the engraving is of mediocre quality, a synchronization could have well been intended. In the allemande from the same partita (separate 1731 edition) we find (with thanks to Arthur Mendel) in measure 1 and 22 the following clear and logical alignment:

Such synchronizations, sporadic in Bach and other polyphonic masters, became more frequent in the homophonic music of the *galant* era. We have an illustration from C.P.E. Bach's treatise where the vertical line-up indicates such intention— —and an almost identical one from Türk. Such

occasional synchronizations are of course a far cry from those allegedly required in the "French overture style" with its extreme rhythmic contractions; the *galant* German ones are, moreover, totally unrelated to the French.

Ex. 8.

a. Cantata 170, third mvt. (autograph)

b. Cantata 127, first mvt.

Organ (sounding a whole tone higher)

c. BWV 827, Allemande (autograph)

d. BWV 829, Sarabande

A *melodic* context for overdotting occurs when dots are followed by one or more pitches that are ornamental in character though written as regular notes. As ornaments they are not of the melodic essence and have no vested interest in metrical coordination with another voice or voices but serve primarily to smooth the transition to the following structural note. In such a context these ornamental pitches can, and often should, be played more lightly and faster than their metrical face value. For instance, in example 9 the note after the cadential trill is a *Nachschlag*. I believe that most practicing musicians will find a delay of this note corresponding roughly to doubledotting to be a more satisfactory rendition than its exact coordination with the eighth-note in the bass. Similarly we find in Bach many a spot where, e.g., a trill will profit from being played as if it had been written hence with a lengthened dot—the more so since Bach practically never used the two small notes to notate a trill's suffix.[41] In all such cases it is of course the shortening of the ornamental notes that incidentally causes the overdotting, not vice versa.

Ex. 9. *Well-Tempered Clavier*, Book I, Prelude 17

The flexibility of the dot provided the performer with the opportunity of lengthening or shortening the dot's value whenever, *as a soloist,* he felt that the expression of a passage called for such alteration. A lengthening of the dot under these circumstances was of course categorically different from the *notes inégales,* since it was not subject to any kind of rule or regulation.[42] The range of this freedom was obviously limited in polyphonic textures and became wider in homophony. Strong overdotting for the sake of expression became in fact something of a mannerism in the Germany of the *galant* style, where rhythmic spice was welcome in an otherwise impoverished texture. It is no coincidence that the first theoretical documents on this matter appear in the mid-eighteenth century in Quantz's and C.P.E. Bach's epoch-making manifestoes of *galant* performance practice. With regard to both of these eminent theorists two basic, general misunderstandings reside in an appraisal of them—common, since Dolmetsch used them as foundation stones for his doctrine—as retrospective sources for a hundred years of the "French overture style," when in fact they are the first heralds for a German *galant* manner of overdotting that has nothing to do with the French and very little with previous generations.

I cannot avoid reverting to these two documents (though I have dealt with them before, in my article "La Note pointée")—to Quantz, because I earlier gave an incomplete accounting, to Bach, because I have been criticized for having distorted his meaning. Of the two, Quantz is unquestionably the crown witness, since in one out of five passages he makes a reference to French dance music, thus establishing a certain link with the French style.

In Quantz's book we have to distinguish several pertinent passages.[43] In the first of these (chap. 5, pars. 20ff.) he stipulates exact rendition for the pattern ♩. ♪ but very sharp overdotting for the smaller note-values. There is no mention of French style or form. Instead we find here the probably first revelation of the recently emerged German *galant* mannerism.[44] In the second passage (chap. 12, par. 24), a somewhat pedantic discussion of the musical portrayal of various emotions ("Leidenschaften"), Quantz lists as one of the ways of portraying brilliant grandeur ("das Prächtige") the use of dotted, sharply articulated notes with a "long sustained dot" and a very short companion note. Again distinct overdotting, again no mention of the French. In the third passage (chap. 17, sec. 2, par. 13), dealing with ripieno violinists, he speaks of slow pieces where dotted eighth- and sixteenth-notes are to be played with a heavy, slow bowstoke, well sustained ("nourissant") to the very end of their value without lifting the bow for the second note. Quantz here cautions only against *shortening* the dot, "so as not to appear impatient and change the adagio into an andante." The text implies no lengthening of the dot and excludes the insertion of a rest. Then he adds that when dashes are placed above the notes, the short companion is to be played "very brief and sharp." Since dashes stand for a sharp staccato, the wording very probably indicates a sharp *tactée* articulation *without* overdotting: ♩̇ 𝅘𝅥 𝄾 𝄾 (ᵗᵉⁿ·). The directive not to lift the bow makes an overdotting technically impractical; besides, the instruction of holding the dot "to the very end of its value" by itself implies that it is not to be held beyond its value. This is rather important, because it indicates that his wording of playing the companion note "very short and sharp" refers to articulation rather than rhythmic compression.[45] In the fourth passage (chap. 17, sec. 2, par. 16) Quantz writes, "when a long note and a rest is followed by thirty-second-notes, the latter must always be played very fast, be it in allegro or adagio," and gives an example in the rhythm ♩ 𝄾 𝅘𝅥𝅘𝅥𝅘𝅥𝅘𝅥 ♩̇ 𝄾 𝅘𝅥𝅘𝅥𝅘𝅥𝅘𝅥 . Here a rhythmic contraction is clearly indicated (though in an allegro it will hardly be practical), yet again without reference to the French.

Finally, (chap. 17, sec. 7, pars. 56-58) Quantz discusses French dance music as actually played for ballet performances.[46] In paragraph 56 he mentions in a general way that dotted notes are to be played "heavily, the following notes very short and sharp." In paragraph 58 he speaks specifically of the loure, sarabande, courante and chaconne, in which "eighth-notes after dotted quarter-notes are to be played not according to their literal value but very short and sharp." The dotted note is accented and for the dot the bow is lifted. In both quotes the wording permits, as in the third passage, the meaning of a short and sharp staccato articulation of the eighth-notes without delayed entrance. [Though at the time tentative, the correction of this explanation was, I trust, conclusively proved in FN5, pp. 170-73. Hence the interpretation as overdotting, proposed as alternative in the future course of this passage, was mistaken. F.N. 1982] This interpretation is compatible with the specification "not according to its literal value" since the eighth-notes in these pieces are rarely, if ever, marked with staccato dots or dashes. Now it is certainly possible, even likely, that Quantz was thinking here of overdotting, though he failed to express himself precisely. Should he have had in mind a sharp overdotting in the sense of the "first passage" of chapter 5, it could, in view of a total lack of corroboration from any French source, and in view of the earlier passages in his treatise, reflect a superposition of the German *galant* mannerism on the mild overdotting of the French *notes inégales* (which Quantz—and Quantz alone among non-French theorists—endorsed within the framework of his ideal of a "mixed style"). Although this passage has been interpreted by everybody (including myself in discussing the *note pointée*) as implying sharp overdotting, on closer scrutiny its meaning is at best ambiguous. Quantz continues by saying whenever thirty-second-notes follow a dot or a rest, they are to be played with greatest speed at the extreme end of their assigned time, and with separate bowstrokes. Such figures, he adds, occur fairly often in overtures, *entrées,* and *furies.*

This paragraph 58 in Quantz is to my knowledge the *only* theoretical source that deals with the execution of dotted notes in French dances and describes, probably, the lengthening of the dotted quarter-note, and, definitely, the rhythmic contraction of the thrusting thirty-second-note figures in overtures, *entrées,* and the like. This latter contraction has, in view of the many notes involved, only a limited range, and its documentary value for the French style is further diminished by the fact that the instructions are practically identical with those of the "fourth passage," which is not focused on any form, style, or nationality.

Whatever question marks need to be attached to this paragraph about French dance music, Quantz's testimony on German *galant*-style overdotting is unequivocal and was echoed with various degrees of reservations by a number of German theorists in the second half of the 18th century. The most important of these is C.P.E. Bach, the second pillar of the Dolmetsch doctrine. Bach discusses the dotted note in two separate passages: the first in his book on solo performance, the second in his book on accompaniment.[47] In neither does he mention French music. Dolmetsch, Geoffroy-Dechaume, and Collins quote only the first of these passages, which is vaguely worded and in part obscure. Dolmetsch, in apparent bewilderment, offers an English version that deviates so grossly from the original that we must write it off as an aberration. Fortunately we do not have to be particularly concerned about the first passage (which I discussed in detail in dealing with the *note pointée)* since the perfectly lucid second one fully clarifies Bach's ideas on this matter.

This second passage nips in the bud any attempt to extract from C.P.E. Bach a rule for obligatory overdotting in any style. He writes: "The notation of the dotted note is often imprecise. Attempts were made to establish in this matter a principal rule which, however, suffers many exceptions. According to this rule the notes following the dot must be played very fast [aufs kürzeste abgefertigt werden], and often this rule applies. However, it does not apply when the disposition of the notes in various voices requires their exact coordination; furthermore, a tender expression which does not tolerate the characteristic boldness [das Trotzige] of the dotted notes, will cause us to shorten the length of the dot. *If one stipulates one type of rendering these notes one loses the other types* [italics mine]." The types he speaks of are 1) overdotting, 2) literalness, and 3) underdotting.[48]

In his violin method of 1756, Leopold Mozart, like everybody else, presents and illustrates at first the standard rule of the dot. Then he notes that "in certain passages of slow movements" [in langsamen Stücken gewisse Passagen] the dot should be "held a little longer" [etwas länger gehalten] to prevent too sleepy or lazy an impression.[49] He also sees a place for such moderate lengthening as a pedagogical device to prevent speeding. However, he recommends for an intended overdotting the use of the double dot (at the time still novel and "strange looking") in order to give more specific guidance. From this remark we can conclude that for composers who used the double dot routinely, as did his son, Leopold's recommendation must not be thoughtlessly "applied."

Collins has also cited in part more specific instructions about doubledotting by Agricola (1757), Georg Friedrich Wolf (1784), Rellstab (1790), Tromlitz (1791), and Türk (1789). He could have added Löhlein, who writes in 1765[50] that dots should be held approximately twice as long as notated. In his third edition of 1779 Löhlein adds that it is much preferable if the composer writes such a rhythm exactly the way he wants it to be played. Of these later theorists Wolf is a treacherous witness. Whereas in his vocal treatise, as quoted by Collins, he only says the dotted note is sung better long than short (which is not saying much) and that new composers use double dots if they desire any lengthening, in his clavier treatise (to be cited below) he rejects overdotting outright. Rellstab qualifies the overdotting directive by adding that occasionally the dot is held precisely. Türk, too, considerably qualifies his directives and likewise, recommends the double dot to eliminate doubts. Tromlitz speaks only of fast and lively pieces, where overdotting in many cases becomes technically impractical.

This practice of German *galant* overdotting was by no means general. Quite apart from the strong qualifications of C.P.E. Bach and similar ones by some of the other theorists already mentioned, we find eminent writers who strongly dissent. Very characteristic is a testimony by Friedrich Wilhelm Marpurg, who has been cited as chief witness for the introduction of French practices into Germany. He writes: "If ♫ is to be played as ♫ one also has to write in this manner, or else like this: ♫ Unless this is done, nobody is under any obligation to divine the composer's thoughts, and since the latter has two methods at his disposal to clarify his intentions ... I cannot see why one should write one way and want to have it perfomred in another way; i.e., why one puts only one dot and expects to have it read as one and a half."[51] Wolf, in his clavier treatise, quotes and endorses these statements from Marpurg. After illustrating the standard meaning of the dot, he adds: "There are some who claim that a dot after short note values ought to be held approximately half again as long as the notation indicates; that one ought to hold the dot as if there were two. Such is Löhlein's opinion...; the opposite is shown with good reason by Marpurg.... If a composer wants to avoid having his pieces spoiled by awkward performance, he must write the way he wants to have it performed and executed."[52] Johann Samuel Petri writes: "For dots, one must count precisely 1, 2, 3, and only after the third quarter-, eighth-, or sixteenth-note, etc., move on to the fourth one. When two dots are placed after a note, the latter is extended by three-fourths of its value."[53] Johann Anton Hiller uses bold type to lend emphasis to the rule: "a dot after a note *always stands for half of its value*. If the [tied] note which is represented by a dot, already has a dot, one has to mark two dots and the second has only half the value of the first."[54] Petri and Hiller are in obvious accord with Marpurg.

For a preliminary balance sheet, we can mark down as facts a practice of overdotting in the (mostly northern) Germany of the *galant* style, limited to solo performance (the quoted authors speak either of the clavier, the flute, the violin, or the voice) and limited also to a notation that was not yet using the double dot (hence the many recommendations to do so)—a practice of overdotting qualified by practically all and rejected outright by others. A relationship to France is nowhere in evidence—with the sole exception of two sentences (with the crucial sentence being at best ambiguous) in one of the five passages devoted to the matter by Quantz, writing at a time when the French overture and ballet suite were breathing their last breath.

Concerning W.A. Mozart, who used the double dot from his earliest youth on (e.g., in the symphony K. 48 of 1768) with ever-increasing frequency, deliberation, and methodicalness, we need not dogmatically bar occasional mild overdotting in a solo setting—with him as little as with nearly any composer of any era. But in his operas, orchestral, and vocal works, from his mature years particularly, there is no justification for deviating from his notation of single dots.

Some of the present fashion of overdotting derives from the fire and excitement that the sharpened rhythms are supposed to engender. It is easy and therefore tempting to make this argument, but just as easy to forget that often such fire or excitement may not have been intended. Lully's overtures, for instance, opened a prologue, dedicated to the fawning glorification of the "Sun King." They were meant to be pompous and regal, not excited and breathless. During the roughly hundred years of the French overture's lifetime, musical style, as is its wont, did not stand still. Thus in the first half of the eighteenth century we see tendencies to greater sharpness, carefully notated with ties, rests, and dashing runs of thirty-second- and sixty-fourth-notes, but these tendencies were not consistent. We still find many a French overture without any trace of rhythmic sharpness, some with a great deal of it, others, again, where in careful notation the sharp and the mild are closely intermingled in succession and simultaneity.

In matters of historical performance we must not be swayed by our own preferences, which might well be reflexes conditioned by an overdose of poorly digested old treatises. Also, it is one thing for a performer to say, "I like it better this way and do not care what the composer had in mind." A case might be made for such an attitude. But it is altogether different to argue, "I like it better this way, and therefore the composer must have intended it." Such argument is vulnerable to the unanswerable riposte: "I disagree."

In addressing myself now to Michael Collins's attempt to buoy up the Dolmetsch doctrine, I can omit those parts of his article that have to do with upbeat figures of three or more notes that follow a dot or rest or start from a tie,

♩ ♪♫♫ ‖ ♩. ♪♫ ‖ ♩ ♫♫♫ ‖ ♩ ♫♫♫   for I have dealt with this
matter in an earlier paper.[55] As a welcome by-product of my arguments there I
was able to show that rhythmic sharpness was not of the essence of the French
overture at any time of its existence. It remains now to take a look at his
presentation of the "missing link," the French sources for obligatory sharp
overdotting that have so far eluded all researchers.

His first witness is Bacilly. Collins himself says that the evidence is
"oblique," since Bacilly is speaking of the *notes inégales*, and that a reference to
the "jerky style" is "obscure." Adding to this Bacilly's above-cited stress on the
near-imperceptibility of the *notes inégales*, one could leave matters at that,
were it not for another argument, based on Bacilly's use of the word *saccades*. I
had used the term *style saccadé* for the "jerky style" of the Dolmetsch school,
whereas Bacilly warns *against* singing *par saccades*, which, he says, would be
most disagreeable. Collins writes: "Bacilly used the very word at the very time
Lully was composing." Ergo, Bacilly confirms Dolmetsch.[56] The fallacy needs
no analysis. Next, Collins cites La Chapelle and Hotteterre giving an
explanation of the *notes inégales* (Hotteterre with the makeshift dotted
notation); here I can pass this over as well.

Collins's citation from Loulié involves a misunderstanding. In the first
part of his treatise—a part addressed to children—Loulié shows how to teach a
dotted quarter-note, c ♩ . ♪ and so clarifies its value. The dotted eighth-note
lacks the help of an intervening beat, so he explains: "One holds the eighth-note
a little longer [italics mine] and renders the sixteenth fast."[57] A useful first
approach, though it might tend to produce underdotting. However can
overdotting be deduced from it? Similar is the case with L'Affilard's
explanation of the dotted quarter-note: "One holds the dotted note and plays
the eighth fast" [Il faut suspendre la Note pointée & passer vite la croche qui
suit].[58] Again a rough indication of a long-short relationship but certainly no
injunction of overdotting. L'Affilard's treatise, too, was on the elementary
level.

Collins then refers to irregularities of notation by Gigault and Couperin.[59]
Gigault often uses from one to as many as six extra beams or flags but says in
his foreword not to be afraid of the extra beams since they do not mean
anything else than sixteenth-notes. Collins comments, "It matters little what
Gigault tells us in the preface. What would be the purpose of the extra beams if
it were not to indicate that the semiquavers were to be played as rapidly as
possible?" The reader is forced to decide which is the more compelling
authority as to Gigault's intentions: Collins's reasoning or Gigault's assertions.
Besides, what "purpose" could be found in the notation shown in example 10,
where Gigault uses eight beams for septuoles filling quarter-note beats, with no
dot anywhere in sight?

Ex. 10.   Gigault, page 103, Fugue a3

Collins then quotes similar irregularities in François Couperin's notation, involving extra beams or flags. Donington had claimed overdotting for such notation in the sixth movement from the *Apothéose de Corelli,* where, however, the tempo is so fast that literal rendition is extremely hard, overdotting totally impractical. Elsewhere I have dealt with this question at some length, giving examples of where overdotting was out of the question because there was no dot, and where the extra beams were meaningless.[60] In addition to those illustrations, how are we to explain example 11a from the Fifth Prelude (from *L'Art de toucher le clavecin)* where we find an eighth-note space filled by a quintuplet with a five-flag rest and four five-beamed notes with two overlapping, two-flagged notes of which the second, three times as short as the first, has the identical length of a five-beamed note? In example 11b from the same prelude the sixty-fourth-notes after the dot *could* be explained in Loulié's sense as extending the dot, but for the preceding sixty-fourth-notes following an eighth there is no rational explanation. And how to explain example 11c from the Second Prelude where the last quarter-note space is occupied by a six-beamed sextuplet? Granted there are cases where after a dotted note an extra beam could or does suggest doubledotting in a tempo where it is feasible. However, as explained above, whenever an exact nonstandard length of the dot is indicated by irregular notation, these are not cases of under- or overdotting, and permit no inference regarding the execution of dotted notes in standard notation. Hence these arguments, too, fail to score.

Ex. 11.   Couperin

a.   Fifth Prelude   b.   Fifth Prelude   c.   Second Prelude

There remain two German quotations to be considered. Johann Mattheson describes the *entrée* as being more sharp, dotted, and impetuous than other melodies. Collins asks: how can one piece be more dotted than another? Quoting Mattheson as saying that in *entrées* and similar dances the very dotted style is often expressly required ("mehrenteils ausdrücklich erfordert") he sees here a proof for overdotting. However, the word *ausdrücklich* implies explicit prescription, and the only way to "expressly prescribe" is either to write more dotted notes or otherwise to write "expressly" sharper dotted rhythms by using ties or rests. Again, the explicitness of such notation in sharpened dots would carry no implication for the over-dotting of the plain dotted note. Finally, Collins cites J.P. Schultz, author of the article of "Ouvertüre" in Sulzer's *Allgemeine Theorie der schönen Künste* of 1775. Schultz writes: "The main notes are usually dotted, and in performance the dots are held longer than their value." Unquestionably he speaks of a measure of overdotting. The wording, however, falls far short of confirming the "jerky style" and is fully in keeping with the lengthening produced by the *notes inégales;* hence it has no more evidential value than the latter. In Germany, the French overture was at that time but a faded memory. No matter whether Schultz may have heard in Paris some old-time overture with its *inégalité,* or have relied on hearsay, this last (German) piece of evidence no more closes the gap to the Dolmetsch doctrine than do any of the others.

All in all, the effort to save the Dolmetsch doctrine must at this point be judged a failure, partly because of confusion with the *notes inégales,* partly by highly vulnerable interpretations of theoretical and musical evidence. Above all, the *French* "missing link" is still missing. If my answers to Collins and the adduced additional evidence shall have clarified the issues, my original conclusion would be reinforced: that Dolmetsch's doctrine, as reflected in all his examples and in the "French overture style" of his disciples, belong in an area of unsupported speculation, surrounding the various kernels of fact identified and described in the course of this study.

Ex. 12.   *Well-Tempered Clavier,* Book I, Fugue in D (Dolmetsch's interpretation)

As a coda, true to its function of emphasizing the conclusion, I shall show how Dolmetsch's instructions for the playing of the D Major Fugue of the *Well-Tempered Clavier,* Book I, endorsed by Donington, adopted by Wanda Landowska and given wide circulation by her recording, is clearly contradicted by theoretical and external evidence. Dolmetsch's interpretation as given in example 12 pervades the whole piece.

Two things are particularly strange about this interpretation. First, the prescribed doubledotting in measure 2 of example 12a and all its parallel spots, contradicts one of Dolmetsch's prime sources, C.P.E. Bach's "first passage," which states that sometimes the disposition of the voices requires exactness of the dot; the pertinent illustration happens to be rhythmically identical with measure 2 of the fugue: . In the "second passage" Philipp Emanuel is even more specific when he says that overdotting does not apply "when the disposition of the notes in various voices requires their exact coordination." And where could such coordination be more vital than in a fugue? The second surprise element is measure 9 of example 12b and parallel spots where a written synchronization in a purely harmonic context is replaced by a rhythmic clash, reversing the pattern of the "jerky style." That both these interpretations are misunderstandings becomes clear when we look at Bach's autograph, shown in plate 4. In his musical handwriting in general, but most strikingly in his fair copies, of which this autograph is a fine example, Bach displays an extraordinary care of vertical alignment. Looking at the autograph we find, first, that among the sixteen passages in which the pattern of measure 2 appears, in fifteen of them the sixteenth-note after the dot is consistently and clearly aligned with the penultimate thirty-second-note in the other voice (the only exception being the second beat of measure 6, where the sixteenth comes too early rather than too late). Second, with regard to example 12b, at the spots in the autograph marked by me with an asterisk we see the clear line-up of the last sixteenth-notes in harmonic simultaneity, which belies any thought of a rhythmic clash through overdotting of the harmonic parts.[61]

Thus, the internal evidence of disturbed polyphonic relationships, and the external evidence of Bach's clear line-up refute the Dolmetsch-Landowska rendition. Alice Ehlers, the late eminent harpsichordist, wrote me ten years ago in a personal letter how, after studying this piece with Landowska, she played it for Paul Hindemith in the overdotted style. He summed up his reaction in one word: "nonsense." Lacking the talent for such laconism, I have had to use many more words to make the same point.

9

Once More: The "French Overture Style" (FN4)

[The following article (FN4) calls for a brief comment. When the editor of *Early Music* accepted the English translation of FN1 for publication, he commissioned for increased interest an article that would represent an opposing point of view. This rejoinder was written by David Fuller in the October, 1977, issue of that journal. Sharp in tone, it focused less on proving the validity of the challenged doctrine that on finding fault with my reasoning. Confident that I could invalidate its many charges I wrote a detailed reply that, however, was too long for the available space. I had to agree to severe editorial cuts that were acknowledged in the following note below the title: "This article has been editorially condensed for reasons of space. We greatly regret that not all of Professor Neumann's specific points in reply to David Fuller could be included."

Today, my publication of new material in FN5 diminishes the need for the restoration of all the cuts made in my original manuscript and I shall therefore reinstate only a few of the excised sections with a view to improving the continuity and to pointing up more weaknesses in David Fuller's brief. The restored sections are placed within brackets.]

The so-called "French overture style" is an astounding psycho-sociological phenomenon. In the course of the last decades many scholars and performers accepted its existence as an unquestionable fact—and keep accepting it at an alarmingly accelerating pace—when a sober examination reveals its evidence to be so elusive that it has to be classed as a myth. What is the "French overture style?" As might be expected from its shadowy origins, we are not dealing with a clearly defined entity, since every one of its advocates—Professor Fuller's "new zealots"—introduces his own variations on the main theme. Hence, the concept is fuzzy at the periphery, but has a solid nucleus: the "rule" that in French overtures and dance movements such as the sarabande, courante, entrée, chaconne, loure, etc.—be they written by French, German, or English composers—the dotted notes have to be strongly overdotted (ranging from circa double to quadruple dotting). Surrounding this nucleus, variants extend the dogma's timeframe, geographical range, and focus on specific forms. Some

Reprinted with permission from *Early Music* 7 (1979), 39-45, (with additions by the author).

(like Dolmetsch) encompass the 16th and 17th centuries, some (like Donington) all baroque music, some (like Collins) Mozart and Haydn, and at least one (Dart) the whole of the 19th century.

My French article, now fourteen years old (translated in *Early Music* 5/3) was, so far as I know, the first printed challenge to the doctrine's existence. Michael Collins answered in 1969; then in 1974 and 1977 I published two more articles on the subject. For the sake of brevity my three articles are cited hereafter as FN1, FN2, and FN3 respectively.[1]

In October, 1977, *Early Music* contained a long essay by David Fuller in answer *only* to FN1: "Dotting, the 'French Style' and Frederick Neumann's Counter-Reformation." Though he lists FN2 in his footnote 1 and mentions it briefly in footnote 7, he ignores its contents in the main text. My third article came out too late to be considered. Yet Fuller, in a brief postscript, finds that its reasoning "stumbles over fallacies similar enough to the earlier ones" to dismiss it along with FN1.

Today FN1 still represents my views, although I would reformulate certain sentences and tone down points that now seem somewhat overstated. My argument was not, as Fuller assumed, my dislike for the "jerky style" but the simple thesis, that "the style" has no basis in provable fact. FN2 and FN3 were designed to complement, refine and buttress this thesis by 1) presenting new evidence, 2) identifying, clarifying, and sorting out the various distinct elements that go into the complex picture of rhythmic alteration as it affects the dotted note, and 3) answering criticism that has been made.

Before considering Fuller's arguments, I might briefly list the various circumstances in which dots were likely to be lengthened (detailed more fully in FN3), then take a look at the background evidence for "the style."

Overdotting was, or could be, practised:

1) in the context of *note inégales* where the dot takes the place of the longer first of two notes evenly written, yet the resulting inequality is too slight to qualify as the strong overdotting of "the style";

2) in the German *galant* style (which, as Fuller concurs, has no connection with French practices) where it is limited to solo performances;

3) in occasional synchronization, when suggested by musical logic (often producing not over- but underdotting);

4) when a dotted note is followed by a *Nachschlag*-type ornament (such as a written-out suffix after a trill);

5) in certain cases of unmetrical notation;

6) in solos where the legitimate or arrogated licence of the performer allows him to manipulate the rhythm with agogic accents, or lengthening and shortening of dots;[2]

7) but not in the figures ♩♪♪♪ let alone ♩♪♪♪ which are not to be contracted (as discussed in FN2).

The alleged strong overdotting of "the style" remains unsupported by any piece of *French* evidence. The search for this "missing link" has so far been unsuccessful[3] and Fuller's citations of French primary and secondary sources all refer to *notes inégales.*

A few sentences in Quantz's famous treatise have so far been the theoretical mainstay of the doctrine.[4] Even Fuller admits that C.P.E. Bach, the other chief authority, speaks only of German *galant,* and not of French practices and he, too, like Quantz in chapter 5, speaks of solo performance only. Here are Quantz's sentences:

> The French use this [2-]metre in various dances such as bourrées, entrées, rigaudons, gavottes, rondeaus etc.... In this metre as well as in the 3/4 metre of the loure, sarabande, courante, and chaconne, the eighth-notes following the dotted quarter-notes must be played not with their literal value [nicht nach ihrer eigentlichen Geltung] but very short and sharp. The dotted note is emphasized and during the dot the bow is lifted. [FN's translation.]

In FN3, I ventured the hypothesis that these sentences, which are generally believed to prescribe sharp overdotting of quarter-notes in French dances and overtures (though its application to the latter is not directly referred to), instead may have implied sharp staccato articulation of the eighth-note rather than its strongly delayed entrance: ♩ ♪ - ♩ ♪♫ not ♩♫♪ (the rest, in lieu of the dot, as Quantz prescribed). Since then I have found further support for this hypothesis. Two paragraphs earlier than the quotation above, Quantz discusses the interaction of dancers and orchestra, and prescribes, for French dance music in general, a bowstroke that is heavy, yet short, sharp and more detached than connected. Here he also insists that the dotted notes must be played heavily, the companion notes short and sharp [die punctirten Noten werden schwer, die darauf folgenden aber sehr kurz und scharf gespielet]. "Heavy" rendition does not imply any lengthening, and "short and sharp" without indicating delayed entry, on the face of it suggests accented sharp articulation, a clipping of the note value at the end, not at the start.

A "short and sharp" delivery would create critical ensemble problems unless done either on the beat or within an established lilt of *notes inégales.* Such ensemble problems do not arise for the next directive, that three or more 32nd-notes after a dot or a rest (the scale-wise *tirades* mentioned by Fuller on p. 535), are to be played as fast as possible at the end of their time. Here the rhythmic alteration is intended, but the unavoidable imprecisions are immaterial, because the resulting glissando-like flourish makes orchestral sense, whereas unsynchronized sharp attacks of single notes do not.

If Quantz's authorization is in doubt, there remains no other unequivocal evidence in support of "the style."

Plate 5. Manuscript British Library: RM 18 c.l. (c1729) 'Handel Miscellaneous'. Overture to *Amadigi*. Nos. 1, 3, 6, 7: 8ths before 16ths: Nos. 2, 8: 16ths aligned with 32nds; No. 4: 8th aligned with 32nds; No. 5: 16ths aligned

Plate 6.   Rm 18 c.1. Overture to *Radamisto*. No. 1: 8th before two 32nds; Nos. 2, 3, 5: 8ths aligned with 32nds; Nos. 4, 6: 16ths aligned with 32nds

True, a generation after Quantz, when the French overture had passed into history, another German, Johann A.P. Schultz, writing in Sulzer's *Encyclopedia of the Arts,*[5] does mention lengthening of the dot in French overtures ("the dotted notes are held longer than their value). I pointed out in FN3 that this wording merely allows the mild overdotting generated by *notes inégales.* Schultz's article on *Punkt, punktirte Note,* offers further confirmation: "generally, the dot extends the value of a note by one half... however, there are cases where the proper execution calls for a *somewhat longer* rendition [eine noch etwas längere Geltung] as was previously pointed out in the article on the overture" [italics mine].

This significant lack of corroborating evidence has so far been ignored by adherents of "the style." Since "the style" postulates a drastic deviation from the established mathematical values of rhythmic notation, the onus of proof of its existence rests with its advocates. If the arguments for "the style" are severely deficient, as I trust I have shown, and if I can now show that the new counter-arguments also miss the mark, then it is highly improbable that "the style" ever existed, I am afraid that my opponents are fundamentally arguing in a circle, by taking as *demonstratum* that which as *demonstrandum* is in need of solid proof.

Some scholars, frustrated by the meagre pickings of theoretical sources, appeal to an alleged "tradition," notably the 19th-century English convention of strong overdotting of the *Messiah* overture. This is a most slippery path to take. For all we know, the 19th-century overdotting of this overture may have started with somebody's idiosyncrasy. That "somebody" may have been William Crotch, whose early 19th-century double-dotted organ arrangements, fully three generations after Handel, are cited by Donington as the earliest source of what he calls "one of our best attested conventions of baroque interpretation." Battishill's keyboard arrangements from the end of the 18th century, which Professor Graham Pont has kindly brought to my attention, display overdotting in erratic, arbitrary patterns. Simply, they show that a soloist could and did take rhythmic freedoms. They cannot be used as evidence for an *orchestral* convention: there, if utter chaos is to be avoided, drastic deviations from the notated values are thinkable only on the basis of total consistency.

Furthermore, the Handelian "tradition" is flatly contradicted by an important manuscript in the British Library: RM 18 c.1., entitled: *Handel Miscellaneous,* (plate 5). Though undated, the manuscript was presumably written in, or shortly after, 1729,[6] and contains harpsichord reductions of seventeen Handel overtures and selected opera pieces. Its adaptation to the harpsichord idiom, instance its written ornamentation, shows the hand of an experienced professional performer, whom one would certainly expect to have been conversant with a convention of overdotting so widely practised (we are led to believe) that nobody saw the need to mention it in any textbook or anywhere else. However, the manuscript's painstakingly careful vertical alignment of rhythmical relationships invariably shows exact standard values for all dotted notes, *no overdotting, no synchronization.* The horizontal disposition of the notes in proportion to their values reinforces the evidence. The specimens (plates 5 and 6) are fairly representative of the whole volume. I have marked certain details with numbers to facilitate comments on their significance.

A contemporary print by Walsh of Handel, *XXIV Overtures fitted for the Harpsichord or Spinet* (London, n.d.), varies in details of transcription from the above manuscript, but offers the same external evidence against over-dotting.

[Fuller charges me with a series of "arguments from ignorance" meaning that failure to find a fact (like, say, the "style") does not prove the non-existence of the fact. True enough, but neither does it prove its existence. Take the following example.]

Quantz specifies that groups of three or more 32nds that follow dots or rests (the above-mentioned *tirades*) are to be played, tempo permitting, as late and as fast as possible. Fuller implies that Quantz must have meant this to apply to 16th-notes as well, though he does not refer to them specifically. My failure to acknowledge this allegedly obvious fact is branded as an argument from ignorance. It is very convenient to adapt a source to fit one's opinion. If one cannot always take an authority at face value, it is up to one to prove an alternative reading. It so happens that in French overtures the difference between a sequence of 32nds and one of 16ths is not one of degree but of kind. The 32nds appear characteristically in the *tirade* form, the "scalewise flourishes" as Fuller describes them. Only such figures (shown in ex. 1a) can be contracted effectively for the glissando effect described above. The 16ths, by contrast, are not only slower, but appear in far more varied melodic designs that would become unintelligible if played at extreme speed. One would have to look long and hard to find the *tirade* of example 1a written in 16th-notes (ex. 1b) in French overtures. And what would be the musical result if—say, in Bach's C major Overture, BWV 1066 (ex. 1c)—each violinist and oboist tried to execute the 16th-notes as late and fast as possible?

In FN1 I pointed out that Quantz's rule about the shortness and sharpness of eighth-notes following dotted quarters, refers to a number of dances, but not to the overture. Fuller questions the logic of calling this omission "important." Whatever the degree of its importance, the omission was hardly inadvertent, as we may see from Quantz's remarks (chap. 17, sec. 7, pars. 56-58) on the interaction of music and dance. Speaking of fast dances, he again refers to the need for sharply articulated bowing—previously stipulated as a general rule for French dance music—in order to spur the dancers to leaps and at the same time

Ex. 1a.    Ex. 1b.

Ex. 1c.

convey musically the dancers' actions to the public. These reflections on the dancers' and the public's requirements provide further support for the argument that the notes following a dot have to be executed in a clearly defined rhythm. We should not forget that Quantz's rule about overdotting in chapter 5 applies primarily to the solo flute, not to the orchestra, and *not to quarter-notes.* (Similarly, C.P.E. Bach, Löhlein, Agricola, Rellstab, Tromlitz, Türk, also speak in this connection only of soloists, never of an orchestra.)

Since overtures are not dances[7] there is no reason for Quantz to mention them in a music-dance context, nor any reason to apply to the overture what he says about the music for the dance. He discusses the overture in the next chapter, 18, paragraph 42, along with other purely instrumental music. In the context of the dance, the overture is mentioned only incidentally, in connection with the flourishes of 32nd-note *tirades* which he says occur in overtures, entrées, and furies. It should be clear now that the previous failure to mention the overture along with the dances was no oversight.

Fuller finds it "quite disingenuous" on my part "not to have pointed out that elsewhere in his treatise Quantz says that the overture demands a *prächtig* and *gravitätisch* [splendid and weighty] opening and says that *das Prächtige* is characterized by overdotting." But Quantz's statement is not of one piece: a) *das Prächtige* und *Gravitätische* of the overture do not directly apply to b) the overdotting. The statement (b) occurs not in connection with the start of the overture (chap. 18, par. 42), or music of a similar character, but in the chapter on how to play the Allegro! There (chap. 12, par. 24) Quantz says that *das Prächtige* (and not *das Gravitätische)* is expressed either by long notes under which another voice executes a fast movement, *or* by dotted notes that are to be overdotted "as explained in chap. 5, pars. 21 and 22." This last reference is to

German and not to French practices, to the *soloist,* not to the orchestra. After explicitly stipulating, in par. 20, literal rendition of dotted quarter-notes, Quantz prescribes overdotting *only* for dotted eighths and shorter values, "because of the liveliness which these notes are intended to express." Fuller's reasoning is a classical "fallacy of the undistributed middle": 1) Overtures are *prächtig* and *gravitätisch.* 2) In the *Allegro, das Prächtige* may be expressed for soloists by overdotted eighths and shorter notes. 3) Therefore the dotted quarter-notes in the *gravitätisch* orchestral overtures have to be overdotted.

Fuller continues: "Since Raison uses double dots, [Neumann reasons that] Lully who does not, is to be played as written. But Lully would only be played as written *if there was not a convention of overdotting* [Fuller's italics], i.e. if Neumann's conclusion from this evidence is true. This is the fallacy of circular argument . . . " I have to return the compliment: according to Fuller, arguing from the "master-circle," "the style" existed, therefore it applies to Lully. Moreover, my reasoning was quite different. It showed how Raison juxtaposes double dots with single dots and it concluded that explicitly different notation implies different rhythmic intent. Speaking of Lully, my point was that he and most other masters of the time did *not* use the double dot, but did use ties or rests to indicate the same or similar effect.

[Fuller continues: "Furthermore the argument depends on what might be called the 'fallacy of the dizzy leap': how does one get from Raison—an organist about whom almost nothing is known—to Lully?" Very simply, by first discussing the musical evidence of Raison, then that of Lully. I made not even an inferential link between the two, did not "apply" what I found in Raison, to Lully. I simply pointed to their outwardly different, but closely related evidence. Their being contemporaries in Paris made it still more natural to move from one to the other. That little is known about Raison's life is of course irrelevant to the issue. If to move, with related but independent evidence, from Raison to his contemporary and compatriot Lully is a "fallacy of the dizzy leap," what would be the proper term for *applying* Quantz, Rellstab, Tromlitz, and even Türk, to Lully (as approvingly cited in Fuller's footnote 7)? Maybe "the trip on the magic carpet?"

A further point about Raison is also ill taken. The first Kyrie in the sixth tone may not be in the "form" of a French overture. But Raison advises the performer in his first book of organ pieces, to find the proper tempo and interpretation of each piece by looking at the time signature, then to consider whether it "relates" to a sarabande, gigue, gavotte, bourrée, or other pieces, performing it accordingly. Certainly, the start of the Kyrie in the sixth tone with its ₵ metre and its solemn dotted quarter-notes *relates* to an overture.

Fuller finds another such "dizzy leap" in my "exegesis" of C.P.E. Bach, who explained that some dots last longer than notated, some less long, but dots have to be exact in value when the disposition of the voices requires their precise coordination. As his illustration indicates (see FN1, ex. 9f), such precise coordination is required especially in polyphonic music. By applying this principle to the polyphonic music of the late baroque, I am not "throwing to the winds" earlier arguments that C.P.E. Bach's and Quantz's precepts cannot, as a matter of routine, be applied retroactively. The principle applies to J.S. Bach and other polyphonic masters not because Philipp Emanuel's treatise is a rule book for his father's performance, which it is not, but because we have to do here with a timeless matter of musical logic—indeed of musical common sense. Genuine polyphony is inhospitable to pronounced rhythmic alterations, in J.S. Bach as well as in Mozart, in the 15th century as well as in the 20th. Important treatises, including Quantz's and Philipp Emanuel's, can never be applied *in toto* to *any* other master, yet they often contain remarks and directives that transcend specific styles, generations, and even centuries. The implied directive about the basic integrity of the dotted note in polyphony belongs in this timeless category.

Fuller finds still another "dizzy leap" when the same principle is related to Lully and Rameau. This is not, as Fuller charges, a "sly" insertion into the syllogism, since both Lully and Rameau have written polyphonic alongside homophonic music (and Fuller has to admit that the one Lully overture [*Alceste*] I quoted in FN1 proves to be polyphonic).

He proceeds: "Having learned that homophony is polyphony, we should not be surprised to find polyphony boldly asserted to be homophony." At issue are the three measures given in example 2 (FN1, ex. 32; Fuller, ex. 1).

Ex. 2. Boyvin Trio

Imitation as such is not synonymous with polyphony. Certainly not in today's commonly accepted meaning of the term "polyphony" as the combination of "several simultaneous voice-parts of individual design" as contrasted to homophony "which combines several voice-parts of similar, rhythmically identical design" (*Harvard Dictionary of Music;* see also Riemann, *Musiklexikon,* 12th ed., *Webster, OUD;* also *MGG* s.v. Kontrapunkt). In this sense, the three measures cited are a prime illustration for an imitation that is patently homophonic. Considering that Boyvin did not use the double dot, the synchronization of the 8th-note g' with the 16th-note e", in this context of parallel sixths is virtually self-evident. Yet by decreeing these measures to be polyphonic, Fuller charges me with "circles within circles!" His circular double-vision was caused by a simple *non sequitur* (a "fallacy of the consequent"): polyphony can be imitative, ergo imitation has to be polyphony.]

Regrettably, Fuller confuses a concept fundamental to the whole issue of rhythmic alteration. He challenges as "false dichotomy" the assertion that there is a categorical difference between the *freedom* to lengthen, shorten, or synchronize according to musical judgement, on the one hand, and the *obligation* to do so by a definite convention such as *notes inégales,* on the other hand. His argument: "since the 'law' is evidently a fiction and taste can run to extremes, the 'profound and categorical' difference easily dwindles and dissolves into union." However, the "law" I was speaking of is not fictional but an obligation to follow the uncontested rules of *inégalité.*[8] It is the failure to distinguish clearly between the two categories that leads to misguided claims for the international validity of the French *inégales* convention. References may be found outside France to the inequality of evenly written notes, but then only as a matter of free artistic choice and not as a requirement of a syntactic rule. Thus when Donington speaks of very sharp inequality in leaps, and tries to connect this with *notes inégales,* he errs on three counts. First, there is no evidence of rules for *notes inégales* outside France and much evidence against it. Second, the French *notes inégales,* linked to specific metres, occurred only in essentially stepwise motion, hence were automatically excluded on leaps. Third, those *notes inégales* were overwhelmingly mild.

[When I denied that Lully's frequent rhythmic clashes in polyphonic textures were meant to be synchronized, Fuller counters by charging a circle. My argument, he says, depends on the nonexistence of a synchronization convention. Certainly, synchronization was occasionally intended when the combination of inadequate notation and of musical logic suggested it. A case was shown in the above example 2 where for the *keyboard,* synchronization was clearly indicated. By contrast, a general convention of synchronization is unrealistic because it could not supply members of an orchestra or chorus with the answers to the questions of *what* to synchronize, *with whom,* and *how.* Yet, keeping within the "master-circle" of the "style," that includes synchronization along with its features of rhythmic contraction, Fuller takes the existence of such a convention for granted and applies synchronization even to the fast part of Lully's overtures. He failed to think through the orchestral-technical unfeasibility of such undertaking. Nowhere does a later statement by Fuller (p. 531) fit more perfectly than here: "a notation that does not mean what it causes a player seeing it automatically to do would seem sheer perversity to my square Yankee mind." This remarkable sentence is a powerful—if unintentional—indictment of the whole "style" with its array of drastic rhythmic alterations. Fuller's sharp-edged word "perversity" cuts through the Gordian knot of the whole tangled issue. Unfortunately, in his complex discussion of the issue, Fuller lost track of the beacon offered by this eloquent statement.]

It is strange that Fuller (p. 527) criticizes me for not having dealt with written dotted notes in a *notes inégales* context, when earlier he quotes my dealing with that very issue (I discussed it at greater length still in FN3). Also, how does the frequency of dotted notes in Italian and German compositions from the early baroque to Beethoven and Schumann bear on the issue, since a notated inequality permits no inference on any inequality that is *not* notated? (See FN3, pp. 122-23.) The written proliferation of the dotted notes in French sources is actually one of the elements that contributed to the emergence of the dogma, because references to the quantity of dots in French music were misinterpreted as hints of their greater intensity. The prevalence of dotted rhythms became such a hallmark of the French style that when Bach changed the theme from the *Art of Fugue* to dotted rhythms he spoke of it as *"stile francese"* (with the assistance of 32nd-note scale flourishes).[9] Couperin's dotted notes where *notes inégales* would apply (as cited by Fuller) are simply further proof of the slightness of *inégalité.*[10] Similar examples are legion in French music of the 17th and 18th centuries.

In addition Fuller charges that I take advantage of my readers by withholding evidence injurious to my "thesis." As proof he offers one example that "will have to do." He quotes me as saying that every single one of numerous French treatises of the 17th and 18th centuries that mentions the dot describes it unfailingly in its standard meaning and that none "mentions in this connection—the obvious place to refer to exceptions—*any* kind of lengthening." Fuller argues that this was not the obvious place because the French "discuss such exceptions, i.e. rhythmic alteration, under the heading of *measure* (metre), *mouvement,* or something similar, in quite a different section of the treatise from the basics of notation" and that I knew it. He is quite mistaken. The French do discuss the *notes inégales* in connection with metre for the obvious reason that the rules of *inégalité* are strictly dependent on the metre (eighths *inégales* in 3-, 16ths in C-metre etc). But the overdotting of "the style" is, according to its advocates, not only much more pronounced, it is independent of metre, tempo, or "something similar" (whatever that may be). The reason why reference to this kind of strong overdotting appears neither in its logical place after the standard rule, nor in a less logical one is simple enough: it appears nowhere so far as has yet been discovered. I did not find it in 50-odd French treatises; all that Fuller found, and "it isn't much," as he admits, is written in connection with *notes inégales*—which is just as I report in my three articles. What, then, have I withheld from my readers?

Now where do we stand? As said before, Fuller has not produced a single piece of genuine evidence for "the style." On the contrary, in his strangely muted and ambivalent summary he actually supports my views on at least two points, and approaches them in others. Thus he agrees that *notes inégales* are a convention by themselves, not connected with "the style"; and that the German *galant* convention of overdotting had no connection with the French.[11] He also says that "the vigor of dotted rhythms is as much a function of articulation ... particularly the sharpness with which the short note is delivered ... as it is of the proportion of values." That statement closely approaches my recent hypothesis that Quantz, in his much quoted sentences about the shortness and sharpness of the eighth-notes, refers to articulation and dynamics rather than to delay. Moreover there is the remarkable statement: "if the short note is delayed so much that there is not time to make it speak properly, the effect will be flabby and neurotic rather than energetic." Here he disavows Dolmetsch, Dart, Leonhardt, Donington (and his "up to quadruple dotting"), along with many members of the "nameless horde."

Fuller also offers interesting information in footnote 19 about the first movement of Handel's Organ Concerto op. 4, no. 2, which opens in the dotted style of a French overture. He finds this the only example known to him on an 18th-century barrel organ, to be *not overdotted,* though such a rhythmic contraction would have posed no problems to the pinner.

Having thus in several crucial issues moved rather far from left to centre, Fuller does not disown "the style." He speaks of a "third convention of special cases" that form a group "because they are occasionally mentioned by name as candidates for overdotting." They include marches, French gigues and canaries, *"and of course the slow parts of French overtures"* [italics mine]. However, overdotting in French gigues and canaries, with their fast speeds and separate bow strokes, is technically impractical. For these dances a 3:1 (and occasionally even smaller) ratio gives by itself the effect of extreme dotting and great bounciness (*par saccades* as Bacilly put it). By including the French overture, Fuller simply continues orbiting in the master-circle: "it existed, therefore..."[12] The term "of course" with its implied assuredness, actually covers up a good deal of insecurity on Fuller's part for this very nucleus of "the style." He admits that "the case of the French overture is by far the most complex and difficult to deal with." That, as one of several "special cases," it is occasionally mentioned as a candidate for overdotting, is saying very little. The "occasional mention" may well be limited to Schultz's mild overdotting of 1777. The only other answer Fuller has about French overture performance is to be sought "in the unanimous references to their splendour, energy and fire ... " But who were the unanimous authorities? Fuller does not say. Quantz, as cited above, mentions splendour and graveness; Schultz, seriousness and fire; Koch, still later, in 1793, seriousness and pathos; but Mattheson in 1713, when the French overture was at its zenith, characterizes its first part as having "a fresh, gay, and also uplifting nature" [ein frisches, ermunterndes und auch zugleich *elevirtes* Wesen],[13] a description that Walther, with due credit, repeats verbatim in his Lexicon of 1732. In *Der vollkommene Capellmeister* of 1739 (p. 234), Mattheson later mentions only 'nobility' *(Edelmuth)* but refers his readers back to his explanation of 1713. Jean-Jacques Rouseau, in his Dictionary of 1768, speaks of the overture as "a slow piece marked *grave"* [un morceau traînant appelé *grave*]. Whoever else can be mustered, one thing is sure, there is no unanimity. Yet even *if* the statement about unanimity were true, it still would prove nothing, since splendour, energy and fire can be conveyed in many ways other than by strong overdotting. Thus another attempt to save the dogma falls short of its aim.

The Overdotting Syndrome: Anatomy of a Delusion (FN5)

There have been collective hallucinations that deceived large majorities....
—Jacques Barzun

I. Structural Infirmities

"French overture style" is a common term for an alleged seventeenth- and eighteenth-century convention that involves acute sharpening of dotted notes, contraction of "upbeat figures" such as ♩ ♪♫♫ ♩ or ♩ ♫♫♫ ♩ , and synchronization of the smallest note values at the end of a beat.

The term "French overture style" (hereafter the "style") is misleadingly narrow because even if we include its satellite dances its application reaches far beyond the French overture. How much of the musical landscape the "style" is supposed to cover is difficult to say, because each of its advocates has different ideas about it. Similar disagreements concern the degree of overdotting, the nature of upbeat contractions, and synchronizations.

This essay intends to show that the doctrine of the "style" is untenable *structurally*, because it requires assumptions that range from highly improbable to the absurd, and *evidentially*, because "proof" cannot survive critical scrutiny.

An article of mine in 1965 was apparently the first printed challenge to the existence of the "style." I discussed this issue again in 1974, 1977, and 1979 and in this essay refer to the four articles as FN1, 2, 3, and 4, respectively [*Editor's note:* For ease of comparison, page references in FN5 to these articles (except note 1) refer to pages in this present volume.] Major answers for the defense came from Michael Collins in 1969, David Fuller in 1977, and John O'Donnell in 1979.[1]

Reprinted with permission from *The Musical Quarterly* 67 (1981), pp. 305-47. This essay is dedicated to the memory of Arthur Mendel, lost mentor and friend.

In all matters of substance, I still stand behind what I have written, but I omitted vital points. I failed to stress the important difference between soloistic and orchestral performance; but, of more consequence, I completely overlooked fatal internal incongruities of the doctrine which I am now addressing. These incongruities will be the main subject of part I and, I believe, are sufficient to dismiss the "style" as a historical probability. Part II will deal with alleged evidence that I had not yet or only insufficiently discussed before.

The doctrine appeared in England in the early nineteenth century when William Crotch published keyboard (solo) arrangements of doubledotted Handel overtures.[2] Ebenezer Prout, the most important of several imitators, transferred the principle to the orchestra by overdotting the Sinfonia to *Messiah* (a French overture). His edition with the overdotting spelled out gave wide circulation to this practice. Arnold Dolmetsch, perhaps inspired by these antecedents, formulated in his famous book of 1915 a sweeping theory of rhythmic sharpening. He thus became the theoretical founder of the doctrine which he based on misinterpreted passages in Quantz and C.P.E. Bach (to be discussed later). Mentioning neither the French overture nor the French style, he gave his doctrine a wide range of validity.[3]

In the 1950s, two respected scholars, Thurston Dart and Robert Donington, endorsed the "style" without producing evidence of its existence. Strangely, the mere consensus of the Dolmetsch-Dart-Donington triumvirate proved sufficient to spread the belief in the "style" among ever-growing numbers of converts, all of whom accepted it on faith. Thus fortified, the "style" has taken hold of most researchers and numerous performers[4] in Europe and America and has resulted in the acceptance of its theory as established fact. By now the "style" has become dogma.

Mistaken identities. There have always been certain discrepancies between rhythmic notation and performance. To avoid misunderstanding, it is necessary to eliminate those discrepancies that did occur but had no relevance for the "style." The main categories for such deviations from the notated—notably dotted—rhythms were: 1) soloistic license; 2) the *notes inégales* in France; 3) notational deficiencies; 4) notational laxness; 5) written-out *Nachschlag*-type ornaments; and 6) occasional synchronization. I have dealt with categories (2) to (6) in FN3 (pp. 119ff) and will discuss them only briefly here. But (1), the solo-orchestra polarity, which is fundamental to the issue and which has been overlooked by everyone, including myself, will be discussed in some detail.

It is uncontroversial that during the baroque and preclassical eras the *soloist* enjoyed great license, which was often freely conceded by composers who left ornamentation, articulation, tempo, dynamics up to the performer, though there were notational symbols available to indicate their intentions. The soloist also took liberties with rhythm: he varied the tempo, applied rubato to melodies, rendered evenly written notes unevenly, or altered the length of the dot in either direction. Some composers actually suggested such freedom. Well known are the rubato illustrations of Caccini and the instructions for tempo changes by Frescobaldi, as well as his directive for short-long unevenness in certain contexts. Similarly, Tosi's description of rubato singing against a steady beat, and Mozart's famous letter about the freedom of the right hand against a steady left, all belong in this category of soloistic rhythmic freedom. Documentation of the rhythmic alterations of soloists—notably a German *galant* mannerism of overdotting single dots (before the double dot became commonly used)—was an important element in the formulation and the subsequent defense of the "style." But it was a textbook case of mistaken identities: confusing the soloist with the orchestra, and unrelated eras and styles with each other. (Not one of the German *galant* advocates of overdotting mentioned the French "style," and some important theorists, among them Marpurg and Petri, rejected the practice altogether.)

Orchestral performance was an entirely different matter. While a soloist was expected to alter the letter of the score, or got away with doing so, an orchestral player or member of a chorus could not. The reason is obvious: arbitrary deviations from the written notes in pitch or rhythm, or both, upset the ensemble and create confusion.

Few theorists of the age deal with orchestral performance but those that do invariably stress the need for precision and the discipline of literal execution. Georg Muffat did so in his famous dissertation of 1698 about the Lullian performance style in which, as has been pointed out repeatedly, he discusses at length the *notes inégales* but fails to mention the overdotting of the "style." A few years later, the eminent theorist Fuhrmann describes the ensemble discipline in Buxtehude's famous *Abendmusiken:* "All these instrumentalists must neither alter a note *or a dot* [italics mine] nor bow differently from the way he prescribed it."[5]

Quantz, the misinterpreted crown witness of Dolmetsch and his disciples, enjoins the orchestra director to enforce ensemble discipline.[6] The orchestra player, he says, "must pay the closest attention to the value of the notes... For if he makes a mistake in this regard, he misleads all the others, and produces confusion in the ensemble." And when a soloist plays a ripieno part, he must relinquish freedom and "so to say accept servitude" (par. 15). The contrast of orchestral precision versus soloistic freedom is further reflected in the fact, later to be discussed in detail, that *all* of Quantz's directives about overdotting refer exclusively to the soloist and that the one directive in which he speaks of orchestral performance of French dances—believed by everybody, including myself, to refer to overdotting—was misinterpreted, as I hope to prove.

In a monograph of 1776 on the orchestra violinist, Reichardt devotes chapter VIII to the "exactness with which orchestra players have to execute the notes in front of them." He says: "The paramount duty of the ripienist from which he must not deviate by a hairbreadth is the greatest exactness in the execution. Not a note, not a staccato dash more or different from what is written."[7] That alone should be sufficient testimony. In an earlier chapter (pp. 20-22) Reichardt speaks of dotted notes, saying that they require "a precise and clear rendition" *(Die punktirten Noten erfordern einen genauen und bestimmten Vortrag).* In a sequence of dotted notes such as "one has to observe in particular that the shortened note has to be done as short as possible in order to give greater weight to the longer one." This last sentence deceptively seems to call for overdotting; but in the fast sequence implied by the denominations, executed by separate bowstrokes (as later directed), overdotting is technically impossible in the face of an overwhelming tendency to shorten the dot. The best way, then as now, to avoid such shortening is Reichardt's directive: "Play the short notes as fast as possible." I am not fabricating this argument since even today's leading virtuosos have problems with this rhythm.[8] As a final confirmation, Reichardt writes that the dotted notes "must be held to the end of their value" *(ganz bis zu Ende ihrer Geltung)* to distinguish them from notes followed by rests. They are to be held "to the end," not beyond it.

A year later, Robert Bremner, a student of Geminiani's believing himself to be the first ever to write about the difference between solo and orchestra performance, emphasizes the sharp contrast between the two.[9] The solo player may "crowd the melody with additional notes, or simplify it.... The concert, or orchestra player, on the contrary, is only a member of that whole by which a united effect is to be produced...." Hence, he has to abide by the text. In this lengthy essay Bremner deals among other things with vibrato, ornaments, pure intonation, and management of the bow, but makes no mention of any kind of rhythmic contraction that, after all, would have a profound effect on the uniformity of the ensemble. Scheibe, who wrote a lengthy essay on the French overture,[10] makes no mention of any rhythmic alteration either, nor do any other contemporary theorists.

The soloistic medium, a free-for-all where anything was possible, beclouds our issue. So we must use the *orchestra* as the touchstone for existence or nonexistence of the "style."

Among rhythmic deviations that did occur in the orchestra, the most striking were the French *notes inégales.* Since in a *notes inégales* setting the dot is lengthened by the ratio of the prevailing lilt, some writers have tried to link *inégalité* with the "style": Dart and Donington did it rather vaguely, Collins and O'Donnell explicitly. For several reasons there can be no connection: the *notes inégales* were 1) severely hedged in by their rules, hence far too limited in application; 2) too mild for the sharpness of the "style"; 3) not traceable outside of France; and 4) useless in explaining the contraction of the "upbeat figures." I shall discuss this later.

For our discussion it is important to keep in mind that the rhythmic alterations of the *notes inégales* could work in a *French* orchestra only because all French musicians had the rules for their use hammered into their heads since their earliest musical training. By contrast the total silence of all theorists on the "style" precludes an assumption that any orchestra members were familiar with its complex procedures.

Notational deficiencies could affect the precise interpretation of a composer's meaning in solo as well as orchestral performance. Perhaps the most important was the unavailability of the modern $\sqrt{3}$ which became current only in the mid-nineteenth century. Until then $\int$ was the only available substitute: a makeshift, still used in a ternary sense by Beethoven, Schubert, and Chopin. By and large these were minor matters that look more important today because we mistakenly tend to apply modern standards of performance practices to that time.

A different category was *notational laxness* that was avoidable but used as a shorthand convenience. A frequent case was the cutting in half of the dot's value when $\downarrow$. $\overline{}$ stood for $\downarrow$ $\overline{}$ though the latter notation was available. Donington acknowledges the synonymity of these two patterns as a case of Baroque "underdotting."[11] Being fairly common, it was presumably understood by most orchestra musicians. Here the dot filled the void left by the following notes. In analogy, a few Frenchmen used such a notation as $\int$ which *can* mean $\int$ but often does not, when the tempo is too fast for doubledotting.[12]

Ex. 1. Bach, Cantata 119/3 autograph score

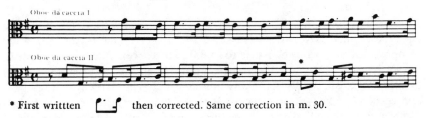

* First writtten $\int$ then corrected. Same correction in m. 30.

Another sample of an inaccuracy that could have been eliminated was the use of an upbeat eighth note in the meaning of a sixteenth. Quantz mentions such use, but it was not a law, as many advocates who see in it a manifestation of the style's synchronization facet wrongly believe. Example 1 offers striking proof for the literal meaning of such upbeat eighth notes and their non-synchronization. In the passage, shown from Bach's autograph score of Cantata 119/3, the double interruption of the dotted rhythm by two eighth notes on the upward leap of a fourth would by itself be indicative of its thematic intent. But most tellingly, at the spot marked by an asterisk, Bach at first wrote a dotted-note pair, which he crossed out and corrected to even eighth notes. The identical correction is then repeated in measure 30.[13]

Other deviations stem from *occasional synchronization* where, in a homophonic or quasihomophonic context, a rhythmic clash of two *parallel* voices makes little sense. The need for such synchronization, which can incidentally produce doubledotting, will be more readily perceived on the keyboard. Once in a while it is desirable for the orchestra, too, but there its execution will be hazardous since it will depend on the correct musical judgment of all the players involved. Under no circumstances can such infrequent synchronization be stretched into a pervasive principle of the kind needed to support the "style."[14]

Another imprecision, always cited in support of the "style," pertains to the *tirades,* the dashing scale figures in thirty-second or sixty-fourth notes, so characteristic of many eighteenth-century French overtures. Quantz in a much-quoted passage refers to them and, provided they start from a dot or a rest, has them played as late as possible, but with detached bowstrokes.[15] In a whole section, the resulting imprecisions blend into a striking orchestral glissando effect.[16] Given the speed and technical difficulty, such rhythmic contraction, if any, could have only been minimal.

The point of this section on "mistaken identities" is this. Except for the *notes inégales* whose clearly structured rules put them into a category of their own, all other rhythmic deviations discussed in the preceding paragraphs were, by the then prevailing standards of orchestral performance, of a cosmetic nature. They either did not exceed the existing tolerance levels for ensemble precision or were innocuous as orchestral effects.

Musical cryptography. The picture of rhythmic alteration for orchestra changes dramatically when we assume the reality of the "style." Now the composer did not want the music to sound even approximately as he wrote it, but desired a drastically different execution. He used a code that the players had to translate in the "clear." Every musician had to be his own cryptographer and needed for the task a conversion table as cipher key. But first of all he had to answer the formidable question: *Which music is in code and which is not?* Without a definite answer to this question, orchestra members could not function. Thus the first hurdle is the *when* of the code's presence or absence.

If we turn to the advocates for an answer, we find that they disagree greatly and are extremely vague. Dolmetsch holds that "the music of the sixteenth and seventeenth centuries abounds in passages that demand [drastic rhythmic sharpening]" hence "we can but feel justified in *treating all the old music alike* in this respect."[17] Thirty years later Dart is no less vague. True, in a chapter on the French style he makes a special point of the French overture (the origin of the term "French overture style") saying that all parts "should move together jerkily [the origin of the "jerky style"] even when their written note-values do not suggest that this is how they should be played. *All* dotted rhythms should be adjusted so that they fit the shortest one in the piece [the origin of the "synchronization law"]. . . . " But for him the overture was only a specimen. Overdotting "was in very wide-spread use over a very great length of time. . . . It is a fashion that lasted from the early years of the seventeenth century down to the last years of the nineteenth. . . . " Then he lists sample composers and works that were subject to the "style," among them Monteverdi, Purcell, Handel and Bach, overtures, marches, sicilianos, jigs, and andantes, *some* Gluck operas, those of Sarti (apparently all); the "style," he continues, is "implied" in Haydn, Mozart, and Beethoven.[18]

This wide and varied assortment of eras, composers, styles, and forms is, like Dolmetsch's directives, useless as a guide for orchestra players.

Donington is also vague. He, too, focuses on the French overture but says that the influence of its style was felt "much farther afield,"[19] and lists, in an interesting contradiction to Dart, the D-major fugue from the *Well-Tempered Clavier,* I (one of Dolmetsch's illustrations). Donington sees in the term "French overture style" "perhaps" a focusing of our attention "upon one particularly recognizable development of the *general baroque practice* of rhythmic sharpening [italics mine]." Then does the "style" apply to *all* baroque music, and if so, what is and what is not baroque music—a convenient but imprecise modern term—which Donington uses in a larger sense than most musicologists, by including Quantz and C.P.E. Bach. Yet he also points to occasional *under*dotting, and general flexibility of the dot in the "baroque." Again we have no useful answer for the cryptographers.

Collins summarizes his findings by saying: "It seems clear that overdotting applies at least from the time of Lully to that of Haydn and Mozart. . . . That it applies at least to the works in French style—*ouvertures, courantes, sarabandes, etc.*— of J.S. Bach, Handel and Telemann is certain, and it no doubt applies to all music except that of a languid, expressive, character in the *galant* and Classical style."[20] Thus Collins appears to apply overdotting from Lully to Bach only to French-style music, then from the *galant* style on, up to and including Mozart, to *all,* except languid and expressive works. (Interestingly, Leopold Mozart had suggested soloistic doubledotting only for occasional slow pieces to keep them from sounding "sleepy.") Collins' answer can give no more direction than the others.

O'Donnell does not address the question of the range for what he calls the "jerky style." He, too, was obviously not aware of the key role for the *when.* His two articles focus on Bach overtures but, since his examples include among others a *pièce de caractère* by F. Couperin and an Allegro movement from a

Vivaldi concerto, he obviously had in mind a much wider scope than French overtures. Significantly, as will be presently documented, he, alone among the advocates, excludes from contraction *all* music beaten in values shorter than half notes.

Clearly, the advocates have formulated their theories about the *when* in an arbitrary fashion. Not having found any clue in primary sources, they had to devise their own answers. These we have seen were a random collection of time spans, composers' names, styles, forms, moods, etc., and *every answer was at odds with every other one.* They may have tried their theories on the keyboard where anything is possible but gave no thought to how orchestra players of the period could have translated such theories into practice.

To strengthen my thesis that the "style" has already come to grief at the first hurdle of the *when,* I shall, in a clinical experiment, assume the most favorable possible circumstances: I shall eliminate all the wide-ranging claims of the advocates and pretend that the answer was pared down to only French overtures and their satellite dances to see whether under such limitation the "style" could be made to work. For experiment's sake let us assume that a title such as "Overture" or "Sarabande," etc., alerted the players to the presence of the code (without worrying how—not having read Dart or Donington—they discovered the special status of such pieces). What happens then with, say, the numerous French overtures in Bach's cantatas (such as Nos. 20, 61, 97, 110, 119, 152, 194)? Some of these were entitled "Sinfonia" or "Sonata" or "Chorus" or "No. 1"; only No. 61 was entitled "Ouverture." How were the players to know that the pieces were in code? This also applied to the numerous instrumental movements, arias, duos, choruses that are in the style or character of a chaconne, sarabande, gavotte, etc., yet never so called. The story is repeated over and over for many composers and compositions.

Thus even within the artificially narrow compass, chosen to give the "style" the best chance of survival, the answer to the *when* is unsatisfactory. The consequence is simple: without an unequivocally clear answer to the *when* that we have a right to assume was known to all orchestra members of the period, the "style" was inoperable. That this condition has not and, as the "clinical experiment" showed, *could* not have been met should now be clear. The first hurdle proved insurmountable.

Let us go a step further and pretend that the *when* was answerable. We now face the *how:* When a player decided a piece was in code, how would he decipher it? Here again, the advocates are vague and discordant.

For the dotted note, Dolmetsch gives no standard conversion ratio. His examples range from double- to quadrupledotting, with different ratios appearing side by side in the same piece. Dart has no precise answers either. He says that as a general rule the disparity between the note pair should be emphasized. For French overtures he mixes double- and tripledotting.

Donington, too, is vague. For the "baroque" he acknowledges a wide range for the dot from underdotting over standard value to overdotting; depending apparently on the expressive need. In French overtures he wants the rhythm to be "as sharp as possible."[21] Collins also fails to commit himself to a specific ratio. Ralph Leavis, in a letter to *Early Music* (1978, p. 309), has a scale reaching from double- to "ultra-dotting." O'Donnell is content with double-dotting for overtures because he wants them to be played much faster than is commonly done. What matters to him is "jerkiness," but by not limiting the "jerky style" to overtures he would need sharper dotting in slower pieces. David Fuller rejects sharp overdotting for overtures. They should have splendor, energy, and fire: "If the short note is delayed so much that there is not time to make it speak properly, the effect will be flabby and neurotic rather than energetic."[22] By contrast, in "flagellation pieces" (whatever they are) "the dotting should be as savage as possible."

Another hurdle is the frequent juxtaposition, both in melodic sequence and in polyphonic interplay, of plain dotted notes and notes that are explicitly doubledotted by either a tie or the insertion of rests such as a) ♩. ♪♩. ⅞♪ b) ♩♪. ♪♩. ♪. ♪ Here the rhythmic sharpening is spelled out, often to the limit of the feasible. Why would composers trouble to specify rhythmic variety and rhythmic clashes when both of these were outlawed by the "style"? If, then, we are forced to assume that such differences in notation were meaningless, then they add a new dimension to the difficulty of deciphering by making the players constantly jump back and forth from what looks coded to what looks "clear." The answer, or the lack of one, from the advocates to this challenge is interesting. Dolmetsch denies the existence of the problem by mistakenly holding (p. 62) that "double dots or combined rests were not used till the end of the eighteenth century." Dart and Donington fail to address the issue. Collins, who records Handel's mixing of 3:1 and 7:1 ratios, tries to dismiss the problem as a "vagary," implying that both had the same meaning.[23] O'Donnell sees the problem and attempts a solution. He posits that the difference between 3:1 and 7:1 ratios in the same piece "is not one of rhythmic ratio but of the amount of silence between the long and short notes. Since the dot in the jerky style was treated as a rest, it automatically carried an articulation significance in addition to its rhythmic meaning."[24] According to this daring theory, illustrated in O'Donnell's example 19 from Lully's *Armide* overture (which mixes 3:1 and 7:1 rhythms), the performed rhythm is uniformly 7:1 while a longer note is to be held *less* long than a shorter one: ♩♪. = ♩♪ but ♩. = ♩. ! Such an interpretation turns elementary notational symbols upside down and becomes still more illusory when we consider that Lully and countless others used rests, or dots *above* notes, not dots *after* notes, to indicate clear breaks of articulation. Also, a sharp articulation will clarify a rhythm without altering it: the shortening of a note at its end must not affect the start of the following note, and it is the latter's start that defines the rhythm and is the main point at issue here.

So far only Graham Pont has recognized the true nature of the problem that a 3:1 versus 7:1 notation creates for the "style" and recognizes that it cannot be ignored or brushed aside as a "vagary." We owe to him a very valuable listing of 157 composers from Byrd and Cavalieri to Gluck and Jommelli, a veritable Who's Who of seventeenth- and eighteenth-century composers who have used the device of either ties or rests to indicate doubledotted rhythms.[25] Needless to say, all these masters used concurrently the singledotted note, and, of course, this notational variety would augment the confusion of the cryptographers.

As though these problems were not enough, the "style" raised the complexities of the code by another power when it extended rhythmic contraction to the "upbeat figures" where no dots are involved. Here, too, Dolmetsch was presumably the originator with his interpretation of Bach's D-major fugue (*WTC,* I).[26] Others simply decreed, obviously inspired by their faith in the overdotting dogma, that rhythmic sharpness in any form is an absolute value, a "consummation devoutly to be wished" and that therefore everything contractible ought to be contracted. For a characteristic manifestation of this faith and as illustration of how advocates, acting on this faith, prescribe rhythmic contractions by fiat, see example 2. It shows O'Donnell's interpretation of the opening measures of Bach's C-major overture.

Ex. 2.   Bach Overture in C

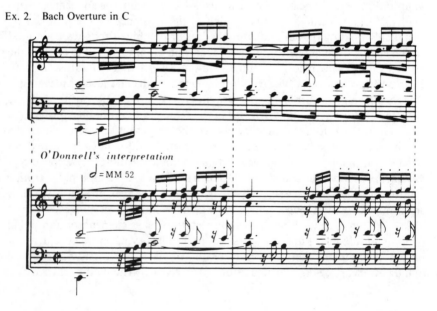

This version interrupts the even flow of sixteenth notes by three brisk jolts in the first three measures. How the amateurs in Bach's Collegium Musicum were to recognize the presence of a code in what even well-indoctrinated overdotting conductors of today have taken as a "clear" message, we are not told, nor is it explained how the players had to solve this cryptographic riddle. What key could have directed the first violins and oboes to contract the second beat in measure 2, but not the analogous third beat in measure 1? Incidentally, Bach wrote C not ¢ (as did O'Donnell), and the piece was certainly beaten in four not in two; hence, according to O'Donnell's own theory, it was not eligible for any kind of rhythmic contraction. And where do the staccato dots come from? I suppose they were to serve (like the dashes in O'Donnell's ex. 23) as surrogates for jerkiness. Yet in measures 103 and 106 Bach's slur marks in this very theme in the continuo part belie such intended articulation.

Another problem with the "upbeat figures" that the advocates have not faced parallels the juxtaposition of 3:1 and 7:1 ratios for the dotted notes; we find similar juxtapositions within the same piece of eighth, sixteenth, thirty-second, and even sixty-fourth note "upbeat figures" of varying numbers of notes, in varying rhythmic contexts, and of varying melodic designs. Surely their intended rhythm cannot be identical, and because of it they would just as surely throw the decoding efforts into disarray.

A further hurdle is the rule of synchronization. The *occasional* need for synchronization, notably on the keyboard, was discussed above. A pervasive principle to that effect is unworkable. David Fuller suggested synchronization for the fast section of Lully's *Armide* overture because it would "sound simply chaotic if played as written."[27] In other words, it has to be decoded. Imagine the problem of a section player who has to figure out whether to synchronize each note and, if so, with whom and how; who was to be the synchronizer and who the synchronized? Since his colleagues are likely to come to different conclusions, the musical result would be chaotic. Fuller may have changed his mind on this point, but the case illustrates the insurmountable difficulties of a would-be orchestral law to eliminate rhythmic clashes.

Forgetting for a moment that the *when* of the code was unanswerable, the *how* could, for the dotted note, be answered speculatively by uncompromising "ultra-dotting" of *every* dotted note regardless of denomination and notated ratio. Even the most devoted advocate would not consider such a solution. But for the "upbeat figures" that range from eighth to sixty-fourth notes—and that can have any number of notes from three upward, can start after a dot, a rest, a tie, or on the beat—I cannot conceive of any speculative deciphering key, however extreme, that could have provided orchestra players with a workable conversion formula. And for synchronization, too, there is no cipher key that could fit the myriad rhythmic combinations between the parts. For these reasons alone both the contraction of "upbeat figures" (outside the extremely narrow scope of Quantz's slightly hurried dashing *tirades*) and consistent synchronization are orchestrally impracticable.

We must not be deluded by the fact that today the "style" is widely practiced. All that is needed to make it work is to edit or rewrite the orchestra parts—the only way in which today's overdotting conductors can safely operate. But the seventeenth and eighteenth centuries knew none of these editorial procedures, and any trace we might find of them would only confirm that cryptography could not stand on its own feet. Yet, if all these incongruities were not enough, worse is still to come.

The chained composer. Suppose that Lully, Bach, Handel, and others wanted the very rhythms they notated, because that is how they conceived them. I submit that these simple, unspasmodic rhythms are neither unnatural, unmusical, illogical, nor illegal. They have been commonplace for centuries and are still common fare. Yet, if the doctrine were true, a composer was, as if shackled by mysterious forces, prevented from *conceiving* them because as soon as written they were, in a King Midas-like miracle, instantly transformed into the pure gold of the jerky pattern. To add to their woes, any idea composers may have had about different rhythms for different voices would also be nipped in the bud and the resultant rhythmic clashes eliminated by the "law" of synchronization. That some of the most ordinary rhythms are among those expurgated; that any sequential rhythmic variety between milder and sharper designs is outlawed; that any polyphony is eradicated de facto by being made inaudible through synchronization; that no moderately paced "upbeat figures" could survive the zealous crusade to contract everything contractible; that we are left with a monolithic rhythmic monotony aggravated by unremitting jerky jolts—all this shows the appalling degree to which composers would have been enchained by the commandments of the "style." I think such tyrannical thought control would be unnatural, unmusical, and nonsensical, because it flies in the face of every tenet of aestheticism.[28]

Thus in order to sustain the "style," hypotheses had to be piled on top of each other, ranging from the highly improbable to the patently absurd, and the "style" has to be dismissed as a historical probability. Here I shall quickly summarize only the most glaring incongruities.

The idea of cryptography is preposterous. Composers who had at their disposal the notational means to clarify their rhythmic intentions chose instead to write how they did *not* want to be interpreted. To explain such irrational behavior, we would have to assume a perverse conspiracy among composers whose interest lay in making themselves as clear, not as inscrutable, as possible. By itself the idea of a code would have been a silly and thoughtless trick to play on orchestral performers. Yet the travesty becomes grotesque when one realizes that apparently all composers of that era mixed—often from beat to beat, and from one voice to a simultaneous one—milder rhythms that looked coded with sharper ones that looked "clear." I hope that I have shown that the critical question of the *when,* that is the presence or absence of a code, was unanswerable, and this alone made the "style" unworkable for an orchestra, and because it was unworkable the "style" could not have existed. Failing this, the question of the *how* of application became academic; but to compound the incongruities, this, too, had no satisfactory answer. Add to this the absurdity of the "chained composer" and the total lack of genuine historical evidence (to be detailed in part II), and we should be prepared to bid good-bye to a cherished phantom friend.

If I have made a strong enough case against the "style" on the grounds of internal incongruities, I would theoretically not need to go further, but several reasons compel me to do so. Trying to avoid disruptive discursions, I have several times made summary statements that are in need of substantiation. Also, knowing the awesome power of faith and the obstinacy of long-held opinions, I have to obviate the criticism that I ignored contrary evidence. I shall therefore proceed to investigate those arguments proffered for the "style" that I have not yet or only inadequately dealt with: those that attended the birth of the "style" and those that were put forward later in an attempt to defend it against criticism.

II. The Evidential Infirmities

The "Handel Tradition"

A leading argument for the "style" is an alleged Handelian tradition of doubledotting his overtures. Of all the research tools available to historical performance, few are as treacherous as the recourse to "tradition." Certainly, tradition is a powerful force in many human pursuits, notably within static institutions. But Western music was not static, and of all artistic endeavors musical performance—prior to the age of the phonograph—was the most elusive, most ephemeral, and the least susceptible of being frozen into a semblance of permanency. It is, after all, humanly impossible to duplicate exactly anybody else's performance, least of all that of a genius. In earlier centuries, when today's concern for "authenticity" was unknown, even the students of great masters rarely attempted to imitate their always variable and highly personal manner of playing. Hummel's monstrous cadenza to Mozart's C-minor concerto would be today considered a model of authenticity, if we did not happen to know so many of Mozart's own cadenzas. Here a "tradition" was already stillborn.

When in later years some performers did try to imitate a model they admired, the best they could do, given its fleeting nature, was to acquire certain details and add traits of their own. These traits in turn might strike the fancy of the next imitator. Such additions then cling like barnacles to the musical hull and in each succeeding generation additional layers are formed in parasitic growth. In FN3 I quoted Gustav Mahler's caustic epigram: "Tradition ist Schlamperei" [slovenliness]; in a similar vein, Toscanini said: "Tradition may only be the memory of the last bad performance"; and Arthur Mendel, in a letter, fittingly characterized tradition as "imitations of imitations of imitations." All considered, the odds are forbidding that we might be heirs to an unbroken, unadulterated tradition over centuries to any early master's performances.

In his "Handel Studies," Jens Peter Larsen outlines several phases for "Messiah Performance Traditions."[29] He tells how the first decisive break with Handelian practices occurred in 1784 with the transfer from the theater to Westminster Abbey and an "enormous enlargement of performance forces" which in turn led to a slowing down of the tempos. The nineteenth century saw a reflection of "vocal attitudes of the Wagnerian era" in corrupt performance editions (such as those of Chrysander); the twentieth century, the tampering with the melodic line in rhythm and ornamentation, "at times beyond recognition...dotted notes become double dotted, and even notes become *notes inégales*" (p. 29). For the tempos of Handel's oratorios in general, Larsen deduces from the available source material (including autograph length indications for the three parts of *Solomon*) five distinct stages which move from Handel's own lively tempos to ever-greater slowness, then gradually rebounding from the worst excesses (pp. 31-40).

At the *Messiah* Symposium of December, 1980, in Ann Arbor, several papers traced a great many other *Messiah* performance traditions including monster presentations in the Crystal Palace with 14,000 participants. The very number of diverse "traditions" that have spontaneously sprung up over the last 250 years, and continue to do so in our time, point up the chimerical nature of the supposedly *one* pure and undefiled "authentic" one.

As discussed in part I, the advocates trace their "Handelian tradition" of overdotting to William Crotch's keyboard arrangements of the early nineteenth century. His doubledotting was prompted, and was almost necessitated, by his funereal tempos which he marked with the aid of a pendulum, using as metrical unit a slow eighth note, when in Handel's time even a Grave C meter was beaten in four, never in eight. Apart from this incongruence, the date of the evidence—three generations after Handel's death—would be reason enough to dismiss it.

Even though soloists could have taken similar freedoms at any time before, it is surprising that none seem to have done so (an insignificant exception remains to be quoted). In FN4 I published two pages from the manuscript: British Library RM 18 c.1. that dates approximately from the late 1720s (plates 5 and 6 of this volume). It contains harpsichord transcriptions of seventeen Handel overtures in a manner that betrays a professional. In the meticulously calligraphic notation the rhythmic symbols are throughout geometrically aligned according to their nominal values. Here I am presenting additional external evidence for Handel and for Lully. The Handel evidence is particularly weighty because it comes from J.C. Smith, Handel's copyist and closest collaborator. It is contained in an important manuscript collection in Smith's hand at the New York Public Library (Lincoln Center).[30] The sizable volume, containing harpsichord transcriptions of Handel works for orchestra, along with original harpsichord compositions, exhibits throughout the same external evidence for the exactness of the dot, as found in the London MS RM 18 c.1. Characteristic of this evidence is the first part of the overture to *Amadigi* shown in plate 7. In almost every measure we see the geometrical indications of both rhythmic clashes and synchronizations which are due to the precise meaning of the dot. None perhaps is as eloquent as the spot in measure 10 with its juxtaposition of a double dot (by means of a rest) in the alto and a single dot in the tenor in exact mutual alignment as well as the geometrical reflection of their respective clash and simultaneity with the soprano. For other graphic reflections of clashes see measures 3, 12, 13, 14, and 15.

Plate 7. Handel, Overture to *Amadigi*, transcribed for harpsichord by J.C. Smith (ca. 1720-22) Courtesy: Music Division, The New York Public Library, Astor, Lenox & Tilden Foundations (Drexel 5856).

Also of interest is a later document in the New York Public Library: a 270-page volume entitled *Manuscript of 18th Century Music,* written between 1760 and 1770. It contains harpsichord transcriptions of many works by Handel and his contemporaries. No overdotting is anywhere in evidence. Though the alignments are not always careful, in many spots, for example in the overture to *Radamisto* (p. 197), the intended exactness is unmistakable.

A Walsh edition of circa 1759 of *Handel's Sixty Overtures from all his Operas and Oratorios* arranged for violins in eight parts has all the original rhythmic notation. In FN4 I mentioned the equally faithful rhythms in Walsh's keyboard arrangements of Handel overtures issued in Handel's lifetime in two volumes of twenty-four overtures each. Many first editions of Handel's operas and oratorios are in the Jacobi S. Hall collection at the Princeton University Library.[31] All carry the subtitle "as performed" in the King's Theatre at either the Haymarket, or the Royal Academy, or the Theatre Royal at Covent Garden; and all are printed as Handel wrote them, that is in would-be code. Later eighteenth-century editions present the same picture. Singling out the *Messiah* overture as the center piece of the "tradition," we find it in its original rhythmic form in the Randall and Abel (successors to Walsh) first complete edition of 1767; in a keyboard version in the Harrison edition of *Songs of Handel* of 1789; in a Harrison edition (of the same year) of the oratorio arranged for voice, harpsichord, and violin; in the Preston edition of the oratorio of 1805 (a reprint of the Wright edition of ca. the same year); in Dr. John Clark's organ or pianoforte transcription of Handel's vocal works, Button and Whittaker, London (ca. 1809 or later); in the Breitkopf edition of Mozart's orchestration in 1803.

Seemingly all editions and manuscripts of scores, parts, and transcriptions during the whole eighteenth century and beyond show no doubledotting that Handel had not spelled out himself by ties or rests. The conclusion is unavoidable that the "tradition" is of nineteenth-century vintage hence of the barnacle species. As such it has be be dismissed as a pipeline to Handel's intentions.[32]

The Lully evidence. The "style" supposedly started with Lully, which gives considerable interest to a number of documents for that master's overtures and dances. Well-known and easily accessible (in a facsimile print and modern editions) are the harpsichord transcriptions by d'Anglebert. In FN2 (ex. 6) I presented the latter's version of the overture to *Proserpine* where inserted ornaments into eighth-note "upbeat figures" ruled out intended contractions.

Many other masters made keyboard transcriptions of Lully's works. Among the most interesting of these is a manuscript volume of nearly 200 pages (British Library, Add. MS 39569), written in 1702 by Charles Babell (father of the well-known William). It contains, along with a number of Lully pieces, works by numerous seventeenth-century French composers and a few English

Plate 8. Lully. Overture to *Persée*, transcribed by Charles Babell (1702). British Library Add. MS 39569. p. 110.

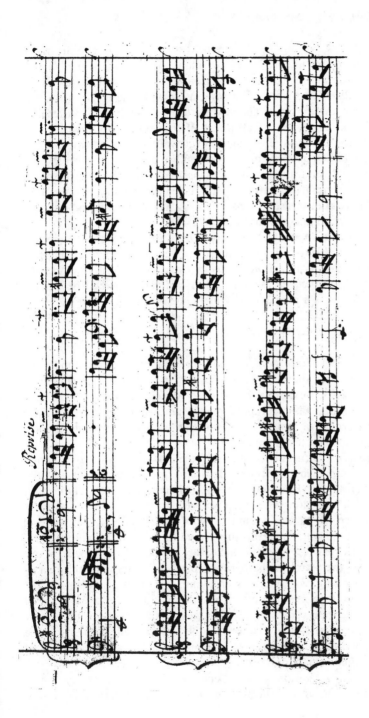

and Italian masters writing in the French style.[33] Babell Senior was a bassoonist at the opera in The Hague, which at the time was under French musical dominance, and he had close connections with the inner circle of the Paris harpsichordists. This fact and his association with The Hague opera add weight to his keyboard versions. The manuscript is throughout a masterpiece of calligraphy; the alignments in all pieces of the volume are invariably of geometrical precision, always reflecting the exact values of the notes as written. Plate 8 gives a characteristic example from Lully's overture to *Persée.*

Since practically all transcriptions had inserted ornaments (mostly *ports-de-voix,* trills, mordents), it is extraordinary, given the freedom of the soloist, that among the mass of transcriptions[34] Professor Gustafson found only one with some spotty rhythmic alterations.[35]

No contraction of "upbeat figures" could be found in any of the keyboard arrangements I was able to consult, though there were plenty of ornaments that would preclude such contraction. Thus it appears that, if the "Handel tradition" was a product of the nineteenth century, a would-be Lullian overdotting tradition is a post-World War II phenomenon.

The Founder's Arguments

Dolmetsch. Since Dolmetsch's doctrine was the theoretical foundation for the "style" and his prestige the propelling force for its widespread acceptance, I shall turn to a detailed examination of his evidence and reasoning. I have discussed Dolmetsch in FN1, but incompletely, and without awareness of the decisive soloist-orchestra polarity and of the futility of his single most important item of theoretical support.

Dolmetsch's first witness is Quantz, and the first citation is from chapter V, paragraph 21, in which Quantz explains that dotted eighth, sixteenth, and thirty-second notes are to be strongly overdotted because of the *liveliness* they are to express.[36] He demonstrates the overdotting in four graphic examples through the device of vertical alignment with smaller note values. Several important facts stand out: 1) overdotting served to sharpen the edge of lively rhythms, not to create a jerky effect in a measured, moderate tempo; 2) for this reason Quantz, in the preceding paragraph, specifically exempted the quarter note from overdotting; 3) Quantz is speaking here of the soloist, not the orchestra; 4) there is no mention of the French style; 5) sharp overdotting of "lively" eighths is at best very difficult, of sixteenths and thirty-seconds, rarely if ever practicable; 6) most likely we see here the first theoretical reflection of a German *galant* soloistic mannerism of doubledotting, not a late reflection of seventeenth-century French practices.

Another Quantz citation is from chapter XII, paragraph 24, which discusses the rendition of the Allegro and the portrayal of various emotions, among them *das Prächtige,* "the splendrous," "the brilliant." Dolmetsch, and several later writers, mistranslated the term as "the majestic," though Quantz used it here and elsewhere in the context of an unmajestic Allegro. For the latter he lists as an alternative of expressing splendor the use of dotted notes, vivaciously executed and overdotted according to the principles given in Chapter V, paragraphs 20-21, hence applied only to dotted eighth and sixteenth notes, not to dotted quarter notes. Again the passage is addressed to the soloist.

Dolmetsch then presents the important passage of chapter XVII, vii, paragraph 58, that deals with a ballet orchestra's performance of French dances. It is important because it alone establishes a link with both the orchestra and the French style. This passage has deceived everyone, including myself, into believing that it prescribes strong overdotting of the quarter notes in French dances. Though rather late, and reflecting Berlin practices, the passage seemed so far the *only* solid theoretical evidence for the orchestral "style." In FN4, I suggested that Quantz speaks here of sharp articulation, not of sharpened rhythm, but I failed to make a strong enough case for the new interpretation. I do so now because by toppling this *sole* theoretical support, the whole doctrine, already unhinged structurally, also becomes unhinged evidentially.

The key sentences are: "... in this 2-meter as well as in the 3/4-meter of the loure, sarabande, courante, or chaconne, the eighth note following dotted quarter notes must be played not according to their literal value but *very short and sharp* [italics mine]. The dotted note is emphasized and during the dot the bow is lifted." It was the combination of "not according to their literal value" and "short and sharp" which gave rise to the overdotting interpretation, when in fact the directive referred to the French, as contrasted to the Italian (and German), *bowing style.* An Italian or German violinist, asked to play ♩. ♪ in slow or moderate tempo, would have played the dotted note with a cantabile downbow stroke and retraced the eighth note on the upbow with the notes well connected. In a more lively tempo, we would have taken both notes in the same bow, stopping briefly between them, with a similar effect. The French, on the other hand, with their shorter bows, from the time of Lully and well into the eighteenth century, practiced a short and sharply articulated bow stroke, leaving a distinct *silence d'articulation.*

The true meaning of the two sentences emerges from several other statements in the book. For the first we need to go back to paragraph 56. Here Quantz speaks for the first time of French ballet music and points out its differences from the Italian style, the French being "generally played with a heavy but *short and sharp* [italics mine] bowstroke, more detached than connected." There is, he says, little gentleness and songfulness: "The dotted notes are played heavily, their companion notes by contrast *very short and sharp*" and the fast dances have to be played "with a very short, strongly accented bowstroke,"[37] in order constantly to move the dancer and impel him to leap and at the same time give the audience a musical portrayal of the dancer's action.

Here we have twice more our key words "short and sharp" in a context that leaves no doubt about their referring to articulation, not rhythmic disposition. In this paragraph the two words contrast the French short and sharp articulation with the songfulness of the Italian style of playing. The second reference is specifically focused on the short note following the dot and here the true meaning is not blurred by the mention of "literal value" which had disoriented commentators. Also a short and sharp on-time eighth note could both inspire and musically reflect a dancer's leap, whereas a strongly overdotted one could do neither.

If, after Quantz's introductory discussion of the French dance performance style and its particular application to the dotted note, we reread the two sentences of paragraph 58, it becomes clear that they represent a reaffirmation and amplification of paragraph 56, not a totally different instruction. Now Quantz only adds that the dotted quarter note is to be shortened by the length of the dot (for which the bow is lifted)—which only confirms the detached, unconnected playing style. Hence the "short and sharp" rendition of the eighth note means . An intended deviation from the notated rhythmic relationships—in repudiation of paragraph 56—would have had to be expressly mandated. Every time Quantz asks for rhythmic alteration he is unfailingly explicit about his meaning. And remember that even a soloist was to play dotted quarter notes in an exact manner.

We find a second confirmation in a passage about the orchestra violinist in chapter XVII, ii, paragraph 13, where Quantz speaks of dotted eighth and sixteenth notes in slow pieces, the very notes which the soloist was to overdot strongly. The orchestra violinist, by contrast, must play these notes with a heavy bow and "in a sustained or *nourissant* manner" without lifting the bow for the second note. The dots must be held to the very end of their value to avoid an impression of impatience that would change an adagio into an andante. "The sixteenth notes following a dot[ted eighth] must always be played *very short and sharp* be the tempo slow or fast, because dotted notes express the splendrous and elevated, hence each note, unless marked by a slur, requires a separate bowstroke, since it is not possible to render the short notes after the dot as *sharply* by detaching the bow with the same stroke, as can be done with a new upbow [italics mine]." I quote the entire passage because it is revealing and because I did not grasp its significance in FN3. By saying that the dotted note is to be held to the end of its value to avoid the impression of impatience, Quantz cautions against *shortening* the dot, but excludes its lengthening. In contrast to the dotted quarter notes in French dances, the bow is *not to be lifted* and the following note played "very short and sharp." The only technically rational way of following these instructions is to play: ♩ . By contrast, an overdotting, especially a marked one, without previously lifting the bow is *violinistically impossible*. Here we have technical proof that this fourth mention of "short and sharp" also refers to articulation, not delay. Significantly, we also see in these passages the clear polarity of soloist versus orchestra. The soloist expressed "splendor" by the overdotting of dotted eighths and shorter values; the orchestra player expressed it, for the same denominations, by sharp articulation and precise rhythm.[38]

A third passage reinforces the proof. Quantz opens chapter XVII, ii, paragraph 26, with the remark that for the accompaniment, especially of lively pieces, the French short and articulated bowstroke *(kurzer und articulirter Bogenstrich)* is more effective than the Italian long and dragging stroke *(langer und schleppender Strich);* he ends by saying that he will explain "the type of bowstroke used in French dance music" in chapter XVII, vii, paragraph 58, which contains the two sentences we are discussing. We are thus explicitly told that the two sentences deal with *bowstroke,* hence with articulation, not with rhythm. This, I believe, closes the ring of the circumstantial evidence about the true meaning of the two sentences. With it, the "style" has lost its sole theoretical mainstay.[39]

Why have these sentences been misunderstood? One reason is the psychological conditioning brought about by faith in the doctrine. A second may be a retroactive effect of the next sentence (briefly mentioned above) in which Quantz speaks of "three or more thirty-second or shorter notes that follow a dot or a rest that are not always played with their literal value, especially in slow pieces, but at the extreme end of the time allotted to them and with the greatest possible speed.... " They have, he says, to be played with separate bowstrokes. He speaks here of the fast scale passages, the *tirades,* as Fuller justly calls them, that were a characteristic feature in many eighteenth-century French overtures and *entrées*. Here rhythmic alteration is made explicit by the words "at the very end of their value"—the kind of explicitness that would have been indispensable in the previous sentence if Quantz had meant to convey a rhythmic alteration of the dotted quarter note.[40]

Dolmetsch's second witness is C.P.E. Bach, who deals with the question of the dotted note in two distinct passages.[41] Dolmetsch cites only the first of these two passages in a regrettable mistranslation that changes its meaning.[42] Suffice it to say here that C.P.E. Bach speaks of the soloist, not the orchestra, and not of the French style, and that he lists besides overdotting the alternatives of exactness and underdotting. For these reasons he is not a practicable witness for the "style." His occasional overdotting was, like Quantz's, an early testimonial to the new, spotty, German *galant* mannerism.

Finally there are Dolmetsch's assertions that strong overdotting was "quite natural" and that the music of the sixteenth and seventeenth centuries "abounds in passages that demand it." Clearly, a judgment based solely on personal taste has no evidential value. Besides, if any rhythm is more "natural" than any other one, it is an even pulse: the basic life rhythm of the heartbeat, of breathing, and sex; and if any rhythm is less "natural" than others it is the strongly overdotted one, because it is antivocal and can be difficult, at times impossible, for instruments to execute.

I believe I have shown that, for the orchestra, Dolmetsch failed to present a single item of valid historical evidence.

Dart and Donington. Thurston Dart made no effort to support the "style" with independent research. He vaguely refers to the *notes inégales,* for which he cites a passage from Couperin's treatise. Under the form of a direct citation, he offers a paragraph of twenty-five lines, of which less than seven correspond to Couperin's text.[43] The rest is a free exposition of Dart's own ideas about the French style not to be found anywhere in Couperin's treatise. This procedure illustrates the relaxed and carefree manner in which the doctrine was shaped by its chief architects. Dart then follows his reference to *inégalité* with his previously cited influential description of the French overture style and with his vague guidelines for its application.

Robert Donington at first simply adopted his teacher Dolmetsch's theory. Later he leans on Collins and refers to the "Handel tradition."[44]

Defense of the "Style"

The arguments just described were the motive force behind the triumphant advance of the "style" to worldwide domination. Since I first questioned the reality of the "style" in 1965, a number of writers have rallied to its defense.[45] For reasons of space, I shall refer the reader to such answers as I have previously given and shall discuss here mainly the most recent arguments.

Regarding Michael Collins, I am referring to FN2, especially pages 104-6, and FN3, pages 116-17, and 129-32. David Fuller, writing in 1977 about FN1 only, charged me with a multitude of sins of logic in a catalogue longer than Leporello's. But since then Fuller has written a remarkable letter to *Early Music.*[46] He starts by quoting a sentence from his article: "It seems to me that the letter of Neumann's conclusion is so far beyond dispute as to require no defense at all: there was no single comprehensive 'style' of extreme obligatory overdotting. . . . " After mentioning my pointing out a circular argument of his—it was not the only one I pointed out—he continues: "I should hate to think that readers of *EM* might come away from this *querelle* with the impression that my purpose was to preach the gospel of overdotting. Gospels are death to musical performance, and besides, no one really knows how Lully or anybody else performed his overtures." (I could not agree more.) He then continues to say that he *did* preach a sermon against my "syllogistic legalisms; if I stumbled," he continues, "it was because I was unused to them." The sentence he quoted from his article condemns the "style" more completely than its wording seems to indicate, since, as shown above, an orchestral overdotting convention would even theoretically be conceivable only if it were universal and extreme. Fuller agreed with me that neither of the two categories, the *notes inégales* and the German *galant* mannerism of soloistic overdotting, can be linked to the "style." That his third category of "special cases," including French overtures, was a less robust hypothesis, I have tried to show in the last paragraph of FN4.

Concerning Professor O'Donnell, I shall not deal here with his first article on tempo. Even if we were to accept his thesis of a rather fast tempo for overtures, such a tempo does not touch the heart of the issue: the principle of obligatory overdotting.[47]

His second article is very complicated and difficult to deal with. If I read it correctly, its main arguments regarding the dotted note pursue the following plan. Their aim is to prove the pervasiveness of the "jerky style" for an unspecified body of music of the seventeenth and eighteenth centuries. This body includes French overtures and dances except those beaten in quarter-notes, but it must also encompass many other kinds of music since the examples include such disparate styles as organ Masses, *pièces de caractère,* and Italian concertos.

The procedure is twofold: first it claims that, given the faster tempo advanced for the overtures, a plain doubledotting of the quarter note suffices to achieve "jerkiness"—thus tempering the sharper contractions of other advocates. Second, the *notes inégales* provide the needed doubledotting. I shall now address this central argument of O'Donnell's.

By and large, French overtures were probably played faster than they are today. But there could have been no unified tempo during the roughly one hundred years of the overture's blossoming in various countries. *Tirades* in sixty-fourth notes, frequent in Handel, technically limit the speed as do the complex textures of Bach's overtures; and many movements in Italian concertos and other pieces within the undefined realm of the "jerky style" were certainly slow enough so that the sixteenth notes did not sound "jerky."

The essayed strategy meets far greater trouble from the *notes inégales.* They could play their role in the scheme only on two conditions: 1) that they were consistently of a 3:1 ratio, and 2) that they were applicable to *all* cases claimed for the "style."

As to the first condition, the required 3:1 ratio, we find overwhelming evidence of much milder *inégalité,* in keeping with the latter's ornamental purpose of adding grace and elegance. Among some fifty-odd theorists who dealt with the *notes inégales,* O'Donnell found only one, the maverick François David, who lists a 3:1 ratio for *inégalité* (and is unlikely to have meant it as a rigid prescription). Saint Lambert, whom O'Donnell singles out as "giving perhaps the best summary," lets the *goût* decide for the harpsichord soloist: for some pieces, he writes, a strong *inégalité (fort inégales)* is proper, for others a mild one. Hence the "strong" unevenness is only an occasional option and besides not necessarily 3:1, since 2:1 is, after all, a rather strong inequality. References to strong *inégalité* are very rare and when they occur are, as in Saint Lambert, limited in application.

In FN3, I presented a body of evidence that pointed to predominant mildness. Among others, I quoted Loulié, Montéclair, Villeneuve, Choquel, Mercadier de Belesta, Jean Jacques Rousseau, who stress mildness by saying that the first of two notes is *a little longer* than the second. Others, like Hotteterre and L'Affilard—among O'Donnell's main witnesses—speak of the first note being long, the second short in a formulation that falls short of requiring the needed 3:1 ratio.

David Fuller sees the range of *inégalité* spanning the gamut "from nearly equal to the equivalent of dotted rhythms of 3:1; preliminary evidence of mechanical instruments suggests that the ratio varied freely within the same phrase or piece, and that it was more apt to be subtle than extreme: 2:1, 3:2 or even 4:3."[48]

O'Donnell, like others before him, was misled by the notational and terminological imprecisions which I briefly mentioned in part I (under "mistaken identities") and discussed at greater length in FN3. The gist is 1) that because ♩ ♪ , let alone ♫ , was unknown, ♫♩ was the only available graphic design to indicate *any* amount of long-short ratio, even a very small one. Only Loulié, in the manuscript additions to his treatise of 1696, used the ingenious design ♩. ♩ ♩. ♩, to indicate *inégalité,*[49] and 2) the linguistic counterpart to dotted notation, the term "pointer" could likewise stand for any lengthening from the smallest increment to standard dotting.[50] Thus, when O'Donnell writes that "vigorous inequality has the full support of the French theorists" (p. 338) and "alternate dotting (3:1) of quavers ... and overdotting (7:1) of dotted crotchets is what the French teach" (p. 339) the statements are invalidated by an overwhelming mass of contrary evidence. And when he writes that "the quavers of overtures were performed ... *fort inégales,*" the French terms derive from the quotation of Saint Lambert given above that has nothing to do with overtures.

Thus, the first condition, the 3:1 ratio, fell far short of fulfillment. The second, the universality of application, is even more problematical. The *notes inégales* are traceable only for France, not Italy or England, and in spite of some attempts to introduce them in Germany (Muffat and Quantz) there is no indication of any noteworthy inroads.[51]

In France itself, the use of the *notes inégales* was strongly limited, as pointed out in part I, besides being subordinated to the *goût*. The eighth notes, which are the center of the controversy because their *inégalité* lengthens the dot of a quarter note, were *equal* in C and even in ₵ meter when the latter was beaten in four rather than in two; as well as in all cases of disjunct motion. It is probably with regard to this metrical limitation that O'Donnell significantly restricts the doubledotting of the "style" to meters beaten in half notes, whereas in meters beaten in four quarters, the dotted quarter note "would not be overdotted, and any desired rhythmic intensification would have to be notated as such" (p. 340). With this statement O'Donnell himself eliminates from the "jerky style" practically all of Bach's, Handel's, and Dieupart's overtures because they are in C meter, and countless other works, including those in ₵ meter that were beaten in four. Even without this remarkable concession that by itself largely subverts O'Donnell's theory of the "jerky style," the fact that both fundamental conditions of his strategic plan were unfulfilled by a wide margin spells its failure.

Concerning O'Donnell's other arguments, he sees "possibly the earliest detailed description of the alleged style" in two essays by Roger North written in 1728 (p. 336). In the first one North points to the vogue of the French style, as initiated by Lully, during the early years of the Restoration in England. He speaks of French orchestral suites in concert form and mentions their theatrical, dancelike character, their having "more regard to the foot than the ear and no one could hear an *Entrée* with its *starts and saults* but must expect a dance to follow.... "

O'Donnell is certain that the "starts and saults" describe the "jerkiness" of doubledotting. I think these terms apply better to single dots whose companion notes are sharply delivered on time (Quantz's "short and sharp" articulation): ♩ ⸽ ♪ 𝄾𝄿 because the latter is far more suggestive of dancers' "saults" than the strongly contracted "jerky" rhythms that would leave no time for them.

North then describes "two modes of the Grave." The first is the *start* "striking upon a semiquaver rest, thus":

whose "desultory action" contrasts with the "sober" bass. Here we have a *written-out* doubledotting in rhythmic clash with the steady movement of the bass. O'Donnell infers: "These remarkably vivid descriptions of the 'style' leave no possible doubt about one aspect of the performance—its jerkiness." On the contrary, the example and its vivid description confirm that a rhythmic sharpening could occur, but had to be specified in notation by rests (as here) or by ties, as was the rhythmic clash between the parts. It certainly does not prove that without such specification a written 3:1 ratio would have had to be played 7:1.

The claim to "jerkiness" is further contradicted by North's second example, illustrating the *stopp* which O'Donnell did not discuss. "The other mode is the stopp, striking after a quaver rest all together in this manner":

According to O'Donnell's conception of the "style," this passage ought to be doubledotted. Yet the explicit mention of striking after the "quaver rest all together" leaves no doubt that, here too, in this "second mode" we have to do with a rendition *as notated,* which happens to have neither jerks nor rhythmic clashes, because the harmony was paramount: "Harmony cannot be had with more advantage than by these stopps."[52] The two examples beautifully summarize the variety of rhythms, both horizontal and vertical, sharpened or mild, clashing or synchronized. Thus the "possibly earliest description of the style" actually disproves it.

O'Donnell's reference (p. 330) to Bacilly's singing "par sacades" or "par sautillement"—expressions sounding like equivalents of the "jerky style"—overlooks Bacilly's rejection of such a rendition as "fort désagréable."[53]

Gigault, O'Donnell continues, made in 1685 "an unequivocal statement demanding both overdotting and synchronization: 'When there is a semiquaver above a quaver they must be played together.'" O'Donnell found one such incidence in Gigault's book (O'Donnell's ex. 12). The principle refers to the infrequent cases where synchronization is a likely intention whenever a rhythmic clash would make little sense for parallel voices. I demonstrated specimens in FN1, example 32, and FN3, examples 8a–d, and pointed out that overdotting as a chance by-product of such rare synchronization cannot support the "style."

Montéclair is listed with "two contributions." In his example 13, O'Donnell gives the start of an *Air* or *Entrée* from Montéclair's treatise of 1709 *(Méthode nouvelle)* where he uses in measures 1 and 3 the unmetrical notation of an excess beam after dotted notes:♪ | ♩ ♩. ♩ whereas all the other dotted notes, including one in measure 2, are metrical. O'Donnell concludes that these two specimens prove that Montéclair "takes for granted the existence of the jerky style." The inference is unfounded. Though such irregular notation does not necessarily imply doubledotting,[54] in this particular case it may well do so. Still, it has no evidential value for the "jerky style" since—I quote from my FN3—"an *irregular notation* that implies an exact non-standard length of the dot does not admit the inference of an obligatory over- or underdotting for a dot written in standard notation—and that is what the whole issue is about." There is no law whereby the sharpest rhythm in a piece has to infect its whole rhythmic fabric and force it into conformity.[55] These two measures only prove again that a composer had to specify an intended sharper rhythm in any of various ways, of which irregular notation was an occasional makeshift alternative.

The second "contribution" (O'Donnell's ex. 14) shows, in a demonstration of ties and dotted notes, along with standard examples, the following superposition ♩ ♩♩ ♩ where the alignment seems to indicate double-dotting. His comment that "the overdotting of dotted crotchets is included as part of the most rudimentary training in music theory" is misleading. We should be told that the example is preceded by two clear statements of the standard value of every dot.[56] On page 22, as part of the most rudimentary training in music theory, Montéclair stipulates that in 2-meter "the quarter-note...when followed by a dot, is worth, or lasts, three fourths of a beat." On the next page, immediately preceding the example given by O'Donnell, Montéclair reiterates and illustrates the value for each dotted note, among them:

La Noire pointée ♩.
vaut trois croches ♫ ♪

In view of this unequivocal, twice-stated principle, the suggestion of a longer value for the dot would have called for comment. In the absence of one, a plausible explanation is that a dotted note could occasionally have the meaning of a doubledotted one, notably in the infrequent cases where musical logic suggests synchronization. Given the complete context of the rudimentary rule, verbally and graphically formulated, one possibility is excluded: that it *had* to have such meaning whenever it appeared. Hence both "contributions" fail to support the "style."

O'Donnell reports that Loulié in his explanation of the dotted note does not imply overdotting, but L'Affilard does. As to the dotted note "...a significant difference exists between the discussion of these two theorists. Loulié is explaining rudiments of *notation,* while L'Affilard is presenting rudimentary instruction in *performance*" (p. 337). I can detect no difference in approach. Loulié says, "in singing one holds the [dotted] eighth note a little longer [*un peu plus longtemps*] and passes over quickly [*passer viste*] the sixteenth note." L'Affilard, speaking of the dotted quarter note says: "To render the dots in their proper value one has to sustain [*suspendre*] the dotted quarter and pass quickly the eighth note." Both address the beginner and for that reason content themselves with a sketchy approximation. That L'Affilard later describes a "departure from the literal notation" is true, when he deals with the *notes inégales* and speaks of eighth notes whose first of a pair is *pointé.*

In another example of *dotted* notes, he marks them *pointez fort.* O'Donnell comments: "Surely we can read these as 'dot' and overdot." We can not do so. This is the first of several cases where O'Donnell, as others before him, misread *pointer* for a standard dot.[57]

The same misreading of the terms *point* and *pointer* is obvious in a passage which O'Donnell quotes from Jullien's organ book of 1690 where the latter writes that one should dot "more or less lightly" according to the indicated character *(mouvement)* of the piece (p. 338). The wording specifies a variability of the dot that tends towards mildness. O'Donnell quotes Gigault as saying that "one can animate one's playing more or less by adding dots whenever one wishes." The option it offers disqualifies it as pervasive principle, and the "dots," in keeping with the prevailing usage, are almost certainly of Jullien's gentle variety.

The misreading of the term from Montéclair is apparent. O'Donnell cites him as instructing the student to sing a passage of conjunct eighth notes "as if they were notated" with dots (p. 338). We are not told that Montéclair precedes the dotted illustration to which O'Donnell refers with the directive that in those cases where the eighth notes are *inégales* "one holds the first a *little longer* than the second" *(on demeure un peu plus sur la premiere que sur la seconde)* which is a clear indication that the notated dots stand for a very mild inequality (italics mine).[58]

In a difficult paragraph on page 338, O'Donnell tries to enlist Loulié as an advocate of vigorous inequality. What Loulié, speaking of eighth notes in three meter, says is simple and straightforward. O'Donnell himself gives at the outset this correct and concise report: "Loulié . . . distinguishes between *Détacher les Nottes* (disjunct motion, performed equally), *Lourer* (conjunct motion, the first of a pair a little longer than the second), and *Piquer* or *Pointer* (the first note much longer than the second but *requiring a dot* [italics mine] in the notation." Then he quotes from my FN3 that "only the *lourer* with its mild unevenness represents *notes inégales,* since the concept of *inégalité* refers solely to evenly written pairs of notes." Since Loulié in the definition of the terms stipulates the need of a notated dot for the indication of vigorous inequality for his *piquer* or *pointer* (for once "pointer" seems to be used in the sense of standard dotting), it is impermissible to argue that Loulié prescribed a 3:1 ratio for evenly written notes.[59]

O'Donnell's theory of doubledotting was predicated on the assumption that evenly written eighth notes were rendered 3:1 and dotted notes 7:1. I trust that I have shown that his witnesses, Gigault, Jullien, Montéclair, L'Affilard, Hotteterre, Loulié, and North, do not bear him out.

O'Donnell "concludes the case for overdotting" with an example from André Raison's *Livre d'orgue* of 1689. I had pointed to Raison's systematic use of double dots and argued that his carefully explicit differentiation between 3:1

and 7:1 ratios, in analogy to the ties or rests used by other masters, indicated different rhythmic intent and literal meaning of the single dot. O'Donnell cites the start of the *Offerte du 5 me ton* (his ex. 20) as the "only real overture" in the book. It is a fine illustration for my thesis. The introduction contains twenty-one singledotted versus three doubledotted quarter notes (of which two occur in the first measure, the third toward the end). Because of the two double dots in the first measure, O'Donnell concludes that "with this evidence the case against overdotting of overtures crumbles." I need not repeat that none of the three double dots was contagious, so that in this particular piece in the form of a French overture, the mild rhythms outweigh the sharp ones at the rate of seven to one. Of course, sharp rhythms occurred occasionally in overtures or anywhere else. The point is that they had to be *spelled out* in notation.

The "upbeat figures." For that aspect of the "style" that calls for the contraction of "upbeat figures" such as shown in the first paragraph of this article, the evidence is even more nebulous.

Michael Collins seems to have been the first to attempt a historical proof.[60] Having dealt with his attempt at length in FN2, I can be brief. First he advanced his theory of "notational development" according to which upbeat figures of thirty-second and shorter notes were a "modernized" notation that corresponded more closely to the composer's intention, as contrasted with figures of eighth or sixteenth notes that were old-fashioned, still in code, and had to be deciphered into strong contractions. The theory was disproved by the pervasive juxtaposition, in the *same* works, of "old-fashioned" and "modern" figures for any eighteenth-century composer.

Second, he compared the two versions of Bach's French Overture BWV 831: the first in C minor with upbeat figures predominantly (not exclusively) in sixteenth notes; the second in B minor, published about five years later as part of the *Clavier Übung,* part II with the upbeat figures predominantly in thirty-second notes. Collins asserts that both versions "obviously" have to be played in the same rhythm. He then tried to bolster this assertion by subjecting the pervasive figure ♩ ♫♫ of the C-minor version to the jurisdiction of Quantz's above-cited sentence that three or more thirty-second or faster notes that follow a dot or a rest (the dashing scalewise *tirades* of overtures) should be played as fast as possible. The argument faltered because the figures in question had neither thirty-seconds, nor dots, nor rests.

Yet the belief in the musical identity of the two versions has been voiced by other scholars, too, among them Walter Emery and Christoph Wolff (Hans David knew better)[61] and has become the mainstay for justifying the contraction of the "upbeat figures." O'Donnell also leans heavily on this alleged evidence.

The theory of identity is untenable. There is hardly a composer who did not revise some of his works, and Bach himself was a tireless reviser. Hence if we find a second version of any piece by a master, the simplest and the most plausible explanation is a revision, a second thought. We are entitled to claim identity of sound *only* if we could convincingly eliminate the alternative of a revision. Since this alternative is not only possible but eminently probable, its elimination is a "reductive fallacy."

For asserting identity of sound of the two versions of Bach's French Overture we would have to make, among others, the following extraordinary assumptions: 1) among the numerous revisions by Bach (and other composers) the second version of this piece, and of this piece alone, embodies no musical change but represents an "orthographic variant": a deciphering of the code for the benefit of those uninitiated in its mysteries;[62] 2) the key of C minor was a code for B minor;[63] 3) the changed final cadence has to be overlooked; 4) the notation ♩ ♫♫ which was a more precise, more "modern" notation for the unmetrical, doubly underdotted ♩. ♫ was suddenly revised to mean ♩. ⅔♫ the tie impersonating a dot plus a rest, the evenly written sixteenth notes torn apart, their right fragment contracted in a manner that defies the most elementary principles of notation; 5) most importantly, as O'Donnell himself points out (p. 343), Bach made no less than *four mistakes* in the final part (in mm. 154, 155, 156, and 159) when he wrote ♫♫ as the wrong cipher for ♩ ♫♫ of the second version; 6) in measures 11-13 of the first version Bach wrote the left hand in the "clear," the right hand in code; measures 17-20 throughout in the "clear"; in measure 157 the third beat in the "clear," the fourth in code; 7) in measure 152 the contractible second beat looked coded (compare the preceding measure) but was to be played as written, etc. etc.[64]

This should suffice to show that in order to sustain the identity theory we again have to pile improbable, even absurd, assumptions on top of each other—reason enough to abandon it.

When Collins and O'Donnell infer from the identity theorem the law of contraction for the "upbeat figures," they argue in a perfect circle. This is spotlighted when O'Donnell admits that "had there not been a tradition of upbeat contraction, Bach's notation of the earlier version of the movement provides few hints of the desired rhythmic interpretation": the tradition (i.e. the "style") existed, ergo the two versions are identical, which proves that the tradition existed—a classical *petitio principii*. No other serious proof has been attempted.[65]

If the argument of part I was convincing, then the negative findings of part II were a foregone conclusion. Their cumulative evidence should secure the thesis embodied in the title: that the "style" is a delusion that needs to be dispelled to save an ever-growing number of masterworks from the rhythmic distortions visited upon them by misguided performers.

Misconceptions About the French Trill in the 17th and 18th Centuries

On Dogmatism in Performance

It is true that all things subsist only through order, and as soon as it ceases, confusion takes its place... But it is also certain that a too rigid regularity is unbearable, especially when the matter in question is not of paramount importance: both sacred and profane books teach us that it is sometime permissible, indeed necessary, to ignore ordinary rules, because rules are made for man not man for rules... Don't we see every day in various compositions... how especially the Italians take liberties which surprise us pleasantly, and how, to our admiration, they break the most essential rules of composition? Why then should we be hemmed in by rules which are far less important than those of composition?

—Jean Rousseau, *Traité de la Viole*, 1687.

Certain beliefs about trills in French music of the 17th and 18th centuries have been held over the years with such uncontested unanimity that they assumed the status of quasi-axioms. The two most important ones are the alleged rules that 1) the trill had to start invariably with the upper note and 2) this start with the upper note had to take place exactly on the beat.

Close study of the theoretical literature does not support these beliefs, which, applied rather dogmatically, still influence our performance practice, and not only in connection with French music. For example since Bach's ornamentation symbols were derived largely from the French, many prominent musicologists have insisted that those ornaments, including, of course, the trills, have to be performed according to what is believed to be the French manner. As a consequence Bach's trills have been subjected to the same confining regimentation that was erroneously ascribed to the French.

In addition to the two beliefs already mentioned, a third one will be analyzed in the following pages. This belief, not as widely held as the first two, has nevertheless been given considerable currency through the advocacy of

Reprinted with permission from *The Musical Quarterly* 50 (1964), pp. 188-206.

influential writers. It has to do with the *tremblement lié,* a trill that is tied to its preceding upper neighbor. The theory is that this preceding note has to be held over the beat in the manner of a suspension, to insure conformance with the upper-note-on-the-beat rule:

In the following, these three main theories will be discussed and after evidence is produced that none can be maintained in its accepted form, the implications of these findings on Bach trills will be examined briefly.

Three Main Theories

The Start with the Upper Note

Eugène Borrel points repeatedly to the remarkable unity that prevailed in French performance style for well over a hundred years, from the middle of the seventeenth century to the outbreak of the revolution. With regard to the trill, he states bluntly that "according to the invariable rule for all trills of the French school, they start with the upper note."[1] With this categorical statement, he voiced a conviction that seems to have been accepted by all scholars.

The reason for this belief is not difficult to find. The authority of Couperin, who states that every trill should start with the upper note, has much to do with it, but he was not the only one: other French authors made the same statement and many composers who printed tables of ornamentation show the trill starting with the upper auxiliary. No doubt such a start was the prevalent practice, but it was by no means the exclusive one. The extreme position some scholars have taken—"there is no exception to the rule"—is entirely unwarranted, as the following documentation, presented chronologically, will show.

Bacilly, in his remarkable book of 1668 on the art of singing, describes the pattern of the trill with its preparation, the trill proper (the repercussions), and the transition to the next note.[2] Then, after mentioning exceptions that are appropriate in "a thousand places" he launches an attack against the tyranny of rules. One of these rules is the preparation of the trill with the upper note:

> Those who imagine themselves to be great experts of the vocal art [*de grands Docteurs dans le Chant*] would not for anything in the world omit that preparation of the trill (of which I just spoke), as if it were of its essence, even in the case of the shortest trills. They consider it a crime to do otherwise and thereby render the performance dull and monotonous without considering that the most universal rules have exceptions which often produce more pleasing results than the rules themselves. There are even cases of cadential trills where the preparation is inappropriate and where one plunges immediately into the repercussions starting them *from the bottom up* [*Il y a même des cadences finales, où cette préparation sied mal, et dans lesquelles on se jette d'abord sur les tremblements de bas en haut*] . . . and after all these observations it would be naive to try to establish rules where such [preparation] fits and where it does not fit; good taste alone has to be the judge.

The passage is significant for two reasons: 1) if even a cadential trill can start with the main note then the conclusion is inescapable that there must be other situations where such a start could not be found objectionable; and 2) it clearly expresses a principle that was to dominate the whole French literature up to the end of the eighteenth century: that the *goût,* good musical taste, has the last word in matters of interpretation and that there are no rules that are not subject to revision by this sovereign authority.

Another eminent witness is Jean Rousseau, who in his treatises on singing (1678) and viol playing (1687) describes four kinds of trills, of which two start with the upper note and two with the main note.[3] The first two are prepared trills with the preparation falling *on* the beat in one and *before* the beat in the other.

The third type is the *cadence sans appui,* sometimes in his books referred to as *cadence simple.* This is an unprepared trill *starting on the main note,* to be "done on the natural note by the simple shaking of the voice." For instrumentalists he explains this trill as one with the preparation cut off *(retranché).*[4] He recommends the use of this trill 1) in an upward motion, 2) with notes that are short and not dotted and either stay on the same pitch or descend, and 3) anywhere ("en toutes rencontres") in a gay piece like a minuet.[5]

Rousseau's fourth type is a trill prepared with the main note. It is used on long notes: the *main* note is sustained for the first half of the trilled note's value and then the trill starts without *appui* on the second half. This type of trill is to be used especially in accompaniment or harmony parts, but may be used also for the melody, preferably when the trilled note is approached from below.[6]

Rousseau adds that all trills that are under a slur are to be performed without preparation, which in his terminology implies the start on the main note.[7] This rule extends the already considerable range he assigns to the main-note trills.

Very interesting are Dandrieu's trills. He presents the following ornaments:

Ex. 1.

| Tremblement simple | Tr't appuyé | Tr't lié | Tr't ouvert | Pincé simple |

As can be seen he introduces a special symbol for a trill starting with the main note, his *tremblement lié.*[8] Though this trill always occurs in stepwise descent, it is by no means limited to the usual pattern of a *tremblement lié:* one tied to its preceding appoggiatura. This can be seen from the following examples, which imply independent start of the trills.[9]

Ex. 2.   From *Pièces de Clavecin*

approximate realization

Bérard in 1775 distinguishes two main types of trills: the *cadence appuyée* in its usual meaning, and the *cadence précipitée,* which starts *with the main note:* "Jetez le premier martellement sur la note ou l'on doit battre cette cadence" [throw the first repercussion on the note on which the trill is to be made].[10]

Duval in 1764 mentions a *cadence subite,* the kind of trill "which is never preceded by the sound of the upper auxiliary."[11] It is to be used if the note that carries the trill sign is short, or when musical taste requires it.

Lacassagne in 1766 distinguishes between a *cadence préparée* and *jetée.*[12] The first differs interestingly from its usual form in that it may be prepared on the main note, as well as on the upper auxiliary.[13]

His *cadence jetée* starts without preparation and may begin *either with the upper note or with the main note.* Most of his examples show the start from the main note:

Ex. 3.

The preceding documentation, spanning a century, shows that the upper-note start was at best a preference and not a law and that the main-note trill occupied a respectable, if minor, place in the French performance practice of the age.

The Start on the Beat

Another belief that seems to be widely held is that the upper note with which the trill is supposed to start, regardless of whether this note is extended in an *appui* or not, has to be sounded strictly on the beat and should be accented to emphasize its appoggiatura-like nature. The following pages will show that no such general rule existed and that there were many instances where the start with the upper note had an unaccented upbeat character and occurred before, rather than strictly *on* the beat.[14]

The common belief in the existence of the above rule is understandable since most of the tables of ornamentation found in French treatises and prefaces to compositions seem to imply such a start on the beat and until fairly recently these tables have generally been interpreted in a very literal way. However, the realization is growing among scholars that ornamentation at all times contained a strong element of irregularity involving rhythmical and dynamic nuances of such subtlety that musical notation is incapable of even suggesting them. All that the tables can do is to present the basic design of any ornament, but it has to be left to the imagination and taste of the performer to fill the dead formulas with life. It is for this reason that the evidence derived from ornament tables alone has only conditional value and has to be interpreted with much reserve. How great this reserve needs to be emerges clearly from this passage from Montéclair: "It is almost impossible to teach in writing how these ornaments should be performed, since the personal instruction of an experienced master is barely sufficient to do so, however ... I shall try to explain them the least poorly that I am able to."[15]

Outside of tables of ornamentation hardly anything is to be found in the texts of the French treatises to confirm the start on the beat. St. Lambert may be the only French writer to make a distinct reference to it.[16] However, when viewed in the light of his statement that the choice of ornaments should be arbitrary and guided only by the *goût*,[17] this rule would seem to lose all rigidity.

Couperin, who specifies the start on the beat for the mordent *(pincé)*, does not do so for the trill[18] and this silence is hardly accidental since there is no exact analogy between these two ornaments. Whereas the mordent invariably emphasizes the main note, the emphasis of the trill may be either on the main note or on the upper note. If it is on the main note, the trill, like the mordent, becomes essentially a melodic accent, underlining linear progression; if the stress is on the upper note, the trill carries a harmonic accent, the emphasis on the dissonance. This ambivalence of the trill adds to its problems, but widens the scope for its imaginative treatment. An arbitrary limitation to the harmonic function of the stressed upper note not only impoverishes the ornamental vocabulary, but will frequently falsify the meaning of a passage where harmonic emphasis is uncalled for and where the melodic outline is blurred instead of sharpened.

The question of emphasis will have an important bearing on the relationship of the trill to the beat. A trill might start with the upper note, but if the emphasis is on the lower one in the manner implied, for instance, by Loulié and Montéclair: , the auxiliary is bound to acquire the character of an upbeat since the accent (whether dynamic, agogic, or both) on the lower note will either be attracted by the gravitational pull of the beat, or in the case of the latter's ambiguity[19] serve itself to convey the feeling for the beat's location.

If, on the other hand, the trill is, in the sense of Marpurg, a series of accented appoggiaturas, its first note will convey its downbeat character to the listener, and its start *on* the beat is foreordained. It is this Marpurg type of trill, and not one gleaned from the French treatises, that those writers have in mind who insist on a rigid on-the-beat start.

If proof can be produced that the main note was frequently stressed, this alone would make a strong case for the anticipation of the auxiliary. However, in addition, the following section will adduce some evidence that is direct and undeniable.

As already mentioned above, one of the trills described by Rousseau that is prepared "par anticipation de valeur et de son" starts with the unaccented upper note before the beat, and is therefore iambic in character. This type of trill is to be used mainly in descending from a shorter to a longer note or to a note of equal value,[20] as shown in this example from his vocal treatise:

Ex. 4.

In his viol method there are many more examples of such anticipation; here are two:[21]

Ex. 5.

Loulié in 1696 defined the trill as a repetition of a *coulé* from a small tone *(petit son)* to a regular tone *(son ordinaire)* a step below and illustrates it as follows:[22]

Ex. 6

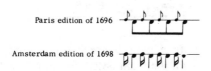

Paris edition of 1696

Amsterdam edition of 1698

That the definition reveals the upbeat character of the auxiliary is evidenced by Loulié's explanation that:

1) The small tones *(petits sons)* indicated by small print are either weaker or shorter than the regular notes.[23]

2) A *coulé* is an inflection from "a small, or weak, or short tone to a lower and stronger tone."[24]

3) His examples of realized *coulés* show the upper note in anticipation as in the following:

Ex. 7.

This shows that Loulié's trill is iambic in character and therefore antithetic to and not, as has been claimed by a prominent writer, identical with Marpurg's trochaic pattern of a repeated appoggiatura.[25]

Montéclair in 1736 adopts Loulié's definition of the trill as a series of *coulés* and for him too, the *coulé* means a descent upon a strong note.[26]

Couperin gives an example that strongly suggests an upbeat start with the auxiliary.[27] He illustrates the *tremblement continu* side by side with the *pincé continu:*

Ex. 8.

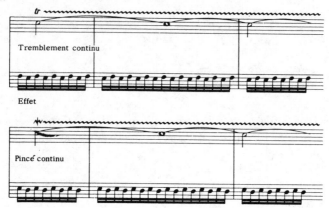

Though this trill starts with the upper note, the second and third measures unmistakably reveal an emphasis on the main note. Such emphasis is logical since this kind of trill is used to sustain the sound of the *main* note, hence the auxiliary cannot have the meaning of an accented dissonance. To stress the first note would therefore make little musical sense, and it happens that this first note is the only one that does not fit into the otherwise painstakingly accurate metrical pattern.[28] To regard it as an upbeat seems the simpler and more logical solution (ex. 9a) than an attempt to force the first note into the downbeat (ex. 9b):

Ex. 9.

Fortunately, Couperin himself offers in one of his clavecin works a confirmation of this reasoning.[29]

Foucquet writes the upper auxiliaries as small notes before each trill, but makes it clear that they should *not* stand for an *appui,* and are used only to make sure that the note is not left out. That the small note is to be played before the beat is already strongly suggested by Foucquet's translation of the *tremblement ouvert:*

Ex. 10.

and becomes all but certain when one compares the *cadence aspirée* (which is shortened at the end) with the *cadence suspendue* (which enters with a delay), in which the upbeat character of the auxiliary is clearly spelled out.[30]

Ex. 11.

In the following example from David (1737)[31] the repeat of the D, as indicated by a circle, makes sense only through the anticipation of the two small notes before the beat.

Ex. 12.

Abbé le Fils in his violin method illustrates the unprepared trill *(tremblement jeté)* like this:[32]

Ex. 13.

The implication of the heavily printed notes can hardly be misunderstood. The main note has the stress of accent or length or both and the preparation is bound to have upbeat character.

This should suffice to show that the iambic, upbeat start with the upper note was a familiar pattern and that the trochaic start, far from being a law, was probably not even a preference. For further proof see note 36.

The Tremblement Lié

The so-called *tremblement lié* is the subject of a third misconception about the French trill. Not of such universal currency as the first two (from which it is derived), it nevertheless is upheld by many prominent writers and its application to Bach has led to some pedantic results.

The claim is made that in a trill that is tied to its preceding upper neighbor, this note should be held over the beat in the manner of a suspension, thus assuring compliance with the "rule" that each trill has to start on the beat with the upper auxiliary:

In what follows I shall try to show that neither documentation nor logic supports the monopoly of this pattern and that two or even three other solutions are not only admissible, but were probably used far more frequently: 1) the start of the trill on the beat with the main note: ; and 2)

the anticipation of the trill, a) entirely: or b) partially:

A. *The Suspension Pattern.* Only a few French writers mention or describe the *tremblement lié* and as to the suspension pattern, I could find only one clear reference, in Corrette,[33] who explains it like this:

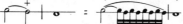

It seems that its modern advocates rely partly on a misinterpreted illustration of Couperin's, but mainly on German authors of the second half of the 18th century. However, since the suspension pattern has its merits we can assume that it was used in certain cases. It can be attractive in a slow tempo provided another voice articulates the beat over which the appoggiatura is to be tied: . On the other hand, in the absence

of a rhythmical support in another voice, the lengthening for the duration of only a trill's repercussion might satisfy the eye on paper as to the dutiful conformance with the "rule," but it will disorient the ear by rendering the rhythm unintelligible.

B. *The Anticipated Trill.* In Couperin's first book of clavecin pieces we find the following illustrations:

Ex. 14.

It is important to note that the quarter notes in b and c are precisely lined up and that the notes in small print representing the trill proper are clearly placed between the first and second quarter notes.[34]

Dannreuther already suspected that the *tremblement lié* "judging from the *'effet'* written out, appears to be an anticipatory shake, slurred, the repercussions of which belong to *the time of the preceding note.*"[35] There are four good reasons that make Dannreuther's thesis a certainty. 1) The exact lining up of the quarter notes clearly points to their identical start. For any other solution this illustration would have been utterly misleading. 2) The phrase "sans être appuyé" implies a shortening of the first note. If the note were to be held for its full value, or even lengthened, the trill would be unquestionably an "appuyé." 3) The melodic and rhythmic logic of this solution is hard to deny. 4) The strongest corroboration is presented by the corollary pattern of the *tremblement détaché* (ex. 14c). According to the alleged on-the-beat rule this trill ought to be played:

If this was the *effet* Couperin had in mind, his description of it would be unbelievably inept. The anticipatory nature of both these trills cannot be doubted.[36]

A documentary proof of such anticipation of the trill is to be found in Bedos de Celles's description of a mechanical organ, where the following examples of trills and their realization appear (in the cylinder cuts as well as in the notation accompanying them; ex. 15).[37]

Ex. 15.

Cadence appuyée et liée   Cadence jetée

If such trills, be they slurred or detached, can be fully anticipated on the authority of Couperin, there would seem to be no reason, considering the general license given to the performer of the period, why an infinity of transitional forms of partial anticipation of such a trill cannot also be applied in places where such a solution would be pleasing.

C. *On the Beat.* Frequently used was also the start of the trill on the beat with the main note: as suggested in example 14a.

Rameau tells us that "the note which is tied to a trill or a mordent serves as a beginning to each of these ornaments" and gives these examples[38] for a trill and a *pincé:*

Ex. 16.

The beginning of the trill's repercussions on the beat can be deduced from the example of the *pincé,* which has to start on the beat if it is not to lose its identity.[39]

Dupuit has this illustration:[40] ♩♩ . Dandrieu's *tremblement lié* was discussed above. Its main-note start on the beat holds good whether we are dealing with a genuine *lié* or not. Abbé le Fils equates ♩♩ with ♩♩ .[41]

Jean-Jacques Rousseau presents the same pattern[42] and most of the realizations of *liés* in Bedos de Celles's cylinder cuts of a *Romance* by Balbastre show the start strictly on the beat.[43]

We have seen that the *tremblement lié* can be played in a great variety of ways: with complete or partial anticipation, on the beat, or after the beat; in fact all theoretical possibilities are available for use in various contexts.[44]

To summarize the results of this discussion regarding the three main misconceptions about the French trill: there was far greater freedom in the execution of the trill than has been hitherto believed. We have seen that trills need not invariably start with the upper auxiliary; that emphasis could be placed on the lower as well as the upper note; that the start with the upper note could occur *before* as well as *on* the beat; that trills could often be entirely or partially anticipated.

The stringent modern interpretations of the rules that have restricted these freedoms are singularly out of place for a period that gave extraordinary latitude to the performer. As heirs to a tradition of spontaneous improvisation, ornaments lose the very essence of their meaning if regimentation deprives them of their vital tie to freedom and imagination.

Implications for Bach

The obvious question arises: what are the implications for Bach? If, for the sake of argument, one were to adopt the theory held by many writers that Bach's ornaments have to be played according to the French manner, then all the freedom now recovered for the French would of course automatically accrue to Bach. A striking example of what this can mean is shown in newly available solutions of the old problems of Bach's trills that produced forbidden parallels when executed according to the "rules." For instance:

Ex. 17.

New possibilities offer themselves: 1) anticipation of the auxiliary, 2) anticipation of the trill (Couperin's *tremblement détaché*), and 3) main-note-trill. So
far the only solution offered was that of the inverted mordent, ⎡♪⎤, and
some scholars like Bodky took great pains to prove its acceptability for such
cases.[45] Recently a new approach was attempted, one that involves nothing less
than the changing of Bach's text by switching trill signs from one note to
another and even altering the notes themselves. Fortunately, it has been shown
that there is no need to tamper with Bach's text for the sake of saving the
"rules."

Ex. 18.

The anticipatory principle will not only prove a remedy against parallels,
but will provide an attractive solution in a thousand other instances. Its use will
be especially indicated in cases where the main note of the trill is dissonant with
the bass and where consequently the rule-dictated emphasis on its upper
neighbor makes very little musical sense indeed.

There are still other benefits that Bach performance can derive from the
widened vistas of French practice. However, it is more than likely that the
freedom of Bach's trills transcends that outlined for the French. After all, why
should Bach be limited to French patterns? Is it not rather absurd to think of
Bach as a timid imitator who would not go beyond the confines of what he
learned from Couperin's book, from D'Anglebert's tables, or what he heard
from French clavecinists in Celles or elsewhere? This is truly the impression
conveyed by a number of eminent writers.[46] How can such a claim be justified?
Aldrich, for instance, tried to prove it by pointing mainly to Bach's interest in
French music, his copying out of keyboard pieces by Couperin and Daquin, his
alleged admiration for the German partisans of the French style, and his
abundant use of French dance rhythms.[47] The argument is far from convincing.
No doubt Bach learned from the French and no doubt he admired some of their
masters. Not unlike Mozart, he looked for and absorbed eagerly musical
stimulations wherever he could find them, but in doing so he transformed,
merged, and assimilated them in a higher synthesis as an integral part of his
own uniquely personal style. Also he was far from limiting his receptiveness to
French models, and if he learned from the French, so did he learn from the
Hanseatic organists, the German violinists, the Italian masters of sonata,
concerto, and opera, and countless others. If he copied out Couperin's pieces,

so did he copy and transcribe Vivaldi, Marcello, Telemann, and Reinken. And as to his use of French dance forms, it is significant that in those dances that like the courante and gigue show distinct differences between the French and Italian types, he divides his favors about equally between the two.[48]

True, the "essential" ornaments were largely developed by the French, but at least one of Bach's symbols: ∿ is of purely German origin. As to the trill in particular, it certainly was no French preserve and it is a well-documented fact that during the 17th century and well into the beginning of the 18th both the Italian and the German trills were predominantly started on the main note. This is formulated by Diruta, Praetorius, Herbst, Falck, Murschhauser, and Printz,[49] and shown in many examples in written-out form in the work of Frescobaldi, Froberger, Kerll, Murschhauser, Buxtehude, Pachelbel, Scherer, and many others. It is therefore certain that during Bach's formative years the main-note trill was part of his musical environment. Who can prove that he found it distasteful?

We shall never be able to reconstruct Bach's exact intention, since no text in any treatise can be considered definite proof of what he did and no silence proof of what he did not do. But the likelihood is great that he took advantage of all the freedoms provided by the French, the Italians, and the Germans and that he sovereignly added to them of his own imagination.

The anticipation of the upper note, the partial or total anticipation of a whole trill (à la Couperin) are freedoms one ought to concede him, and as to the main-note start, the French license in this respect would seem vastly enlarged by Bach's German and Italian models. In other words, there is no kind of manipulation of the trill that we can confidently declare to be forbidden for his music. However, since the French did prefer the start with the upper note and since it was during Bach's lifetime that in Germany the former preference for the start with the main note gradually gave way to one with the upper note, it is very probable that the upper-note start, *on or before* the beat, ought to be given the first consideration. On the other hand, there is no reason why the main-note start should not be used whenever a performer of discrimination and taste decides that in a given context it makes better musical sense. There is no need to try to categorize the instances where such a start is permissible, as some writers have done who found the "no exception to the rule" stand too constraining. Permission can be granted from case to case by musical judgment, the highest authority of the period.

Bach's exact ideas about the performance of his works will forever elude us, but we have reason to think that small details mattered little to him as compared to the meaning of the whole. He certainly was no pedant, and if in playing trills and other ornaments we invest them with that measure of freedom and imagination that their nature demands we can be sure to be more in keeping with Bach's spirit than if we treat them with rule-ridden inhibitions and rigidity.

12

A New Look at Bach's Ornamentation

I

In matters of Bach interpretation almost everything is controversial. The reasons for this state of affairs can very often be traced to improper use of historical treatises, in particular to unjustified generalizations of their teachings and their unquestioned and categorical application to the music of J.S. Bach. The old treatises are invaluable for shedding light on certain contemporary practices and conventions, but they have to be handled with great care if errors of logic are to be avoided. The reasons are several. In the first place, practices and conventions vary not only with the passage of time (sometimes rather rapidly) but also differ on national, regional and local levels, and also with individuals in direct proportion to their individuality. There was no such thing as a general Baroque convention and many treatises are therefore bound to contradict each other on many points. The only thing that we can generally assume about a treatise is that it speaks for the author at the time of writing. And even then the author must not be taken too literally: many treatises are elementary textbooks, and in conformance with sound pedagogical practice the author will formulate rules to point out certain regularities without necessarily intending to proclaim unbreakable laws. Instead he expects the student to find out with growing experience about the many exceptions which, in any field of aesthetics, invariably temper every prescription. For these reasons all treatises, including those bearing famous names, have only a limited validity in time and space and only a conditional one in matters of their wording.

In the field of ornamentation the uncertainties surrounding historical sources are further increased by the nature of the ornaments themselves and by the problems the old writers had to face in explaining the practice of embellishments in words or notation. Musical ornaments, born of a seemingly instinctive urge to manipulate playfully the raw materials of melody and

Reprinted with permission from *Music & Letters* 46 (1965), pp. 4-15; 126-33.

rhythm, have always, in all cultures, led to shapes of fancy and freedom whose very nature resists precise definition and hence theoretical description. When, in the sixteenth and eighteenth centuries, this decorative urge was given free rein by the Italians and their German, Spanish and English disciples, ornamentation burst forth into an unparalleled luxuriance. The composers wrote down only the outline of the melody; the performer was expected to embroider it lavishly with improvised embellishments. Several treatises, like those of Ganassi, Bovicelli, Ortiz, Praetorius, and Simpson, attempted to teach this difficult performing skill through the formulation of principles and the demonstration of examples. Though such documents give us a good general idea of this practice, they cannot begin to recapture the exuberant flight of the Italian ornaments in their living actuality.

The French did not follow this lead. Their rational mind was averse to a licence that could lead to chaotic excesses. They chose instead to channel the ornaments into certain patterns, for which they developed the shorthand device of symbols. Composers and pedagogues then tried as best they could to explain these symbols in words or ornament tables. It is these tables, more than anything else, that gave rise to many misconceptions. Such misconceptions arose partly because of many discrepancies in terms, symbols and their transcription; partly, and more importantly, because the tables gave the false impression that the French ornaments had frozen into rigid and stereotyped patterns. However, though disciplined into smaller shapes and into a limited number of designs, French ornamentation still had not lost its link with its improvisatory origin; and within their narrower confines French ornaments retained a considerable measure of freedom and flexibility. Because of this many Frenchmen of the period stressed the difficulty of teaching ornamentation by book, since even the *vive voix,* the live demonstration of a teacher, was barely capable of doing so. Several German authors, like Heinichen and Mattheson, expressed complete agreement.

The many ornament tables which have come down to us, including the one by Bach himself, written for the instruction of his son Friedemann, were therefore only stylized approximations showing the fundamental design, but they never pretended to show how the formulas were to be brought to life. The relationship of formula to artistically performed ornament can be likened to that between the straight lines, triangles and ellipses with which a draftsman outlines a human figure and the completed drawing. To ignore this and to take the tables at their metrical face value is a misunderstanding of their nature and purpose (without mentioning the fact that many of the formulas in these tables were metrically irregular). It is this misunderstanding which has led so often, not only with Bach, but with the music of the whole period, to the most rigid and pedantic treatment of ornamentation—one that runs counter not only to the spirit of ornamentation itself but to the whole spirit of the Baroque. Trills, slides, appoggiaturas, and whatever their names may be, when pressed into metrical straitjackets, fail in their fundamental artistic function: instead of dissolving rigidity, they enhance it.

From these considerations one can derive a general principle that all ornaments have to be liberated from metrical pedantry and have to receive a strong injection of life-giving rhythmical freedom. This principle applies fully to Bach and his contemporaries and largely still to the following generations in spite of some manneristic hardenings that began to take place in the second half of the eighteenth century.

The "Arbitrary" Ornaments

Like many other Germans of his time, Bach learned in matters of ornamentation from both the French and the Italians. He uses both types and for obvious reasons favours the Italian in works leaning towards the Italian style, and similarly for the French.

He was in the habit of writing out the "arbitrary" ornaments of the Italian style. This, among other things, led to violent attack from the contemporary musical theorist Scheibe; at the same time it bequeathed to us the priceless treasure of Bach's own "arbitrary" ornamentation practice. Though his writing out of these so-called *coloratura* or *fioriture* has solved the most difficult problem, that of design, it has also created some new ones. One is that of identification. A florid passage may or may not be an ornament. If not an ornament, then each note has structural meaning, is part of the essence, of the body of the melody. If it is an ornament, then it only decorates, embroiders, winds itself around salient features of the melody, but does not represent its essence. It is clear that the difference has important interpretive implications. A passage, recognized as an ornament, has to be played with this fact in mind, that is, it has to be rendered with a sense of spontaneity which gives the impression that it was improvised on the spur of the moment. It has to flow out almost imperceptibly from one keynote of the true melody[1] and flow smoothly into the next one connecting the two with lightness, elegance and grace. Moreover, its tempo is defined within fairly narrow limits since it has to be such as not to stress or unduly magnify the ornament to the point of obscuring the underlying structural design of the melody. Ignorance about the ornamental nature of such written out *fioriture* often leads to misrepresentations.

If we take as an example the preludes from the G minor or A minor sonatas for violin alone, or the second movement from the E major violin and harpsichord sonata, there can be little doubt that the demisemiquavers in these works are not the melody proper but only embellishments of the latter. Bach wrote the beginning of the G minor prelude like this:

If he had heeded Scheibe's admonition he would, in conformance with contemporary Italian practices, have written it approximately as follows:

With this in mind, we can tell that the piece should be played in very slow four rather than in eight to avoid nailing to the ground at every eighth beat the free meandering of the melisma. Yet some modern editions mark the movement as 16/16 and many a violinist plays it accordingly at a tempo so inordinately slow that each demisemiquaver pours out sentiment with an impassioned vibrato.

Bach's willful defiance of the convention presents a further problem. The question arises whether he wrote out all the ornaments he wished or whether he did leave some leeway to the performer to add others. Since he was never consistent in his habits, no categorical answer is possible. The fact that his handwritten parts of vocal and instrumental works often carry many more ornaments than the score makes it clear that the score itself was not the last word in this respect. Cadential trills are often not notated and probably ought to be inserted in most cases. In many a *da capo* aria the end of the middle section seems to require a cadenza-like transition to the repeat. A striking example is the alto aria from Cantata No. 12, where the oboe could not possibly be left stranded on a trill:

In the soprano aria "Blute nur," from the first part of the St. Mathew Passion, the first flute consistently doubles the soprano part, with just a few graces added here and there for the instrument. In the last measure before the *da capo,* however, the flute, in contrast to the voice, breaks the connection of the cadential trill with its preceding appoggiatura. Would not the most plausible explanation of this unusual inconsistency point to Bach's intention of letting the flautist draw a deep breath before playing an improvised transitional cadenza leading into the *da capo?*

In the first movement of the E major violin concerto the two adagio bars at the end of the middle section probably also require a cadential transition to the repeat of the first part, just as the two chords connecting the two movements of the third Brandenburg concerto would seem to call for cadenzas of the first violin on each chord. Many similar instances can be quoted. More difficult is the question of what to do with a repeated section or with a *da capo*. Whenever a piece seems to be richly embellished, no further addition would seem to be necessary. However, if a performer of taste who combines a sense of style with a sense of proportion wishes to add occasional trills, mordents, *coulés,* etc. he may well have stylistic sanction to do so and need not be accused of blasphemy. Whoever is in doubt about his own personal qualifications for such additions will do far better to refrain from further embroidery, since the latter will hardly ever be missed. On occasion perhaps some thought ought to be given to the possibility of reserving Bach's fully ornamented text for the repeat and leaving out a few of the ornaments the first time through.

The "Essential" Ornaments

Far more complicated are the questions surrounding the "essential" orna-ments, that is the interpretation of the various symbols that were largely developed by the French. The subject is far too big to be treated in a limited space; in the following discussion only a few new considerations will be presented.

In general it can be said that many of the solutions advanced by modern writers, especially when clad in the form of definite rules, are too narrow and too rigid, and that most of these rules show an unjustified prepossession with the downbeat start of ornaments. The narrowness and rigidity have their sources in precepts distilled with insufficient logical safeguards from treatises and ornament tables. The obsession with the downbeat is essentially a legacy from the books of C.P.E. Bach and a number of other German writers who, like Marpurg and Agricola, largely followed in the former's footsteps. It is usually recognized that because of his complete stylistic re-orientation Philipp Emanuel cannot be considered to speak for his father in matters of musical aesthetics. This is very evident in the field of ornaments, where in his extensive chapter on this matter he treats of some patterns that had never been used by his father and explains others in a way that is patently inapplicable to Johann Sebastian.

For these reasons Philipp Emanuel and his followers ought to be disqualified as authorities on Bach ornamentation and not used as primary sources. Yet we find over and over again that rules about Bach's ornamentation are formulated in terms of Philipp Emanuel's directions, taken simply at their face value. In particular the downbeat rule would have never won such wide recognition were it not for Philipp Emanuel's book. Neither the French, nor the German contemporaries of Bach, nor Quantz or Leopold Mozart, nor even Marpurg and Agricola show this one-sided prepossession with the downbeat, of which Philipp Emanuel made something of a fetish. The raising of this artificial barrier alone will permit many ornaments to flow across this hitherto forbidden line in many forms of anticipation that will greatly enrich the ornamental repertory yet be completely in line with contemporary practices, as the following discussion of a few ornaments will show. The appoggiatura, the trill, the compound trill and the slide will be discussed and arguments presented which point to a much wider licence in their treatment than has been generally assumed to exist.

The appoggiatura. One of the difficulties in discussing the essential ornaments derives from the chaotic condition of terminology. As far as the appoggiatura is concerned we have, among others, these terms to contend with: long or short, variable or invariable appoggiatura, *Vorschlag, Vorhalt, coulé, port de voix, accent, acciaccatura, Überwurf, Überschlag,* and *Nachschlag.* Sometimes several of these terms will mean one and the same thing, sometimes one of them will mean different things at different times or with different writers. For the sake of easier communication I shall in the following use the term *Vorschlag* to cover all varieties of ornaments consisting of a single note, whether short or long, whether on or before the beat. I shall then refer to "appoggiatura" as the type that varies from short to long, is emphasized and played on the beat. I shall further use the modern term "grace note" for the short *Vorschlag* that is played before the beat.

The grace note as a Bach ornament is either ignored or violently rejected by many writers who cannot tolerate the notion of an anticipated ornament. However, not only documentary evidence but also musical logic require that the grace note should be given its rightful place as one of the more important and frequent of Bach's ornaments. As a matter of fact I would express the belief that in many, perhaps the majority of, cases where Bach writes a little note and perhaps even where he writes a hook, it is a grace note that is in order and not an appoggiatura (far more frequently than, say in Mozart, where 𝄞♪♪

usually meant an appoggiatura: 𝄞♪♪). In other cases an interpretation as a short appoggiatura is either indicated or at least possible. By contrast, a reading as a long appoggiatura seems to be justified only on comparatively rare occasions. Whereas eighteenth-century writers, including C.P.E. Bach, Quantz and Leopold Mozart, give us definite rules about the long appoggiatura, such as

♪ = ♪♪ or ♪♪ , and the overlong one, such as ♪· ♪ = ♪· ♪♪ (which is usually associated with dotted notes), these interpretations are rarely applicable to Bach, because, as Arthur Mendel has pointed out, they often lead to absurdities.[2] The reason for this is to be found in the fact that Bach, here too, as in the case of the arbitrary ornaments, deviated from convention and made a habit of writing out his long appoggiatura in regular notes. It is a clear-cut case: since Bach departed from the notational convention, his notation cannot be read according to convention. Apart from this easily verified fact of Bach's nonconformance, and apart from the "absurdities" referred to by Mendel, the bass figuring in the vast majority of cases provides undeniable evidence that the long interpretation according to the rules is hardly ever possible. However, since Bach was never consistent, there are exceptions, but they are few and far between. One of these exceptions is shown in the following example from Cantata No. 19 where the bass figures in the soprano aria indicate "long" quaver value for the appoggiaturas:

They occur here as preparation for cadential trills, which is naturally the likeliest location for a long appoggiatura in the first place.

On the other hand the often quoted case of the Sinfonia No. 5 (three-part invention in E-flat major) is not convincing. I think it very doubtful that ♪♪♪ should be consistently read as ♪♪♪ in conformance with the "rules." Apart from the fact that the little notes were entered at a later date, which would decrease the likelihood of profound changes in the profile of the melody, there are the following considerations which, perhaps not singly, but in combination point to a much freer and less rule-bound interpretation. 1) Some long appoggiaturas are written out in full, and they happen to occur just in those places where such long appoggiaturas can be logically expected: in bars 22 to 24, to stress the intensification of expression preceding the F minor cadence in bar 24 (including the written-out appoggiatura preparation for the cadential trill proper). 2) In bar 20 the long interpretation leads to parallel fifths, as Bodky has pointed out, unless, of course, one makes the heretical assumption that the E-flat "appoggiatura" is only a grace note (which in turn would only prove my point). 3) Whereas the long interpretation in the case of the written out double-dotted crotchets is a least musically possible, except for bar 20, the same interpretation is generally not possible where the little notes precede a dotted quaver. This dilemma is soluble only at the cost of severe inconsistencies. 4) The impression of deadening monotony created by the unrelenting repetition of the same appoggiatura pattern. Bodky's suggestion of holding the appoggiaturas as quavers throughout instead of dotted crotchets does not at all relieve the problem of monotony.

With the long appoggiatura as featured by the books practically never in the picture, the whole problem of Bach's *Vorschlag* centers almost exclusively on the alternative of grace notes *versus* short appoggiatura. In deciding between the two solutions we have to be aware of their different musical functions.

The anticipated *Vorschlag* is a melodic lubricant which eases and adds more grace to the transition from one main note to another. It is played lightly and shortly without emphasis and therefore has its logical place before the natural accent of the beat. (In this it is related to the *portamento* of the singer or violinist, which serves a similar purpose.) The grace note softens the edges of the linear design without altering its fundamental shape, and because of its inconspicuous place in the rhythmical shade of the bar, and because of its short duration, it has no effect on the harmony. Its presence will therefore never be strongly felt and this quality of discretion and unobtrusiveness alone favours its frequent use; provided, of course, it can be shown that such use is legitimate.

The French used it extensively under various terms. In France, too, there was chaos in terminology and an ornament of one or two notes connecting two main notes, whatever its name, was used sometimes before, sometimes on, the beat. These two types of ornaments were the counterparts of the grace note and the appoggiatura. Of the various terms involved, *accent, chute* and *demi port de voix* referred to a grace that almost always occurred before the beat (d'Anglebert's down-beat *accent,* which Bach adopted in his ornamentation table, is one of the rare exceptions). The *coulé* and *port de voix* were used, according to context or individual preferences, in either of the two guises, as grace notes or appoggiaturas and countless transitional forms that straddle the beats. Some writers expressed preference for the trochaic downbeat interpretation, others left the rhythmical shape to the judgment of the performer, yet others express definite preference for the iambic, upbeat version—in other words, for the grace-note treatment. Among the latter is Jean Rousseau, who wrote one treatise on viol playing and one on singing. In the former all examples of *port de voix* are iambic, e.g.:[3]

He even suggests this grace-note rhythm for certain final cadences where the penultimate note is not longer than a crotchet and ascends to the final note:

In his vocal treatise he presents the iambic grace note and the trochaic appoggiatura pattern as alternative possibilities.[4] Loulié calls *coulé* the descending, *port de voix* the ascending type. His examples of *coulés* are all iambic, e.g.:[5]

and for the *port de voix* he presents side by side the iambic and the trochaic reading without giving any rules for their choice. The obvious implication is that the all-important *goût* of the performer makes the choice according to context.[6]

Saint-Lambert quotes d'Anglebert's trochaic pattern for the *port de voix,* but declares his own preference for the grace note treatment of which he gives among others these examples:[7]

port de   voix ·simple   port de voix appuyé demi port de voix

André Raison's only example of a *port de voix* in his ornamentation table of 1687 is iambic:[8]

Couperin's *coulé* and *port de voix* were, according to his own instructions, meant to be played mostly on the beat, but his works are full of *accents* and *chutes* whose anticipatory nature is clearly indicated by their tie to their preceding note. These are the prototypes of the German *Nachschlag.* The following example (a) shows a combination of downbeat *coulés* in the melody and anticipatory *chutes* in the bass. Also, Couperin's use of a line connecting two neighboring notes symbolizes an anticipatory grace ranging from one to about seven notes. Example (b) shows its grace-notes meaning:

(a)   7e Concert, Sarabande Grave

6   6   #6   6   4   6
3   b3   3   6   3

[The meaning of Couperin's connecting lines is uncertain. They *might* stand for legato.FN 1982] *(b)*   'Pièces de Clavecin', 20ᵉ Ordre, 'La Croûilli''

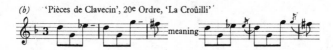

After Couperin, Villeneuve clarifies the upbeat character of both the *port de voix simple* and *port de voix double* (the slide) in the following illustration:[9]

Jean-Jacques Rousseau in his dictionary of 1768 presents only the grace-note version of the *coulé*.[10]

It is also significant that to an outsider the grace-note treatment of the *coulé* was considered the typically French manner. Quantz emphasizes that it would be wrong to perform the following *Vorschläge:*

in the Lombard rhythm instead of treating them as grace notes or *durchgehende Vorschläge,* as he calls them. He argues that this *agrément* was invented by the French and therefore ought to be played in the French manner, which he asserts to have met with general acclaim.[11] He was by no means the only German to admit grace-note interpretation. Agricola mentions anticipatory graces in the guise of *Nachschlag, Überwurf,* and *Überschlag*—the counterparts of the French *accent, chute,* and iambic *coulé.* Played very shortly within the time value of the preceding note, so Agricola tells us, one-note *Nachschläge* are never written out, those of two notes only rarely—which implies that they were freely added by the performer.[12] Even Marpurg admits *Nachschläge* and introduces a special symbol—a little note with its flag turned to the left: 𝄽𝄽 as indication that it is to be played before the beat.[13] In Walther's Lexicon the article 'Accentus' seems to imply downbeat start of the *Vorschlag.*[14] However, in his article 'Cercar della Nota' Walther tells us that this grace—which was always anticipatory—is practically indistinguishable from the *accent* except that the latter occurs mostly at the beginning or the end of a note. Both these remarks—the practical identity with the *cercar* and the occurrence at the end of a note as *Nachschlag,* as true *accent* in the sense of most French writers—indicate that Walther's *accent* can have grace-note character. Moreover, in articles under the titles "Accento doppio," "Anticipatione della Nota," and "Anticipatione della sillaba" he presents a number of grace-note patterns that are illustrated in table I, figures 3, 6, 7, and 8. In his article on "Port de voix" he points to the discrepancies in French terminology and to the different schools of thought as to down-beat or up-beat treatment. In his illustrations on table XVIII, figures 17 and 18, he presents both the appoggiatura version of d'Anglebert and the grace-note versions of Saint-Lambert and Loulié.

Whereas Walther in his article on the "Anticipatione della sillaba" expresses a certain doubt as to the merit of this grace, because of its effect on musical declamation, Bach himself demonstrates its use in the first soprano aria of Cantata 84, shown here side by side with Walther's illustration from his table I, figure 7:

What is interesting about the Bach theme, which occurs many times, is the fact that it is in conflict with the phrasing of the instruments, which articulate the same and similar melodic ideas in the following manner:

Mattheson's definition of the *Vorschlag* as a note to be touched "quasi-twice" very softly and very fast[15] seems to describe the above grace-note patterns of Saint-Lambert's *port de voix simple* or *appuyé*. It certainly does not suggest an emphasized appoggiatura. Long before Mattheson, Schütz's pupil Christoph Bernhard (1627-92) presents under the names of *accento, antici-pazione della nota* and *cercar della nota*[16] a number of examples of iambic grace-note ornamentations which, though derived from Italian origins, nevertheless agree with the French iambic *coulé* and *port de voix* patterns. This Italo-French-German agreement and would seem to show that the anticipatory *Vorschlag* was part of the international musical vocabulary of Bach's time. As to modern scholars, Walter Emery feels that the anticipatory treatment to which he refers as *Nachschlag* is not as rare in Bach as it is supposed to be.[17] He points in particular to parallel octaves or fifths that result on occasion, when they are played on the beat, and mentions bar 17 in the 13th Goldberg variation. In the same variation Bodky found two more parallels in bars 25 and 26 in the case of downbeat treatment. Another striking example is the last full bar of the Sarabande of the 6th Partita where downbeat performance is out of the question:

Alfred Kreutz in his important analysis of Bach ornamentation expresses certainty that the passing *Vorschläge* of the *tierces coulées* type, the kind mentioned by Quantz, were always meant by Bach to be played as grace-notes.[18] He brings the following telling illustration of bar 46 of the D major Invention, which appears in the final manuscript as 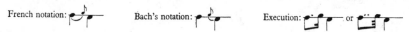 whereas

in Friedemann's "Klavierbüchlein" it was written like this: Kreutz also states that the French *accent,* which was invariably played before the beat, is often to be understood when Bach writes a little note:

French notation: Bach's notation: Execution: or

If in addition to all these considerations it can be shown that in many instances the downbeat start does not make musical sense, then there can be no doubt that grace-note treatment in Bach's music is thoroughly legitimate. The only question is when it is to be used in preference to the trochaic downbeat treatment. In order to gain a better perspective on that alternative we have to examine the nature and function of the appoggiatura.

II

In contrast to the unobtrusive grace note, the appoggiatura is very conspicuous indeed and makes its presence far more strongly felt than the former. Placed in the rhythmical spotlight of the measure it displaces a melody note for varying length of time and thereby actually changes the contour of the melody itself; it implies a harmonic accent, stressing the dissonance, and carries strong expressive emphasis, and when too short to do so, carries a strong rhythmical stress. In other words, it is a powerful ingredient. Because of this it stands to reason that its use requires far greater circumspection than that of the grace note, which can hardly do any damage even if improperly applied. On the other hand, the strong flavour of the appoggiatura can, in a favourite simile of the period, easily spoil the broth by too much seasoning. The over-use of its long variety will first saturate, then irritate: the over-use of the short variety will make for ruggedness where smoothness would have been the wiser and more artistic choice. In other words, the appoggiatura must never be used as a matter of routine, but only in those instances where the very kind of emphasis it imparts is called for by the context. They are the places where a sensitive performer of the period would have added one of his own, had it not been indicated.

Once we realize that Bach's little notes did not invariably stand for appoggiaturas, we shall find many places where their interpretation as appoggiaturas simply does not fit. Apart from the forbidden parallels already mentioned, the most obvious case is one where the *Vorschlag* precedes a long appoggiatura that, as usual, is written out by Bach. Nothing could be more incongruous than to top one appoggiatura with another one, since the second would, like a parasite, drain from the first the very essence of the melodic, rhythmic and harmonic emphasis which it was meant to convey. Quantz points to this instance and tells us that a *Vorschlag* written before another one that is spelled out has to be played before the beat—in other words, as a grace note. [19] His example:

Agricola makes a similar statement vetoing the cumulation of two appoggiaturas and admits only rare exceptions, such as a 6/4 chord which may on occasion be preceded by a descending appoggiatura. For an ascending appoggiatura he admits no exceptions. Moreover, he makes the significant statement that an appoggiatura makes no musical sense on top of a melodic dissonance that occurs on the beat. [20] Nothing could be more logical. Yet we find the compound appoggiatura interpretation over and over again in books and in performance. Kirkpatrick, for instance, a consistent advocate of the downbeat ornamentation, repeats this pattern of a doubled appoggiatura in many cases in his edition of the Goldberg variations. [21] A good example is the thirteenth variation. It so happens, as was pointed out before, that this interpretation leads in no fewer than three cases to forbidden parallels. One is shown here:

    Grace-note treatment is therefore unavoidable in some, and is indicated in a great many other, cases. How should the choice be made? If any directive can be given it is this, that the decision be based on musical and not dogmatic grounds; that the emphasized downbeat start can be applied only when an appoggiatura is suggested on harmonic, expressive and melodic grounds; that a grace note should be used, not just by default, to avoid forbidden parallels, not as an embarrassed second choice when an appoggiatura obviously makes little sense, but as the first choice whenever melodic smoothness seems the point at issue. To put it simply, it can and should be used whenever it sounds better to a discriminating ear. And this decision can be made without selfconsciousness, since authority for it is plentiful.

    Moreover, a performer is not forced to choose squarely between one or the other. Grace notes and appoggiaturas are only opposing prototypes and their characteristics can be mixed in an infinite variety of ratios. A *Vorschlag* can be played on the beat yet be unaccented and thus give the effect of a grace note with a delayed entrance—the kind of delay that Couperin calls *suspension*. A *Vorschlag* can also straddle the beat in many different rhythmical shapes which in turn can be treated to an imaginative variety of dynamics. The combination of all these possibilities will then provide the very diversity that is the essence of ornamentation.

The trill. It is commonly assumed that the trill in Bach should always start with the upper auxiliary and that the latter should enter precisely on the beat with an appoggiatura-like emphasis which it retains throughout the repercussions. This rule was derived mainly from Philipp Emanuel Bach and from Marpurg and is generally believed to accord with French practice. The latter is assumed to feature invariably the upper-note-on-the-beat start. That this interpretation is far too rigid I have shown in a recent article.[22] In it I have, I hope successfully, tried to prove that even in France the trill was accorded far more freedom of manipulation than was hitherto suspected. The particular points were: 1) that the trill did not invariably start with the upper note; 2) that the emphasis could be on the main note instead of the upper one; 3) that the start with the auxiliary often took place, grace-note fashion, before the beat, and finally 4) that whole trills could be anticipated. It was also pointed out that Bach, though he learned from the French, never imitated them slavishly; and that German composers he admired offered him models of ornamentation that deviated from the French. Some of these composers, in matters of trills, for instance, not only tolerated a main-note start but distinctly favoured it.

But quite apart from these considerations the thesis that Bach's trills should be accorded a far wider freedom than commonly assumed is a logical consequence of the following reasoning. If an appoggiatura-like emphasis on the auxiliary is built into the trill by definition, then the trill is simply a sub-form, an ornamented variety of an appoggiatura. This is how Marpurg explains the trill and this is what modern scholars such as Kirkpatrick, Bodky, and Aldrich consider to be its essential nature. If we accept this premise, does it not stand to reason that the trill could be used only where an appoggiatura on the same note would make musical sense? If trills should occur only in such instances, it might be difficult to disprove this theory. However, one needs only to open almost at random any of Bach's works to find trills in places where an appoggiatura would be inappropriate. And of course where an appoggiatura is out of place an appoggiatura-trill is *ipso facto* also impossible. Here too there is an opposition between the two extremes of an impossible appoggiatura-trill on the one side and a near-required one on the other. On the negative side there are first of all the instances of offensive parallels, such as:

Next to this we find trills in places where an appoggiatura is musically senseless (among these ranks high the above-mentioned case of one appoggiatura on top of another), or, in the sense of Agricola, a downbeat trill whose main note is dissonant with the bass (Ex. (a)):

Other cases are trill chains, especially when they ascend chromatically like those in the second organ sonata (Ex. (b) above) (since nobody would think of saddling chromatic sequences with appoggiaturas) and trills on organ points or other long-held notes *(tremblement continu)* which serve the purpose of sustaining the sound of that note. Next in line are cases where, if a trill had not been written, an enlightened performer would not conceive of adding an appoggiatura as an improvised ornament. Next will be cases where the alternative between yes and no hangs in the balance; after that we arrive finally at those instances where an appoggiatura is well-nigh required, as in most cadential trills.

How then should Bach's trills be performed? Considering the various types that are available one could simply say that the one should be chosen that in a given situation makes the best musical sense. For more specific directives it may be practical to divide Bach's simple trills into four main categories and call them:

1) The appoggiatura trill, whose emphasized auxiliary may or may not be extended in an *appui:*

2) The grace-note trill, starting with the unaccented auxiliary before the beat and stressing the main note:

3) The main-note trill, which may or may not start with an *appui:*

4) The anticipated trill:

To find out which of these types is the best choice in a particular case, it is suggested at first to leave out the trill, then to consider which of the other possibilities listed below in the left column would have been a likely choice for improvised ornamentation. The second column indicates on the same line the type of trill that is likely to fit best for this particular instance:

(a) long appoggiatura	appoggiatura trill with *appui*
(b) short appoggiatura	unprepared appoggiatura trill
(c) grace note	grace-note trill
(d) none of these ornaments	main-note trill, sometimes anticipated trill

The compound trills. The ornament which Bach called a *Doppelt-cadence* is explained in his table in conformity with d'Anglebert:

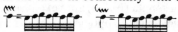

It has been taken for granted that in this type of trill, which starts with a turn or an inverted turn, the first note has to coincide with the beat. However, except for the evidence of the metrical patterns in the tables, which is very thin indeed,[23] there does not seem to be any convincing documentary confirmation from the first part of the eighteenth century that a downbeat start was obligatory. Again the rule was made retroactive and deserves all the scepticism of the analogous rules about the appoggiatura and the simple trill.

Couperin, for instance, does not use d'Anglebert's symbol. Instead he writes out the turn preceding the trill in little notes, which through their spacing in print and their musical context suggest anticipation. This can be shown for instance in the sarabande "La Majestueuse" from the first *ordre* of harpsichord pieces. A *petite reprise* at the end of the piece is followed by another *petite reprise* which is more ornamented. A simple trill in the former (a) is changed into a compound trill in the latter (b) by the insertion of a turn whose anticipatory nature would be hard to deny:

In the gigue from the eighth *ordre* bar 37, a compound trill is written out in regular notes:

In the second Air of the twenty-second *ordre,* bars 17-19, three compound trills follow each other in sequence. In the first of these a change from F to F-sharp in the left hand makes sense only if the turn anticipates the beat:

Since Bach wrote the symbol only for keyboard instruments and not for strings or wind, it is instructive to look for written-out patterns in nonkeyboard works. In the G minor prelude for violin alone we find two such patterns in the first bars. They are written as in (1), whereas in a keyboard version they would most likely have been notated as in (2):

If we can only free ourselves from the downbeat complex which has fenced in Bach ornamentation for so long, we can see how one single ornament like the *Doppelt-cadence* can assume a great variety of shapes by combining the anticipation of any number of notes—one, two, three, four or five—with occasional rhythmic variants like the one in example (1) above. For instance, the compound trill in the third bar of the Goldberg aria is shown here in its original notation and in Kirkpatrick's transcription:

This version seems particularly ill-chosen. The repeat of the two crotchets is a key motive throughout the aria, but Kirkpatrick's interpretation obscures this motive because it deprives the second note of its identity by the double device of downbeat start of the turn and appoggiatura-trill. I submit the following interpretation, which permits the ornament to display all its elegance and at the same time helps to underline the crucial melodic idea instead of nearly destroying it:

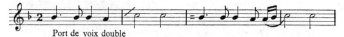

The slide. We need touch only briefly on the matter of the slide for which Bach uses sometimes the symbol: ⌐, sometimes two little notes: ♪. Similar considerations apply here too. The ornament was occasionally played on the beat, in which case the first note was usually lengthened: ♪. On other occasions it was played before the beat, and on still others it may well have been done in a mixed manner, straddling the beat, so to speak. As usual, the accepted version is the downbeat interpretation.

The French called it *port de voix double* and seemed to have preferred its upbeat start. In L'Affilard we find the following example:[24]

Port de voix double

Fifty years later the same pattern is shown in the illustration from Villeneuve which was presented earlier,[25] in which the two little notes in front of a downbeat note are placed to the left of the bar-line. That Couperin used anticipatory slides can be deduced from examples like the following:

1er Ordre, Allemande: 1er Ordre, Rondeau: Sylvains', bars 12-13
(a)   'L'Auguste',bar 2   (b)

In the case of (a) where the lower note of the slide is tied over into the chord, a downbeat start would have undoubtedly been notated like this: ♪ . In the case of (b) a downbeat start would produce ugly octaves in the outer voices. As to the Germans, Walther in his "Praecepta" of 1708 shows both ascending and descending slides as anticipating the beat.[26] Agricola distinguishes two kinds of slides *(Schleifer):* the fast and even ones, and the slow and dotted ones. The fast ones he says are sometimes written out by the composer ♫. in a manner belonging to the Lombard taste, whereby the short notes are strongly accented. Then he adds: "In contrast thereto a slide which fills in a leap and belongs properly to the weak part of the bar must be played more discreetly."[26]

These documents give added significance to the fact that several slides in Bach produce forbidden parallels if played on the beat. The following is an example of fifths in bar 23 of the sarabande from the sixth Partita:[27]

In the "Aria variata alla maniera italiana," bar 2, a slide occurs which precedes a little note that could stand for either a grace note or an appoggiatura. In either case the slide has to be anticipatory:

In the violin obbligato to "Erbarme dich" from the St. Matthew Passion an upbeat interpretation of the slides is suggested by the following considerations. The start of the melody which carries the slide in the violin part is unadorned at the entrance of the voice:

The anticipation of the slide in the violin would closely parallel the *portamento* with which the singer is likely to bridge the interval smoothly and expressively. On the other hand, an accented downbeat start of the slide with its intrusion into the domain of the melodic keynote would alter the contour of the melody to a point where its identity with the vocal line would be strongly blurred. Also, the anticipation gives far more unity to the phrase, which contains several more upbeat slides which are written out and give the phrase its pleading, submissive character.

To sum up, it may be said that it is necessary to take a new look at the many restrictive rules and taboos which surround so much current thought on Bach ornamentation. If we subject all these rules to a thorough scrutiny of their legitimacy in terms of the soundness of their logical foundation, in terms of their compatibility with what we know about the vast licence accorded to the performer of the time, with what we know about the essential freedom of ornamentation as such, and above all, in terms of their compatibility with internal evidence from Bach's own works, we can be sure that many of these rules will stand revealed to be without foundation.

13

Notes on "Melodic" and "Harmonic" Ornaments

I

Musical ornaments are referred to as "melodic" if their impulse in embellishing a phrase is predominantly linear; they are called "harmonic" if their impulse is strongly vertical and results in the enrichment of the harmony. For reasons that will emerge below, the difference between the two types turns mainly on a question of rhythm: ornaments are melodic when they are placed *between* the metrical beats; they are harmonic when placed *on* the beats provided they change by such placement a consonance into a dissonance. In this sense the one-note grace of example 1(a) is melodic if executed in the manner of (b). It is harmonic if executed in the manner of (c). By straddling the beat as shown in (d), the characteristics of the two contrasting types can be mixed in many different combinations.

Ex. 1.

This melodic-harmonic antithesis commands our interest on several counts. Chief among them is the prevalent doctrine that links the preferential, indeed the exclusive, use of one or the other types to definite style periods. We are told, for instance, that melodic ornamentation reigned supreme during the renaissance; but that during the baroque harmonic ornamentation drew into its

Reprinted with permission from *The Music Review* 29 (1968), pp. 249-56.

orbit those small-scale graces of one to three or four notes which became first standardized, later prescribed by symbols. In other words we are to accept as a fact that during the middle and late baroque and lasting through the rococo and the classical eras, ornaments such as the *appoggiatura,* the slide, the turn, the mordent and the trill-family, etc., had to be played strictly on the beat to insure the full harmonic effect of which they are capable.

Pending a thoroughly documented refutation of this theory in a lengthy forthcoming study, the present article proposes simply to examine the nature of the two ornamental prototypes in question with a view to showing how internal reasons alone militate against the current downbeat doctrine.

II

In order to gain a perspective on the melodic-harmonic antithesis, we have to recognize the important fact that the structural character of a melodic line is determined by the *starting points* of its constituent tones. (The term "structural" is used with reference to such tones as are needed and sufficient to convey the basic meaning of a given musical phrase.) These starting points establish not only the purely melic design of a phrase, but also its internal rhythm, *i.e.,* the pattern of length and shortness from note to note. They establish this rhythm, regardless of whether the tones are sustained to form a continuous flow of sound or whether they are separated by rests. For, within a musical phrase, a tone once announced, is understood to carry the melic thread across to the next melodic impulse. Whenever rests, the *"silences d'articulation"* separate notes, aural imagination integrates the disconnected sounds into the psychological unit of an uninterrupted line. With percussion instruments the moment of impact is obviously the only thing that counts and to a large degree the same is true of all plucked instruments, and of the harpsichord, as well as the modern piano. Yet even for media capable of sustaining sound, as a rule, it is the start that matters, whereas what happens after the start is of secondary importance: it influences articulation and nuance, but does not alter the fundamental shape of the melody. Because the melodic energy is thus focused in the starting points, these latter represent the active phase of the linear drive, the power stroke so to speak of its motor energy.

The time after the impact, where the tone is either sustained or carried by implication across the void of silences, represents the passive phase where the energy flow is decreased occasionally to the point of near-disappearance. These differentials in energy flow create a pattern comparable to alternating high and low pressure, with the lowest points at the end of the time span before the new note is sounded. Graphically, the energy pattern of four structural quarter notes in example 2(a) can be represented by the wedge-like triangles (b). When ornaments of the connective type[1] (for instance two-note slides) are introduced into such an energy structure, the new subsidiary melodic particles are then in an almost physical sense drawn in by the suction of the low pressure phases, whereas the firmly implanted pillars of the structural starting points put up high pressure resistance to being displaced. Graphically this is illustrated in (c) and (d), showing the anticipation, or more precisely, the inter-beat, or inter-tone rendition of the ornaments. In the four-note melody (e) the inserted ornaments (f) will then be rendered approximately as in (g), gracing the transition from one note to the next inobtrusively in the spot of lowest pressure, hence of lowest melic-rhythmic sensitivity. By not interfering with the crucial starting points of the principal notes, the graces do not impinge on the structural integrity of the melody and consequently play their role in complete conformance with the chief esthetic function of an ornament which is to embellish the structural design without altering its fundamental character. (Also, the connective function of such embellishment is clearly best fulfilled when the ornamental elements are inserted in such a way that they strengthen a link between notes where the link is weakest.)

Ex. 2.

This procedure is the prototype of "melodic ornamentation." Its natural-ness, inescapable to the unprejudiced ear, accounts for its almost exclusive use in the linear music of the Renaissance and its vast, uninterrupted importance from the baroque to the present day.

To show the force of this natural tendency and to dispel widespread prejudices to the contrary, it might be sufficient to look at Quantz's tables of improvised embellishments,[2] written at the time of the alleged high water mark of harmonic ornamentation, and written by a man whose precepts for the rendition of certain *appoggiaturas*—too narrowly interpreted—has become one of the principal pillars of the harmonic down-beat doctrine. In examining these tables we find that in all but the fewest cases, the starting points of the structural notes remain rocklike in place with the graces all inserted between them, in the truest maner of melodic embellishment. Quantz postulates the principle of structural integrity at the outset of the discussion when he says:

"One must take care at all times not to obscure the principal notes which are to be embellished [literally: altered]. When quarter notes are to be embellished, in most cases, the first of the added ornamental notes must be identical with the simple, *i.e.*, the principal ones, and that procedure applies to all types of notes, be they longer or shorter than quarter notes. It is possible, though, to pick another note from the harmony of the bass, provided the principal note is sounded soon afterwards."[3] (See also chap. XIV, par. 14.)

For several reasons this passage is significant. It establishes the integrity of the structural notes as a general principle and where, as an exception, it does admit the substitution of a different note, this note has to belong to the "harmony of the bass." This implies, of course, that the ornament is not a harmonic one since a *consonance* would strike on the beat. The examples are mostly in complete accord with the pronounced principles. Here and there we find a genuine downbeat *appoggiatura*, but far more rarely than would appear at first glance, because the detailed commentary which Quantz furnishes for his examples makes it clear that not only two- and three-note graces of the *Anschlag* and slide species are anticipated,[4] but also a good number of the one-note graces which are meant as "durchgehende" and not as "anschlagende" Vorschläge, in other words as grace notes in the modern sense and not as appoggiaturas.

The principle of safeguarding the structural integrity of a melodic line has far-reaching importance for polyphonic textures. The starting points, being the determinants of a melody's basic structure, are by necessity also the determinants for the relationship between two or more contrapuntal voices. Thus a melodic ornament that does not affect the basic structure of a melody, will have little if any effect on the relationship to the other voices; by contrast a harmonic ornament which displaces a structural note will bring about a transformation and often a telling disturbance.

However natural the prebeat melodic ornaments may be, the harmonic, downbeat species began to emerge as an important variant, most prominently in the case of the one-note grace, the so-called "long *appoggiatura*." It is typified by an ornamental tone that ventures in the best *Serva Padrona* style from its normal, subservient role in an inconspicuous place to the prominence of a leading part, displacing a structural note in the very spotlight of the heavy metrical beat. By so doing it will change the harmony, turning, in its most typical application, a consonance into a dissonance; moreover, by delaying the entrance of the principal note, it will affect the rhythm of the phrase, and in a polyphonic texture, as mentioned, affect strongly the relationship to the other voices. The most characteristic use of the harmonic downbeat appoggiatura is a design in which the dissonance is either prepared in the manner of a suspension or approached stepwise; in either case the resolution is stepwise down or up. Such preparation—dissonance—resolution pattern if, of course, a procedure that has been used from medieval times as a structural, mensurally notated element, and must not as such be equated, or confused with harmonic ornamentation, because in its written-out form it partakes neither of improvisation, nor flexibility of rendition, nor freedom of choice, all three of which are earmarks of a genuine ornament. It is, therefore, advisable to speak of a harmonic ornament only in cases where it is either not indicated at all and left to insight and imagination of the performer, or where it is indicated by a symbol that leaves the exact execution at least partly indeterminate. As a matter of fact, when in the second half of the eighteenth century theorists tried to legislate such exact execution of *appoggiaturas* or dictate their exact length by the symbol itself, one ought to question whether, in terms of musical logic, we still have to do with an ornament and not with a structural note in ornamental disguise; for what we are concerned about is the ornament that has not yet petrified into a rigid shape, the execution of which is therefore still fluid and flexible.

The harmonic down-beat grace has made occasional chance appearances within Renaissance diminutions but its true debut can be traced to the declamatory style of the early Baroque where it became linked with the emergence of homophonic tendencies and strong metrical accents. This linkage is understandable since a turn against the horizontal "lines of force"—created as in a magnetic field, by the linear flow of energy—presupposes the existence of a different source of power. An explanation for this phenomenon can be found in the newly developing relationships of melodic and harmonic elements and the strange ambivalence that characterizes it. Melody and harmony are at the same time complementary and antithetic, collaborators and competitors. Their complementary character, manifest in the enrichment they can mutually bestow, is self-evident; their antithetic nature is less obvious but no less real: they interact upon one another; their impulses take effect in different dimensions of the musical time-space continuum[5] and consequently they make competitive claims to aural perception and orientation. It is in this antithetic complex that the polarity of melodic and harmonic orientation has its chief roots.

The horizontal thrust of the melodic impulse is acted upon by the vertical pull of harmony not unlike the way a flying object is affected by gravitation. But whereas gravitation is continuous, the pull of harmony is intermittent, because it is strongest when focused in, and reinforced by, the pulse of strong metrical accents.[6]

The link between metrical accent and harmonic impulse is understandable because an accent that cuts through the whole musical tissue illuminates by this emphasis the simultaneity of tones and thereby brings the harmonic aspect of this musical instant into sharper relief. Conversely, a chordal sub-structure provides the vertical lines of conductivity for the flow of the metrical impulse through the musical texture.

As a counterpart and complement to the linear energy pulsation, the metrical pulse of the vertical element creates, like the systole and diastole of the heartbeat[7] a periodic alternation of strong and weak vertical energy; and this polarity, embodied in the old concept of the "good" and "bad" parts of the measure affects the way in which the ear organizes, assimilates and interprets the given sound pattern.

Due to the interaction of the horizontal and vertical pulsation patterns, of which the latter has a regular periodicity, the former, the free irregularity of the melodic rhythm, the vertical element will be in relative prominence for the systolic, the "good" phase, whereas the horizontal element will assert itself in the diastolic, the "bad" phases.

In this relationship of the two energy systems lies the reason why in the same sequence of notes e″ g′-d″ f′-c″ e′ in examples 3(a) and (b) the d″ f′ in (a) are perceived horizontally as passing notes, i.e., as melodic bridge between the neighbouring tones, because the easing of the vertical pull in the "diastole" permits the linear element of this relationship to come to the fore. By contrast in (b) the "systole" of the downbeat emphasizes the vertical aspect, hence the same notes are perceived as part of the dissonant chord: they are heard less in relationship to their predecessors and successors than to their contemporaries in the other voice parts.[8]

Ex. 3.

If we think of these same notes as ornaments with the passage of (a) written perhaps like (c) and the passage of (b) written like (d), the melodic grace of (a)-(c) would be an anticipated "coulé", the harmonic grace of (b)-(d) a long appoggiatura conforming to one of its most typical patterns: stepwise approach and stepwise resolved dissonance.

If such an ornament is shortened and the note in example 4(a) played instead of on the weak beat, on the weakest part of it, then the purely melodic character is still far more in evidence and every possible trace of vertical perception vanishes:

Ex. 4.

In the case of 4(b) the shortening will have quite a different effect. The shortness of the grace weakens its harmonic character, because it might prevent a thorough aural absorption of the chord; however, the combination of brevity and down-beat introduces the new element of a decisive rhythmic change. This is the case because the metrical systole and diastole has strong implications for the rhythmic perception as well as for the linear—vertical complex. In example 4(a) the 16th note, occurring at the lowest ebb of the diastole, at the very end of the beat, will be only faintly perceived as a rhythmic variant because its place in the deep metrical shade makes it rhythmically inconspicuous and leaves the graces a predominantly melodic physiognomy. By contrast, when the short note of a short-long pair is placed "Lombard" style in the spotlight of the systolic beat, its rhythmic nature assumes an obtrusive prominence. It produces a syncopation-like surprise effect because it runs counter to a natural tendency of lengthening an accented tone and vice versa. In such instances where such a strong rhythmic ingredient obscures or near-eclipses a weakened harmonic one it makes sense to speak, as the case may be, of a "harmonic-rhythmic" or just plain of a "rhythmic" ornament.

III

In summary the preceding discussion would seem to suggest the following hypotheses.

In linear music, connective ornaments will be primarily melodic,

1. because the prevailing "lines of force" strongly favour the insertion of such ornaments between the starting points of the melody;

2. because the inter-note ornament affects hardly if at all the relationship to other voices and can therefore be applied with ease and impunity, whereas a harmonic ornament such as the long *appoggiatura* if improvised could vitiate the counterpoint, and even if indicated by symbol could, due to its indetermined length, throw the other voices into disarray.

For these reasons alone we can expect to find genuinely polyphonic music the less hospitable to harmonic ornaments, the denser the texture, the faster the *tempo* (because more notes in other voices would be affected) the stronger the linear impulse, the less prominent its chordal penetration and metrical organizaton.

If polyphonic music offers an unlikely habitat for harmonic ornaments, homophonic music will provide far more favourable conditions for their appearance because the vertical impulse of the metrical accent, in concert with the chordal energy exerts an attractive force strong enough to overcome the linear resistance against ornamental displacement of structural notes.

Moreover, such intensification is welcome in a context where an impoverished musical texture is often in need of the harmonic or rhythmic enrichment that downbeat ornaments are capable of providing. This was especially true of the period of the *style galant* and the *Empfindsamkeit* where the sentimental impact of the appoggiatura-sigh became almost a stylistic hallmark.

However, the favorable conditions for harmonic ornamentation do not at all imply that with the advent of homophonic textures all small connective ornaments have to be attracted by the downbeat. Firstly, the lines of force, unequivocally horizontal in linear music, are not the simple vertical opposite in homophonic music, but are the result of the dynamic interaction of both horizontal and vertical impulses. As has been shown, the interplay of these divergent directional forces always favors the horizontal ones *between* the beats and therefore strongly supports the blossoming of melodic inter-tone ornaments even in purely homophonic textures.

Secondly, the strong impact, harmonically, rhythmically or both, of the downbeat ornament, militates strongly against its frequent use, because frequency of an ornament has to be in inverse proportion to its prominence or obtrusiveness. In a favorite simile of the times, used by scores of old theoreticians, ornaments are compared to the spicing of a dish: necessary to make it delectable, they have to be judiciously applied because their over-use is certain to spoil the broth. The downbeat *appoggiatura* for instance, is such strong musical spice that, if used routinely, it will have an enervating, thoroughly unmusical effect. By contrast, the inconspicuous quality of the melodic type, the weakness of its spice value, is a further strong reason in its favour.

Musical logic would, therefore, seem to suggest that a stylistic watershed between melodic and harmonic ornaments did neither lie between Renaissance and baroque nor between early and late baroque. Instead, a criterion resides in the musical texture: whereas linear music favors melodic ornamentation, homophonic music provides a favorable climate for a flourishing coexistence of the melodic and the harmonic species, and such coexistence can be expected to produce through cross-fertilization a mixed breed that in straddling the beat, partakes of the nature of both parent types.

This hypothesis is at odds with the exclusive downbeat theory for small ornaments, a theory so firmly entrenched as to have almost become an article of faith. However, it can be proved that the hypothesis of these pages is supported by historical fact. The presentation of such evidence, however, would far exceed the frame of an article and, as mentioned above, will have to await the publication of a forthcoming book.

14

Couperin and the Downbeat Doctrine
for Appoggiaturas

I

Couperin's famous treatise on the art of harpsichord playing contains a
sentence that has loomed large as a proof for the prevailing theory that in the
seventeenth and eighteenth centuries all small ornaments had to be played *on*
and not *before* the beat. The sentence reads: "The small note of a *port de voix or
of a coulé* must strike with the harmony: that means at the time in which the
following principal note should be played."[1] This article proposes to show that
Couperin's rule often did not apply to his own music and consequently can not
be invoked to confirm the exclusive downbeat doctrine. This doctrine, by dint
of a half-century's uncontested rule, has become an institution of unquestioned
authority, having achieved this status, as it were, by usucaption—the juridical
concept that confers legal ownership after extended uncontested use. However,
any principle, regardless of its tenure, must be reexamined whenever its claim
admits the slightest reason for doubt. Such doubt is very much in order with
regard to the doctrine in question which, as closer examination reveals, is
founded mainly on C.P.E. Bach's principles of ornamentation.[2] This can be
said even though C.P.E. Bach was not of course the sole advocate of downbeat
execution of ornaments; but he was the only writer who was uncompromising
about the downbeat and consequently the only one who fully supports the
modern, by and large equally inflexible doctrine.[3] Thus C.P.E. Bach's
principles served as a beacon to modern researchers who projected them
geographically from Berlin into the whole of Europe and backward and
forward in history until they flooded the eighteenth century and spilled over
into a good part of the seventeenth and even the nineteenth centuries.[4]

Reprinted with permission from *Acta Musicologica* 41 (1969), pp. 71-85

Researchers felt justified in so doing because they saw in C.P.E. Bach's principles only a convenient codification of rules that had been valid for previous generations. These writers based their belief on a number of fragmentary source indications that began with chance occurrences in Renaissance diminutions, appeared in Italian recitative formulas, showed up in ornamentation tables of seventeenth-century English and French keyboard players, were reflected in, among others, Bach's own small table (which he excerpted from D'Anglebert); these writers were, of course, spectacularly supported by the quoted sentence of Couperin's. In the mind of modern writers such indications form a solid chain linking the masters of the middle and late baroque with the rules of the *Galant* Berlin school, thus vindicating the daring retroactive application of C.P.E. Bach's principles. For a balanced view, however, we must not overlook a number of important facts.

1. The backward extrapolation of C.P.E. Bach took place over the chasm of one of the most striking stylistic breaks in musical history: the change from baroque polyphony and complexity to *Galant* simplicity and lightheartedness. Some writers were seemingly unaware of the extreme hazard inherent in any projection of aesthetic principles across a borderline of drastic change.

2. Even the so-called "Berlin School" is by no means in full agreement on this matter: C.P.E. Bach's colleagues and followers like Marpurg and Agricola did not share his extreme attitude. Though these two writers also emphasized strongly the downbeat aspect, they accepted anticipated ornaments in the guise of *Nachschläge*. They are the same *Nachschläge* that C.P.E. Bach condemns as "ugly" while at the same time admitting they were extremely fashionable.[5] This admission is highly significant in itself because it testifies to the widespread practice of anticipation.

3. Quantz, though usually included under the label of the "Berlin School," assumed a far more flexible attitude in matters of ornamentation than is commonly known. More cosmopolitan in outlook than his colleagues and an eclectic by principle, he counterbalanced his much publicized downbeat pattern for the long appoggiaturas with a strong admixture of French-type, prebeat *coulés and ports de voix* which he called the *durchgehende Vorschläge*. Moreover his tables of diminutions, when studied in the light of his detailed instructions, reveal not only a most sophisticated finesse in phrasing, nuance, and dynamic shadings, but also an imaginative and highly diversified treatment of many small ornaments.

4. The downbeat pattern of French ornamentation tables like those of d'Anglebert, Dieupart, Le Roux, etc. was limited to certain types of *Vorschläge*, namely those in the very definite melodic-harmonic contexts of a prepared and step-wise resolved dissonance; such *Vorschläge* were indicated by abstract symbols (mostly hooks) whereas the little notes had generally the meaning suggested by their pictorial symbolism: to be executed *between* the principal notes, hence in anticipation.

5. Downbeat *Vorschläge* appeared in France almost exclusively in clavier works, yet they were far from standardized even in this medium: a number of keyboard players in both the seventeenth and eighteenth centuries, among them Nivers, Gigault, Raison, Saint-Lambert, Siret, Luc Marchand, definitely favored the upbeat pattern.

6. In France, for the media of the voice and of the melody instruments, anticipation was the favored style throughout the seventeenth and the better part of the eighteenth centuries. Not surprisingly, four foreign observers writing almost a century apart (Janowka in 1701, Quantz in 1752, Agricola in 1756, and Türk in 1789), saw in the anticipation of the *Vorschläge* a characteristic of the French style.[6]

7. There are many indications for upbeat graces in German and Italian as well as in French music. Consequently one must be aware that in the climate of permissiveness that is congenital to ornamentation, the upbeat and downbeat types would inevitably be mixed to form specimens straddling the beat in an infinite variety of rhythmic designs.

In summary, it can be said that the exclusive downbeat dogma is the offspring of incomplete research procedures, mainly in the form of unjustified generalizations, wrong evaluations, too narrow interpretations, and the failure to realize that occasionally even direct and seemingly incontrovertible evidence, like Couperin's rule, can be deceptive.[7]

II

Couperin's rule is interesting because it is one of the early instances, if not the earliest, where the downbeat rule for the *Vorschlag* is associated not with abstract symbols but with the little notes *(notes postiches)* themselves. Couperin writes his little notes in two distinct ways, tying them either to the preceding, or to the following principal note. Only in the rarest instances will he leave them untied. When he ties them to the preceding note he does so in the manner characteristic of two distinctly French ornaments: the *accent* and the *chûte*. The *accent* is, most typically, a stepwise ascent prior to a fall (ex. 1(a)), or a stepwise descent prior to a rise (1(b)) involving therefore a reversal of direction. The *chûte*, as the name indicates, is a fall to the level of the next note (1(c)). As the tie reveals, they were played in the time of the preceding parent note.

Ex. 1.

Couperin does not limit himself to these three patterns but uses the tie to the preceding note in an unrestricted variety of melodic designs to indicate unquestionably an inter-note rendition, as for instance in the following examples:

Ex. 2.

Theoretically, these graces may belong to the *accent-chûte* family (the counterpart of the German *Nachschläge*); practically, they will mostly be undistinguishable from anticipated *coulés* and *ports de voix*. When, on the other hand, Couperin links the little notes with a slur to the following principal note, then they represent genuine *coulés* when they descend, and ports de voix when they ascend. These alone are the cases, and they are very frequent, where his downbeat rule is to apply. That it applies in many cases is, of course, unquestionable. That, however, there are many cases where it does *not* apply will be shown with a number of examples that could be multiplied at will, where a downbeat rendition would lead to musical incongruities.

Before proceeding to analyze such purely musical evidence it will be necessary to examine the context and background for the theoretical ruling in order to place the latter into the right perspective.

III

Couperin is unquestionably the most famous and most frequently quoted of all French authors on performance and particularly on all matters of ornamentation. Modern researchers, impressed with his prestige, have applied what he has to say not only to his immediate circle of influence but rather indiscriminately to many non-French contemporaries as well. Bach, in particular, has been subjected to many of Couperin's rules with the alleged justification that Bach studied and admired the Frenchman's work. Bach may well have admired Couperin, but some researchers keep forgetting the common-sense fact that admiration is not synonymous with complete and unconditional surrender.

Couperin's pedagogical writings are embodied in an ornamentation table that accompanied the first book of clavecin pieces (1713),[8] in his above quoted treatise from 1716-17, and in a few prefaces to compositions. Concerning the *coulé* and *port de voix,* the ornamentation table fails to explain the *coulé* proper as an independent grace, though the term *coulé* as an adjective referring to slurred rendition is used in connection with other graces, among them the *port de voix* as we shall immediately see. Of the three types listed for the *port de voix* the first is designated as *Port de voix coulé* the second as *Port de voix simple* the third as *Port de voix double* (see ex. 3).

Ex. 3.

These illustrations keep the reader guessing by failing to offer any explanation for type one, and by using small, unmetrical notes for types two and three. The ensuing ambiguity was probably intentional in order not to force into a rigid metrical mold what was meant to remain flexible and variable. However, if such vagueness has the virtue of suggesting an imaginative treatment, it leaves us in the dark with regard to the basic rhythmic design that Couperin had in mind. Three years later the quoted downbeat rule seems to clarify some of the previous ambiguity, but by failing to indicate the relative length of the downbeat grace, leaves the door open in this respect to varied interpretations.

Couperin's sentence in the treatise is an isolated statement of a general rule that is neither illustrated in the text nor alluded to anywhere else. To take general rules in treatises on performance on face value is always dangerous, even if the author uses great care in weighing his every word. If an author is less than meticulous in his formulations, the danger of literal interpretation is greatly enhanced. Couperin's book, coming from a man of his stature and influence, would be a document of great value under any circumstance, even if it did not contain its many fascinating flashes of illumination; but good organization, clear expression, and methodical presentation are not among its outstanding qualities. The book does not read like a work that has been carefully planned and thoroughly thought through, but rather like the transcript of an impromptu lecture in which the author talks in turn, and in no apparent order, about matters of pedagogy, problems of technique, and questions of interpretation, just as they happen to come to his mind. It is quite typical that our key sentence is haphazardly sandwiched between a discussion of fingerings for *ports de voix* and the admonition to teach children how to trill with all the fingers. The highly informal, conversational setting does not encourage the assumption that Couperin has carefully weighted every single statement and verified each for its completeness and unconditional validity.

It is, therefore, no surprise to find that his ornamentation table, too, is unsystematic, ambiguous, and incomplete. Its ambiguity, as said before, may possibly have been intentional, but hardly its incompleteness. No less than four of Couperin's ornamentation symbols are not listed. Besides the *coulé* proper, the omissions include two other frequent ornaments: the dash connecting two notes ♪⌐♪, and a trill-turn combination ∾, as well as a fourth one: Ω that seems to occur in one piece only *(L'Enfantine* from the 7th *Ordre)*. Couperin was apparently still not aware of these omissions when he wrote the treatise, for he made no attempt to correct them, though he supplemented the information on some of the other ornaments, notably the trill.

These considerations suffice to elicit skepticism about the completeness and unconditional nature of any of Couperin's statements, but they are not in themselves sufficient to disprove them. To do this we shall now turn to musical evidence.[9]

IV

The prevalent opinion about the execution of the *coulés* and *ports de voix* is expressed by Brunold in the formula:

which he claims to be valid for all French clavecinists.[10] For shorter note values this formula is unquestionably meant to be applied in analogy:

First it will be necessary to show the defectiveness of this widely accepted equation.

In example 4(a) the *coulés* in the upper voice cannot have an 8th note meaning, and for that matter, neither can the *coulé* in the bass. (The symbol over the d″ indicates delayed entrance). In 4(b) an analogous rendition in 16th notes would be impossible for the first *coulé*, highly improbable for the second one.[11]

Ex. 4.

a) I Les Sentiments
   m. 12

b) VI Les Bergeries
   m. 3

In ex. 5(a) the formula is inapplicable to both the *port de voix* and the *coulé* of the second measure. In ex. 5(b) the difference in the notation of the two measures would seem to point to a difference in their rhythmic rendition or else this notational discrepancy would confuse the issue.

Ex. 5.

In most of these cases, a downbeat execution of the graces can be restored to musical sense by a very short rendition of the "Lombard" type rhythm . Unquestionably this, rather than Brunold's formula, is the way in which Couperin intended many of his *coulés* and *port de voix* to be played.[12] But not less unquestionably there are many instances where an anticipated execution was intended and many others where the beat was straddled. Various reasons suggest such solutions.

One is voice leading. Couperin was meticulously careful about his voice leading, and we can assume that in deliberate performance he would have avoided progressions that were objectionable to him in writing. He never would have condoned such blatantly conspicuous parallels as would result from downbeat execution in examples 6(a), (b), (c), and the obvious way of avoiding them was by anticipation.

Ex. 6.

Moreover these *coulés* occur in contexts that suggest anticipation for other reasons as well. They are in descending thirds where the filling in of the space is the *locus classicus* for melodic, that is, inter-beat ornamentation. Even Agricola tells us that in thirds the purpose of the inserted graces is to connect the melody rather than to enrich the harmony.

Secondly, these *coulés* occur on light beats where the stressed dissonance would be out of place. The occurrence of the graces on light beats is especially typical of feminine endings, where the terminal tapering of the musical impulse would be disturbed and distorted by the accent-implying downbeat appoggiatura. See examples 7(a) and (b). Such disturbance would be still more obtrusive on the harpsichord as it cannot indicate the tapering by dynamic means.

Ex. 7.

In both of these examples, as well as in ex. 8(a), the downbeat execution of the grace would obscure the true character of the harmonic progression, inasmuch as the sound of a consonance suggests that what we hear is a basic progression. A similar case is that of the third quarter beat of ex. 8(b) with its would-be stress on the consonance and "resolution" to dissonance. A dissonance that is kept from striking on the beat is emasculated and prevented from fulfilling its function in the harmonic scheme. The sharper the dissonance, the more incongruous its delay.

Ex. 8.

In ex. 9(a) the factor of dissonance treatment is reinforced by the location of the *coulé* in the bass with no "harmony" to strike against[13] except the held-over note in the upper voice. In the second measure of ex. 9(b) the same harmonic logic opposes a delayed entrance of the e-flat half note in the bass that certainly could not sound later than the top note of the arpeggiated chord.

Ex. 9

In ex. 10 the consonant *coulé* g-sharp before the 32nd notes is clearly of the connecting and not the intensifying type: *a tierce coulée* on the weakest part of the beat linking at great speed two notes of the same dissonant chord.

Ex. 10.

In example 11(a), the simultaneousness of the *port de voix* in the bass with a *coulé* in the second voice, both on the same scale tone, would make little harmonic sense on the downbeat. Similar considerations apply to ex. 22(b) (m. 2) with simultaneous *port de voix* in the soprano and *coulé* in the bass on the same scale tone. Here, too, simultaneous anticipation would seem the likeliest solution, though anticipation of the bass *coulé* and downbeat rendition of the soprano *port de voix* is a distinct possibility. The same can be said of an analogous spot in XXIV, *Les vieux Seigneurs,* m. 23-24.

Ex. 11.
(a) III Gavotte   (b) XIII L'âme en peine
                                             m. 5

In ex. 12(a) a downbeat rendition of the *port de voix et pincé* on the 3rd quarter would make sense only against the G in the bass and not against the *coulé* a. Hence the only possible alternatives are an anticipation of the bass *coulé* alone, or a simultaneous anticipation of both graces.

Ex. 12.

(a) 7ᵉ Prelude (L'Art de toucher le Clavecin)   (b) III Gavotte
         m. 2   m. 12

When such graces appear simultaneously in all voices, as shown in ex. 12(b), then, of course, there can be no "striking against the harmony," not even in the widest, the modern sense of the word; there can be no enrichment of the harmony, and the logical solution would seem to point either to simultaneous anticipation (with possibly a light straddling effect) or to anticipation of the bass alone.

When only one of two simultaneous mordents is preceded by a *port de voix,* as is shown in examples 13(a) and (b), the necessary synchronization of the mordents leaves to the grace no alternative except anticipation. See also example 5(b) above.

Ex. 13.

Where a *coulé* or *port de voix* coincides with a different type of ornament, as shown in ex. 14(a) and (b), a confusing clash can often be avoided only by anticipation of the *Vorschläge.*

Ex. 14.

In ex. 15 anticipation is spelled out by Couperin in placing the bass *coulés* at the end of the second and third measures before the barline.

Ex. 15.   IV Tendresses Bachiques

In ex. 16 anticipation would seem to be the only practical solution, not to speak of the missing slurs which fail to indicate to which parent note the grace belongs, and whether we have to do with *coulés* or *ports de voix*.

Ex. 16.

XXIV L' Amphibie
Modérément

If the little note in ex. 17 is played on the beat a main note trill results, which is anathema to downbeat advocates who will probably consider anticipation to be the lesser of two "evils."

Ex. 17.

VI La Bersan
m. 2

Where a *coulé* occurs at the start of a piece, as shown in ex. 18, or of a phrase, anticipation is more logical, because a downbeat appoggiatura which is supposedly harmony-enriching, has its proper place between two notes, of which the first typically functions as preparation, or at least as introduction, the second as resolution.

Ex. 18.

II La Garnier
m. 1

In example 19, a downbeat rendition is out of the question since it would be incongruous melodically, technically, and rhythmically.

Ex. 19.

5ᵉ Prélude
m. 20

In ex. 20 the two *tierces coulées* are of the familiar type. What is new are the two other small notes which are both clearly tied to an identical principal note. Since downbeat rendition of this note would be understood without the grace, the only possible meaning of the latter can be that of anticipation.

Ex. 20.   XI La Castelane, 2d ending

The alternative of downbeat versus prebeat rendition of a *Vorschlag* has important implications for rhythm as well as for harmony and melody because the rhythmic spotlight is centered on the strong metrical beats that are comparable to the systole of the heartbeat. Any change occurring *on* those beats will affect the rhythmical essence of a phrase. By contrast, the moment before the strong beat represents the darkest rhythmical shade, the diastole, as it were, and what happens in it affects the rhythmical physiognomy only superficially: it represents a truly ornamental, and not structural modification. For these reasons, considerations of rhythmical logic will often determine the appoggiatura execution of an ornament.

　*Such is the case for instance when a rhythmic design that is clearly of structural importance is obscured or even disguised by downbeat treatment. In ex. 21 the anapestic motive ♪♪♩ in the alto part of the first measure would lose its identity on its repeat in the second measure unless the *port de voix* is anticipated.

Ex. 21.

VIII La Raphaéle
m. 1

In ex. 22 the characteristic counter rhythm of the second voice would be distorted by downbeat rendition of the *tierce coulée*.

Cases are frequent in keyboard music where, as in the preceding example, a grace precedes a note that belongs in unison at the same time to another voice.

Ex. 22.   II La Garnier
m. 24

In all such cases the rhythmic-melodic integrity of the unembellished voice can be assured only by anticipation. Other illustrations for these occurrences can be found in examples 9(a) and (b), 11(a) (for the bass), and 21.

Many are the situations where a number of different considerations combine to favor anticipation. Example 23 might serve as an illustration: 1) the grace is a *tierce coulée* on the weak beat, 2) there is no harmony to strike against, 3) following the written out anticipated *coulée* before the trill, melodic logic suggests analogous anticipation of the grace, and 4) rhythmic logic is also in support because downbeat execution would disturb the characteristic counter rhythm of the bass.

Ex. 23.   V Les Agrements, 2ᵉ Partie

V

The reader may be justified in questioning the persuasiveness of one or the other example when taken by itself. However, many examples are convincing on their own merit and certainly their combination ought to prove the point at issue: that in Couperin's music anticipation of *coulés* and *ports de voix* was a frequent occurrence in spite of Couperin's express ruling to the contrary.

This finding naturally complicates the problems of interpretation for Couperin's music. No longer can we apply to the *Vorschlag* a ready-made formula à la Brunold. Instead, each case has to be decided on its individual merits with such considerations as have been discussed in this article. General directives can be given only in the broadest terms and with the proverbial grains of salt. With such a proviso it can be said that the downbeat rule is most likely to apply to such *coulés* and *ports de voix* that are in the upper voice or voices, that strike a dissonance against the bass, and that do so on the heavy metrical beats; that the *coulés* in these circumstances will be short, resulting in a "Lombard" type pattern and will rarely if ever extend to the length of Brunold's formula. On the other hand, the *port de voix*, especially in the *port de voix et pincé* combination, has a wider scope of rhythmic freedom and is more likely to be, on appropriate occasions, of the long, expressive suspension type.[14] *Anticipation* is most likely to occur on light beats, especially on feminine endings; at the start of a piece or a phrase; between descending thirds; in the bass line; in an unaccompanied voice; where anticipation clarifies two or more simultaneous ornaments; where downbeat rendition would impoverish the harmony, or would interfere with a rhythm pattern that is of structural importance, or infringe on the integrity of a second voice that happens to coincide on the embellished note. In summary, it can be said that anticipation is indicated wherever it is favored by melodic, harmonic, or rhythmic logic.

While these directives may be helpful, the last word always belongs to the *goût* that all French authors extolled as the supreme arbiter in all matters of interpretation. *Goût,* which combines taste, musicianship, instinct, and imagination is also the highest and sole authority to decide when and how the two principles of prebeat and downbeat rendition are to be combined rubato-like in the mixed breeds that straddle the beat.

Though the above discussion was limited to one composer, it sheds some light on a situation that had many parallels in the rest of Europe, where in Couperin's and Bach's time the ornamental situation was both extremely varied and extremely fluid. As far as Bach is concerned, what was said of Couperin's anticipation would be an understatement in spite of the vastly overrated downbeat "accent" of *Explicatio* fame (Bach's small ornamentation table in the *Clavier Büchlein vor Wilhelm Friedemann Bach).* This is not the place to branch off into these matters but a forthcoming book by this writer will present evidence that the anticipation of the *Vorschlag* or of other small ornaments was commonplace in the music of Bach and his contemporaries. For the time being, a single illustration may do double duty as a postscript to the present article and as a single token for forthcoming abundant documentation.

I believe it to be obvious that in the following passages from the *Art of the Fugue,* the *Vorschläge* have to be played in full anticipation, in other words, as modern type grace notes:

Ex. 24.

Canon per Augmentationem in contrario motu

Their performance on the beat would result in undesirable parallels. Though in more informal settings parallels may not provide an exclusive guide for ornamental execution, here the clue can hardly be mistaken: it is inconceivable that parallels of penetrating offensiveness should occur within the formal strictness of a two voice canon, let alone in a didactic work of the highest order, the supreme manifesto of voice leading. Hence we can conclude from this single example that, if the little note *must* have upbeat meaning here, it *can* have upbeat meaning elsewhere. This alone is sufficient evidence to puncture the pretense of downbeat exclusivity.

[*Author's note:* The preceding article elicited three responses: "The Downbeat Doctrine for Appoggiaturas: Ergänzungen zum Aufsatz von Frederick Neumann," *Acta Musicologica* 42 (1970), Friedrich Neumann, pp. 252-53; Robert Donington, pp. 253-55; and Klaus Hoffmann, "Noch einmal: Couperin and the Downbeat Doctrine for Appoggiaturas," *Acta Musicologica* 43 (1971), pp. 106-8.]

15

Ornament and Structure

A discussion of ornamentation regardless of period must first approach the difficult and not fully soluble problem of defining what constitutes an ornament and how the latter can be set apart from the nonornamental, i.e., from the structural, components of the musical fabric.[1] Whereas in all the arts the existence of a similar ornament-structure polarity is a matter of aesthetic-theoretic concern, in musical performance the differentiation between the two categories, aside from any other consideration, becomes a matter of practical importance. For this reason an attempt will be made to clarify to some extent the fundamental concepts of ornament and structure, and to examine the relevance of their definition for a historically correct performance (especially of baroque music).

In the fine arts, ornament is generally conceived as the antithesis of structure, in the sense that structure embodies all the elements of the art work that are essential to its meaning and purpose, whereas ornament is a nonessential accessory made for additional aesthetic gain. Ornament and structure, thus conceived, are categories in a relationship of polarity. Either can appear in its pure state, or the two can be mixed in an alloy that might defy neat separation into its components yet permit an evaluation of their approximate ratios.

In architecture both the functional purpose of a building and its engineering imperatives will identify certain elements as unequivocally structural, whereas at the opposite pole certain surface decorations that are not artistic entities in their own right (as would be, for instance, a frieze or a statue), will be easily recognized as pure ornament. In music the identification even of the polar extremes is harder. The utilitarian purpose of a composition, where such a purpose exists, influences its form and its overall character, but does not have a bearing on the structure-ornament issue; also, musical construction is not subject to laws of nature comparable to those which govern mechanical

Reprinted with permission from *The Musical Quarterly* 56 (1970), pp. 153-61.

construction; and if we use the yardstick of "essential meaning," we face the difficulty of definition, because "meaning" in music is an elusive quality which can not be equated with any palpable outside concept. Even though undefinable, such a thing as "essential meaning" in music does exist, however, and with it the polarity of structure and ornament. Normally the musical fabric contains a hard core in which is vested the quintessence of the composer's thought. As a rule, this hard core is embedded in material of lesser specific weight, thinning out occasionally to near weightlessness. It is, on the whole, immaterial whether one thinks of such anatomy in terms of layers (as did Heinrich Schenker with his concepts of background, middle ground and foreground), or in terms of polarities between the structural and the ornamental, the central and the marginal, the vital and the nonvital, or the greater density (or weight) and the lesser; the choice of a simile is more a matter of semantics than of substance.

The contrasts within the musical fabric were implied in notational habits of the baroque era that go back at least into the Renaissance, when composers frequently wrote down only what was, to them, of the essence, leaving further elaboration to the performer; the contrast was also evident in such terms as the "fundamental" and "ornamental" instruments of the early baroque orchestra and, still more clearly, in the distinction of German theorists who, beginning perhaps with Christoph Bernhard, speak of *figurae fundamentales* as opposed to *figurae superficiales*.[2]

The existence of a structural core and the approximate outline of its confines can in individual cases be ascertained by removing successively different parts of the fabric and evaluating the nature of the resulting changes. If the change is felt to obliterate the basic identity of thought, we can assume that the excision has penetrated into structural matter. If, on the other hand, the basic thought seems to stand unimpaired and, in spite of the change involved, the identity of the two versions remains unquestioned, the material removed must have consisted of nonvital tissue.

The expendable outermost sphere of lightest specific weight is generally composed of pure ornaments whose function is strictly decorative, being limited to adding grace and elegance and having no intent of deeper artistic communication. A clear characterization of such pure ornaments was once given by the French gambist-composer Marin Marais. Speaking of groups of little notes, he says they stand for "certain *coulades* [i.e., slurred and usually scalewise figurations] which one may do or not do without altering the piece, and which I have written down solely for the sake of some variety."[3] The stated fact that these *coulades* would not be missed marks them as pure ornaments *par excellence*. Not all ornaments are "pure" in the same sense, however. There are many cases where an ornamental or quasi-ornamental addition has the weightier purpose of enriching the musical texture by intensifying its communication or, if this overworked term may be excused, its expressiveness. In these cases they partake of structural characteristics and carry as an alloy greater weight in the musical fabric. It is, by the way, not the design which determines the weight but the function assigned to the ornament in a particular case; and almost any musical element: melody, harmony, counterpoint, rhythm, dynamics, can affect the nature of this function. Thus a one-note grace may be a pure, weightless ornament if rendered softly and swiftly before the beat, but may assume considerable weight in the form of a long downbeat appoggiatura that changes a consonance into a dissonance; even florid figurations, usually purveyors of mere elegance, are at times entrusted with a weightier message and so become, to varying degrees, part of the musical essence.

These matters have more than academic interest. If a musical work contains elements of various density, these differences ought to be clarified by the interpreter if he is to do justice to the composer's thought. In this clarification of structure-ornament polarity two main principles are involved. One flows from the quasi-weightlessness and surface characteristics of pure ornaments and suggests the latter be not endowed with either the intensity, solidity, or gravity that are appropriate only for weightier elements. In other words, a pure ornament must not be rendered in such a way that it could be mistaken for a structural part. Usually the implications will call for a more flowing tempo and easier dynamics. The second principle issues from the improvisatory heritage of musical ornaments, a heritage still very much alive in the eighteenth century. This principle indicates for the rendition of ornaments a touch of spontaneity, rhythmic freedom, and imaginative nuance that are all earmarks of inspired improvisation. For ornaments that are not in their pure state but weighted down with structural admixtures, both of these principles will have to be modified accordingly. Of the two, the second principle—the need for flexibility—will be more persistent and assert itself even when the ornamental alloy tends strongly toward the structural pole.

In considering the proper interpretation of ornaments, we have first to identify them as such and then assess the degree of their purity, i.e., the ratio of structural admixtures. The difficulty of identifying ornaments in either their pure or alloyed state varies greatly. There is no great problem with unwritten embellishments that are left to the performer's discretion, and there are not too often problems when ornaments are indicated by symbols, though once in a while a composer uses a symbol as convenient abbreviation for structural elements. By and large the problem of identification is centered on these ornaments that are spelled out in regular notation and are, therefore, outwardly indistinguishable from structural components.

Identification may be fairly simple in cases where the melody is presented first in a plain and later in a more elaborate version. This pattern, frequently found in the classical era, is illustrated by an example from Haydn's "Lark" Quartet (ex. 1). However, a comparison of two such versions has its pitfalls. The first, simple one is not necessarily all structural (the thirty-seconds in ex. 1(a) are certainly ornaments), and the second version may exceed the scope of ornament and become, partly or entirely, a free variation.[4]

Ex. 1.   Haydn

A similar situation obtains when the melody is known in its simple unadorned form, though the composer presents it only in an elaborate version. We find such cases frequently in chorale figurations, for instance, in Bach's *Allein Gott in der Höh'* (ex. 2(a), with the melody of the chorale shown in ex. 2(b)). The figuration of the melody is, therefore, basically ornamental.

Ex. 2.   Bach, BWV 662

Identification of ornaments is harder when we encounter melismas without any direct clue as to whether or not they hide a simple, basic melody. The appropriate test would be related to the one described for probing the musical anatomy of a phrase, except that now the experiment is focused on reducing the florid melody into a simpler form, extracting its square root, so to speak, in order to find out whether the substance of its thought stands unimpaired. The question is not whether the removal of any particle will be felt—leaving out a well-placed ornament will always be a certain loss—but whether the process of compression and simplification violates the essence of the phrase. For instance, when Bach writes in the St. Matthew Passion the passage of example 3, it is, of course, technically possible to simplify the melismas, but by so doing we would seem to cripple their message; every note appears to be part of the structural core.

Ex. 3.   Bach, BWV 244/46

und wei - - - - - - - ne - te bit - ter-lich

In this particular instance the words gave a helpful clue. If the words were less affect-laden, or if the passage were to occur in a purely instrumental setting, the diagnosis might have been more difficult.

Many are the instances where knowledge about the performance practices of a given style can be a help. We know, for instance that arias in the Italian style and slow movements of concertos and sonatas required florid embellishments. Though the latter were mostly left to the performer's improvisation, some composers preferred to write them out. Whereas a few—Locatelli, Geminiani, Bonporti, for instance—did so occasionally, Bach did so as a matter of principle. Thus, if we find many florid passages in a setting of Bach's Italianate arias or instrumental adagios, there is a strong presumption for their ornamental nature. If, in addition, these figurations start after a tie, occur as thrity-second notes,[5] move largely by step or by broken chords, and have a legato articulation either marked or implied, then the presumption gathers weight, because the just-mentioned qualities are all typical attributes of melismatic ornaments and, therefore, helpful clues in their identification. If, to give an example, we find the first adagio movement of Bach's G minor Sonata for unaccompanied violin, which is patterned after the Italian-style *sonata da chiesa*, filled with this very kind of melismas (example 4(a)), there can be little doubt that we have to do with ornaments. Their reduction will yield approximately the basic melody shown in example 4(b); the eighth-note g' on the third quarter of the first measure could be considered an appoggiatura, but it seems to have structural importance and was left in the skeletal design. The latter is, incidentally, something like the form in which most Italian composers—or Purcell or Handel or Telemann—would have actually written it.[6]

Ex. 4.   Bach, BWV 100

a.

Adagio

b.

Further important factors in the ornament-structure polarity are tempo, meter, and rhythm. A slow beat, an unobtrusive meter, a great diversity of note values involved, and a melodic rhythm that appears free and rhapsodic, will all tend to provide a fertile soil for melismatic ornaments. By contrast, a fast beat, a sharply defined meter, incisively contoured melodic figures, and a fundamental sameness of note values will offer little opportunity for them. Hence, florid figurations are much more likely to be ornaments under the first than under the second set of conditions. We thus have a number of clues at our disposal to help us recognize the presence of ornaments and at the same time to evaluate the degree of their purity. However, since no formula will provide us with ready answers, in the end it is the performer who has to supplement the clues by his own musical insight.

The preceding remarks were chiefy aimed at the ornaments made up of many notes best known as diminutions, but the same principles apply to brief ones as well. Those among them that are *pure* ornaments have to be rendered with the lightness and unobtrusiveness that is in accord with their small specific weight. If, for instance, such graces serve the sole function of smoothly connecting structural notes, this function should be carried out discreetly without an attempt to usurp rhythmic or dynamic prominence. If, on the other hand, they are given a more significant assignment such as the enrichment of the harmony, they assume, as mentioned above, greater weight, but their ornamental nature still manifests itself in its need for greater rhythmic freedom. For instance, when Bach, who spelled out most of his long appoggiaturas in regular notes, writes the passage of example 5(a), the identification of the slurred quarter-notes as written-out *Vorschläge* implies that a literal rendition is out of place, that a touch of pliancy, as intimated in example 5(b) or 5(c), is musically more satisfactory, precisely because it is in keeping with the ornamental nature of the note.

Ex. 5.   Bach, BWV 893/1

Wilhelm Rust, the first editor of the old Bachgesellschaft edition, recognized over a hundred years ago that certain written-out *Vorschläge* must not be taken literally. He cites two spots from Cantatas 21 and 32 (example 6) where the clash of the sixteenth-notes in the voice with the bass would render the feminine endings "brusque and angular," if the notation were to be taken too seriously. Instead the *Vorschlag* should each time suggest a "gentle transition" [ein sanftes Hinüberleiten]. He wisely stressed the need to identify such *Vorschläge* as the graces they are and to treat them accordingly.[7]

Ex. 6.   BMV 32/5 (a); and BWV 21/2 (b)

Literally countless are the instances where similar considerations apply to *Nachschläge,* i.e., afterbeats, that are written out in regular notes. In example 7, taken from the A-flat major prelude of *Well-Tempered Clavier,* I, the eighth-note after the trill can and probably ought to be shortened, not because of a widely held, but mistaken, idea that all such dotted notes must be "overdotted," but because the eighth-note is an ornament that should be passed over lightly.

Ex. 7.   BWV 862/1

An interesting case is presented by the long trill. Before Couperin had started indicating its exact length by extending the wave symbol, there was no means available for conveying this directive. Therefore, many composers, among them Frescobaldi, Froberger, Kerll, Pachelbel, and Buxtehude, wrote out trills for measures on end in regular notes to insure their proper extension. These figures, nevertheless, remain trills with all the characteristics and privileges of an ornament. Frescobaldi made that very clear in the preface to his Toccatas and Partitas of 1615/1616 when he said: "Whenever a trill occurs in either the right or the left hand, while at the same time the other hand plays a passage, one must not synchronize the notes, but simply see to it that the trill be played fast and the passage less fast and expressive: else it would create confusion."[8] Dannreuther, who reproduced the whole preface (albeit with a few misprints), already made the point that only a nonmetrical, faster execution of the written-out trill in the middle voice, according to Frescobaldi's instruction, restores musical sense to the passage of example 8.[9]

Ex. 8.   Frescobaldi

Performers have so far largely overlooked the ornament-structure dichotomy when analyzing a work with a view to gaining a well-informed conception of its proper interpretation. This neglect should be remedied, because the identification of pure ornaments and, in the case of alloys, the recognition of an ornament predominance will often hold the key to questions of nuance and phrasing, of tempo, rhythm, and dynamics, and at times, indeed, to the true spirit and character of a composition.

The Appoggiatura in Mozart's Recitative

I

Of the many problems we meet in the performance of Mozart's recitatives, this study will address itself only to the question of the added appoggiaturas. More specifically, it will deal with those appoggiaturas that take the place of the first of two notes written on the same pitch on feminine endings (ex. 1). We can exclude from consideration such endings following the fall of a fourth because Mozart, along with most of his contemporaries, invariably wrote out this formula the way it was meant to be sung (ex. 2). Appoggiaturas on masculine endings, such as those in example 3, will be considered only marginally. They are rare because they introduce a melisma into the typically syllabic setting of recitative and are fitting only for occasional words with a strong emotional tone such as "amor," or "pietà." In the case of feminine endings, we are dealing with a convention, still fully alive for Mozart, whereby the insertion of a stepwise falling appoggiatura was often obligatory, or else optional, but also from time to time undesirable. The main purpose of the following discussion is to provide approximate guidelines for identifying the three categories of the obligatory, the optional, and the undesirable in Mozart's recitatives.

Ex. 1.

Ex. 2.

Ex. 3.

Reprinted with permission from the *Journal of the American Musicological Society*, Spring 1982.

The convention of adding appoggiaturas had long been forgotten, and until recently most recitative formulas were sung as written. With the rising interest in historically accurate performance, however, awareness of this convention was revived; but now a new problem arose marked by an exaggerated swing in the opposite direction, coupled with a misunderstanding of the underlying principles. We can observe this situation in several volumes of the *Neue Mozart Ausgabe* (hereafter: NMA), where editors suggest not only too many appoggiaturas, but appoggiaturas of the wrong kind.

By the mid-eighteenth century, earlier differences between church-, chamber-, and theater-recitative had lost their meaning. For Mozart we have to be concerned mainly with the difference between *recitativo semplice,* better known by the nineteenth-century term *"secco"* (which I shall use hereafter), and *recitativo accompagnato.* The *secco* is accompanied by cello, bass, and cembalo or fortepiano, whereas the *accompagnato* involves the whole orchestra. Both types serve different purposes. The *secco* often contains very fast exchanges that carry the action forward like the spoken dialogue in *Singspiel* or *opéra comique.* The *accompagnato* is often a monologue that sets the stage for a following aria. As such it is also used in *Singspiele* (e.g., in *Die Entführung aus dem Serail* or *Die Zauberflöte*). As a dialogue, it usually occurs at moments of dramatic gravity or tension. Concerning both types of recitative, theorists of the period agree on several general points: that recitative represents musical prose declamation which often approaches everyday speech ("halfway between speech and song" as some put it); that as such it is syllabic, not melismatic: that it is rhythmically and metrically free, and not bound by a specific key or key scheme. They also agree that a stepwise descending appoggiatura is often necessary to do justice to the prosodic accent on the penultimate syllable of a feminine ending; and that the function of such an appoggiatura is not one of expression, but of musical diction. This is the crux of the matter. In Italian, in German, and in English, the speech accent is rendered by a combination of greater loudness and an elevation of the voice. Both loudness and elevation can range from almost imperceptible to considerable, depending on the emphasis placed on the word. But never will either loudness or speech melody be *lowered* for the accented syllable. For these reasons a recitative appoggiatura on a feminine ending has to be applied from above, not from below; moreover, since Mozart writes out those syllabic appoggiaturas that fall a fourth (and are extremely frequent at phrase endings), as well as those involving larger intervals, the appoggiatura that is to be, or may be, freely inserted, can only be the stepwise descending one.

If recitative is to approximate speech, then the prosodic accent on a word will vary with the weight of that word within the sentence as well as with the overall degree of emphasis on a particular passage: it will be stronger in an oratorical delivery that might be proper for certain accompanied recitatives, weaker in the fast give-and-take of daily conversation as so often encountered in the *secco* style. Thus often in the middle of sentences rendered in fast *parlando* fashion the accents are minimized to near or total disappearance, obviating the need and often the desirability of added appoggiaturas. Their proliferation in such contexts would be unnatural and impart a sing-song quality to a fast dialogue that is theatrically unjustified. In the *accompagnato*, by contrast, the words are generally rendered with more deliberaton; in addition, the participation of the orchestra will tend to limit the speed of delivery and with it the range of rhythmic freedom for the singer. But those are differences of degree, not of kind.

The need for an inserted appoggiatura will normally be greatest for the falling third at the cadence, because there, a stepwise descent, along with the prosodic accent, would reflect the gradual tapering of a falling speech melody better than a downward leap to the accented syllable. The need is less obvious for the falling second, because there is no angular leap to be bridged. The need will be smallest when the repeated pitches are approached from below because the upward step or leap can often by itself be sufficient to mirror the tonic accent. That is most evident with such characteristic intervals as, say, the augmented fourth.[1] (See ex. 4 in note 1.) The need will also be small for words so casually spoken that they call for no accentuation. At the other end of the spectrum, an appoggiatura will be improper for words of such forcefulness that they would be weakened by the smoothing effect of the grace.

In order to gain a better perspective on the problem of Mozart's recitative, we shall first examine the historical sources for the appoggiatura convention.

II

Georg Philipp Telemann is among the authors most frequently cited on the question of the recitative appoggiatura. He offers an illustration that shows how singers do not always sing as written but "occasionally" [hin und wieder] use an appoggiatura [Akzent].[2] Since his illustration served a pedagogical purpose, the fact that he added appoggiaturas to all masculine and feminine endings does not really undermine the reservation of "occasionally." His example shows eleven descending appoggiaturas and one that, ascending chromatically, fills in the interval of a whole step. Several factors disqualify the transfer of this rising appoggiatura to Mozart: its date, solemn religious tone, and generally poor diction that was later to be devastatingly criticized by J.A.P. Schulz (see below).

Johann Friedrich Agricola in 1757 joins in the widespread agreement that on feminine endings the falling fourth preceding two identical pitches should always be delayed by an inserted appoggiatura, as illustrated above in example 2, whereas for the falling third, a connecting, stepwise appoggiatura should be inserted only "occasionally" [zuweilen].[3]

In a lengthy serialized essay on recitative, Friedrich Wilhelm Marpurg criticizes the notation of the feminine cadence with the falling fourth on the beat: "This notation is unquestionably reprehensible because one ought not naturally and without good cause write differently from the way one sings" because by so doing one confuses the singers.[4] From this principle alone we can infer that when Marpurg writes a tone repetition, he means it, and his many examples contain numerous tone repetitions. He is even more explicit on the matter when, in speaking of half-cadences [schwebenden Absätzen], he lists as one of their alternatives an execution with repeated pitch [mit dem wiederholten Einklange]. A few of his illustrations are given in example 5, where we see a fall of a fifth in (a), of a fourth in (d), and tone repetitions in (b), (c), and (e). The remarkable fact that among his many illustrations, including those for full cadences, he shows not a single appoggiatura filling in a descending third, would seem to indicate that he found the tone repetition preferable.

Ex. 5

Marpurg, *Kritische Briefe über die Tonkunst* (1762)

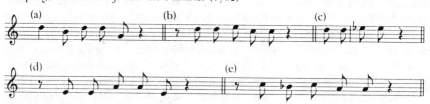

Like many other writers, Johann Adam Hiller warns against the use in recitatives of ornaments other than the appoggiatura; trills and mordents, he says, may be applied only once in a while.[5] Appoggiaturas *may* be used for all falling thirds; also, after three or four stepwise ascending notes, the last one may receive an appoggiatura from above. Surprisingly, these appoggiaturas [Vorschläge] do not replace the written note but are of the very short species [unveränderliche] that resolve in Lombard rhythm into the written note. Even if such a *Vorschlag* is indicated by symbol, as in example 6(a), it is to be sung as in (b), not as in (c).

Ex. 6

Hiller, *Anweisung zum musikalisch-richtigen Gesange* (1774)

und   Eh - re   Eh - re   Eh - re

Johann Abraham Peter Schulz offers a long and thoughtful disquisition on recitative,[6] which was later admiringly cited by the eminent theorist Koch.

Schulz reconfirms for recitative the lack of an exact meter and key scheme and its non-lyrical, syllabic nature that should allow no melismatic ornaments. For full cadences he gives the models of example 7 without indicating a rendition differing from the notation.

Ex. 7

Schulz, "Recitativ," in Sulzer's *Allgemeine Theorie der schönen Künste* (1771)

For feminine endings he restates the principle that the formula of the falling fourth to the repeated note should be written as sung, i.e., as a downward leaping appoggiatura. Since Schulz, like Marpurg, obviously wants the cadences written as sung, we must assume that in his numerous examples the many repeated notes that follow the fall of a third or other melodic progressions were intended to be rendered literally. In the same vein he objects to altering a masculine fall of a fourth, as shown in example 8, which would sound "dragging and unpleasant" [höchst schleppend und widrig]. He admits such appoggiaturas that result in melismas only exceptionally in spots of unusual expression and then only when sung by first-class artists. He makes an exception only for masculine endings on a falling third where, in the passage of example 9(a), the last note receives an appoggiatura as if it had been written like (b).

Ex. 8

Schulz, "Recitativ"

Ex. 9

Schulz, "Recitativ"

Very interesting and logical is his rule that cadences expressing questions, violent exclamations, or strong injunctions must emphasize not the final syllable of the sentence but the principal word [Hauptwort] carrying the meaning. For questions he lists the formulas of examples 10(a) and (b), then sensibly corrects the solution of (c) with an upward leaping third, to (d) with the repeated pitch.

Ex. 10

Schulz, "Recitativ"

In Germany we find more theoretical mention of appoggiatura inserts as the eighteenth century nears its close. Johann Carl Friedrich Rellstab points out that in recitative the appoggiaturas are not written out but left to the judgment of the singers.[7] Significantly he adds that "in the theater, a singer who knows what action means will add few if any appoggiaturas, and even in church or chamber...I prefer the plain rendition" (example 11(a) as opposed to 11(b)). As a good compromise he suggests the notation of 11(c), which the singer "obviously" sings as in 11(d).

Ex. 11

Rellstab, *Versuch über die Vereinigung der musikalischen und oratorischen Declamation* (1786 or 87)

Johann Baptist Lasser shows the descending appoggiatura inserted on the fall of the third in feminine endings (ex. 12(a)) and on the last of several ascending pitches (ex. 12(b)). Johann Friedrich Schubert limits the use of the appoggiatura to "every so often" [öfters] in order to bring out a declamatory emphasis as shown in example 12(c). Neither he nor Lasser mentions any rising appoggiaturas.[8]

Ex. 12

Lasser, *Vollständige Anleitung zur Singkunst* (1798)

(c) J. F. Schubert, *Neue Singe-Schule* (1804)

Johann Christoph Koch, in two partly overlapping articles, stresses the declamatory, syllabic nature of recitative and its freedom from meter and key. He largely follows Schulz, mentions no appoggiaturas, and gives no examples.[9]

All these German theorists took the Italian vocal art as their model and offer Italian as well as German texts for their examples. Though the degree of relevance for Mozart is uncertain for these or any other theorists, we cannot ignore the large role that many of them assign to tone repetition on feminine endings.

We have few Italian documents on eighteenth-century recitative. In Pier Francesco Tosi's famous treatise, *Opinioni de' cantori antichi e moderni* (Bologna, 1723), the chapter on recitative is disappointingly lacking in specifics. For the latter part of the century, however, we find some interesting accounts in Mancini, Manfredini, and Corri. Giambattista Mancini, like the German theorists, stresses the declamatory character of recitative which, he says, is at its best when the notes imitate natural speech ("perfettamente imitano un discorso naturale"). He stresses the importance of the "valuable appoggiatura" [accento prezioso] performed *one tone higher* than written and used notably when two syllables of the same word are written on the same pitch. Such a stepwise falling appoggiatura is characterized as a prosodic accent that underlines the declamatory nature of recitative.[10] Important, too, is Mancini's precept that, even in an aria, where melody is far more independent from declamatory intonation patterns, exclamations of invective, great fervor of action, or the passion invested in words like "tiranno," "crudele," or "spietato," would be denatured by an added appoggiatura. *A fortiori* this principle has to apply to recitative. (The same idea, this time specifically aimed at recitative, is expressed by Daniel Gottlob Türk, who writes: "when an idea is to be rendered defiantly... appoggiaturas would be totally improper because they impart a certain smoothness to the melody that is unfitting for such occasions."[11])

For the first of two notes of equal pitch and value, Vincenzo Manfredini stipulates the need to sing an appoggiatura stepwise *from above*. By contrast, an instrumentalist is under no clear obligation to insert such an appoggiatura unless it is prescribed by the composer. Manfredini considers other ornaments undesirable for both *secco* [semplice] and *accompagnato* [obbligato] recitative and admits some very brief embellishments only for uninteresting and indifferent words, but never for an animated, tender, or expressive text.[12]

In his collection of arias and duets from operas, Domenico Corri, a student of Nicola Porpora, shows how specific Italian singers render the musical text.[13] As was to be expected, these virtuoso singers take considerable liberties even with, say, Gluck, who would have hardly welcomed their lavish embroidery and their altered melodies (e.g., in "Che farò senza Euridice"). In recitatives, both *secco* and accompanied, Corri almost always replaces feminine endings on the same pitch with a stepwise descending appoggiatura, never with an ascending one, as shown in example 13(a). (See also the recitatives to Giordani's *Artaserse,* pp. 1-2, and Sacchini's *Perseo,* pp. 48-49.)

Ex. 13

(a) Corri, *A Select Collection* (*ca.* 1779)

(b) Gluck, *Orfeo,* I, 1 (Gluck, *Sämtliche Werke,* Vol. 1, part 1)

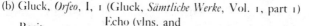

We have significant proof for Gluck's disagreement with Corri in the first act recitative from *Orfeo.* We see in example 13(b) a written-out appoggiatura on "cara," but the exclamation "Euridice!," and the question "dove sei?" are each followed by an instrumental "echo" that unmistakably indicates the absence of vocal appoggiaturas.

Because of the scarcity of Italian theoretical sources on recitative, several editors of the NMA had recourse to a vocal treatise by Manuel Garcia (son), written in French fifty years after Mozart's death.[14] The editors attach great importance to a sentence in which Garcia, speaking of the *accompagnato* only, admits the use of a stepwise rising appoggiatura, which he characterizes as being more "moving" [plus pathétique]. This is an elaboration of a previous statement concerning recitative in general, in which he defined the appoggiatura as a "raising of the voice for the tonic accent." Garcia's testimony has to be viewed with great reserve. Even if his father, who was Rossini's first Almaviva, had bequeathed Rossinian principles to him, they are no reliable guide for Mozart. Rossini, born a year after Mozart's death, was heir to an extravagant tradition of vocal embellishment from which the mature Mozart had thoroughly emancipated himself. We need only look at Garcia's interpretation of Donna Anna's great opening recitative (ex. 14) to realize that he should be dismissed, not summoned, as an expert witness for Mozart's recitative. The same conclusion is inevitable when, in the dialogue between Don Giovanni and Zerlina in act I, scene 9, Garcia has the impertinence to recompose Mozart's text. Apparently bothered by Don Giovanni's threefold repetition of the triadic formula on the words, "quegli occhi briconcelli, quei labretti si belli, quelle dituccie candide e odorose," Garcia tried to "correct" an imagined monotony. He was unaware of the psychological masterstroke with which Mozart revealed Don Giovanni's insincerity by the very mechanical way in which he rattles off his flatteries.

Ex. 14

Garcia, *A Complete Treatise on the Art of Singing* (1847 and 1872)

(*Don Giovanni*)

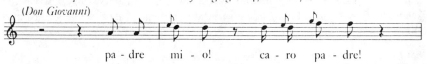

        pa - dre   mi - o!   ca - ro   pa - dre!

Garcia is further disqualified when he authorizes the singers to change the melody of *secco* recitative (the "récitatif parlant," as he calls it), on the grounds that it is "only a platitude" to begin with.

Considerable inconsistency characterizes the approach of the various editors of the NMA to the recitative appoggiatura. Nearly all of them underplay the role of tone repetition, but they do so to different degrees: some admit no such repetitions at all, others only a carefully limited number. They diverge more strongly in their treatment of the appoggiatura from below. Some editors limit this type to the stepwise ascending formula and use it sparingly. Others use it more generously and extend it to upward leaps by thirds and fourths. In the following section, I shall apply the criteria of diction, speech melody, word meaning, and affect to some characteristic passages of recitative from Mozart's operas, in order to arrive at some working principles about advisable, questionable, and inadvisable procedures.

III

In Mozart's recitatives masculine endings rarely pose a problem: in general we ought to leave them alone to avoid melismas unwarranted by diction. Once in a while, when word meaning and length of syllable combine, however, an appoggiatura may be advisable, as in examples 15(a) and (b), whereas (c) and (d) will best be sung as written.

Ex. 15*

(a) *Così fan tutte*, II, 8

Ferrando

Ab - bi di me pie - tà,   -tà,

(b) *Idomeneo*, III, 2

Idamante

che ap - pa-gar-ti e mo - rir.

(c) *Così fan tutte*, II, 9

Don Alfonso

in - fe - del a voi fu.

(d) *Così fan tutte*, II, 1

Despina   Dorabella   Despina

per voi.   Per noi?   Per voi.

*Appoggiaturas with inverted stems in this and all following examples are suggestions of the NMA unless otherwise indicated. My own suggestions are indicated in square brackets.

For a feminine ending, the *locus classicus* is of course tone repetition after a falling third. Here the tendency to fill the gap will be strongest when the speech contour was already one of gradual descent, as in examples 16(a) and (b).

Ex. 16

(a) *Le nozze di Figaro*, I, 1

Figaro

fi - gu-ra in que-sto lo-co.

(b) *Don Giovanni*, I, 15

Don Giovanni

le vo-glio di -ver-tir   fin che vien not-te.

The humble, pleading tone of example 17(a) calls for a gentle articulation pattern, hence for an appoggiatura on "ubbidisco," and probably also on "Signore." (The NMA omits an appoggiatura on "Signore," certainly a reasonable option.) In German, the urgency of the plea in example 17(b) requires an appoggiatura.

Ex. 17

(a) *Don Giovanni*, II, 11

Leporello

Pia - no pia - no, Si - gno - re, o -ra ub- bi - di - sco.

(b) *Die Zauberflöte*, I, Finale

Tamino

Ihr Un - sicht - ba - ren   sa - get mir:

In a stepwise fall, or when a note is preceded by one of the same pitch, the need for an appoggiatura is lessened because there is no disturbing break in the speech contour. When the repeated pitch is approached from below, the need for an appoggiatura fades still more, because the melodic rise will often be sufficient to take account of the tonic accent. In all of these cases an appoggiatura will be suggested by either a need for distinct emphasis, or, in an *accompagnato*, by a sense of warmth or tenderness. Thus, in example 18 no appoggiatura is needed for "momento" after the stepwise rise; for "affanno" the decision could go either way, but for "idol mio," where warmth of feeling coincides with a falling third, an appoggiatura is obligatory.

Ex. 18

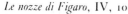

In the stepwise descent of example 19(a) the word "bella" pronounced by Don Giovanni calls for emphasis. In example 19(b) the stepwise rise alone is sufficient for the weak speech accent on "vestirla" and an appoggiatura would be pointless for the two "E poi." In 19(c), "questo" is not important enough to require extra emphasis, while in (d), the leap of a fourth is sufficient to render the speech accent and obviates the need for an appoggiatura.

Ex. 19

(d) *Così fan tutte*, II, 9

The need for caution in adding appoggiaturas after upward leaps is underscored by numerous instances in which Mozart, in cases where they are clearly called for, specifically writes them out, as shown in examples 20(a)-(c). See also below example 32(c).

Ex. 20

Don Giovanni

(a) I, 13

(b) I, 13   (c) II, 12

Such examples suggest reserve, not prohibition. Where the meaning of a word calls for special emphasis, appoggiaturas sometimes may, sometimes should, be added. The pleading of Zerlina in example 21(a) would be pale without an appoggiatura, and so would Susanna's flirtatious "Figaretto" in example 21(b).

Ex. 21

(a) *Don Giovanni*, I, 16   (b) *Le nozze di Figaro*, I, 1

The meaning of the words is not always the main criterion, however. What often matters more is the way they are rendered: whether spoken soft or loud, fast or slow, *legato* or *staccato*. Phrases and sentences will often give a clue and so occasionally will the composer, by tempo markings or by specifying the character of the declamation. The *sotto voce sempre* in example 22 suggests a minimum of inflections, hence the NMA with good reason omits appoggiaturas on "sei" and "voi"; the one on "disgrazia" follows the natural speech flow. See also below (in ex. 32) the directive "con risolutezza" and its presumable implications.

Ex. 22

Don Giovanni, I, 2

Don Giovanni *sotto voce sempre*   Leporello

Le-po-rel-lo, o-ve se - i?   Son quì per mia dis-gra-zia;   e   vo - i?

Although an appoggiatura from below contradicts the prosodic accent, once in a while it can be harmless when introduced discreetly as in Luigi Ferdinando Tagliavini's interpretation of example 23(a). Here the rising appoggiatura on "rivedi" is unnecessary, but unobtrusive, being prepared and rising only a half step. The prosodic infraction is small and the result in the frame of the whole phrase is pleasing. The appoggiatura on "felice" is unobjectionable, the one on "Mitridate" necessary.

Ex. 23

(a) *Mitridate*, I, 10

Mitridate

ma quel più non ri - ve - di   fe - li - ce   Mi - tri - da - te,

(b) *Le nozze di Figaro*, I, 5

Susanna

Po - ve - ro Che - ru - bin,   sie - te voi   paz-zo!   paz - zo

Though melodically similar, the case of example 23(b) is not comparable. Occurring at the end of the recitative, Susanna's exclamation: "Cherubino, you are crazy!" calls for emphasis on the key word "pazzo"—which has to have an appoggiatura from above, not from below; the word does not call for a gentle ingratiating inflection, but a musical exclamation point.

More serious still are appoggiaturas that leap upward a fourth or more, because here the infraction against proper declamation is so drastic as to subvert the basic principle of the recitative. This is true of such cases as shown in examples 24(a) and (b). Related to it and even more objectionable are such cases as those shown in example 24(c), where the rising appoggiatura is approached by an upward leap for words that should have no appoggiatura to begin with, because their expression of contempt and fury must not be softened by a "pathetic" ornament.

Another frequent application of the rising appoggiatura that has crept into several volumes of the NMA involves questions. It is true that in Italian, as well as in German and English, a question will more often than not involve a rising inflection of the voice. Such rise is clearest in masculine endings where it

will be the more evident, the more pointed the question, and less so—
occasionally to the point of disappearance—the more casual and timid it is.
Such shadings are reflected in examples 25(a)-(c).

Ex. 24

(a) *Le nozze di Figaro*, I, 5

Susanna

Cor vo-stro! Co - sa av - ven - ne?

(b) *Idomeneo*, III, 2

Ilia

che sco-prir la mia fiam-ma?

(c) *Idomeneo*, I, 6

Elettra

Oh sde - gno!   oh sma - nie!

Ex. 25

Don Giovanni

(a) II, 4   (b) I, 16   (c) I, 16

Masetto   Masetto   Masetto   Zerlina

Chi va là?   Eb-ben che c'è?   Non mi toc - car!   Per-chè?

By contrast, in feminine endings of questions, the voice contour will
generally rise to the accented first, then fall to the unaccented second, syllable.
In a monotone delivery the voice may not rise at all, and may even fall to the
accented syllable, but it will never rise from the accented to the unaccented one.
Mozart himself confirmed the tonal descent from the penultimate to the final
syllable in countless instances for which two examples (exx. 26(a) and (b)) are
typical. Example 26(c) shows both the descent for the feminine and the rise for
the masculine ending.

Ex. 26

Don Giovanni

(a) II, 5   (b) I, 15

Don Giovanni   Don Giovanni

E po - i?   Co - me va tut - to ma - le?

(c) II, 11

Leporello   Don Giovanni

Chi mi chia - ma?   non co - no - sci il pa - dron?

Given this characteristic of Italian and German diction, the introduction of a rising appoggiatura for questions is a misunderstanding. Nevertheless, we find it being suggested on many occasions in the NMA, notably in *Idomeneo, Le nozze di Figaro,* and *Die Zauberflöte,* as shown in a few instances in example 27. (See also examples 24(a) and (b)).

(a) *Le nozze di Figaro*, I, 2   (b) *Le nozze di Figaro*, I, 1

(c) *Le nozze di Figaro*, I, 5

(d) *Die Zauberflöte*, I, Finale   (e) *Idomeneo*, III, 1

Ex. 28

Die Zauberflöte, I, Finale

Tamino's famous recitative, from which the next example is taken, merits closer scrutiny for the overuse of both types of appoggiaturas. While in example 28(a) the appoggiatura on "Knaben" is appropriate, the one in (b) on "Pforten" is unnecessary and disturbs the musical line, with its ascent to "Säulen" portraying Tamino's growing astonishment at the grandeur of the temple. Next, the NMA has falling appoggiaturas on "Klugheit" and "Arbeit,"

and a rising one on "weilen." All three would better be left out. Tamino's wondrous awe is better reflected by the simple, dignified, unornamented line with its striking ascent by thirds, than through the appoggiatura clichés, while the idea of "weilen" (to endure, to reign) finds a far better pictorial reflection in the persistence, the "Weilen" on the pitch than in a would-be "expressive" rising appoggiatura.

In Donna Anna's narrative of Don Giovanni's intrusion into her room at nightfall (see example 29), it seems that the slow stepwise ascent from "quando nella mia stanza" builds up its tension to the climax of "istante" far more stirringly if its linearity is not interrupted by appoggiaturas on "stanze," "sventura," and "avvolto," as suggested by the NMA. The only advisable appoggiatura is that on "alquanto" in the first measure of the example.

Ex. 29

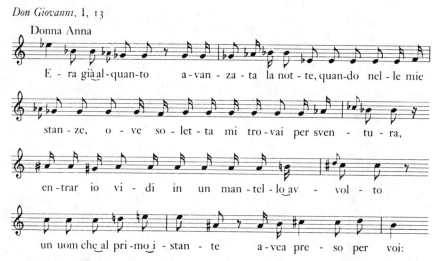

Don Giovanni, I, 13

In example 30 from the same recitative, the NMA suggests, with good reason, appoggiaturas for the three falling thirds in measures 64-65. In measure 66 an appoggiatura on the falling second is even more necessary to do justice to "più forte," but in the following measure I would suggest eliminating the appoggiatura on "suo." By repeating the words "compie il misfatto suo"—a rare occurrence in a recitative—Mozart achieves an extraordinary dramatic effect; yet the intensification inherent in the repetition on a higher pitch level is weakened by the suggested appoggiatura. In another passage from *Don Giovanni*, given in example 31, the appoggiatura in measure 2 on "vuoi" is unnecessary, while the one in measure 3 is optional; if the latter is left out, then the obligatory one in measure 4 will more effectively bring out the augmentation from "importante" to "importantissimo." In measure 5, Don Giovanni's "finiscila," as a cool command, could normally do without an appoggiatura, but the Don mimics Leporello's inflection, hence the appoggiatura is needed; so is the one on "collera"; in measure 9 one is unnecessary on "soli," optional on "vedo"; and in measure 10 "sente" can do without one.

Ex. 30

Don Giovanni, I, 13

Whenever the rounding, softening effect of an appoggiatura is unfitting, we should avoid inserting one. Much will depend on the prevalent tone of the monologue or dialogue in question, whether fast and casual, excited, solemn, determined, and so forth. Generally, words expressing authority, decisiveness, threats, violence, terror, stubbornness, finality, and similar affections will be more fittingly rendered by tone repetition.

A striking example is the first accompanied recitative in *Don Giovanni*, where Donna Anna comes upon the body of her slain father. Her anguished terror is poignantly rendered by the upward rushing triadic figure of example 32. The two appoggiaturas suggested by the NMA in the first measure weaken the dramatic impact of the outcry—its force underlined by the powerful interjections of the orchestra. That Mozart did not have appoggiaturas in mind, becomes clear four measures later when terror yields to compassion at the sight of the wound and Mozart writes out the appoggiaturas of example 32(b) accompanied by tender woodwind figures, indicating thereby that their insertion would not have been understood without such notation. To bring this contrast into still clearer focus, the recurring feeling of terror brings forth a similar triadic outcry (ex. 32(c)), again punctuated by dramatic orchestral interjections, followed, above a soothing chord in the strings, by "padre amato," which should have an appoggiatura from above, not from below, as suggested by the NMA (presumably to provide a change from their proposed appoggiaturas on "mio" and "padre," which again would be better left unsung).

Ex. 32

Don Giovanni, I, 2

In the preceding brief *secco* that starts scene 3 (ex. 33), Mozart's directive "con risolutezza" strengthens the case for tone repetition on "periglio," which would be weakened by an appoggiatura.

Ex. 33

Don Giovanni, I, 2

Although on a less pathetic level, the words "ingrato" and "crudele" in example 34(a) ought not to be softened by appoggiaturas from above and below. Similarly, in example 34(b), "perfidia" is stronger when sung as written and in example 34(c) the command can easily dispense with an appoggiatura.

Ex. 34

(a) *Don Giovanni*, I, Finale

(b) *Le nozze di Figaro*, I, 7   (c) *Don Giovanni*, I, 20

There is a revealing passage in Mozart's insert in Gluck's *Alceste: Popoli di Tessaglia* (ex. 35(a)), where, in addition to the grimness of the word "funesto," the orthography of a-sharp and a-natural following closely the high b-flat, definitely precludes an appoggiatura. The latter would even theoretically be feasible only if Mozart had written a b-flat instead of an a-sharp, since the solution given in example 35(b) is irrational.

Ex. 35

"Popoli di Tessaglia," K. 316 (300b)

In example 36(a) the word "resto" is more congenial to literalness than to the rising appoggiatura in the NMA. Similarly, the solemn authority of the old priest in example 36(b) is better served by omitting an appoggiatura on "Gründe."

Ex. 36

(a) *Idomeneo*, III, 2   (b) *Die Zauberflöte*, I, Finale

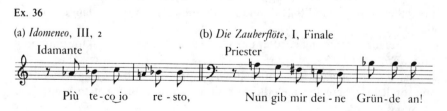

As a final illustration for the three options open for tone repetitions, an appoggiatura on "Susanna" in example 37 is possible, but unnecessary; one on "l'istoria" is necessary, whereas "finita" should be sung as written, since tone repetition better conveys a sense of finality.

Ex. 37

Le nozze di Figaro, II, 2

Summing up the insights gained from theoretical and musical evidence, we can tentatively formulate the following principles for Mozart's recitatives:

1. Appoggiaturas on tone repetitions range from necessary to undesirable, with a grey area of ambivalence between the two.

2. The appoggiaturas should descend stepwise from above. They mirror the prosodic accent and should be used whenever a distinct accentuation is warranted by the situation.

3. Ascending appoggiaturas on questions should be avoided. They involve a misunderstanding of Italian and German diction.

4. Appoggiaturas leaping from below are never appropriate because they conflict too sharply with proper declamation.

5. In rare cases, in an *accompagnato,* a chromatically rising appoggiatura may be admissible if prepared and fitted smoothly into the melodic line; but it is never necessary and is best avoided.

6. For the fall of a third, even where the speech accent is very weak, an appoggiatura is often used in a lubricating function to avoid an unwarranted break in the speech melody.

7. An appoggiatura is undesirable:

    a. when it infringes a characteristic melodic design

    b. for words expressing firmness, finality, resolution, hatred, terror, or any other state of mind that should not be subjected to the softening effect of the grace

    c. for commonplace utterances in fast *parlando* style and for unimportant words.

8. An appoggiatura is optional when approached from below by either step or leap, where the melodic rise alone is often sufficient to render the prosodic accent.

In general, I see wisdom in moderation. Excess is always tiresome. A good speaker, always cited by seventeenth- and eighteenth-century writers as a model for proper musical interpretation, will not give equal emphasis to every word accent. By the same token, the appoggiatura will be the more effective, the more discriminately it is used, and the more its use is attuned to word meaning and speech melody in a given passage.

Notes

Chapter 1

1. "La Note Pointée et la soi-disant "Manière Française," *Revue de Musicologie,* 51 (1965), 66-92 (FN 1).

2. Putnam Aldrich, "The Principal Agréments of the Seventeenth and Eighteenth Centuries," unpublished Harvard dissertation (1942), p. 457.

3. A few are listed here to point to the risk of such reasoning: Tomás de Santa Maria, "Libro llamado Arte de Tañer Fantasia" (Valladolid, 1565), folio 46v, calls it *Quiebro senzillo* (simple shake); Michael Praetorius, *Syntagma Musicum* (Wolfenbüttel, 1619), iii, p. 235, lists it under *tremoletti;* Daniel Friderici, *Musica Figuralis,* 4th ed. (Rostock, 1649) and identical 6th ed. (Rostock, 1677), chap. 8, *regula* 13; Johann Andreas Herbst, *Musica Moderna Prattica* (Frankfurt, 1658), p. 7, based on Praetorius; Johann Crüger, *Musicae Practicae Praecepta Brevia* (Berlin, 1660), p. 25, sub-form of *tremulus;* Wolfgang Caspar Printz, *Musica Modulatoria Vocalis* (Schweidnitz, 1678), pp. 45 and 53, *figura corta;* id., *Compendium Musicae Signatoriae & Modulatoriae* (Dresden, 1689), p. 47, species of *accentus;* Moritz Feyertag, *Syntaxis Minor zur Sing-Kunst* (Dudenstadt, 1695), p. 206, *accentus circumflexus.* Quite apart from these and other quotations, a single look at the extravagance of improvised coloraturas and cadenzas that were still current in the eighteenth century would seem to discredit the idea that nobody used the *Schneller* because it was not yet invented.

4. Johann Gottfried Walther, *Praecepta der Musicalischen Composition* (1708; first printed: Leipzig, 1955, ed. by P. Benary), pp. 38-39, 152-53.

5. Johann Joachim Quantz, *Versuch einer Anleitung die Flöte traversiere zu spielen* (Berlin, 1752).

6. Michel de Saint Lambert, *Les Principes du Clavecin* (Paris, 1702), p.v: Un bon Maître ... n'embarrasse point la mémoire de ceux qu'il instruit par des distinctions hors de saison. Il enseigne une règle generale comme si elle était sans exception, attendant que l'occasion amène cette exception pour en parler, parce qu'il sçait u'alors elle se conçoit mieux; et que s'il en eut parlé d'abord elle eût empeché l'impression de la règle generale.

7. Bach himself indicates as much in his heading, which reads "Explication unterschied-licher Zeichen, so gewisse *manieren* artig zu spielen, andeuten" (Explanation of various symbols suggesting the way in which certain ornaments are to be properly played). The word *andeuten* implies an approximation, not a definition.

8. The passage in question is C.P.E. Bach, "Versuch über die wahre Art das Clavier zu spielen (Berlin, 1753), chap. III, par. 23; Arnold Dolmetsch, *The Interpretation of the Music of the XVIIth and XVIIIth Centuries* (London, [1916], p. 59.

9. See my article "External Evidence and Uneven Notes," *The Musical Quarterly, 52* (1966), pp. 448-64. (Chap. 5 in this volume.)

Chapter 2

1. Bach, who started using the natural sign regularly around 1717 and the double sharp around 1732, and who may never have used the double flat, indicates the latter in the autograph of the very late second book of the *Well-Tempered Clavier* by adding a single flat to the flat of the key signature (see Preludes and Fugues Nos. 17 and 22). In the penultimate measure of Fugue No. 17 the double flat so indicated on the second quarter is followed in the same bar by three more single flats, all written by plain unaltered notes.

2. Donington tries to belittle forbidden parallels as a consideration for the proper use of ornaments. On p. 218 he gives this rule: "When, of two notes moving in parallel fifths, one is an accented passing note resolving by step before the other note has changed, the progression is correct." This, he adds, can also happen with long appoggiaturas. Donington, as he has revealed in an earlier article, learned this rule in Oxford. I have never found anything remotely resembling it in primary sources. True, some writers tolerated parallels that were very short and inconspicuous, especially in the middle parts of thick textures, but many other theorists condemned any ornament-generated parallels from Christoph Bernhard in the mid-seventeenth century to C.P.E. Bach, who writes that ornaments must never interfere with the purity of voice-leading and gives as an illustration a trill that is objectionable because it would create fifths. Why disregard him in this matter, yet quote him constantly as a supreme authority for the whole eighteenth century? He, and I am sure, Couperin would have objected to Donington's interpretation of ex. 65, billed as "normal baroque progression," especially when stripped of the trill before the fifths, added despite Couperin's injunction neither to omit any marked nor to add any unmarked ornaments.

3. Donington's translation of Quantz's passage (citation 85) is inaccurate, in that the word "attacked," which is suggestive of an accent, should read "articulated" for the German noncommittal "angestossen" (Reilly rendered it: "tipped with the tongue."). In chap. 8, par. 4, Quantz writes: *"man muss die Vorschläge mit der Zunge weich anstossen."* (*Vorschläge* must be gently articulated with the tongue.)

4. The discrepancies are not felt at all as dissonant clashes, because they occur off the beat and are very brief. We find similar combinations in Oriana's aria "Oh caro mio" in Handel's *Amadigi* or, for that matter, in Don Ottavio's aria "Il mio tesoro," mm. 8, 11, and parallel spots. Mattheson in *Der vollkommene Capellmeister*, chap. 12, par. 20, observes that vocal melody does not admit the same sharp dotting as do instruments.

Chapter 3

1. Johann Joachim Quantz, *Versuch einer Anweisung die Flöte traversiere zu spielen...* (Berlin, 1752), chap. II, par. 12. Translation by Arthur Mendel used with permission of G. Schirmer, Inc., New York:

Ich muss hierbei eine nothwendige Anmerkung machen, welche die Zeit, wie lange jede Note gehalten werden muss, betrifft. Man muss unter den Hauptnoten, welche man auch: *anschlagende,* oder, nach Art der Italiäner, *gute* Noten zu nennen pfleget, und unter den *durchgehenden,* welche bey einigen Ausländern *schlimme* heissen, einen Unterschied im Vortrage zu machen wissen. Die Hauptnoten müssen allezeit, wo es sich thun lässt, mehr erhoben werden, als die durchgehenden. Dieser Regel zu Folge müssen die geschwindesten Noten, in einem jeden Stücke von *mässigem Tempo,* oder auch im *Adagio,* ungeachtet sie dem Gesichte nach einerley Geltung haben, dennoch ein wenig ungleich gespielet werden, so dass man die anschlagenden Noten einer jeden Figur, nämlich die erste, dritte, fünfte, und siebente, etwas länger anhält, als die durchgehenden, nämlich, die zweite, vierte, sechste, und achte: doch muss dieses Anhalten nicht so viel ausmachen, als wenn Puncte dabei stünden. Unter diesen geschwindesten Noten verstehe ich: die Viertheile im Dreizweitheiltacte; die Achttheile im Dreiviertheil—und die Sechzehntheile im Dreiachttheiltacte; die Achttheile im Alla-breve; die Sechzehntheile oder Zwei und dreissigtheile im Zweiviertheil—oder im gemeinen geraden Tacte: doch nur so lange, als keine Figuren von noch geschwindern oder noch einmal so kurzen Noten, in jeder Tactart mit untermischet sind; denn alsdenn müssten diese letztern auf die oben beschriebene Art vorgetragen werden. Z.E. Wollte man Tab. IX. Fig. I die acht Sechzehntheile unter den Buchstaben (k) (m) (n) langsam in einerley Geltung spielen, so würden sie nicht so gefällig klingen, als wenn man von vieren die erste und dritte etwas länger, und stärker im Tone, als die zweite und vierte, hören lässt. Von dieser Regel aber werden ausgenommen: erstlich die geschwinden Passagien in einem sehr geschwinden Zeitmaasse, bei denen die Zeit nicht erlaubt sie ungleich vorzutragen, und wo man also die Länge ùnd Stärke nur bei der ersten von vieren anbringen muss. Ferner werden ausgenommen: alle geschwinden Passagien welche die Singstimme zu machen hat, wenn sie anders nicht geschleifet werden sollen: denn weil jede Note von dieser Art der Singpassagien, durch einen gelinden Stoss der Luft aus der Brust, deutlich gemachet und markiret werden muss; so findet die Ungleichheit dabei keine Statt. Weiter werden ausgenommen: die Noten über welchen Striche oder Puncte stehen, oder von welchen etliche nach einander auf einem Tone vorkommen: ferner wenn über mehr, als zwo Noten, nämlich, über vieren, sechsen, oder achten ein Bogen steht, und endlich die Achttheile in Giguen. Alle diese Noten müssen egal, das ist, eine so lang, als die andere, vorgetragen werden.

2.   Edward Dannreuther, *Musical Ornamentation* (London, n.d., [1893-95]), I, p. 54.

3.   Arnold Dolmetsch, *The Interpretation of the Music of the XVII and XVIII Centuries,* new ed. (London, 1946) [1st ed., 1916], pp. 78ff.

4.   Sol Babitz, "A Problem of Rhythm in Baroque Music," *The Musical Quarterly* 38 (1952), pp. 533-65.

5.   Idem, "On Using J.S. Bach's Keyboard Fingerings," *Music and Letters* 18 (1962), pp. 123ff.

6.   Arthur Mendel, Introduction to Vocal Score of J.S. Bach's *St. John's Passion* (New York: G. Schirmer, 1951), pp. XIVff. Mr. Mendel tells me that he would express himself today with even greater caution on this point.

7.   Curt Sachs, *Rhythm and Tempo* (New York, 1953), pp. 296ff.

8.   Alfred Dürr, *Neue Bach Ausgabe,* Series II, Vol. 3, Kritischer Bericht (Kassel and Basel, 1955), pp. 47ff.

9. Robert Donington, *Tempo and Rhythm in Bach's Organ Music* (London-New York, 1960), p. 42.

10. To use the term in a wider sense, as Donington has done in his article on *Inégales* in Grove's Dictionary, to include other kinds of rhythmic alteration, and even such pairs of notes whose inequality is indicated by the notation, is inadvisable. It is out of keeping with the French use of the term and is bound to lead to misunderstandings.

11. Tomás de Santa Maria, *Libro llamado Arte de tañer Fantasia...* (Valladolid, 1565), fols. 45v-46r.

12. Loys Bourgeois, *Le Droict chemin de Musique* (Geneva, 1550), facsimile reprint (Basel, 1954), chap. X.

13. Pedro Cerone, *El Melopeo y Maestro* (Naples, 1613), p. 542.

14. This may be the last non-French reference to inequality before Quantz. Between the rising concerto style with its sharply profiled themes and concise rhythms, on one hand, and the luxuriance of the diminutions on the other, inequality lost its *raison d'être* and seems to have vanished from Italy before it blossomed in France.

15. Since Santa Maria also mentions *"glosas"* which are diminutions, as appropriate places for his long-short and short-long interpretations, he, too, might be classed in the category of Ganassi.

16. The following is a reference list of historical treatises dealing with the *Inégales:* Michel L'Affilard, *Principes très faciles pour bien apprendre la Musique,* 6th ed. (Paris, 1705),   pp. 32ff.
    Bénigne de Bacilly, *Remarques curieuses sur l'art de bien chanter...* (Paris, 1668), pp. 232ff.
    (Antoine) Bailleux, *Méthode pour apprendre facilement la musique vocale et instrumentale*   (Paris, n.d. [1770])
        This book as well as its third edition under the title *Solfèges pour apprendre facilement   la Musique...* [1785?] is a word-for-word plagiarism of the two treatises by Montéclair   that are listed below.
    Bordet, *Méthode raisonnée pour apprendre la Musique...* (Paris, n.d. [1755?]), pp. 7ff.
    (Louis Charles) Bordier, *Nouvelle Méthode de Musique...* (Paris n.d. [1760]), pp. 38ff.
    C.R. Brijon, *Réflexions sur la musique et la vraie manière de l'exécuter sur le violin* (Paris, 1763), pp. 23ff.
    Loys Bourgeois, *Le Droict chemin de Musique* (Geneva, 1550), facsimile reprint (Basel, 1954), chap. X.
    Buterne, *Méthode pour apprendre la Musique vocale et instrumentale* (Paris, 1752), pp. 12ff.
    François Bedos de Celles, *L'Art du Facteur d'orgues,* 4th Part (Paris, 1778), pp. 602ff.
    (Henri Louis Choquel), *La Musique rendue sensible par la Méquanique* (Paris, 1762), pp. 106ff.
    (Michel Corrette), *Méthode pour apprendre aisément à jouer de la Flute traversière...* (Paris, 1735), pp. 4-6.
    Michel Corrette, *L'Ecole d'Orphée...* (Paris, 1738), pp. 4-5.
    _____, Méthode pour apprendre en peu de temps le Violoncelle (Paris, 1741), pp. 4ff.
    _____, Méthode pour apprendre aisément à jouer de la Flute traversière (Paris 1770), pp. 4ff.

François Couperin, *L'Art de toucher le Clavecin* (Paris, 1717) pp. 39-40.

Dard, *Nouveaux Principes de Musique* (Paris, n.d. [1769]), p. 10ff.

François David, *Méthode nouvelle ou principes généraux pour apprendre facilement la musique, et l'art de chanter* (Paris, 1737), pp. 22ff.

(Démotz de la Salle), *Méthode de Musique selon un nouveau systeme...* (Paris, 1728), pp. 155ff.

(Pierre) Denis, *Nouveau systeme de musique pratique...* (Paris, 1747), pp. 5ff., 2nd ed. under title: *Nouvelle Méthode pour apprendre en peu de temps la Musique et l'art de Chanter* (Paris, n.d. [1762]), pp. 5ff.

Henri Bonaventure Dupont, *Principes de Musique par demandes et par réponses* (Paris, 1718), pp. 9ff.

Jean Baptiste Dupuit, *Principes pour toucher de la viele* (Paris, n.d. [1741]), p. VI.

Duval, *Méthode agréable et utile pour apprendre facilement à chanter juste avec Goût et Précision* (Paris, n.d. [1741]), p. 9.

L'abbé Duval, *Principes de la Musique par Demandes et par Réponses* (Paris, 1764), pp. 42ff.

Père Engramelle, *La Tonotechnie ou l'art de noter les Cylindres* (Paris, 1775), pp. 32ff.

Jacques Hotteterre, *Principes de la Flute Traversière...* (Amsterdam, 1708 [1st ed. Paris, 1707]), p. 22.

_____, *Méthode pour la Musette* (Paris, 1738), p. 18.

Jacob, *Méthode de Musique sur un nouveau plan* (Paris, 1769), pp. 55ff.

G. Jullien, *Premier Livre d'Orgue* (Paris, 1690), preface.

L'abbé Joseph Lacassagne, *Traité général des éléments du chant* (Paris, 1766), pp. 51ff.

De la Chapelle, *Les vrais principes de la Musique...* vol. I (Paris, 1736), p. 5.

(Etienne) Loulié, *Eléments ou Principes de Musique, mis dans un nouvel ordre...* (Paris, 1696), pp. 32ff., also (Amsterdam, 1698), pp. 35ff.

Mercadier de Belesta, *Nouveau systême de Musique théorique et pratique* (Paris, 1776), pp. 67ff.

B. Métoyen, *Démonstration des Principes de Musique...*, (Paris, n.d.,) pp. 7 and 17.

Michel Pignolet de Montéclair, *Nouvelle Méthode pour apprendre la Musique* (Paris, 1709), pp. 15ff.

_____, *Principes de Musique* (Paris, 1736), pp. 20ff.

Georg Muffat, *Florilegium Primum* (1695), DTÖ. I, 2 (Vienna, 1894), p. 20.

_____, *Florilegium Secundum,* (1698) DTÖ. II, 2 (Vienna 1895), p. 49.

Nivers, *Livre d'Orgue...* (Paris, 1665), p. 5.

Johann Joachim Quantz, *Versuch einer...*, chap. II, par. 12, chap. VII, par. 3, chap. XVII, sec. VII, par. 40.

Raparlier, *Principes de Musique, les agréments du chant...* (Celles, 1772), pp. 10ff.

Rollet, *Méthode pour apprendre la Musique sans transposition...* (Paris, n.d. [1760?]), pp. 27ff.

Jean Rousseau, *Traité de la viole* (Paris, 1687), p. 114.

Jean-Jacques Rousseau, *Dictionnaire de Musique* (Paris, 1768), s.v. "Pointer," p. 387.

Michel de Saint Lambert, *Les Principes du Clavecin...* (Paris, 1702), pp. 25ff.

Le Menu de Saint Philbert, *Principes de Musique courts et faciles* (Paris, n.d.), pp. 12. 38, 66.

Tomás de Santa Maria, *Libro llamado ado Arte...*, fols. 45vv-46vv.

(Didier Saurin), *La Musique théorique et pratique dans son ordre naturel* (Paris, 1722), pp. 26ff.

Vague, *L'art d'apprendre la Musique...* (Paris, 1756), pp. 53ff.

Alexandre de Villeneuve, *Nouvelle Méthode très courte et très facile . . .*, new aug. ed. (Paris, 1756), pp. 4ff.

F.C.X. Vion, *La Musique pratique et théorique, réduite à ses Principes naturels . . .* (Paris, 1742), pp. 18, 21ff.

Among modern discussions of the *Inégales* the two most important are probably: Eugène Borrel, "Les Notes Inégales dans l'ancienne Musique Française," *Revue de Musicologie* (November, 1931), pp. 278ff.; and Newman Powell, "Rhythmic Freedom in the Performance of French Music from 1650 to 1735" (Stanford University diss., 1958), pp.75ff.

17. Loulié, speaking of the *"Lourer"* which he defines as long-short inequality, says: "One applies it to melodies that move stepwise." [On s'en sert dans les chants dont les sons se suivent par Degrés non interrompus], (1696), p. 34, (1698) p. 38. Montéclair, after presenting the following example of long-short ♫ in 3-meter:

adds: "When the melody moves by skips, the eighth-notes in 3/4 meter are normally even" [Quand le cant procède par intervalles disjoints, les croches sont ordinairement égales dans le triple 3/4]. Example:

Nouvelle Méthode, p. 15. Couperin says: "We dot eighth-notes that follow one another stepwise and yet we write them as equals." [Nous pointons plusieurs croches de suite par degrés conjoints; et cependant nous les marquons égales . . .], *L'Art,* p. 39. Vague: "Disjunct notes are normally equal." [Notes en degrés disjoints sont ordinairement égales], p. 54. L'Affilard, p. 33; Bordet, p. 6; Bordier, p. 47; David, p. 46.

18. Loulié, (1696), p. 62: On avait oublié de dire dans la 2. Partie en parlant de Mesures de trois temps, que les premiers demi-temps s'exécutent encore d'une quatrième manière, savoir en faisant le 1. plus court que le 2. Ainsi.

19. Michel L'Affilard, *Principes très faciles . . .*, pp. 33-34. The examples in brackets were added by this writer.

20. Saint Lambert, *Principes du Clavecin,* p. 25.

21. Dard, *Nouveaux Principes . . .*, p. 10.

22. Bordet, *Méthode raisonnée . . .*, p. 7: Il faut observer surtout, lorsque l'on donne ce Mouvement inégal à des Notes, que celle que l'on fait longue soit la première d'un nombre pair, soit après la ligne qui sépare chaque mesure, soit après une note d'une autre valeur, ou soit après un silence; car si des notes inégales commençaient par nombre impair, il faudrait pour lors, faire la première brève et la suivante longue, afin de ne point déranger le rang naturel qu'elles soivent avoir, & ce nombre impair proviendrait de ce qu'il y aurait avant, un point ou un silence de même valeur, lequel tiendrait lieu de première note longue, & de première du nombre pair.

23. Further specific statements about the long-short nature of inequality can be found in Démotz, p. 155, Choquel, p. 106, Denis, p. 5, Dupont, p. 39, Brijon, p. 23, Bordier, p. 47, Corrette, *Méthode pour . . . le violoncelle,* p. 5, Muffat, *Flor. Sec.,* p. 48.

24. Robert Donington, *Tempo and Rhythm in Bach's Organ Music* (London-New York, 1960), pp. 42-43; also *Grove's Dictionary*, 5th ed. (London, 1954), *s.v.* "Inégales".

25. Some of Babitz's other arguments are easily countered. His attempt to read short-long inequality into one of Hotteterre's tonguing patterns ("A Problem of Rhythm. . . . ," p. 557) is incompatible with Hotteterre's own confirmation of the long-short nature of inequality. Babitz then states: "Further evidence that the normal English phrasing was short-long is provided by the fact that while there are many written long-shorts to provide contrast, there are no written short-longs, obviously because they were already being played without being written." (p. 555). This is an argument in a circle, a *petitio principii:* what needed to be proven, the *demonstrandum*, that a short-long convention existed, is taken as a fact, as *demonstratum:* the convention existed, therefore the lack of short-long notation proves the short-long performance, which in turn is to furnish "evidence" for the existence of the convention.

26. This *Agrément* occurs in two forms, of which one is related to the descending appoggiatura and was often added by the performer's initiative. When written out by the composer it appears as a small note played sometimes on, sometimes before, and sometimes straddling the beat. The second type of *Couler* is a kind of arpeggiation between the held-out notes of a chord and was usually indicated thus: a)

  played b) ⸙ or else c) ⸙ to indicate an arpeggiation from above.

27. Bedos de Celles, in *L'Art du Facteur,* calls it *Secondes Coulées* and interprets it (pl. 111) as a short-long pattern:

28. Dupuit, *Principes pour toucher . . .*, presents a pattern that is similar but has the dot on top of the first instead of the second of a pair of slurred notes which he explains as short-longs:

effet   Again, this is not inequality but a notational device (p. VI).

29. This episode should give pause to those writers who look upon old treatises, especially if they bear such famous names as Couperin, Quantz, or C.P.E. Bach, as if they were binding codes of law. It should bring home the fact that the only thing we can safely assume about a treatise is that it speaks for the author himself, *at the time of his writing*. It is this quasi-religious faith in the old treatises and their infallibility in proclaiming universal verities which is responsible for most of the dogmatism that besets the field of interpretation of old music. This reflection ought also to help us view the Quantz Remark with a better sense of proportion and at the same time help us realize that, before we accept any text as even possibly relevant to such a mysterious and complex phenomenon as Bach's music, we have to check again and again with other evidence and above all with the internal evidence from Bach's works themselves.

30. *Principes*, p. 20, ". . . il faut bien partager . . . chaque temps en deux parties très égales."

31. David, *Méthode nouvelle . . .*, p. 22.

32. Saint Lambert, *Principes du Clavecin*, p. 25. See also Muffat (*Flor. Primum*, p. 20),

where he tells us that ♩♩ in **c** because ineligible for inequality, have to be played "Rigoureusement l'une égale à l'autre."

33. Loulié, *Eléments ou Principes...*, (1698), p. 38.

34. Corrette, *Méthode pour... le violoncelle*, p. 4.

35. Corrette's statement is clearly borne out by the violin works of such masters as Francoeur, Senallié, and Leclair, which follow throughout Italian models in their general stylistic bearing, in their consistent choice of Italian-type *Gigas* and *Correntes*, in their Italian tempo markings, in their lack of typically French ornamentation symbols, and in their lack of any reference to inequality. One of Francoeur's Sonatas: 1er livre, Sonata VIII, for instance, is so closely patterned after Corelli's Op. 5, No. 1, that it almost borders on plagiarism. Some of these same composers put on a different air when they write in the French manner. They conspicuously change their idiom and one immediately senses the different stylistic climate, one in which inequality is fully at home.

36. Couperin, *L'Art*, pp. 39-40.

37. Jean-Jacques Rousseau, *Dictionnaire de Musique*, p. 387: Dans la Musique Italienne toutes les Croches sont toujours égales à moins qu'elles ne soient marquées *Pointées*. Mais dans la Musique Française on ne fait les Croches exactement égales que dans la mesure à quatre temps.

38. In the second half of the 17th century, while the convention was still in its formative stage, one finds sporadic references to eighth-note inequality in **C** meter. Nivers in 1665 *(loc. cit.)*, and Jullien in 1690 *(loc. cit.)* mention the long-short inequality of successive eighth notes, and each uses as an illustration an example written in **C** meter. After 1700 this would have been rather unthinkable, as a look at table 2 will readily show.

39. It is interesting and revealing that Quantz, as he expressly points out, has taken his three examples of inequality from the first of his Tables of Diminutions: tab. IX, fig. i, (k) (m) (n).

40. As to the striking disagreement about the 3/4 meter, it could be explained by the fact that the character of this particular meter was not clearly defined. Its quarter notes could be fairly slow, not unlike those of the **C** meter, in which case it was a natural candidate for the first category. On the other hand, the meter could be the equivalent of a 3, or even faster than the latter. Then the quarter note loses its character as a foundational beat, the meter would be conducted, as were the faster triple meters in France, in two uneven beats with the thesis comprising one and two, and the arsis the three: ♩↓♩↑♩ rather than in three even beats. The eighth notes are then likely to be predominant as the fastest notes and the meter will fall naturally into the second category.

41. Paul Henry Lang calls Couperin "the Cynosure of Rococo art." *Music in Western Civilization* (New York, 1941), p. 542.

42. Muffat tells us in the Preface to his Concerti Grossi of 1701 (DTÖ. XI, 2) that he was the first who brought Lully's ballet style to Germany, referring, of course, to his two *Florilegia* with their prefaces.

43. On the other hand Quantz can be absolved of the reproach made by Babitz of another alleged inconsistency in connection with the slur over more than two notes.

According to Babitz ("A Problem...," p. 558) Quantz states in a different place that the first note under a slur covering four or more notes ought to be held longer. However, Babitz's allegation is not footnoted and I could not locate it. The nearest I could find is a passage (chap. VI, sec. iii, par. 15) in which Quantz states that in a *"Figur"* of three, four, or six notes, the first one should be held a little longer to insure synchronization of tongue and fingers, and proper value to all the notes. (A *"Figur"* in Quantz's terminology is a group of notes under a common beam [chap. 5, par. 8]). This ruling was meant chiefly as a safeguard against rushing. But even if Quantz should speak elsewhere of lengthening the first note under a slur there would be no contradiction involved since the latter principle, which will be referred to as "agogic articulation," is independent of the *Inégales*. This, too, will be discussed later in more detail.

44. Babitz's statement that the convention was so well-known that nobody thought it necessary to write about it ("A Problem...," p. 536) is again an argument in a circle since it takes the existence of the convention for granted.

45. Babitz, "A Problem...," p. 550. This might be an indication that Quantz did not practice what he preached.

46. *Virtualiter*, not a genuine Latin word, is a Latinization of the French *virtuellement* which means "potentially" as contrasted to "actually." It thus deviates importantly from the meaning of the English "virtually."

47. Johann A. Scheibe, *Uber die musikalische Komposition*, I (Leipzig, 1773), p. 230. Friedrich W. Marpurg, *Anleitung zur Musik überhaupt und zur Singkunst* (Berlin, 1763), p. 76.

48. Babitz, "A Problem of Rhythm," p. 536.

49. Sachs, *Rhythm and Tempo*, pp. 296ff.

50. Johann G. Walther, *Musicalisches Lexicon* (Leipzig, 1732): Die äusserliche und innerliche Geltung der Noten; nach jener Art ist jede Note mit ihres gleichen in der *Execution* von gleicher; nach dieser aber, von ungleicher Länge: da nämlich der ungerade Tact-Theil lang und der gerade Tact-Theil kurz ist.

51. That occasionally, especially in media not capable of dynamic nuance, an agogic emphasis will supplement or even replace the accent is certainly true, but does not contradict the above statement. Such small rubato is a coincidental freedom of flexible performance, not an indispensable element of musical diction.

52. Wolfgang Caspar Printz, *Phrynis Mitilenaeus*, (Dresden & Leipzig, 1696), pp. 18ff.

53. Diese unterschiedliche Länge etlicher, der Zeit oder Währung nach gleich langer Noten wird genennet *Quantitas Temporalis Intrinseca*, die innerliche Zeitlänge.

54. Georg Simon Löhlein, *Clavier-Schule...* (Leipzig & Züllichau, 1765), p. 68.

55. The application of "inner" length and shortness to whole measures is confirmed 70 years later by J.P. Kirnberger *(Die Kunst des reinen Satzes*, II, (Berlin, 1776), p. 131.

56. Johann Georg Ahle, *Musikalisches* [sic] *Frühlings Gespräche...* (Mühlhausen, 1695), pp. 36-38. "Die langen Silben müssen auf die ungeraden Noten gesetzt werden, die alle *quantitate intrinseca* lang sind, damit *Accentus melicus & metricus* consoniere."

57.   Johann G. Walther, *Praecepta der musikalischen Composition* (1708) first published edition by T. Benary (Leipzig, 1955), pp. 23-24.

58.   J.A. Scheibe, *Critischer Musikus,* new enlg. ed., (Leipzig, 1745), 37th piece (12 May 1793), pp. 347ff.: Es unterscheiden sich alle gerade Noten, oder alle diejenigen, welche dem Takte nach, von einerlei Grösse sind, unter sich selbst durch den natürlichen Accent, so wie sich in der Aussprache der Worte und Sylben eine Sylbe vor der anderen durch den gewöhnlichen Accent unterscheidet. Wenn also im schlechten oder geraden Takte allein halbe Takte stehen, so ist der erste halbe Takt, nämlich der Niederschlag lang, der zweite halbe Takt, oder der Aufschlag aber kurz. Das ist, der Niederschlag is natürlicher Weise accentuiert, der Aufschlag aber nicht. Sind in der geraden Taktart vier Viertel vorhanden, so hat das erste Viertel des Taktes den Accent, das zweite Viertel aber nicht, mit dem ersten Viertel aber kommt alsdann das dritte, mit dem zweiten das vierte überein. *Dieses nun heisst in der Musik Quantitas intrinseca;* und die accentuierten Noten nennt man anschlagende, die unaccentuierten aber durchgehende Noten. (Italics by this writer).

59.   Ich nenne aber all hier das lang, was den natürlichen Accent hat, als da sind alle anschlagenden Noten; das nenne ich hingegen kurz, was keinen Accent hat, als nämlich alle durchgehenden Noten.

     For further documentation see also Johann Mattheson, *Critica Musica* (Hamburg, 1722), p. 44; F.W. Marpurg, *Anleitung zur Musik,* p. 76, Daniel G. Türk, *Klavier-Schule,* Facs. of 1st ed. of 1789 (Kassel, 1962), p. 91.

60.   Johann Samuel Petri, *Anleitung zur praktischen Musik,* 2nd ed. (Lauban, 1782 [1st ed., 1767]), p. 160: [... die guten und schlechten Taktteile] welche einige Musiker auch die langen und kurzen zu nennen belieben, obgleich ohne Grund. Denn das Zeitmass wird nicht verändert, sondern der Unterschied liegt nur in der Stärke des Vortrages und seiner abgewechselten Schwäche und die stärker vorzutragenden Noten heissen gute; hingegen heissen schlechte welche etwas schwächer vorgetragen werden müssen.

61.   Leopold Mozart, *Versuch einer Gründlichen Violinschule,* (Augsburg, 1756), facs. reprint (Vienna, 1922), chap. XII, pars. 9 and 10. A highly misleading impression is created in this respect by a passage in Babitz's article in which he tries to link the good and bad with long and short notes. ("A Problem...," p. 542). He presents a quotation from L. Mozart in such a manner that the reader is led to believe he is reading one sentence only and that the three dots in the middle of it represent the omission of a few words that are immaterial to the train of thought. However, the dots stand for a whole printed page and a change of paragraph: the first sentence of the quotation is from the beginning of paragraph 9, the second from the middle of paragraph 10. It is not impossible that this is the source for Sach's erroneous statement.

62.   They agree even more than shown in Babitz's chart, since the inclusion of the C signature for ♪♪ in Muffat's column is incorrect.

63.   Johann David Heinichen, *Der Generalbass in der Composition* (Dresden, 1728), p. 257 ff., p. 293.

64.   Because of lack of distinct accents in the French language, musical prosody is based more on the length of syllables and the emphasis of meaning and expression.

65. Jacob, *Méthode de Musique...*, p. 55.

66. Michel de Saint Lambert, *Nouveau Traité de l'accompagnement...* (Amsterdam, 170?), p. 121.

67. Dard, *Nouveaux Principes...*, pp. 8, 10ff.

68. Muffat's explanation of the good and bad notes is less mechanical and more flexible than that of other authors. He refers to the good ones as those which seem to permit the ear naturally a moment of rest, "un peu de repos." They are those that are either of long value, or start an essential part of the measure, or are dotted, and among those of equal duration the odd numbered ones. They are the ones, that according to Lullyan principles, are usually played with the down-bow. By contrast the bad ones are those that leave a desire that they pass on. They are "comme passagères" and are usually played with the up-bow. With this definition Muffat easily covers the fact that in different melodic contexts the same place in the measure can accomodate sometimes a good, sometimes a bad note as shown in this example, when the third quarter is *"vilis"* in the second measure, *"nobilis"* in the third.

It may be added that through the link of good and bad notes with down and upbow the letters n and v probably became the bowing symbols of ⊓ and ⋁ .)

69. Mozart, *Versuch einer...*, chap. 12, par. 10, chap. 7, sec. I, par. 20; and chap. 7, sec. 2, par. 5.

70. Ibid., chap. 7, sec. I, par. 20 (ex. 23) and chap. 7, sec. 2, par. 5 (ex. 33c).

71. Babitz, "A Problem...," pp. 542-43, "J.S. Bach's Keyboard Fingerings," p. 123.

72. The instinctive out-of-tune playing of violinists (which Muffat describes in *Flo. Sec.*, sec I: "Du toucher Juste") could be elevated as "expressive intonation" to a stylistic requirement; the instinctive tendency to slow down for difficult passages could be hailed as "expressive tempo" in accord with the "Affektenlehre" expressing, as it were, the "Affekt" of fearful caution, etc., etc.

73. Quantz, *Versuch einer...*, chap. XVII, sec, VI, par. 18: Wie es denn bei manchem, wenn er einen Lauf von etlichen Noten stufenweis zu machen hat, nicht anders klingt, als wenn er über die Noten hinwegstolperte.

74. F.W. Marpurg, *Anleitung zum Clavierspielen* (Berlin, 1755), p. 61.

75. Jean Philippe Rameau, *Code de Musique Pratique* (Paris, 1760), p. 11.

76. Rameau, *Pièces de Clavessin avec une Methode pour la mechanique des doigts...*, (Paris, n.d. [1724]), p. 4: Observez une grande égalité de mouvements entre chaque doigt, & surtout ne precipités jamais ces mouvemens: car la légèreté & la vitesse ne s'acquierent que par cette égalité de mouvemens...

77. Dolmetsch, *The Interpretation of...*, pp. 380-81.

78. Babitz, "A Problem...," pp. 542-43.

79. P.F. Penna, *Li Primi Albori Musicali...* (Bologna, 1672), Book III, pp. 12, 13, 81.

80. C.P.E. Bach too, presents most of his scale-fingerings in an abstract pattern of unstemmed black notes without meter or measure.

81. St. Lambert, *Les Principes du Clavecin,* p. 42. Michael Praetorius had previously expressed his contempt for the pedantic authors of fingering patterns and declared that all that matters in a passage is that it is played agreeably and precisely, even if one has to use one's nose to do so. (*Syntagma Musicum,* II [Wolfenbüttel, 1619], p. 44).

82. Couperin, *L'Art,* p. 28.

83. Rameau, *Pièces de Clavecin* (Paris, 1731).

84. Santa Maria, *Libro llamado Arte...*, fol. 39r ff.

85. Ibid., fol. 45v-46r.

86. As further alleged proof for inequality as caused by fingering, Babitz, ("A Problem...," pp. 554-555) reproduces the picture from the title page of *Parthenia* which he claims provides "visual evidence" of short-long fingering. The picture shows a young lady sitting in front of a virginal that has no recognizable chromatic keys. The low quality of the draftsmanship is evident from the right hand of the player, which seems severely malformed. The left hand which is to provide the evidence, shows the second and third finger at extreme spread and poised above the keyboard of the virginal, the fourth and fifth fingers curled up in front of, and slightly below the keys. Babitz claims that his picture shows clearly the playing of a descending scale, where the fourth finger after having just paused on the "long" of a short-long pair has just slipped off the key and the third is about to strike for the corresponding short note. Barring the intervention of clairvoyance it is hard to see how anybody can deduce all these facts from one picture. There is no suggestion to be found in the picture that the fourth finger has just played at all, not to mention which note, and how long it had held it, nor is it clear whether the third finger is on the way up or down from the keys. But suppose it were about to strike: there is no way in which a painter, even if he were a genius, could suggest that it would stay only for a "short" of a short-long pair, followed in "compensatory" fastness by the fourth finger. As a matter of fact, if there is anything the picture can possibly tell us, it is that, of the infinity of possibilities, the one given by Babitz is the least likely: since for the claimed pattern (p. 555 with the asterisk indicating the instant of the picture)

where the fourth finger has to come immediately into play again, its slipping off the keyboard below the level of the keys would be a most inappropriate manner of execution. The most likely interpretation is: the lady did not play anything at all but held for hours on end a pose which the artist had selected for her.

87. The fingering is not nearly as bad or as primitive as some pianists believe who by years of training with the modern scale fingerings are prevented from appraising a different one on an equal basis. C.P.E. Bach, who knew the modern fingering, accepts in a number of keys both types as equally good and so did Santa Maria 200 years earlier.

88. On the violin the different tone qualities of the four strings, possibilities for expressive slides, or else the avoidance of audible shifts, more intense tone quality of the stronger fingers, to name but a few matters, make often for a great difference between the two types of fingerings.

89.   Babitz, "J.S. Bach's Keyboard Fingerings," p. 124.

90.   Dürr, *Neue Bach Ausgabe,* p. 11.

91.   Ibid, p. 47.

92.   This latter book dealing with mechanical instruments contains among others, instructions on how to reproduce the *Inégales* on cylinder cuts and presents as examples, of course, French compositions.

93.   Dürr, *neue Bach Ausgabe,* p. 58.

94.   Georg v. Dadelsen, "Friedrich Smend's Ausgabe der h-moll Messe von J.S. Bach," *Die Musikforschung* 12 (1959), p. 331; Dürr, ibid, p. 48; Mr. Mendel told me that he thinks a mildly short-long performance of all the descending seconds is very possibly what was intended.

95.   G. v. Dadelsen, ibid, p. 332, speaks of "ausnehmend kalligraphische Anlage der Stimmen." He convincingly disproves Smend's thesis that the parts were written for Leipzig rather than for Dresden.

96.   Quantz himself tells us in his autobiography that he derived the ideal from Pisendel in Dresden whom he revered as the most decisive artistic influence in his career.

Chapter 5

1.   Frederick Neumann, "The French *Inégales,* Quantz, and Bach" in *Journal of the American Musicological Society,* XVIII (1965), pp. 313-58. (Chap. 3 in this volume.)

2.   On the other hand, the writing of any grace *after* the barline does not by itself carry the analogous implication of downbeat rendition, since the little notes of ornaments, regardless of their rhythmical design, were routinely notated in close connection with the parent note.

3.   The usual editorial procedure of straightening out such irregularities according to the German motto "Ordnung muss sein" may provide a neat and practical solution but not necessarily an artistic or authentic one.

4.   Robert Donington, *The Interpretation of Early Music* (2nd ed., London, 1965), p. 395.

5.   The Rondo theme of Beethoven's *Spring Sonata* (a) is dotted throughout on its last occurrence (b), and, of course, neither inadvertence nor *notes inégales* are involved. Granted, the style has changed but the underlying principle of *variatio delectat* is universal and perennial. (See also Bach's Trio in G major, BWV 1038, 1.)

6.   Donington, *The Interpretation...,* pp. 396-97.

7.   In the autograph of the transcription (BB Bach P 234) Bach wrote even notes at first, then changed them to the "Lombard rhythm." This might further support the second-thought hypothesis.

8.   Ray McIntyre, "On the Interpretation of Bach's Gigues," in *The Musical Quarterly,* LI (1965), pp. 478-92.

9. See chapter 3, pp. 17-19, and note 1, where the passage is reprinted in the original and in translation.

10. McIntyre, "On the Interpretation...," pp. 484-85.

11. See chapter 3, note 16.

12. The examples were not specifically written by Quantz to illustrate inegality, but were taken from a table of diminutions. This further underlines the purely incidental nature of the slurs.

13. McIntyre, "On the Interpretation..., p. 485.

14. Almost two generations after Bonporti, Leopold Mozart tells us that the first of two or more notes under a slur should be "slightly" *(ein wenig)* accented and lengthened (see chapter 3, pp. 40-42). Even if we ignore the problem of pertinence of this source for Bonporti and his transcriber, Mozart's wording, which indicates only a very subtle dynamic-agogic accent, could never be stretched to imply the lengthening to a 2:1 relationship that is necessary for McIntyre's thesis.

15. The term "pirated" commonly used in this connection is actually a misnomer in a period that knew no copyright. Royal privileges gave only a brief protection that never reached beyond the border and there were neither legal nor moral barriers that would prevent a publisher like Roger from printing anything he expected to sell at a profit. It was the same situation that obtains today with regard to works in the public domain.

16. They are foreign even to many modern transcribers, whose countless musical crimes of exploitation, disfigurement, and assault perpetrated against unprotected masterworks are hardly in need of illustration. If some of these arrangers feel called to "improve" on Mozart's harmony, or Bach's counterpoint, can we be surprised if Roger's editor wanted to improve on Bonporti's rhythm?

17. B.B. ms. Bach P 416, recently moved from Marburg with the other holdings from the Berlin library to a new location in Berlin-Dahlem.

18. Paul Kast, *Die Bach-Handschriften der Berliner Staatsbibliothek* (Trossingen, 1958), p. 29.

19. When we encounter in a manuscript or print any kind of notational incongruity, the first possibility to explore is simply that of a slip of the pen or a misprint before we go off into daring speculations about deep meanings or mysterious hints that such irregularities were meant to convey. Mr. McIntyre undertakes such speculations in a few more instances as well. One is an obvious slip of the pen where an unidentified manuscript copy from a posthumously published work by Purcell reads $\frac{6}{8}$ ♩ ♪ ♬ instead of ♩ ♪ ♬ (McIntyre's ex. 6a on p. 488). "The copy is too clear and careful to account for the group of four sixteenth notes as an error." With this verdict he claims the measure as a proof for a convention that permits transformation of ♬ into ♬ However, the reader remains unconvinced that neatness is an absolute guarantee against human error.

Another such case is the puzzling φ signature in the original print of Bach's Sixth Partita. This symbol for *tempus perfectum diminutum* had been obsolete at that time for well over a century. It indicated triple mensuration with three semibreves to one breve: φ ◦ ◦ ◦ but duple mensuration below this level. Approximately equivalent to the modern 3/4 (or 3/8), it makes no sense in a piece that is clearly written in a duple meter (4/2 or double ₵). Also it is hard to see how this symbol, as McIntyre claims, can communicate ternary rhythmic alteration within single beats, inasmuch as the signature implied *duple* subdivision for the beats: ♩ ♩ I see only one solution of the puzzle: somebody made a mistake and the question is only who made it: Bach, the copyist, or the engraver? It really does not matter a great deal but I would venture the suggestion that it was not Bach. He never used obsolete symbols and was never known to use any symbol wrongly; in the analogous cases of both the *Gratias* and the Credo from the B minor Mass he used ₵ and in the motet *Lobet den Herrn,* 1 he used C for an 8/4. The prime suspect would seem to be the engraver and he was, as Spitta convincingly suggests, most likely the young Philipp Emanuel. As Walter Emery writes me, the engraver was "a poor engraver but a musician" and this would fit Spitta's identification. On this basis I would suggest that Philipp Emanuel, with possibly only a hazy idea of the symbol's meaning, may have naively thought that 2 x ₵ = ₵. But whatever the definite explanation may be, it can have human interest but hardly any musical one. Meanwhile the ₵ should be corrected to ₵.

20.   There are several more reasons why *notes inégales* cannot be in the picture. The only possible candidates for the latter could be the 24 ternary sixteenth notes (since Quantz tells us the *notes inégales* are always the "fastest" notes), certainly not the 12 ternary eighth notes and still less the 8 binary eighth notes for which inegality is claimed. Moreover, the unevenness of the *notes inégales* is never tied to another rhythm in assimilation, nor ever tied to a mathematical relationship such as 2:1. One of their characteristics is the freedom of the performer to choose the degree of unevenness for each individual case.

21.   McIntyre, "On the Interpretation . . . ," pp. 486-88.

22.   Ibid, p. 486.

23.   See chapter 3 above, p. 18.

24.   Couperin felt the need of an explanation because a twin meter was very rare in France. The idea that Couperin wanted the simple ternary effect claimed by McIntyre and chose the round-about way of a twin meter and binary notation relying on a would-be law of transformation is too far-fetched to be considered. Moreover, the *notes inégales,* quite out of place in an octave-tremolo, would have to be applied by pairs: the one-in-four inegality is an idea of Quantz, not, as far as I am aware, endorsed by any French source. The previous arguments about the degree of lengthening of the *notes inégales* and their tying to a definite rhythm would apply here too, of course.

25.   The borderline between rubato and tempo variation is not always clearly drawn and the terms are sometimes used interchangeably. It might be helpful to reserve the term "rubato" to that kind of imaginative rhythmic modeling of a melody that takes place against the background of a steady beat in other voices.

26.   McIntyre contests this interpretation (p. 481) for which he quotes Naumann and von Dadelsen, and claims for the Gigue from the First French Suite triplet meaning for the thirty-seconds. However, the reader need only look at the autograph facsimile of this Gigue shown in McIntyre's article opposite p. 484, where in m. 9 the clear line-up confirms von Dadelsen's interpretation.

McIntyre attempts to prove the triplet character of the thirty-seconds by reference to m. 12 of the same piece; he claims that the rests preceding the three thirty-seconds are an eighth rest followed by a sixteenth rest:

However, a careful look at the same facsimile reveals for the second rest a third flag which is partially merged with the first line, and therefore, less readily visible at first glance. (Its writing is comparable to that of the second flag of the sixteenth rest in the bass of m. 6.) The alleged thirty-second triplets are then to prove the ternary character of the whole beat:

¢ ⅂ ⅂ ♬♬ = ⅂⅂ ⅃ ♬♫ How they can do that is difficult to see: even if the thirty-seconds *were* triplets, they would occupy one fourth of the beat, which would therefore remain binary. And there is no apparent reason—and none presented—why triplets in an even fraction of a beat have to infect the whole beat with triplet character. It would seem that Mr. McIntyre equated triplets with ternary meter.

27.   See chapter 6.

Chapter 6

1.   Robert Donington, *The Interpretation of Early Music* (London, 1963), p. 375. [New Version, 1974, p. 441.]

2.   Thurston Dart, *The Interpretation of Music* (London, 1954), p. 81.

3.   Arnold Dolmetsch, *The Interpretation of the Music of the XVIIth and XVIIIth Centuries* (London, n.d. [1915]), p. 63.

4.   Geoffroy-Dechaume, *Les "Secrets" de la Musique Ancienne*... (Paris, 1964), pp. 37ff.

5.   Johann Joachim Quantz, *Versuch einer Anweisung die Flöte traversiere zu spielen*... (Berlin, 1752). The second and third editions (Breslau 1780 and 1789), except for a few modernizations of spelling, are identical with the first.

6.   Quantz does the same in a passage (XVII, 11, par. 10) where he limits this type of shortening expressly for thirty-second notes.

7.   Geoffroy-Dechaume, *Les "Secrets"*..., p. 53.

8.   C.P.E. Bach, *Versuch über die wahre Art das Clavier zu spielen,* First part (Berlin, 1753); 2nd edition, unchanged (1759); 3rd edition enlarged (Leipzig, 1787). Second part (Berlin, 1762); 2nd edition enlarged (Leipzig, 1797).

9.   Dolmetsch, *The Interpretation*..., p. 59.

10.   Geoffroy-Dechaume, *Les "Secrets"*..., p. 37.

11.   The correct meaning of these terms, which are of very common usage in German treatises, is made clear by Bach in chap. 11, par. 67. If the dot meant prolongation, it would follow the long note, and not the short. The word for an additional flag would have been either *geschwänzt* or *Balken.*

12.   We are then faced with another snare to avoid regarding the interpretation of the treatises, namely erroneous translations. The version of this passage by Dolmetsch, for example, is less translation than fantasy on a theme, since under the pretence of direct quotation he inserts entire sentences which are not found in any of the three original editions.

13.   It is not a question as Geoffroy-Dechaume indicates in his translation of this sentence (p. 38), of inserting a rest in place of the dot: "what the notation demands" refers to the rhythmic relationship, and not, especially in the period in question, to articulation.

14.   The translation of Donington is imprecise, and results in a contrary interpretation: "when four or more short notes follow a dot, they are rapidly disposed of, being so numerous." It is

the expression "kurz genug" that gives us the key for the correct interpretation of this sentence.

15. Another question on the subject of dotted notes on which the two authors contradict each other, concerns the combination of triplets with dotted notes in duple or common time. According to Bach the dot is shortened in order to obtain sychronization of the short note with the third triplet; according to Quantz the dot is lengthened to stress the non-synchronization.

16. Bach, *Versuch über...*, Part II (Berlin, 1762), chap. 29, (15).

17. More probably there were, strictly speaking, no unified practices either in Berlin or elsewhere, but a variety of individual practices everywhere.

18. Georg Muffat, *Florilegium Secundum* (1698), DTÖ II, 2 (Vienna, 1895).

19. Lully, *Amadis*, 2nd ed. (Paris, 1721), shelfmark: Opéra A 16b.

20. Unequal notes also have no place there: in the third measure only, where we might consider introducing them, the disjunct figure of sixteenth-notes would oppose it.

21. Therefore we cannot explain this change as a reminder of a forgotten convention. First, because this period was scarcely concerned with forgotten conventions, and second, because such a reminder would have had its logical place at the beginning and not in the middle of the opera.

22. French manuscript from the seventeenth century, *Pièces de Clavecin* (B.N., Rés. Vm^7 675).

23. The manuscript belonged to the Deutsche Staatsbibliothek in East Berlin, but is presently at the library Stiftung Kulturbesitz, in West Berlin-Dahlem.

24. Donington, *The Interpretation...*, p. 380. [New Version, 1974, p. 446].

25. Gigault, *Livre de Musique pour l'Orgue* (Paris, 1685).

26. Ibid.

27. Jacques Hotteterre, *Méthode pour la Musette* (Paris, 1738), p. 35.

Chapter 7

1. I am greatly indebted to Walter Emery, who has prepared the edition and the *Critical Commentary* of this work for the *Neue Bach-Ausgabe*, for sending me Xerox copies of those pages of his manuscript that are pertinent to this paper. All further references to Mr. Emery will be to this still unpublished manuscript.

2. I am very grateful to Mr. Ernest D. May for lending me his photocopy of the Preller manuscript.

3. It was engraved twice because the first edition contained too many mistakes.

4. Erwin Bodky, *The Interpretation of Bach's Keyboard Works* (Cambridge, Mass., 1960), pp. 229-30; Rudolf Eller, "Serie und Zyklus in Bachs Instrumentalsammlungen," in *Bach-Interpretationen*, ed. Martin Geck (Göttingen, 1969), p. 131.

5. Hermann Keller, *Die Klavierwerke Bachs* (Leipzig, 1950), p. 206; Christoph Wolff, "Ordnungsprinzipien in den Originaldrucken Bachscher Werke," *Bach-Interpretationen*, p. 149.

6. A. Dolmetsch, *The Interpretation of the Music of the XVII & XVIII Centuries* (London, 1916), pp. 62-65.

7. Thurston Dart, *The Interpretation of Music,* new ed. (New York, 1963), p. 81.

8. F. Neumann, "La Note Pointée et la soi-disant 'Manière Française,'" *Revue de Musicologie* (1965), pp. 66-92. (FN 1.) I refer the reader to this article and devote only a few sentences here to the briefest resumé.

9. C.P.E. Bach, *Versuch über die wahre Art das Clavier zu spielen...,* second part, Berlin, 1762, chap. 29, par. 15: Wenn man also nur eine Art vom Vortrage dieser Noten zum Grundsatz leget, so verliehrt man die übrigen Arten.

   The first passage is contained in the first part of the treatise, Berlin, 1753, chap. 3, par. 23. See also FN 1, pp. 79-81.

10. J.J. Quantz, *Versuch einer Anweisung, die Flöte traversiere zu spielen...,* Berlin, 1752. The general German practice is discussed in chap. 5, par. 21; the principles regarding French dances in chap. 17, sec. 7, pars. 56-58. In this latter statement Quantz may have superimposed German *galant* manneristic overdotting on the French *notes inégales,* the use of which he advocated. The significance of this passage may also be reduced by a circumstance which to my knowledge has not so far been pointed out. Quantz speaks in these latter paragraphs neither of instrumental Suites nor of opera Overtures but strictly of an orchestra accompanying dancers (the pars. 56 and 57 discuss largely problems of coordination of dancers and musicians). By speaking of such ballets being inserted within Italian operas it is also clear that he had Berlin, not Paris performances in mind. It is not a matter of course that rhythms sharpened for actual dancing, had to be integrally transferred to the stylized Overture-Suites of purely instrumental music. (For a revised interpretation of this Quantz passage that eliminates it as directive for overdotting see FN5 pp. 171-73.)

11. When one or the other French writer, like Hotteterre (presently to be quoted) illustrates the unevennes of the *inégales* by the dotted pattern ♫ they did so for lack of a milder rhythmic symbol ♩₃ ♪ being unknown). Loulié ingeniously indicated the milder character by the following device: ♫♫♩♫

12. See FN 1, p. 95, and chap. 5, p. 72.

13. See FN 1, p. 95.

14. See chapter 5, pp. 71-72.

15. Friedrich Wilhelm Marpurg, *Anleitung zum Clavierspielen...* (Berlin, 1755), p. 13, where he explains that there are two ways in which to indicate an extension of the dot beyond its regular value: a second dot: ♩..♪ or a tie: ♩ ♫ and that one has to use one or the other if such lenthening is desired. "Otherwise one has no obligation to divine the composer's intentions; and since he has two ways to clarify his intentions to the performer, namely the tie or the double dot, I do not see why one should write one way and want to have it performed another way; i.e., why one would write only one dot wanting to have it interpreted as a dot and a half." Georg Friedrich Wolf, *Unterricht im Klavierspielen,* Part 1, 3d ed. (Halle, 1789), p. 26, quotes and fully endorses the passage from Marpurg; Johann Adam Hiller, *Anweisung zum musikalisch-richtigen Gesange* (Leipzig, 1774), p. 111, stresses the precision of the dot's value.

16. Michael Collins, "A Reconsideration of French Overdotting," *Music & Letters* 50 (1969),

pp. 111-23; concerning the theory of underdotting: "The Performance of Triplets in the 17th and 18th Centuries," *JAMS* (1966), pp. 289-99, dealing with "The French Style."

17. Collins, "Reconsideration," p. 113.

18. The rests Quantz had in mind are those that separate the fast notes from their left neighbor in analogy of the dotted patterns: 𝅘𝅥𝅮   or   𝅘𝅥𝅮

19. Collins, "Reconsideration," p. 112.

20. Collins quotes (pp. 112-13) an example of mine from Lully's *Amadis* where some editorial revisions for a performance in 1720 illustrate both the stylistic evolution which now includes sharper rhythms, and the fact that "in the first half of the 18th century" *(dans la première moitié du XVIII siècle)* no convention of rhythmic sharpening existed without exact prescription of the notation (FN 1, pp. 73-75). By substituting "in the time of Lully" for "first half of the 18th century" Collins changed the meaning of my argument.

21. Thirty-seconds after dots or rests in the overtures to: *Rodrigo*, 1707; *Agrippina*, 1709; *Rinaldo*, 1711 (and again in its second version of 1731); *Pastor Fido*, 1712; *Amadigi*, 1715; *Radamisto*, 1720; *Floridante*, 1721; *Flavio*, 1723; *Rodelinda*, 1724; *Admeto*, 1727; *Riccardo*, 1727; *Ezio*, 1731; *Orlando*, 1732; *Arianna*, 1733; *Alcina*, 1735; *Alexander's Feast*, 1736; *Arminio*, 1736 (in the third part of the overture); *Serse*, 1737-38. Thirty-seconds after a tie: *Mucio Scevola*, 1721; *Giulio Cesare*, 1724; *Partenope*, 1730.

22. Emery's speculating that they may be additions by a later owner is not borne out by the fact that the handwriting for *all* ornaments is identical.

Chapter 8

1. Frederick Neumann, "La Note pointée et la soi-disant 'maniére française,' " *Revue de musicologie* (1965), pp. 66-92. (FN 1.)

2. "Overdotting," a term coined by Erwin Bodky, is more fitting because frequently more than "double dotting" is alleged to be involved, and often the lengthening is less than double.

3. Peter Larsen, *Handel's "Messiah,"* 3rd ed. (New York 1972), p. 103, note 2. Larsen sees no justification for this interpretation. (The word "tradition" always evokes Gustav Mahler's pungent aphorism: "Tradition ist Schlamperei" [*Schlamperei*, a Viennese colloquialism, means, roughly, "slovenliness"]).

4. Arnold Dolmetsch, *The Interpretation of the Music of the Seventeenth and Eighteenth Centuries* (London, 1915), pp. 53-65.

5. Thurston Dart, *The Interpretation of Music*, reprint ed. (New York, 1963), p. 81.

6. Robert Donington, *A Performer's Guide to Baroque Music* (New York, 1973), p. 279.

7. Michael Collins, "A Reconsideration of French Overdotting," *Music and Letters* (1969), pp. 111-23 (hereafter, "Reconsideration"). In this study Collins replies to arguments presented in my article "La Note pointée." His intention is not only to support the prevalent concept of the Dolmetsch doctrine but greatly to expand its application, as the quotation above indicates.

8. A. Geoffroy-Dechaume, *Les "Secrets" de la musique ancienne* (Paris, 1964), pp. 53-54. Eugène Borrel, in his pioneering *L'Interprétation de la musique française de Lully à la Révolution* (Paris, 1934), does not mention overdotting, nor does Jane Arger in *Les Agréments et le rhythme* (Paris, 1921). When in 1965 I read a paper before the Société française de musicologie in which I presented the gist of "La Note pointée," Norbert Dufourcq told me, "we French musicologists all agree with you."

9.   Included of course will be French musicians abroad and their slavish imitators.

10. Pére Engramelle, *La Tonotechnie* (Paris, 1776), and Bedos de Celles, *L'Art du facteur d'orgues* (Paris, 1778), Vol. IV; facism, ed. (Kassel, 1936).

11. Engramelle, *La Tonotechnie,* pp. 25-27.

12. Michel Corrette, *Méthode pour apprendre à jouer de la vielle* (Paris, n.d.), pp. 3-4.

13. C.R. Brijon, *Réflexions sur la musique, et la vraie maniére de l'exécuter sur le violon* (Paris, 1763), pp. 22-30.

14. See also FN 1, exx. 29 and 30 on pp. 90-91, from the overtures to *Bérénice* and *Serse.*

15. A similar effect is aimed at in Handel's *L'Allegro, il Penseroso ed il Moderato,* No. 5, where the voice proceeds in even eighth-notes, while the melodically unison violins play in Lombard rhythm.

16. The unvocal character of extended dotted rhythms prompted Bach to write in the *Trauerode* (Cantata 198/I) rhythmically even choral parts against melodically unison, but dotted, instrumental parts, with brief exceptions (lasting no longer than a measure at a time), in order to intensify two cadential climaxes and their parallel spots (mm. 27, 36, 60, 69).

17. See also BWV 659, m. 33; BWV 653, mm. 5, 14, 62, 69; VWV 654, m. 10.

18. For a detailed discussion of the *notes inégales,* see chapter 3 above.

19. Donington, *A Performer's Guide,* p. 259.

20. Bénigne de Bacilly, *Remarques curieuses sur l'art de bien chanter...*(Paris 1668), p. 232.

21. Jacques Hotteterre, *L'Art de préluder sur la flûte traversière* (Paris, 1718), p. 57.

22. Charles Buterne, *Méthode pour apprendre la musique vocale et instrumentale* (Rouen, 1752), p. 11.

23. Duval, *Methode agréable et utile pour apprendre facilement à chanter...* (Paris, 1775), p. 15. Since the eighth-notes were most frequently affected by the *inégales* rules, many French writers often speak only of "pointer" or "inégaliser les croches." The eighth-notes are here used as *pars pro toto,* standing for the whole complex of the *notes inégales* rules.

24. Specification for *inégalité,* however slight, was necessary in an allemande, which, as noted before, was normally not subject to this practice.

25. Etienne Loulié, *Éléments ou principes de musique...*(Paris, 1969), pp. 34-35.

26. These incomplete supplements were first published as inserts in the English translation and edition by Albert Cohen, *Elements or Principles of Music* (Brooklyn, N.Y., 1965). The design for the *lourer* is on p. 67.

27. Michel Pignolet de Montéclair, *Nouvelle Méthode pour apprendre la musique...*(Paris, 1709), p. 15.

28. Montéclair, *Principes de musique* (Paris, 1736), p. 21.

29. Alexandre de Villeneuve, *Nouvelle Méthode...pour apprendre la musique et les agréments du chant* (Paris, 1733), p. 4.

30. Henri-Louis Choquel, *La Musique rendue sensible par la méchanique...*(Paris, 1762), p. 106.

31. Jean-Baptiste Mercadier de Belesta, *Nouveau système de musique théorique et pratique* (Paris, 1776), p. 67.

32. Jean Jacques Rousseau, *Dictionnaire de musique* (Paris, 1768), s.v. "Pointer."

33. As calculated from the rather complex data of the *Tonotechnie* by Hans-Peter Schmitz in his *Die Tontechnik des Père Engramelle* (Kassel, 1953), p. 10.

34. Engramelle, in *L'Art du facteur d'orgues,* IV, 602.

35. "Unavailable" has to be taken with a grain of salt. There are few sporadic cases where this triplet notation was used; once in a while by Kuhnau, and in at least two instances by Bach: in the autographs of Cantata 105 (final chorale, mm. 18-19) and of the *Orgelbüchlein* in *In dulci jubilo,* mm. 25-26. They are insignificant exceptions compared to the infinite mass of dotted notes with 2:1 meaning.

36. C.P.E. Bach advocates synchronization, Quantz the execution after the third triplet. Löhlein, beginning with the second edition (1773) of his *Clavierschule,* advises synchronization in fast, standard execution in slow tempo.

37. Johann Peter Sperling. *Principia musicae* ... (Budissin, 1705), pp. 55-56; Simpertus Schmelz, *Fundamenta musica cantus artificialis* ... (Yresee, 1752), pp. 31-32.

38. See, about this, Wilhelm Rust, Bach-Gesellschaft edition, Vol. XXIII, preface, p. xx; also Alfred Dürr, *Neue Bach-Ausgabe, Kritischer Bericht* to Vol. I/2, p. 79.

39. Loulié, *Elements or Principles,* p. 67. See also J.B. Métoyen, *Démonstration des principes de musique* ... (Paris, n.d.), p. 17.

40. Gigault, *Livre de musique pour l'orgue* (Paris, 1685), preface: Lorsqu'il y a une double croche audessus une croche il les faut toucher ensemble.

41. In the organ chorale BWV 653b, *An Wasserflüssen Babylon,* an exact rendition of such a suffix in the penultimate bar would create very audible fifths.

42. Certain documented instances of inequalities (both long-short and short-long) rooted, outside of France, in the performer's license, have misled Donington and others to call them *notes inégales* and to see proof for the latter's international currency in such categorically different occurrences.

43. Johann Joachim Quantz, *Versuch einer Anweisung die Flöte traversiere zu spielen* (Berlin, 1752).

44. Collins tried to predate this German mannerism and establish a link to seventeenth-century French style by his claim that "the practice was introduced to Germany along with French ornamentation by Muffat and J.K.F. Fischer." The claim is arbitrary, since neither of the two master makes any mention at all of overdotting.

45. Collins, in discussing Quantz, makes the statement that it is "absolutely impossible to shorten short notes after dots without either lengthening the dotted note or inserting a rest" ("A Reconsideration," p. 11, n. 3). The statement is incorrect. Any note can be shortened vis-a-vis its notation by either entering later or stopping earlier. The second method has of course always been by far the most frequent one (and in almost exaggerated form was demonstrated by Engramelle).

46. Incidentally, we can gather from Quantz's mention of these ballet performances taking place between acts of an Italian opera that he had Berlin, rather than Paris performances in mind. Berlin performances had their own style, as we can gather from a statement of C.P.E. Bach

that here (meaning Berlin) the Adagios are played much slower, the Allegros much faster than is customary elsewhere. Also we have to consider that principles appropriate for actual ballet music are not necessarily valid for the stylized overtures and dance forms in chamber music or solo settings.

47. Bach, *Versuch über die wahre Art das Clavier zu spielen* (Berlin, 1753), chap. 2, sec. 3 par. 14; second part (Berlin 1762), chap. 29, par. 15.

48. The same idea of the three possibilities can be extracted even from the opaqueness of the first passage. The overdotting is clouded by a confusing first sentence: "The short notes after dots are always played shorter than indicated by the notation, hence it is superfluous to place dots or dashes above them." It is confusing because the superfluousness of dots or dashes suggests that he speaks of sharpness of staccato articulation. However, overdotting seems implied, because the next sentence describes by way of contrast cases where the dot is to be rendered exact. Underdotting is suggested in the sentence: "...when many dotted note-pairs occur in succession, especially in fast tempo, they will often not be held as indicated by the notation" [so werden sie oft nicht gehalten, ohngeacht die Schreib-Art es erfordert]. Yet Collins derives from this sentence the injunction to *overdot.* Apart from overdotting being totally impractical "in fast tempo," this inference is wrong even if one were to accept Collins's claim that the German "halten" (which in fact is as unspecific as its exact English equivalent "to hold") has to mean to hold the finger down; why should not-holding-the-fingers-down cause overdotting? Actually the simplest connotation of "holding a note" is that which refers to the time span that elapses before the next note is articulated.

49. Leopold Mozart, *Versuch einer gründlichen Violinschule* (Augsburg, 1756), chap. 1, sec. 3, pars. 8-11.

50. Löhlein, *Clavier-Schule* (Leipzig und Züllichau, 1765), p. 69.

51. Friedrich Wilhelm Marpurg, *Anleitung zum Clavierspielen* (Berlin, 1755), p. 13.

52. Georg Friedrich Wolf, *Unterricht im Klavierspielen,* 3rd ed. (Halle, 1789), p. 26.

53. Johann Samuel Petri, *Anleitung zur praktischen Musik* (Lauban, 1767), p. 21; 2nd ed. (1782), p. 142.

54. Johann Anton Hiller, *Anweisung zum musikalisch-richtigen Gesange* (Leipzig, 1774), p. 111.

55. Frederick Neumann, "The Question of Rhythm in the Two Versions of Bach's French Overture BWV 831," *Studies in Renaissance and Baroque Music in Honor of Arthur Mendel* (Kassel, 1974), pp. 183-94. (FN 2.)

56. Collins, "Reconsideration," p. 117.

57. Loulié, *Eléments,* pp. 15-16.

58. Michel L'Affilard, *Principes trés-faciles pour bien apprendre la musique* (Paris, 1694; 2nd ed., 1697), p. 22.

59. Collins, "Reconsideration," p. 118. I have discussed this matter in "La Note pointée." (FN 1)

60. Neumann, "La Note pointée," FN 1, exx. 33-35.

61. The alignments for both patterns are equally perfect throughout in Altnicol's copy of 1755 (Deutsche Staatsbibliothek P 402) and in Walther's calligraphic copy (P 1074).

Chapter 9

1   Frederick Neumann, "La note pointée et la soi-disant 'manière française,' " *Revue de Musicologie* (1965), pp. 66-92; English tr. by R. Harris and E. Shay. "The dotted Note and the so-called French Style," *EM* 5/3 (July 1977) pp. 310-24 (FN1); "The Question of Rhythm in the Two Versions of Bach's French Overture, BWV 831," *Studies in Renaissance and Baroque Music in Honor of Arthur Mendel* (Kassel, 1974), pp. 183-95 (FN2). "Facts and Fiction about Overdotting," *Musical Quarterly* (April 1977), pp. 155-85 (FN3); Michael Collins, "A Reconsideration of French Over-Dotting," *Music & Letters* (Jan 1969), pp. 111-23.

2.   The overdotting survives, especially in Italian opera, to the present day; in a recent performance of *Otello*, the singer of the title role strongly overdotted the last *a'* on his first entrance, with fine effect: "Dopo l'armi lo vince *l'u*—ragano."

3.   Regarding Collins' attempts to find the "missing link" see FN2 & 3.

4.   J.J. Quantz, *Versuch einer Anleitung die Flöte traversiere zu spielen* (Berlin, 1752), chap. 17, sec. 7, par. 58. The sharp overdotting rule of chap. 5. par. 21 for eighths and shorter note values applies to solo performance only.

5.   Johann Georg Sulzer, *Allgemeine Theorie der schönen Künste* (Leipzig, 1777), 2, s.v. *Ouvertüre.*

6.   1729 is the date given by William Barclay Squire in his *Catalogue of the King's Music Library* (London, 1927). Mr. O.W. Neighbour, present Music Librarian of the British Library, to whom I owe this information, adds in a letter: "Whether or not this date is a little too exact I think there can be no doubt that the manuscript dates from Handel's lifetime; it comes from the Aylesford Collection, and was presented to the Royal Music Library by Barclay Squire in 1918."

7.   Quantz indicates their different musical character by describing the start of an overture as "splendid and solemn" [prächtig und gravitätisch] whereas the dances range from "seriousness" to gaiety and sprightliness.

8.   Couperin very cleverly compares the nonliteral rendition of *notes inégales* to the unphonetic French pronunciation which, after all, is not a matter of personal preference.

9.   Overdotting of the quarter-notes and synchronization of the eighth-notes with the 16th-notes in the diminution of the theme, as suggested by Leonhardt, is musically self-contradictory since such procedure would obliterate the 2:1 ratio that is the essence of diminution.

10.   Étienne Loulié (1696) explained that where inequality is intended to be sharper than the mild *lourer* of the *notes inégales,* one has to write a dot. (See FN3, p. 118.)

11.   Yet in another internal contradiction he approvingly cites Collins's invocation of German galant theorists as witnesses for "the style" (see his n. 7).

12.   I wonder whether it occurred to Fuller that his above-cited remark about the "sheer perversity" of a notation that does not mean what it says, would have to apply to "the style" as well. Here we see the difference with a piece like the C minor Partita of Bach, which Fuller mentions to illustrate the complexity of the issue. This Partita is a solo piece where no ensemble problems arise, and if the *goût* (not any "convention") suggests some moderate overdotting at its start, why not? I myself would recommend it.

13.   Mattheson, *Das Neu-Eröffnete Orchestre* (Hamburg, 1713), pp. 170-71.

Chapter 10

1. FN1: "La Note pointée et la soi-disant 'manière française,' " *Revue de musicologie,* LI (1965), pp. 66-92; English trans. R. Harris and E. Shay, "The dotted Note and the so-called French Style," *Early Music,* V/3 (July, 1977), pp. 310-24; FN2: "The Question of Rhythm in the Two Versions of Bach's French Overture, BWV 831," *Studies in Renaissance and Baroque Music in Honor of Arthur Mendel* (Kassel, 1974), pp. 183-95; FN3: "Facts and Fiction about Overdotting," *The Musical Quarterly* (April, 1977), pp. 155-85; FN4: "Once more: the 'French overture style,' " *Early Music,* VII/1 (Jan., 1979), pp. 39-45; Michael Collins, "A Reconsideration of French Overdotting," *Music and Letters,* L (Jan., 1969), pp. 111-23 (hereafter: "Collins"); David Fuller, "Dotting, the 'French style' and Frederick Neumann's Counter-Reformation," *Early Music,* V/4 (Oct., 1977), pp. 517-43 (hereafter: "Fuller"); John O'Donnell, "The French Style and the Overtures of Bach," *Early Music,* VII/2 (April, 1979), pp. 190-96 and (Part 2), VII/3 (July, 1979), pp. 336-45 (hereafter: O'Donnell Pt. 1 and Pt. 2 respectively); Graham Pont, forthcoming in *Early Music.*

2. They may have been preceded by manuscript entries of ca. 1795 (tentatively attributed by Graham Pont to Battishill) into the old Walsh edition of keyboard transcriptions of Handel overtures. These entries show occasional irregular and inconsistent overdotting. Such erratic rhythmic changes are unrealistic for the orchestra unless spelled out, in which case they cease to be "overdotting." Not having been published, their influence was presumably nil.

3. Arnold Dolmetsch, *The Interpretation of the Music of the XVIIth and XVIIIth Centuries* (London, [1915]). Robert Haas in his great book *Aufführungspraxis der Musik* (Wildpark-Postsdam, 1931), does not mention the "style." Neither does Arnold Schering in his *Aufführungspraxis alter Musik* (Leipzig, 1931), nor Eugène Borrel in his pioneering study *L'Interprétation de la musique française (de Lully à la révolution)* (Paris 1934), nor Jane Arger in *Les Agréments et le rythme* (Paris, 1921).

4. The forces at work here, according to modern sociology, are those that govern mass responses to rumor and propaganda. Some asserted fact gains momentum by appeal to authority: "professor X has determined ... professor Y concurs ... " soon turns into "all experts are agreed."

5. Georg Muffat, *Florilegium,* II (Passau, 1698), Preface; Martin Heinrich Fuhrmann, *Musicalischer Trichter* (Berlin, 1706), p. 78.

6. Johann Joachim Quantz, *Versuch einer Anweisung die Flöte traversiere zu spielen ...* (Berlin, 1752), chap. XVII, i, pars. 5 and 14. (I lean heavily on Edward Reilly's translation *On Playing the Flute* [London, 1966]).

7. Johann Freiderich Reichardt, *Ueber die Pflichten des Ripien-Violinisten* (Berlin, 1776), p. 79.

8. In Beethoven's String Quartet, Op. 127, there is in the Scherzando vivace movement a recurring phrase of the rhythm ♪♩♩ ♪ ♩♩ ♪ ♩♩. In all performances I have heard, and on all records I have listened to, including the Guarneri, Amadeus, Busch, Budapest, and other quartets, those passages are rendered in triplet rhythm, because the literal ratio is technically unmanageable.

9. Neal Zaslaw reproduced Bremner's essay in its entirety with informative introduction and commentary in "The Compleat Orchestral Musician," *Early Music,* VII/1 (Jan., 1979), pp. 46-57.

10. Johann Adolf Scheibe, *Der critische Musicus,* new enl. ed. (Leipzig, 1745), pp. 667-70. The melody of the overture, he says, is graced mostly with dotted quarter—sometimes with dotted

eighth notes, and occasionally with groups of sixteenth- and thirty-second-notes. He mentions no rhythmic alteration.

11. Robert Donington, *A Performer's Guide to Baroque Music* (New York, 1973), ex. 117.

12. See FN1, ex. 33.

13. The exact meaning of such upbeat eighth notes is also certain in Cantata 109/1 where mm. 2 and 8 clarify this intention. I could cite many more examples from Bach, Handel, Buxtehude, Steffani, et al.

14. The above-listed extension of the dot when followed by a *Nachschlag*-type ornament has only marginal importance for the orchestra. The matter is discussed in FN3, p. 124.

15. Quantz, *Versuch,* Chap. XVII, vii, par. 58.

16. See FN4, p. 143.

17. Dolmetsch, *Interpretation,* p. 62. (Italics mine).

18. Thurston Dart, *The Interpretation of Music* (London, 1954); reprinted (New York, 1963), pp. 81-83.

19. Donington, *Guide,* p. 297.

20. Collins, p. 123.

21. Donington, *Guide,* p. 281.

22. Fuller, p. 535.

23. Collins, pp. 113-14; see also FN3 pp. 115-17.

24. O'Donnell Pt. 2, pp. 339-40.

25. Graham Pont, "Rhythmic Alteration and the Majestic," *Studies in Music,* No. 12 (1978), pp. 87-89.

26. See FN3, pp. 132-33, about Dolmetsch's ideas on the rendition of this fugue.

27. Fuller, p. 529.

28. *Inégalité* did not similarly inhibit French composers: they could cancel it either by such words as *notes égales, marqué, détaché,* or by placing dots or dashes above the notes.

29. Jens Peter Larsen, *American Choral Review* 14 (1972) (special issue).

30. Its title: *Airs, Overtures and other Pieces for the Harpsichord* (call number: Drexel 5856). Terence Best told me that the Smith penmanship is unquestionable and that the manuscript date is ca. 1720-22.

31. To name a few: *Floridante,* 1722; *Flavio,* 1723; *Admeto,* 1727; *Parthenope,* 1730; *Ezio,* 1732; *Atalanta,* 1736; *Ariadne, Berenice, Arminio,* and *Tolomeo,* all 1737; *Semele* 1744; and many more.

32. Terence Best, in a letter to *Early Music,* VI (April, 1978), p. 310, tries to invalidate my assertion that the overture to *Rinaldo* (1710), of which I published an autograph page in *Early Music,* V. (July, 1977) p. 322, (see plate 3, this volume), was to be played as written (though at a faster than "traditional" tempo). He points to a conducting score by J.C. Smith of 1717 in which the groups of eighth notes are "dotted throughout." The simplest explanation is that Handel revised the score seven years later for the 1717 revival of that opera. Surely it does not

prove that all evenly written eighth notes were a code for dotted ones. If they had been, why would Smith bother to write out the dotting if it was understood to begin with?

33.   I owe to Professor Bruce Gustafson all the information about this volume, its author, and other Lully transciptions. The latter are all catalogued and described in Gustafson's *French Harpsichord Music of the 17th Century* (Ann Arbor, 1979). The manuscript in question is 24-Babell in Gustafson's catalogue.

34.   Gustafson has traced no less than seven for Lully's overture to *Isis* alone and knows that many more exist.

35.   In Menetou's harpsichord version of Lully's overture to *Persée* (46-Menetou No. 98 in Gustafson's catalogue), written a decade or two after 1689, some dotted notes are doubledotted for keyboard-idiomatic reasons, while others are left intact. As said before, such *selective* doubledotting is practicable only when spelled out, hence permits no inference on the orchestral rendition of plain dotted notes.

36.   The references to Quantz are in Dolmetsch, *Interpretation*, pp. 53-59.

37.   Die [französische] Tanzmusik muss mehrentheils ernsthaft, mit einem schweren, doch kurzen und scharfen, mehr abgesetzten, als geschleiften Bogenstriche, gespielet werden. Das Zärtliche und Cantabile findet darinne nur selten statt. Die punctirten Noten werden schwer, die darauf folgenden aber sehr kurz und scharf gespielet. Die geschwinden Stücke müssen ... mit einem ganz kurzen, und immer durch einen Druck markirten Bogenstriche, vorgetragen werden. ...

38.   When Quantz writes that dashes over the notes indicate emphasis, he speaks of the dotted note: ♩ ♪ and of the dash as accentual sign that was common throughout the eighteenth century before the modern > was introduced. I was mistaken in FN3 to refer the dash to the companion note, that is to be played "short and sharp" without the need of such notational indication.

39.   Two more thoughts might be added. 1) If, as everybody assumes, the meaning of the passage is one of strong overdotting, why would Quantz shorten the dotted note by lifting the bow for the dot? The result of ♩ ♫ | ♩ seems particularly incongruous with the gaping hole between the two notes. 2) Why would Quantz who is always explicit about delayed entries say: "For the dot the bow is lifted," when he allegedly meant: for the dot and the following rest?

40.   For purely technical reasons, even at a slow tempo the contractibility of *tirades* of thirty-seconds (let alone sixty-fourth notes) with detached bowstrokes is at best minimal, as mentioned before. I suspect that the directive was primarily pedagogical, to counteract a tendency to fall behind because of the difficulty of execution.

41.   C.P.E. Bach, *Versuch über die wahre Art das Clavier zu spielen,* Part I (Berlin, 1753), chap. III, par. 23; Part II (Berlin, 1762), chap. 29, par. 15.

42.   For details see FN1 pp. 79-82, and FN3 p. 129.

43.   Dart, *Interpretation* (reprinted, 1963), pp. 80-81.

44.   Donington, *Performer's Guide,* pp. 279-82; *The Interpretation of Early Music,* New Version (New York, 1974), pp. 448-51. Donington points in particular to Collins' citation of J.P. Schultz's article on "Ouverture" in Sulzer's *Allgemeine Theorie des schöen Künste* of 1775, written at a time when the French overture had gone out of fashion. In the overture, Schultz writes, "The dots are held longer than their value." I discussed this in FN3, p. 132, and FN4, p. 142,

showing that the stipulated overdotting remains within the scope of *inégalité* and that its mildness ("a somewhat longer rendition") is confirmed in the article on *"Punct, punctirte Note."* A reference to the dotted quarter note in the article on the "Loure" is ambiguous: it may refer either to overdotting or to sharp articulation. The articles on "Chaconne," "Passacaglia," and "Sarabande" mention no rhythmic alteration. Uniqueness, lateness of date, and mildness of alteration disqualify this document as credible evidence for an allegedly longlasting, wideranging international style. Characteristically, Heinrich Christoph Koch, exact contemporary of Schultz, "the outstanding theorist-composer of his time" *(MGG)*, has a chapter on the French overture in his *Versuch einer Anleitung zur Composition* (Leipzig, 1793), Part III, pp. 293-301. He gives a detailed description of the overture's nature, supplemented by an illustration of its first part, that contains dotted quarter, eighth, and sixteenth notes and many *tirades* of thirty-second notes. Again, there is no mention of any rhythmic alteration.

45. For the references see n. 1.

46. V/4 (April, 1979), 279. The letter was in response to FN4.

47. All further references will be to the second article.

48. Preface to Armand-Louis Couperin, *Selected Works for Keyboard* (Madison, 1975).

49. These additions were first published in the English translation of the treatise: *Elements or Principles of Music,* trans. and ed. Albert Cohen (New York, 1965).

50. See FN3, pp. 119-20.

51. On this subject see my article, "The French *Inégales,* Quantz, and Bach" in *Journal of the American Musicological Society* 18 (1965), pp. 313-58 (chapter 3 above).

52. John O'Donnell, *Roger North on Music,* ed. John Wilson (London, 1959), p. 185.

53. Bénigne de Bacilly, *Remarques curieuses sur l'art de bien chanter* (Paris, 1668), p. 232. The *inégalité* he says should be almost unnoticeable: "Il faut donc faire ces sortes de Nottes pointées si finement que cela ne paroisse pas. . . . " On occasion, he continues, *inégalité* may be stronger, on others it should be avoided altogether.

    O'Donnell's later mention of the *style saccadé* (p. 339) sounds like a historical French reference, whereas I coined the term in FN1 to describe the effect of the Dolmetsch doctrine.

54. In FN1 and FN3, I showed instances where such notation had to be meaningless and so did Fuller in his exx. 5a and b.

55. Graham Pont persuasively argues against such arbitrarily imposed conformity in any aspect of performance. "A Revolution in the Science and Practice of Music," *Musicology,* V (Sydney, 1979), pp. 3-5.

56. Michel Pignolet do Montéclair, *Principes de Musique* (Paris [1736]), pp. 22-23. In his earlier treatise, *Nouvelle Méthode* . . . (Paris, 1709), p. 13, a similar explanation of the dotted note through alignment shows the standard value throughout.

57. Michel L'Affilard, *Principes très-faciles pour bien apprendre la musique* (Paris 1694), 2nd ed. 1697, p. 26, where he equates *pointer* with rendering "the first [note] long, the second short."

58. L'Affilard *Principes,* p. 30.

59. The arguments by which O'Donnell arrives at this conclusion involve the claim that Loulié did not have to define *lourer* since its accepted meaning was "to slur." Yet a few lines earlier O'Donnell reported, as just quoted, Loulié's very definition of *lourer* as a mild long-short

inequality. Loulié reaffirms this definition in his manuscript additions using the above-shown ingenious graphic design; Brossard confirms the definition in his *Dictionnaire de musique* (Paris, 1703), s.v. *lourer*. Even Demoz de la Salle whom O'Donnel summons in his footnote 61 in support of his claim about the meaning of *lourer* defines the latter as succinctly emphasizing *(en marquant sensiblement)* the first of two stepwise notes. The current terms for slurring were *lier (liaison)* or *couler*.

60. Collins, pp. 112-13. See FN2, pp. 104-6.

61. See Hans David's Schott edition of the C-minor version.

62. I am not aware of any other second version that showed drastic notational deviations, for which a claim of acoustical identity has been made.

63. If that sounds too silly, are we to permit Bach a second thought on the key but not on the rhythm?

64. When, among other arguments, I pointed in FN2 to the incompatibility of the notation of mm. 11-13 (notably 13) and 17-20 (see FN2, ex. 4 or O'Donnell, ex. 25) with the identity theory, O'Donnell counters with a doctrine of "metrically dependent" and "metrically independent" sixteenth notes. Dependent are those than can not be contracted; independent those that can and therefore *have* to be contracted. The compulsion to contract is an ad hoc construction that can refer to no historical source. It is aesthetically objectionable as another manifestation of the "chained composer" who again is denied the freedom of rhythmic choice; it is logically objectionable as another "reductive fallacy" that arbitrarily excludes the feasible and far more plausible alternative of literalness.

65. O'Donnell's exx. 21-24 are to provide additional evidence but they, too, fail to make their point. For ex. 21 Couperin (with his "capricious" notation) it is again the case of notated sharp rhythms that have no automatic *simile* meaning. The same would be true of ex. 22 from Fux, even if its spelled-out "upbeat figures" were less leisurely. Ex. 23 from a Vivaldi concerto has the figure ♩ 𝄾 𝅘𝅥𝅯𝅘𝅥𝅯 three times repeated. O'Donnell comments: "... the *fermate* over the semiquaver rests can only be indications of rubato, the upbeat figures being 'robbed' of much of their value." Since each fermata indicates a stopping of the pulse on the rest—of which, in the Italian style, one or more call for a brief florid embellishment—it does not infringe the value of the following notes, hence suggests neither rubato nor contraction. In the didactic ex. 24 from Muffat the notational irregularities simply suggest ornamental freedoms in the vein of small unmetrical notes. Such irregularities do not occur in Muffat's compositions.

Chapter 11

1. Eugène Borrel, *L'Interprétation de la musique française* (Paris, 1934), p. 66.

2. Bénigne de Bacilly, *Remarques curieuses sur l'art de bien chanter...* (Paris, 1668), p. 178ff.

3. Jean Rousseau, *Méthode claire, certaine et facile pour apprendre à chanter,...* 1st ed., 1678 (the edition used was the 4th, Amsterdam, 1691), p. 54ff; *Traité de la Viole* (1687), p. 77ff.

4. Though the intent to begin on the main note emerges clearly from the context, the reader might like further confirmation of this important fact. In a question and answer annex to the vocal treatise the fourteenth question is: "Why do you call *cadence simple* a trill that is done in an upward motion without preparation [*en montant sans appui*] when the term *cadence* signifies descent and something done in falling?" "I use the term *cadence* to designate the unprepared trill which is done on the rise [*qui se fait en montant*] because one does not use a

distinctive sign to differentiate it from the trill that is made from above [*en descendant*] and with preparation: because in all music books either of these trills is marked by a *t* or by a +. However, one ought to distinguish between them and by not doing so students are often deceived, and by seeing them marked in the same manner they perform them in the selfsame way."

5. Rousseau, *Traité*, p. 83: *Méthode*, p. 56.

6. Rousseau, *Méthode*, p. 57.

7. Ibid.

8. Jean François Dandrieu, *Livre de pièces de clavecin* (Paris, 1729), and *Premier Livre de pièces d'orgue (Archives des Maîtres de l'Orgue des XVI, XVII, et XVIII siècles,* Vol. 7 [Paris, 1906]). The symbol for the *tremblement lié* must not be confused with the similar one of D'Anglebert's *cadence* and Bach's *Doppeltcadence.*

9. Dandrieu uses the different symbols with remarkable logic and consistency. The above examples can be multiplied many times to show that the main-note trill as well as the mordent are often used to strengthen the melodic line. In 5), for instance, the trill in the second measure reinforces the repeated thematic pattern of the first. The upper-note trill in m. 3 being cadential, it appropriately stresses the dissonant upper auxiliary and ends with a turn. In mm. 5 and 6 the mordent and the main-note trill are used to bring the descending scale pattern into sharper relief.

10. Jean Baptiste Bérard, *L'Art du chant* (Paris, 1755), p. 115. That the main note is understood by *la note ou l'on doit battre cette cadence* becomes clear from the definition of *cadence appuyée:* "[qui] se forme par un son soutenu majeur ou mineur, au dessus de celui sur lequel on la doit battre."

11. Abbé Duval, *Principes de la musique pratique* (Paris, 1764), p. 63.

12. Abbé Joseph Lacassagne, *Traité général des éléments du chant* (Paris, 1766), p. 47ff.

13. Lacassagne expresses his dislike for a special type of prepared trill, the *cadence à progression,* which he claims is becoming old-fashioned and should be avoided. It is interesting that of three examples he presents for this type, two are prepared on the *main* note:

This is closely related to a *tremblement sangloté* described by Lécuyer (quoted by Borrel, p. 61), a trill also anchored on the *main* note, which starts in slow dotted rhythm, accelerates gradually, and ends with a fast trill. It is the *ribattuta* of the Italians.

14. The anticipation may be as old as the start with the upper note. In 1565, Tomás de Santa María at first describes the trill as starting with the main note, then he adds that it is now the fashion to start the trill with the upper note, but in so doing one has to take care to play this first note all by itself, whereas the second note must coincide with the consonance that belongs to it ("El primer punto . . . ha de herir solo, y el segundo punto ha de herir en la Consonancia, que entonces se diere.") Tomás de Santa María, *Libro llamado Arte de Tañer Fantasia . . .* (Valladolid, 1565), p. 47.

15. Michel Pignolet de Montéclair, *Principes de musique* (Paris, 1736), p. 78. Rameau has this to say on the subject: "an ornament may be executed as perfectly as possible, if it is not guided by feeling it will lack a certain indescribable something which gives it all its value; too much or too little, too soon or too late, longer or shorter in *suspensions* [i.e., small agogic delays], in

the swelling and diminishing of tone, in the shaking of trills; if that precise expression is missing that is required by the situation, every ornament becomes insipid." Jean Philippe Rameau, *Code de musique pratique* ... (Paris, 1760), p. 13.

16. Michel de Saint-Lambert, *Les Principes du clavecin* (Paris, 1702), p. 44.

17. Ibid., p. 42.

18. François Couperin, *L'Art de toucher le clavecin* (Paris, 1717), p. 22.

19. In a performance that is sensitive and rhythmically flexible the beat can on occasion not be exactly pinpointed. Such blurring of the beat is the most obvious with arpeggiated chords, but slight anticipations, or belated entries of the *suspensions* and shortenings of the *aspirations* (the latter two *agréments* introduced by Couperin) as well as other agogic devices will often produce an effect of tantalizing ambiguity. Couperin writes that he has devised such methods to leave "the ear in doubt" in order to inject soulfulness into the playing of the harpsichord (*L'Art de toucher*, p. 16). In all these instances the question of the trill's start on or before the beat can become an academic one. What matters alone is then the question of emphasis on the lower or the upper note.

20. Rousseau, *Méthode claire*, p. 55.

21. Rousseau, *Traité de la Viole*, pp. 79-81.

22. Etienne Loulié, *Eléments ou Principes de musique* (Paris, 1696), p. 70; (Amsterdam, 1698), p. 81.

23. Ibid., p. 66.

24. Ibid., p. 68: Le Coulé est une inflexion de la Voix d'un petit son ou son faible, ou d'une petite durée, à un son plus bas et plus fort.

25. It may be added that further corroboration can be found in the illustration from the Amsterdam edition in ex. 6. That edition had no type for small notes and therefore resorted to the sharp contrast of metrical value to express the emphasis on the main note.

26. Montéclair, *Principes*, pp. 78, 80.

27. François Couperin, *Pièces de clavecin, Premier livre* (Paris, 1713), p. 47.

28. When we compare this pattern with the *pincé continu*, where regularity and metrical accuracy of the "effet" leave no doubt about the downbeat start, the above-mentioned fact that Couperin specifies on-the-beat start for the *pincé* but not for the trill takes on heightened significance.

29. In the Sarabande *La Majestueuse* from the *1er Ordre* of the *Piéces de clavecin (1er Livre*, 1713) the last phrase is repeated in a "petite Reprise" with a few new ornaments added. The passage a appears in the reprise as b. If we compare in the bass

the three small notes at the end of the measure in a with the two small notes in b it becomes obvious that the missing third note is the *anticipated auxiliary of the "tremblement continu"* (the latter term is printed in the original). The melodic logic of this interpretation is further supported by its harmonic logic. The E-flat forms a strident dissonance which makes sense only on the downbeat. A start of the trill with an F-natural on the beat would not only obscure the meaning of the dissonance but intensify the latter to a point of irrationality.

30. Foucquet's treatise on *Agréments,* written probably around 1755, was not available. The documentation is based on the reprint of his table of ornaments and of his explanatory remarks by Paul Brunold, *Traité des signes et agréments employés par les clavecinistes français...*(Lyons, 1925), p. 56.

31. François David, *Méthode nouvelle ou Principes généraux pour apprendre facilement la Musique et l'Art du Chant* (Paris, 1737), p. 131.

32. Abbé le Fils, *Principes du violon* (Paris, n.d. [1761]), p. 14.

33. Michel Corrette, *Méthode pour apprendre en peu de temps le Violoncelle* (Paris, 1741), p. 36.

34. The pictorial pattern of these examples has to be viewed in the light of Couperin's comment in the Preface, in which he extolls the intelligence and precision of the engraving, which was due to "extreme attention" and the lavish expenditure of his own time, effort, and money. Among the special assets of this great care he mentions the observation of the exact value of beats and notes in their *perpendicular alignment.* It is impossible therefore to argue that the alignment of the quarter notes was accidental rather than intentional.

35. Edward Dannreuther, *Musical Ornamentation* (London, n.d. [1893-95]), I, 104.

36. Such anticipation of a whole trill, which thus assumes unaccented, iambic upbeat character, is, of course, another conclusive proof against the monopoly of the trochaic downbeat start and *a fortiori* adds further support to the anticipation of the first note alone.

37. Bedos de Celles, *L'Art du facteur d'orgues, 4e Partie* (Paris 1778), Plates 106 and 107.

38. Rameau, *Pièces de clavecin,* Paris, 1731.

39. The fact that Rameau gives only seven notes for the trill does not at all imply a suspension, as Dannreuther has assumed. Rameau's example of a *cadence appuyée:* is similarly unmetrical, which serves only to underline the imaginative irregularity that ought to be brought to the execution of ornaments.

40. Jean Baptiste Dupuit, *Principes pour Toucher de la Viele* (Paris, n.d. [1741]), p. III.

41. Le Fils, *Principes,* p. 14.

42. Jean-Jacques Rousseau, *Dictionnaire de Musique* (Paris, 1768), Planche B.

43. De Cellas, *L'Art,* vol. 4, plate 121.

44. The *tremblement liè* is related to and occasionally overlaps with the *tremblement appuyé,* a trill prepared by an appoggiatura of varying duration, which was either not written out at all or indicated by a note in small print. There is no reason to doubt that the *appuyé* can make use of all the possibilities outlined for the *lié.*

45. Erwin Bodky, *The Interpretation of Bach's Keyboard Works* (Cambridge, Mass., 1960), p. 163ff. It is generally believed that the inverted mordent made its first appearance as the "Pralltriller" in C.P.E. Bach's treatise of 1753. However, Tomás de Santa María knew both the regular and the inverted mordent, which he calls *Quiebros senzillos* (simple shakes): and , *Libro llamado Arte de Tañer Fantasia...*, p. 47. So does Printz, under the name *accentus* with this illustration and Wolfgang Caspar Printz, *Compendium*

Musicae signatoriae... (Dresden, 1714), chap. V, par. 8.

46.   Emery puts it well when he says "Some authors really seem to think that Bach was born and bred in Paris." Walter Emery, "The Interpretation of Bach," in *Musical Times* (April 1955), p. 190ff.

47.   Putnam Aldrich, "On the Interpretation of Bach's Trills," in *The Musical Quarterly* 49 (1963), p. 290.

48.   The French types are favored in his clavier works, the Italian types in his string and chamber works.

49.   Girolamo Diruta, *Il Transilvano* (Venice, 1625 [1st ed. 1593]), p. 19: Michael Praetorius, *Syntagma musicum,* 1619 (facs. reprint 1958), III, p. 235; Joh. Andreas Herbst, *Musica practica* (Nuremberg, 1642), p. 7; Georg Falck, *Idea boni Cantoris* (Nuremberg, 1688), p. 100; Franz X. Murschhauser, *Prototypon longo breve organicum* (1703), in *Denkmäler d. deutschen Tonkunst,* 2. Folge, 18. Jg., p. 122; Printz, *Compendium Musicae signatoriae...,* chap. V, par. 9. In addition, Reinken's "Admonitio" in his *Hortus Musicus* describes, without illustration, either an inverted mordent or a brief main-note trill.

Chapter 12

1.   It is for this reason that Bach's *coloratura* characteristically start after a brief tie, at the least conspicuous moment within the bar.

2.   Arthur Mendel, introduction to the vocal score of Bach's "St. John Passion," (Schirmer, New York, 1951), p. xxii.

3.   Jean Rousseau, *Traité de la viole* (1687), pp. 85-86.

4.   Jean Rousseau, *Méthode claire, certaine et facile,* 4th ed. (Amsterdam, 1691), p. 50 (1st ed. 1678).

5.   Etienne Loulié, *Eléments ou Principes de Musique* (Paris, 1696), p. 68.

6.   Ibid., p. 69.

7.   Michel de Saint-Lambert, *Les Principes du clavecin,* (Paris, 1702), pp. 49-50.

8.   André Raison, *5 messes ou 15 magnificats (Archives des maîtres de l'orgue,* vol. 2 [Paris, 1899], p. 8).

9.   Alexandre de Villeneuve, *Nouvelle Méthode très courte,* 2nd ed. (Paris, 1756), p. 38.

10.   Jean-Jacques Rousseau, *Dictionnaire de Musique* (Paris, 1769), Planche B.

11.   Johann Joachim Quantz, *Versuch einer Anweisung die Flöte traversiere zu spielen* (Berlin, 1752), chap. 8, par. 6. See also chap. 17, sec. 2, par. 20.

12.   Pier Francesco Tosi, *Anleitung zur Singkunst,* German translation and additions by Johann Friedrich Agricola (Berlin, 1757), pp. 81ff. Agricola's extensive additions are set off by different type.

13.   Friedrich Wilhelm Marpurg, *Anleitung zum Clavierspielen* (Berlin, 1755), p. 50.

14.   Johann Gottfried Walther, *Musicalisches Lexicon* (Leipzig, 1732).

15.   Johann Mattheson, *Der vollkommene Capellmeister* (Hamburg, 1739), part 2, chap. 3, par. 20.

16. Christoph Bernhard, *Von der Singekunst oder Manier*, reprinted by J.H. Müller-Blattau (Leipzig, 1926), pp. 34-35. It is interesting and perhaps significant that some of his examples, like the following:

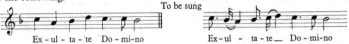

show a grace-note treatment which, like the one from Bach's quoted Cantata No. 84, is not suggested by the natural declamation. Another point of interest is his *cercar della nota*—a portamento-like anticipated gliding into the note from below. When prescribed, the symbol is the letter *c* (from *cercar*) which may possibly be the origin of the clamp or hook symbols. If this is the case it would indicate their anticipatory origin.

17. Walter Emery, *Bach's Ornaments* (London, 1953), p. 77.

18. Alfred Kreutz, *Die Ornamentik in J.S. Bach's Klavierwerken*, supplement to the Peters Urtext edition of the *English Suites* (1950), p. 3.

19. Quantz, *Versuch einer Anweisung*, chap. 8, par. 6.

20. Agricola, in Tosi, *Anleitung zur Singkunst*, pp. 75, 78.

21. Ralph Kirkpatrick, *Goldberg-Variations*, (New York, 1938).

22. Frederick Neumann, "Misconceptions about the French Trill in the XVIIth and XVIIIth Centuries," *The Musical Quarterly* 1 (1964), pp. 188-206 (chapter 11 above).

23. In Walther's *Lexicon*, table V, fig. 2, the pattern is not even metrical.

24. Michel L'Affilard, *Principes très faciles pour bien apprendre la musique*, 6th ed. (Paris, 1705), pp. 26-27.

25. See p. 206.

26. J.G. Walther, *Praecepta der musikalischen Composition* (1708, first published Leipzig, 1955), p. 37.

27. Agricola, in Tosi, *Anleitung Zur Singkunst*, p. 88.

28. Other instances are objectionable unisons of voice and viola da gamba in bar 46 of the aria "Komm, süsses Kreuz" and of voice and viola in bars 16 and 18 of the aria "Mache dich, mein Herze" both from the St. Matthew Passion; and highly improbable unisons in the tenor aria from Cantata 62 in bars 28, 53, 61, 115, and octaves in bar 33.

Chapter 13

1. Ornaments are "connective" if their function is to embellish the transition from one structural note to another. Their counterpart are ornaments that could be called "intensifying" because they have reference to one parent note only, brightening, colouring, intensifying it.

2. J.J. Quantz, *Versuch einer Anweisung die Flöte traversiere zu spielen* (Berlin, 1752), chap. XIII, tables IX-XVI.

3. Ibid., chap. XIII, par. 7: Ueberhaupt muss man bey den Veränderungen allezeit darauf sehen, dass die Hauptnoten worüber man die Veränderungen machet, nicht verdunkelt werden. Wenn Veränderungen über Viertheilnoten angebracht werden: so muss auch mehrentheils die erste Note der zugesetzten ebenso heissen wie die simple: und so verfährt man bey allen Arten, sie mögen mehr oder weniger gelten, als ein Viertheil. Man kann auch wohl eine andre

Note, aus der Harmonie des Basses erwählen, wenn nur die Hauptnote gleich wieder darauf gehöret wird.

4. The anticipation as such is not spelled out but implied by their invariable softness and heavier dynamic emphasis on the principal note. A typical example is table IX, fig. I, a where the instructions (chap. XIV, par. 26) read: "The 32nds weak the quarter notes C, C, C, growing."

    This means:

    According to modern doctrine the dynamics would be the exact reverse: the first note d″ would hit the beat with a decisive accent and the following notes would taper off:

5. The usual reference to the horizontal aspect of melody and the vertical of harmony is of course, a matter of symbolism derived from the pictorial aspect of musical notation. The symbolism coincides, not entirely by accident, with a geometrical graph in which the ordinate registers pitches and the abscissa even units of time, thus clarifying the musical concepts of successiveness (the unfoldment in time) and simultaneity. Although the contrast between the melodic and harmonic principle reaches further and deeper than is suggested by a two-dimensional graph, the horizontal-vertical simile can be used to advantage, if only for its familiarity and plastic descriptiveness.

6. Such rhythmic pulsation which derives from metrical organization has been present in secular song and dance from early medieval times. In polyphonic music metrical accents made their appearance only at a later date when the harmonic principle began to penetrate the linear structure. Commonly considered a baroque phenomenon, this happening has to be antedated to the Renaissance according to the important study of Dr. E.E. Lowinsky, "Early Scores in Manuscript," *JAMS* 13 (1960), pp. 126-73.

7. I naïvely believed I had devised this simile until I read in Dr. Lowinsky's above mentioned article that Zarlino had used it 400 years ago.

8. This is the reason why in metrical music place in the measure is of such importance in matters of dissonance treatment, in matters of ornaments and their melodic and harmonic implications, and many other matters as well, such as prosody and thorough bass realization.

Chapter 14

1. F. Couperin, *L'Art de toucher le clavecin* (Paris, 1716, 1717), p. 22: Il faut que la petite note perdue d'un port-de-voix ou d'un coulé, frape avec l'harmonie: c'est à dire dans le tems qu'on devrait toucher la note de valeur qui la suit.

    The French *port de voix* is usually translated as ascending appoggiatura, the *coulé* as a descending one. However, "appoggiatura" is an infelicitous term, because it implies "leaning," hence an emphasized downbeat rendition. Pending the coinage of a better English term, I shall for the time being use the German term *Vorschlag* which is neutral concerning its rhythmic-melodic design.

2. These principles are presented in great detail in chap. 2 of C.P.E. Bach's treatise: *Versuch über die wahre Art das Clavier zu spielen* (Berlin, 1753).

3. In fairness it has to be said that not all writers follow the line of complete intransigence. Though probably all of them pay too large a tribute to the downbeat idea, there are a few who qualify their stand. We find the latter more among the early writers on the subject (e.g.

Dannreuther or Beyschlag) than among more modern ones, a fact which seems to reflect a hardening trend. Walter Emery in his book on *Bach's Ornaments* (London, 1953) and Georg Von Dadelsen in his article "Verzierungen" in *MGG* are among the few today who take a more flexible stand. At any rate it is the orthodox school which has shaped the image of historical authenticity in the eyes of today's music editors and performers alike. The reader will most probably recognize the downbeat rule as the one he himself was taught to follow. Only a random few among the many advocates of the exclusive downbeat principle can be mentioned here. Andreas Moser, "Zur Frage der Ausführung der Ornamente bei Bach," in: *BJ* 1916, pp. 8-19, sees a problem for the *Vorschläge* in their length only, but takes the downbeat for granted. Ralph Kirkpatrick in his edition of the *Goldberg-Variations* (New York, 1938) leans heavily on C.P.E. Bach in his introductory discussion and transcribes every ornament without exception on the downbeat. Hans T. David does the same in his edition of Bach's *Musical Offering* (New York, 1944). Putnam Aldrich, in his unpublished Harvard dissertation "The Principal Agréments of the Seventeenth and Eighteenth Centuries" dismisses Saint Lambert's upbeat *Vorschläge* of 1702 as old-fashioned; they were "overruled," he says, whereupon the downbeat principle was "scrupulously followed" during the greater part of the 18th century. The same author's monograph: *Ornamentation in J.S. Bach's Organ Works,* (New York, 1950) brooks no exception to the downbeat rule either. Hermann Keller, *Die Klavierwerke Bachs,* (Leipzig, 1950) p. 34: "Alle Verzierungen fallen in den Taktwert der Note, über der sie stehen." Robert Donington, *The Interpretation of Early Music,* 2d ed. (London, 1965) p. 135: "All appoggiaturas take the beat." Reporting later on Quantz's "durchgehende Vorschläge," Donington passes them over lightly, declaring them to be a fashion "of no great duration" resting "only on the opinions of a few mid-eighteenth-century authorities." Rudolf Steglich, editing Händel's Clavier Suites for the new *Hallische Händel-Ausgabe* (vol. IV, 1) shows in his musical illustrations on pp. XVII-XXII complete allegiance to the downbeat principle. Paul Brunold and his analogous treatment of French clavecinists will be discussed below. This list could be extended indefinitely.

4.   When we hear, as we so often do, the many slides in the slow movement of Beethoven's Seventh Symphony:

played accented on the beat, we can feel the long arm of C.P.E. Bach.

5.   Bach, *Versuch über die wahre,* part I, p. 70: "...die hesslichen Nachschläge...die so gar ausserordentlich Mode sind..."

6.   Of the four references only Janowka's needs to be quoted because the other three are readily accessible in facsimile prints. Thomas Balthasar Janowka, *Clavis ad Thesaurum Magnae Artis Musicae...* (Prague, 1701) p. 17. After explaining the *circuitus,* an anticipated slide, he continues: "Solet autem in simili accipiendo modo aliqua mora temporis a priori nota... rapi, ut debito tempore ad sequentem notam perveniri possit; et huic similes modos Galli, ut in eorum Operis expresse videre est, per notulas minori ad distinctionem substantialium notarum typo, apponere solent." It is interesting that Janowka sees in the "Gauls" use of the little notes an express sign of their anticipation. J.J. Quantz, *Versuch einer Anweisung die Flöte traversiere zu spielen* (Berlin, 1752) chap. 8, par. 6; chap. 17, ii, par. 20. J.F. Agricola, *Anleitung zur Singkunst,* tr. from P.F. Tosi, with extensive additions (Berlin, 1757) p. 68. D.G. Türk, *Klavierschule* (Leipzig and Halle 1789) p. 223.

7.   Although such faulty procedures plague all humanistic research, it seems that a higher than usual incidence is found in the field of *Aufführungspraxis.* This may be the case because this fairly young discipline has failed so far to refine all of its tools and to sort out questionable methods.

8.   F. Couperin, *Pièces de clavecin, premier livre* (Paris, 1713).

9.   The examples are taken from the original edition of the four books of clavecin pieces and from the eight Preludes in *L'Art de toucher le clavecin.* The Roman numerals refer to the *Ordres,* prelude numbers to the treatise. Original clefs are indicated in front of either the treble or bass clefs that were used for all examples.

10.   Paul Brunold, *Traité des signes et agréments employés par les clavecinistes français des XVIIe et XVIIIe siècles* (Lyon, 1925) pp. 24-25, 31. His equation can be said to be a standard formula for many an editor of 18th-century music from Couperin and Bach to the classical masters. (Mozart in particular is a frequent victim of its application). For French usage we find this formula of halving the principal note endorsed by Jane Arger, *Les agréments et le rythme* (Paris, n.d. [1921]), p. 37. The exception she lists when the little note is tied to the preceding rather than the following principal note, is based on a misunderstanding, as such notation indicates a different type of ornament: a *chûte* or *accent,* not a *coulé* or *port de voix.* Putnam Aldrich, *The principal agréments,* p. 95: "The interpretation which gives the appoggiatura approximately half the time value of the main note prevailed in all French keyboard works from about 1690 on." It should be added that Von Dadelsen, "Verzierungen," admits anticipation for certain slides and *coulades* in Couperin, but takes, understandably, the latter's downbeat rule for *coulés* and *ports de voix* on face value.

11.   Ex. 4(b) is interesting because the piece is contained in Anna Magdalena's Notebook in her own handwriting in a version that shows certain revealing adaptations and some written-out ornaments. Thus the second measure of ex. 4(b) appears with the *coulés* in full anticipation and the slide on the downbeat with a lengthened first note:

This is, of course, no proof of Couperin's intentions, but it certainly shows that the anticipation of the *coulé* was not outlawed in the Bach household. Couperin's own interpretation was probably closer to the following ex. (b) with the *coulés* shortened and the slide, too, in anticipation:

It is interesting to note that in the third couplet, as shown in ex. (c), the *coulé* is unsatisfactory in anticipation (parallel octaves), impossible in downbeat rendition as ♪♪ , and only barely

possible in a very quick downbeat version as ♫ . It may well have been an oversight or misprint and, interestingly, Anna Magdalena left it out altogether.

12.   When Couperin wanted the long *coulé* effect à la Brunold, he wrote it out as shown in ex. (d) and more strikingly still in ex. (e), where the difference in notation of the two measures implies a difference in execution:

(d) XIII Les Rozeaux   (e) XIX L' Ingénue

On occasion we find the short, Lombard-style downbeat rendition written out, as in ex. (f).

(f) Les Folies Françaises (La Persévérance)
    6ᵉ couplet

13.   To strike "against the harmony" meant at that time to strike against the bass. This is how Boyvin formulated his downbeat rule explicitly (J. Boyvin, *Premier livre d'Orgue* [Paris, n.d.] Preface; also *Traité abrégé de l'accompagnement . . .* 2d ed. [Paris, 1705], Preface), and that is how Couperin's wording has to be understood.

14.   It is no coincidence that Boyvin specifies shortness for the *coulé*, longer value for the *port de voix*.

Chapter 15

1.   This article is an altered and enlarged version of a chapter from the author's forthcoming book, *Baroque and Post-Baroque Ornamentation*.

2.   Christoph Bernard, *Ausführlicher Bericht vom Gebrauche der Con- und Dissonantien*, chaps. 10-22 of MS (from after 1664), published as part of *Die Kompositionslehre Heinrich Schützens in der Fassung seines Schülers Christoph Bernard*, ed. Müller-Blattau (Leipzig, 1926), 2nd ed. (Kassel, 1963). See also Johann Christoph Stierlein, *Trifolium Musicale . . .* (Stuttgart, 1691), p. 18; Johann Baptist Samber, *Manuductio ad Organum . . .* (Salzburg, 1704), p. 219; Johann Gottfried Walther, *Praecepta der musikalischen Composition* (1708), first published, ed. Benary (Leipzig, 1955), p. 152.

3.   Marin Marais, preface to *Pièces à une et à deux Violes* (Paris, 1686): . . . certaines coulades que l'on peut faire, ou ne pas faire sans altérer la pièce, et que j'ay marquées seulement pour une variété d'exécution.

4.   The two notions, ornament and variation, are related as a narrower to a wider concept. Any ornamental addition is a variation, but of course not every variation is an ornament. Whether a change is to be classed as ornament or as nonornamental variation will depend chiefly on whether or not most of the structural notes remain in place while a number of intervening tones are added. If they do remain, it is an ornament. If, on the other hand, many structural notes are changed, or if no increase in the number of notes has taken place, we have to do with a nonornamental variation. There are, of course, the inevitable borderline cases which will arise, for instance, when an extended ornamental melisma takes too free a flight and loses temporarily its close rapport with the basic melody.

5. Up to Bach's time and beyond, there still prevailed a definite link between meter and tempo and, therefore, between relative and absolute note values: a quarter-note could never be very fast nor a sixteenth very slow. It was not till Beethoven's time that this link was fully severed.

6. The failure of some modern performers to recognize the essentially decorative rather than deeply meaningful character of such coloraturas as shown in ex. 4 frequently leads to misrepresentation. Many modern violinists play such a movement too slowly, often changing the bow two or three times within one coloratura in order to extract the maximum of resonance and expressiveness from every single note. With lightweight ornaments thus impersonating structure, such rendition is wrongly focused and misses the forest for the trees. In a modern edition it might be advisable to print the ornamental figurations in smaller notes to suggest graphically their ornamental nature, hence their smaller specific weight and their need for lightness and rhythmic flexibility.

7. Bachgesellschaft edition, Vol. VII, p. XV.

8. Girolamo Frescobaldi, *Toccate et Partite d'Intavolatura di Cembalo*, new corrected ed., Book I (Rome, 1616), preface *(Al Lettore)*, under number 6: Quando si trouera un trillo della man destra, o, vero sinistra, e que nello stesso tempo passeggiera l'altra mano non si deve compartire a nota per nota, ma sol cercar che il trillo sia ueloce, et il passaggio sia portato men uelocemente et affettuoso: altrimenti farebbe confusione.

9. Edward Dannreuther, *Musical Ornamentation*, Vol. I (London, n.d. [1893]), p. 51.

Chapter 16

1. That the augmented fourth was a commonplace in Mozart's recitatives and in no need of being hidden by the fig leaf of an appoggiatura is clear from numerous cases of masculine endings where the direct leap is unquestionable as, for example, in the following spots from *Cosi fan tutte*, II, 8 and *Le nozze di Figaro*, I.7 (ex. 4). (All of the Mozart examples are taken from appropriate volumes of the NMA with the exception of those from *Cosi fan tutte*, which are taken from *W.A. Mozarts Werke*, XIX).

Example 4

    Ferrando   Conte

    e_a ven-di - car   E   voi re - sta - te qui, pic-ciol ser - pen - te!

2. Georg Philipp Telemann, *Harmonischer Gottes-Dienst* (Hamburg, 1725-26).

3. Johann Friedrich Agricola, *Anleitung zur Singkunst* (trans. of Pier Francesco Tosi, *Opinioni de' cantori* [Bologna, 1723]); (Berlin, 1757; repr. Zurich, 1966). p. 154.

4. Friedrich Wilhelm Marpurg, *Kritische Briefe über die Tonkunst* 3 vols. in 2 (Berlin, 1762; repr. Hildesheim, 1974), II, pt. 3.

5. Johann Adam Hiller, *Anweisung zum musikalisch-richtigen Gesange* (Leipzig, 1774), p. 202.

6. Johann Abraham Peter Schulz, writing in J.G. Sulzer's *Allgemeine Theorie der schönen Künste* (Berlin, 1771-74; repr. Hildesheim, 1967-70), s.v. "Recitativ."

7. Johann Carl Friedrich Rellstab, *Versuch über die Vereinigung der musikalischen und oratorischen Declamation* (Berlin, n.d. [1786 or 87]), pp. 47-48.

8. Johann Baptist Lasser, *Vollständige Anleitung zur Singkunst* (Munich, 1798), p. 160. Johann Friedrich Schubert, *Neue Singe-Schule* (Leipzig, n.d. [1804]), p. 145.

9.   Heinrich Christoph Koch, *Versuch einer Anleitung zur Composition,* III (Leipzig, 1793; repr. Hildesheim, 1969), pp. 233ff. *Musikalisches Lexikon* (Frankfurt/Main, 1802), s.v. "Recitativ."

10.   Giambattista Mancini, *Riflessioni pratiche sul canto figurato,* 3rd ed. (Milan, 1777), pp. 237-39, 143.

11.   Daniel Gottlob Türk, *Klavierschule* (Leipzig and Halle, 1789), p. 206, n. 3.

12.   Vincenzo Manfredini, *Regole armoniche,* 2nd corr. and enl. ed. (Venice, 1797), pp. 65 and 71.

13.   Domenico Corri, *A Select Collection of the most admired Songs, Duetts, etc. from Operas in the Highest Esteem,* I (Edinburgh, n.d. [ca. 1779]).

14.   Manuel Garcia, *A Complete Treatise on the Art of Singing,* part II, editions of 1847 and 1872, ed. and tr. Donald V. Paschke (New York, 1975).

Index

accent (French), 229. *See also* grace note, *Nachschlag, Vorschlag*
accent, prosodic, in recitative, 252-53
accento, Bernhard, 207
accidentals, 12; Bach and, 274 n.1
agogic articulation: L. Mozart and, 41
agogics, 70
Agricola, Johann Friedrich: and *Nachschlag,* 206, 228; and recitative appoggiatura, 253; slide, 214-15; and *tierce coulée,* 238; and *Vorschlag,* before written-out appoggiatura, 209
Ahle, Johann Georg: and good and bad notes, 37
Aldrich, Putnam: and Bach's trills, 195; and downbeat start of ornaments, 307 n.3; and trill, 210
alignment, vertical: in Altnikol, 68; in Bach, 60, 66, 123, 133, 134; in Handel, 140, 141, 142-43, 165-67; in Kirnberger, 68
Anglebert, Jean-Henri d': and *double cadence,* 212; and Lully, transcriptions of, 167; and upbeat figures, 105, 108; and *Vorschlag,* 228
anticipatione della syllaba: Bach and, 207
anschlagende und durchgehende Noten. See notes, good and bad
appoggiatura: Bach and, 202-10; Donington and, 12; emergence of long "harmonic," 220-21; function of, 208; in *style galant,* 224; "short" harmonic-rhythmic, 223; terms and meanings for, 202; and trill, 13. *See also coulé, port de voix, Nachschlag*
appuyé, meaning of, 27
articulation: in Bach, 61; in Balbastre, 114; in dotted note passages, 126; in Engramelle, 113; in Quantz, 171-72

Babell, Charles: Lully, transcriptions of, 167-70
Babitz, Sol: keyboard fingerings of, 42-48; and inequality, 284 n. 86; and notes, good and bad, 34; and *notes inégales,* 27-28, 38-39; and Quantz's *notes inégales,* 18

Bach, Anna Magdalena, 99; and prebeat *Vorschlag,* 308 n.11
Bach, Carl Philipp Emanuel (C.P.E.), 12; and Donington on dotted notes, 133, 173, 294 n.48; and dotted notes and articulation, 79; and dotted notes in polyphony, 145; and downbeat doctrines of ornaments, 227-28; and keyboard fingerings, 283 n.80; and Lombard rhythm, 81; ornaments, onbeat start of, 201-2; and overdotting, 79-81, 102, 124, 127, 139; and Quantz, 4; relevance for J.S. Bach, 201-2; rhythmic assimilation, 124; *Schneller,* 6; uneven notes, 56; treatise, application of, 82-84; treatise and baroque style, 4
Bach, Johann Sebastian: *accent* (French), 204; accidentals, 274 n.1; agogics, 70; *anticipatione della syllaba,* 207; appoggiatura, 202-10; appoggiatura, long, written out, 203; appoggiatura-trill, 210-11; articulation discrepancies, 61; cadenzas, 200-201; *Doppelt-cadence,* 212-14; dotted notes, 103, 117-18, 121-22, 148; *Explicatio,* 7-8; grace note, 202; grace note vs. appoggiatura, 209-10; keyboard fingerings, 47; key change in *French Overture,* 99, 182; parallels forbidden, 194; *Nachschlag,* 249; *notes inégales,* 15, 19, 47, 57-58, 64-70; ornaments, addition of, 200-201; ornaments, Italian vs. French, 199; ornaments, written-out, 60-61, 199-201, 246; overdotting, 112, 123, 124, 133; prebeat *Vorschlag,* 240-41; rhythmic alterations, 64-70, 101; rhythmic assimilation, 60, 68, 121-24; rhythmic clashes, 61; rhythmic freedom of ornaments, 248-49; *Schneller,* 6, 195; slide, 60, 214-15; structural melismas, 246-47; symbol ϕ , 286-87 n.19; trill, 210-12; trill, anticipated, 195; trill, cadential, 249; trill, main-note, 195, trill, prebeat start of, 195; trill, four types of, 211-12; trill, performance of, 196, 211-12; triplet